Essential Topics for the Helping Professional

Sheri Bauman
University of Arizona

Boston   New York   San Francisco
Mexico City   Montreal   Toronto   London   Madrid   Munich   Paris
Hong Kong   Singapore   Tokoyo   Cape Town   Sydney

Series Editor: Virginia L. Blanford
Series Editorial Assistant: Matthew Buchholz
Marketing Manager: Erica DeLuca
Production Editor: Mary Beth Finch
Editorial Production Service: TexTech Inc.
Composition Buyer: Linda Cox
Manufacturing Buyer: Linda Morris
Electronic Composition: TexTech International
Cover Administrator: Elena Sidorova

For related titles and support materials, visit our online catalog at www.ablongman.com.

Between the time website information is gathered and then published, it is not unusual for some sites to have closed. Also, the transcription of URLs can result in typographical errors. The publisher would appreciate notification where these errors occur so that they may be corrected in subsequent editions.

ISBN 10:   0-205-41401-X
ISBN 13: 978-0-205-41401-7

Library of Congress Cataloging-in-Publication Data

Bauman, Sheri.
        Essential topics for the helping professional / Sheri Bauman.
        p.   cm.
    Includes bibliographical references and index.
    ISBN 978-0-205-41401-7
    1. Mental illness.   2. Mental illness—Case studies.   3. Mental health personnel.
    4. Counselors.   I. Title.
        [DNLM: 1. Mental Disorders—psychology.   2. Mental Disorders—therapy.
    3. Case Reports.   4. Psychotherapy.   WM 140 B347e 2008]
        RC454.B395   2008
        616.89—dc22   2007019540

Printed in the United States of America
10   9   8   7   6   5   4   3   2   1   11   10   09   08   07

ABOUT THE AUTHOR

Sheri Bauman, Ph.D. is an associate professor in the Department of Educational Psychology at the University of Arizona, Tucson, AZ, where she directs the school counseling master's degree program. Prior to earning her doctorate in counseling psychology from New Mexico State University in 1999, Dr. Bauman was an educator for 30 years, including 18 years as a school counselor. She is currently a licensed psychologist, with a small private practice in Las Cruces, New Mexico.

CONTENTS

6 Suicide   167

PREFACE

In the course of my professional training, first as a counselor and later as a psychologist, I took the many courses prescribed by my programs to prepare me for these careers. With all that work under my belt, I believed I had a firm foundation of knowledge, and solid basic skills. I even had selected a theoretical orientation! What I lacked was knowledge about specific issues or common client problems that my training could not provide.

It was not until field experiences in practica and internships that I directly confronted some of the issues that I would need to deal with as a clinician, and I recall being acutely aware of my own ignorance. When I was finally ready to practice independently, I still harbored doubts about my competence as I anticipated the range of issues and clients I would need to be prepared to address, and that I knew little or nothing about. I had already learned that the "presenting issue" is often not the only issue; indeed, it may not even be the primary issue. Clients may have a situational problem, for example, that temporarily impedes their functioning, and so they seek counseling. As the treatment unfolds and a strong therapeutic alliance develops, the client may feel safe enough to reveal and explore deeper issues.

Although I often read announcements of workshops that offered training on important topics, time and financial constraints limited the number I could attend. There was (and is still) always another one that looks exciting and useful. I was aware of the vast numbers of books available in any given topic, and realized I could never read them all. What I needed was an overview of many topics rather than in-depth information about a few. And how was I to know which of the many books available would provide the overview I wanted? I often wished for a single volume that I could consult to get a basic orientation to the many topics I needed to know about. The seeds of this book were planted.

As a beginning practitioner, I doubted my knowledge about the range of issues I might face, and the skills I would need to treat them. I was aware of the ethical standard that admonishes counselors to "practice only within the boundaries of their competence, based on their education, training, supervised experience, state and national professional credentials, and appropriate professional experience" (Herlihy & Corey, 1996, p. 34). The ethical standards also say, "Counselors practice in specialty areas new to them only after appropriate education, training, and supervised experience" (p. 34). How are neophyte counselors to become competent in the wide range of issues they might encounter, particularly when their education and training have not covered a particular client type or concern?

Many models of training for helping professionals are based on the triad of Awareness, Knowledge, and Skills. This book addresses the first two prongs of the triad. The reader will gain an awareness of these important issues, and will acquire basic knowledge.

There are volumes of material available on each of the topics in the book, and my intent is to distill essential information so that the reader will have a solid foundation from which to develop competencies and skills (the last prong of the triad).

As a counselor educator, I strive to provide my students with the best possible preparation. However, at a master's level, there are only so many courses a student is able to take. Program requirements are to some extent dictated by professional standards for preparation, and this limits the number of electives that a student is free to choose. Training standards of the Council for Accreditation of Counseling and Related Educational Programs (CACREP) do not require specific training in any of the topics discussed in this book. In some programs, a few of these topics are briefly touched upon in more general courses, such as Crisis Intervention. More often than not, limited resources (both financial and personnel) restrict the number of specific courses that can be offered and taken.

One of the refrains I often hear from my students is, "What will I do if I get a client who . . . [fill in the problem]?" Even more urgent are the anxious questions when the student does meet such a client! Although it would be ideal to offer a course on each of the topics that will be presented in this book, students would be in training forever. Although some professionals choose to specialize in certain kinds of clients, or age groups, or issues, and thus may believe they will never have to work with individuals who . . . [fill it in again], the reality is that most clinicians are generalists to some extent. Those who practice in a rural area may be the only professional available, and find themselves serving a wide range of client issues. Even clinicians in more populated areas may not always be able to find a specialist in a particular problem, and cannot simply abandon a client when the problem surfaces. All good clinicians need to have a working familiarity with many issues so they can, at a minimum, make appropriate referrals (and do so effectively), work with a client in a crisis situation, and consult intelligently with other professionals.

Thus, this book is intended to provide that working familiarity with a range of topics that clinicians in schools and community and other mental health settings are likely to face at some point in their careers. In other words, I am writing the book I want to have on my shelf because I could not find one that offered this material in one volume. I hope after going through the book readers will feel more knowledgeable about the many issues their clients may bring. My intent is to provide an awareness of important topics that will enhance professional competence, along with sufficient basic information about treatment and recommendations for resources to consult for more information. This book is *not* intended to provide complete training to become a specialist in any of these issues. Hopefully, readers will find some topics of sufficient interest that they will seek further in-depth reading and training to become highly skilled, but will feel sufficiently prepared to respond professionally to any issue they may face.

I chose topics to include based on my own clinical experience as a school counselor, a counselor in a university counseling center, as a counselor educator, and as a psychologist in private practice. I also listen to the questions my students ask, and pay attention to their anxiety. The topics were selected because they are rarely (with the possible exception of substance abuse) covered in depth in the course of a graduate training program, but they also are issues that counselors will face in their clients.

In many ways, the separate issues overlap. For example, chronic sexual abuse is a trauma, and some survivors develop PTSD. Others may develop eating disorders, engage in self-mutilation, or have problems with substance abuse. Suicide is included as a separate chapter, but is clearly related to all the other topics in the book. A clinician will find that it is difficult to treat any of these issues without touching on others. This is to say that each of the chapters can stand alone in terms of information, but in reality they are all linked and inter-related.

How This Book Is Organized

I have organized all chapters using a similar format to facilitate using the book as a reference as well as a text. That is, each chapter is designed to stand alone, and while the order appears logical to me, reading the chapters in any order should not present a problem. Each chapter begins with a brief introduction, followed by an authentic case study that illustrates the topic of that chapter and provides a context for the rest of the chapter. Then most chapters follow a consistent format:

- An initial section including a definition and description of the problem offers a foundation and vocabulary for understanding the chapter.
- A section on Prevalence provides information on the relative frequency of the problem in various populations.
- The Developmental Influences section discusses what is known about how the problem unfolds over the life span and highlights particular events that may increase the risk for the problem and examines how problems may impact people differently at different points in their lives.
- A section on Assessment outlines the current state of knowledge in that critical area.
- The Treatment Options and Considerations section reviews the available treatments and factors that influence the effectiveness of treatment.
- Issues of Diversity impact the way counselors work with clients; these variables deserve special attention with many topics. In some cases, multicultural factors are not yet understood, but the reader is alerted to potential concerns. Clients with disabilities will be discussed in this section.
- The section on Counselor Issues is a very important one, as it raises readers' sensitivity to factors that may influence their ability to work with clients with a given issue. I have included a note to school counselors in this section, as their role is different from that of other mental health professionals.
- Finally, the Ethical Concerns section addresses particular ethical dilemmas associated with the topic.

A summary concludes each chapter, followed by a section recommending resources—print, electronic, film, and television, and in the community—that interested readers may wish to consult to increase their understanding of the topic. Although I will include important reference books for clinicians, I will also include novels and self-help books when applicable. As a psychologist and avid reader, I have often found that I deepen my understanding of an issue by understanding the characters in a well-written novel, and believe that literature is a valuable resource for psychology. Novels can also be useful as bibliotherapy for some clients, and it is important for clinicians to know which books are appropriate for which clients.

Finally, I have included in each chapter a number of exercises or activities that can be used in classes to deepen students' understanding and engage them more personally with the material. Instructors might wish to assign some or all of these to students or groups and use them as the basis for expanded discussions of the chapter.

A Word about Language

I used the terms counselor, mental health professional, clinician, and therapist interchangeably and consider them to be synonymous. I use the term *counseling* in a generic sense of providing support, guidance, information, and understanding to others to help them overcome obstacles and barriers to optimal functioning. Certainly counselors do this, but so do counseling and clinical psychologists, social workers, and nurses. The book is for helping professionals in a variety of settings and from a variety of disciplines, although those settings often determine professional titles.

At times, I will use terms that may not be familiar to all readers. I will provide a definition in a box close to the first use of the term. The reader will also note references to the DSM-IV-TR throughout the text. This refers to the *Diagnostic and Statistical Manual of Mental Disorders—Text Revision* (4th ed.), which is used by practitioners from all disciplines to arrive at a diagnosis of any mental disorder. In the DSM, criteria for a diagnosis of each disorder are specified, including time markers (how long symptoms have to be present), criteria for ruling out the diagnosis, and subtypes. Many students will study the current version of the DSM in their course in Diagnosis and Treatment Planning.

Who Will Use This Book?

This book can be a basic text for a graduate or upper division undergraduate seminar on Topics for Helping Professionals in programs for counselors, psychologists, social workers, and nurses, but will also be useful to students in practica and internship courses. Instructors may wish to use the book to introduce future clinicians to all of these topics, or use it as a resource when students confront these issues in their field experiences. Note that there are eight chapters. In my experience as a teacher, covering a new chapter every week of a 15-week semester, particularly when each one is dense with information, leads to rushed and sometimes superficial treatment of the material. I hope that having fewer chapters will allow for more in-depth coverage, provide time to utilize some of the recommended media, and an opportunity to do some of the exercises to enhance students' learning.

Although I would like the book to be useful for all helping professionals, some may find a particular chapter of special interest, and may wish to pursue this topic more in depth. For such readers, this book can be a springboard for further study and training.

I hope that students will find this book to be a useful resource that will become part of their professional libraries and consulted often during their careers as helping professionals. This is the book I have always wanted on my shelf!

Other Resources for Instructors and Students

- **Instructors:** Additional exercises and sample responses to the in-text exercises are available to instructors at the Allyn & Bacon Instructor Resource Center. To access this material, go to www.ablongman.com and click on the Instructor Support button.
- **Instructors and Students:**

myhelpinglab is the online destination designed to help students in Counseling and Psychotherapy make the transistion from academic coursework to professional practice. The online content consists of video clips of authentic practitioners/client sessions, video interviews with professionals in the field, an interactive case archive, and a licensing center with valuable information for students who are beginning their in-service careers. For a demonstration of the website and to find out how to package student access to this site with your students' textbooks at no additional cost, go to www.myhelpinglab.com.

Acknowledgments

There are many individuals I wish to thank for their roles in creating this book. I think it is appropriate to begin by thanking all my clients, who have taught me so much over the years, and who inspired me to keep learning. For putting their trust in me, and sharing their struggles and triumphs, I sincerely thank each one. In addition, the individuals who shared their personal journeys and allowed me to include them in the book as case studies made an enormous contribution to this work, which I deeply appreciate. I also must thank my students, whose challenging questions and quest for learning have kept me on my figurative toes.

Seth Osborne's willingness to brainstorm ideas for this book was the first step in this project, and I thank him for his encouragement. Virginia Lanigan, the original editor, believed that I could do this, and was patient with delays, which I appreciate. I value the fine work of Ginny Blanford, the editor who saw this project through to publication and whose suggestions have made this book much more user-friendly. I am very grateful to the reviewers of earlier drafts of this work for their honest and useful comments. They have undoubtedly made this a much better product: Patricia Anderson, Midwestern State University; James J. Bergin, Georgia Southern University; Adam L. Hill, Sonoma State University; David Hof, University of Nebraska at Kearney, Mary H. Jackson, Georgia Southern University; Robin Lewis, California Polytechnical State University; Jonathan Osborn, Hope College; Charles V. Proyor, University of Louisiana at Monroe; Tommie H. Radd, University of Nebraska—Omaha; Lucila Ramos-Sanchez, Santa Clara University; Kathleen M. Salyers, The University of Toledo;

Jobie L. Skaggs, Bradley University; Barry Shreve, Greenville Technical College; Michael Sunich, Troy University—Florida Region; Jim Verhoye, Minnesota State Correctional Facility—Shalopee; Julia Yang, Governors State College.

I would like to sincerely thank several particular former and current students who provided special help during the writing: Sibyl Cato for her assistance locating web resources and articles, Francesca Lopez for her thoughtful comments on earlier chapter drafts, and Kathleen Hoppa, whose assistance locating references, proofreading, and providing thoughtful feedback, were invaluable.

To my former supervisor, current colleague, and valued friend, Greg Kopp, whose clinical skills are a model for me, and whose encouragement has been unwavering, I extend my heartfelt thanks.

Most of all, I am deeply grateful for the constant support and patience of my husband Bob, who never doubted that I could write this book, and who did so many things to allow me the time to devote to this project. His understanding and nurturance made this book possible.

References

American Psychiatric Association. (2000). *Diagnostic and statistical manual of mental disorders—Text revision* (4th ed.). Washington, DC: Author.

Council for Accreditation of Counseling and Related Educational Programs. (n.d.) *2001 Standards*. Retrieved December 15, 2005, from http://www.cacrep.org/2001Standards. htm

Herlihy, B., & Corey, G. (1996). *ACA ethical standards casebook*. Alexandria, VA: American Counseling Association.

Sexual Abuse

Sexual abuse is not a new phenomenon. What is new is the increased attention to the issue by the media and the widespread implementation of programs to teach young children how to protect themselves. Greater public awareness of the problem may encourage more people to report abuse and seek treatment if they experience abuse. In addition to those who come to counseling as a direct result of sexual abuse, it is often at the root of other problems that bring clients to your office—substance abuse, depression, anxiety, eating disorders, acting out, suicide, and so on. Childhood sexual abuse often leaves psychological, emotional, and interpersonal scars that persist and affect victims' functioning throughout life. Surprisingly, a survey of the Council for Accreditation of Counseling and Related Educational Programs (CACREP)-approved graduate programs in counseling discovered that only 9% of graduate programs offered a required course in treating sexual abuse, and another 22% offered an elective course, although 95% of respondents rated such training as important or very important (Kitzrow, 2002). This is why I begin with this chapter—counselors will be more effective with a variety of client issues if they are informed about and sensitive to sexual abuse and its many and serious consequences, but graduate training programs are unlikely to cover sexual abuse in any depth.

Case Study

Mark is a 37-year-old Caucasian who is overweight and in need of dental care. He is currently unemployed and living in his mother's home. He grew up in a small community about 20 miles from a city in the central United States in a neighborhood where several other children close to his age also lived. He remembers playing cowboys and Indians with other boys as a child, and also playing with their toy cars. At the back of the lot of the family home was an empty trailer that the neighborhood children sometimes used as a fort or playhouse.

Mark recalls that his father made a miniature town in the sand where the children played with their cars, and that his father sometimes joined them in play. However, Mark also vividly remembers the strict discipline his father imposed on all the children, such as grounding without meals, forcing a child to stand in a corner for hours, and beatings. His mother was more passive, reporting the children's infractions to her husband, who administered disciplinary measures when he got home. Neither his parents nor his older siblings ever provided Mark with any sex education.

When Mark began school in first grade, teachers quickly detected his learning disability. Throughout school, Mark took "basic classes," which he agrees would now be called Special Education. During high school, he worked at a local establishment for all three years, and was very conscientious about his job.

When Mark was 10 years old, an older boy, Sam, a neighborhood friend of his older siblings, often came over to play. If the older siblings were not available, Sam played with Mark and his friends, joining in their activities. Mark isn't certain how much older Sam was, but believed at the time he was the age of his older siblings, which would make him at least 5 years older than Mark. One day when Sam came over and Mark was alone, Sam suggested that they "do something different." He suggested that they go to the trailer where Mark expected they might pretend to be under attack. Once in the trailer, Sam began rubbing Mark's legs and then his genitals. He suggested they both remove their clothes, and then he proceeded to molest Mark and instructed Mark to fondle him. Mark observed that Sam was sexually mature. The sexual activity proceeded to oral sex.

Mark remembers that Sam came over very often after that incident to repeat the sexual activity. After three to four months, the activity progressed to penetration. Sam told Mark not to tell his parents because they might "get in trouble." Mark did not know anything about sex and trusted Sam who was older and a friend of his siblings.

Mark enjoyed this activity, and looked forward to Sam's visits. He received affection and love from Sam, which he did not get from his family. This sexual relationship continued for over a year until Sam suddenly stopped coming over. Mark did not understand this abrupt termination and never asked about it, although he felt terribly hurt and abandoned. He felt as though he had been merely a sex object and that he had not been valued as a person. He was terribly fearful of discovery and the consequences should that occur.

Mark later overheard several boys at school talking about "gays" and what they do. He realized that they were describing what he and Sam had done, and became more frightened of discovery. He understood from the overheard conversation that being "gay" was a bad thing, and he felt ashamed and confused, but was too fearful to approach anyone to talk about his pain. He feared his father's wrath and was convinced that if he told his parents they would assume he was the instigator and punish him severely. He wondered why he was the one Sam chose, and was unable to understand why Sam would do such things knowing they were wrong. Although he was not actively suicidal, he thought he did not deserve to live.

Mark managed his fears by withdrawing from social interactions and repressing his emotions. He never had a single date with either a male or female. He volunteered to work at his job the night of his school prom. No one in the family ever commented on the lack of normal socialization with peers. Mark managed his sexual desires by masturbating to pictures in a men's health magazine. He believes his sexual preoccupation is higher than that of most other men. To compensate for the absence of meaningful relationships in his life, Mark directed all his energy into his jobs where he always gave "more than 100%" effort.

When he was about 34 years old, Mark was lonely, had yet to have a date, and felt socially isolated. He met a customer through his work, who was a single mother of two boys aged 10 and 11. Mark and this woman became friends and he had frequent contact with her sons. He was delighted that they seemed to like him, and basked in their affection. He felt he was in a surrogate father role and that he was an important male figure in their lives, which was very gratifying to him. After a period of time, the boys began to visit Mark and stay overnight on alternate weekends, often playing with Mark's adolescent cousin. Mark eventually molested the boys, convincing himself at the time that he was educating them about sex so they would be more knowledgeable than he had been. Although Mark told the boys not to tell anyone of their activities because it was "private between guys," one of the boys told a coworker of Mark's, who reported the incident. Mark pled guilty to two third-degree felony counts of criminal sexual contact with a minor and one count of misdemeanor sexual contact. He served a short jail sentence and was on probation for five years. He registered as a sex offender and attended a therapeutic treatment program for sex offenders for two years.

In therapy, Mark acknowledged for the first time to himself, to his group, and eventually to most family members, that he was gay. He has yet to have a serious relationship, but eagerly anticipates the time when someone will love him and value him for himself.

As an adult, Mark repeatedly lets others take advantage of him. He is eager to have relationships, and attempts to please anyone who pays him any attention. Mark recently lost a job he valued because a customer persuaded Mark to request sexual favors from a third man on the customer's behalf. Mark's employer was notified, and he fired Mark immediately. Although he believes that admitting and acting on his interest in adult males is an important step in avoiding future sexual offenses, Mark still struggles with issues of self-esteem and lack of assertiveness that interfere with his well-being.

Definitions and Description of the Problem

Although the federal government first enacted legislation to protect child welfare in 1912, it is only since 1974 and the passage of the Child Abuse Prevention and Treatment Act (CAPTA) that it has been mandatory to report cases of child abuse in the United States. *Child sexual abuse* refers to sexual exploitation of a child by a parent or someone who has temporary (such as a teacher) or permanent responsibility for the child, or by a family member (sibling, grandparent). Sexual abuse of a child includes fondling, requests for sexual touching, forcing a child to look at the genitalia of someone older, forcing a child to undress or expose genitals or pose in a sexual manner, any sexual contact or penetration, or exposing a child to pornography. Force is not necessary for an act to be considered child sexual abuse: children may agree to participate because they are manipulated, bribed, threatened, or confused. Sexual abuse reports are typically referred to Child Protective Services or a similar agency responsible for investigating the complaint and removing the child from the home if necessary for the child's safety. That agency contacts law enforcement to handle the legal aspects of a case. *Sexual assault* refers to any unwanted sexual act or behavior imposed by one person on another, and is reported directly to law enforcement agencies. With children, sexual assault is the legal term used when the alleged perpetrator is unrelated to the child and is not temporarily responsible for the care of the child. Sexual assault is the term most often used when the perpetrator and victim are both adults. The age at which a person can *legally* consent to sexual behavior varies from state to state, with 16 being the age of consent in many states. If the reader would like more specific information about legal issues and definitions, http://www.prevent-abuse-now.com/law3.htm provides links to state and federal documents with definitions and statutes.

Data from the Bureau of Justice Statistics on crimes reported to law enforcement agencies give a perspective on the pervasiveness of the problem. The data indicate that 67% of all victims of sexual assault were under 18 and 34% of all victims were younger than 12 (www.protectmefirst.com). In 1999, children under 17 were the victims of 70% of the forcible sex offenses reported to the National Incident Based Reporting System (NIBRS), and were the victims of 97% of the non-forcible sex offenses (www.unh.edu/ccrc). Rates of childhood sexual abuse are particularly high in runaway youth, with some estimates exceeding 50% (Tyler, Hoyt, Whitbeck, & Cauce, 2001).

Different agencies and researchers use slightly different definitions of the term *sexual abuse*. Most definitions include both contact (e.g., sexual touching, penetration, oral sex) and non-contact sexual abuse (e.g., exhibitionism, voyeurism, and using children in producing pornography). In general, the term describes sexual activities involving a child and some level of "abusive condition" (Finkelhor, 1994). The upper age limit for *child* varies, but is generally between 16 and 18. Some experts include verbal remarks (sexual comments about a child's body or sexual invitations) in the category of sexual abuse. An area of debate concerns whether abuse by peers (such as date rape) is sexual abuse, and if so whether there needs to be a significant age difference between those involved. Another inappropriate behavior that arguably would be considered sexual abuse is parenting that ignores the effect on the child of such experiences as witnessing parental intercourse, or frequent close examination of children's genitalia. Even when these actions do not violate the child or stimulate the adults, the behaviors may have detrimental effects on a child's sexual development. The discussion here will not make fine distinctions but will consider sexual abuse in the generic understanding of the term.

Sexual abuse is widely believed to cause a variety of problems in victims, although individuals vary considerably in the way they react to abuse. Victims of sexual abuse frequently exhibit such emotional difficulties as fear, anxiety, sadness, anger, and shame. Some of the behaviors often associated with sexual abuse are social withdrawal, defiance, aggression, and sexualized behavior. Sexual abuse may appear in the histories of individuals with eating disorders, substance abuse problems, and self-mutilating behaviors. An innovative study of twins, one of whom had experienced childhood sexual abuse, found elevated risk for substance abuse, including earlier and more frequent use, in the twin with a history of childhood sexual abuse (Nelson et al., 2006). Some victims experience physiological symptoms such as stomach upset, headaches, and extreme startle reactions. Enduring psychological disturbances such as low self-esteem, difficulties trusting others, and sexual dissatisfaction are prevalent as well (Deblinger & Heflin, 1996). Researchers have detected reduction in short-term memory in college women with a history of sexual abuse; the greater the duration of the abuse, the greater the reduction in memory scores (Navalta, Polcari, Webster, Boghossian, & Teicher, 2006). Victims of child sexual abuse are also at higher risk for later sexual victimization (Krahe, 2000).

Some victims of sexual abuse may develop post-traumatic stress disorder and others may exhibit symptoms of the disorder without meeting the criteria for a diagnosis. The severity of the problems appears to be influenced by the nature and duration of the abuse, the presence or absence of force, the developmental stage of the victim, the nature of the relationship with the perpetrator, the context of the abuse, and the reaction of others to the disclosure. The damage attributable to sexual abuse is considerable, and mental health professionals must be familiar with the variety of presentations that may develop.

The legal and investigative activities that often follow discovery of the abuse can create additional problems. Some would view these procedures as "re-traumatization" of the victim, who may be asked to tell the story over and over to different interviewers, and who may even be involved in some legal proceedings. If the abuser is a family member, authorities may remove the offender (and on occasion, the child) from the home to ensure a safe environment, but the disruption may be traumatic for the child. If the abuser leaves the home, the child may experience guilt and feel responsible for any strain the family experiences. Sexual abuse treatment must deal with all of these aspects to be effective.

In this chapter, I will discuss sexual abuse to help counselors and counselors-to-be to increase their awareness and sensitivity to this issue. Most professional graduate degree programs in mental health fields lack specific training on working with childhood sexual abuse (Alpert & Paulson, 1990). As with other topics in this book, it behooves mental health professionals to be well informed about this issue whether or not it is an area of specialty. Many clients will seek treatment for other issues that may in fact be effects of the abuse. Clinicians must be alert to the possibility that sexual abuse has occurred, and be aware of appropriate interventions and services whether they will be providing treatment or a referral.

Prevalence

The prevalence of sexual abuse is almost impossible to quantify. The secrecy and shame that often accompany sexual abuse also keep victims from reporting incidents. *Incidence* data report events that come to the attention of authorities, whereas *prevalence data* refer to the proportion of people in the population who are sexual abuse victims. The following figures are tentative at best, but they will help readers develop a notion of the extensiveness of the problem. One widely quoted figure is that reported by Finkelhor (1994), who concluded that 25% of females, and 14% of males are sexually abused prior to the age of 18. Botash (2006) estimates that child sexual abuse affects more than 100,000 children per year. National data compiled on child maltreatment reporting in 2001 documented 86,688 cases of *substantiated* sexual abuse. This actually represents a slight decrease in the rate of sexual abuse based on five-year trends. Readers should not be unduly optimistic about the decline, however, which may reflect changes in Child Protective Service criteria for abuse more than any actual reduction in offenses. Nevertheless, as only a small percentage (as little as 10%, according to Leventhal, 2001), come to the attention of authorities, the number of instances of sexual abuse is staggering!

Incidence: A count of the number of reported occurrences of the behavior (e.g., 5,000 cases).

Prevalence: The percentage of a population that has had an experience (e.g., 25% of females).

Developmental Influences

Development both affects and is affected by sexual abuse. Finkelhor (1995) describes these processes in his theory of "developmental victimology." The levels of risk and the likelihood of disclosure of sexual abuse vary with the age and developmental stage of a child. For example, we know that the risk for sexual abuse increases significantly from ages six to ten. Children under six are less likely to disclose sexual abuse, while victims older than twelve are most likely to report to adults. Puberty increases the risk for sexual molestation, although some pedophiles are less likely to target post-pubescent children.

The stage of development also affects the ability of children to protect themselves from harm. Older children have greater capacity to flee, to argue with or dissuade a potential abuser, or to physically resist. On the other hand, older children and adolescents are more likely to use substances or engage in other behaviors that put them at increased risk for sexual abuse.

Although sexual abuse of infants is mercifully rare, it does occur. A startling 14% of all victims of sexual assault reported to law enforcement were under six years old; of all victims under age 12, 4-year-olds were at greatest risk. Forty percent of offenders against such young children were juveniles under age 18 (Snyder, 2000). Infants and babies will not remember the incidents (Alessi & Ballard, 2001), but the physical trauma from the abuse is likely to have an effect. Some experts think infants may retain "body memories" of the abuse, which are physical sensations that correspond to the abuse experience (Classen, 1995). Toddlers may have a greater awareness of social norms and may exhibit signs of distress following abuse, although they are unlikely to retain any memories about the trauma or to be able to articulate the source of their distress. One woman interviewed by Williams (1994) and who was abused at age 2 years 9 months, remembers the "itchy beard" of her molester, and reports the memory persists and interferes with her relationships with bearded men.

Defense mechanisms are psychological processes that protect us from being consciously aware of a thought or feeling we cannot tolerate. The defense mechanisms only allow the unconscious thought or feeling indirect expression in a disguised form. Preschool children often use the defense mechanisms of denial and dissociation. Preschool children are most likely to cope with the abuse by dissociating, which may become a chronic pattern (Finkelhor, 1995).

Denial: Rejecting the reality of an event or situation to avoid the emotional pain of doing so.

Dissociation: An altered state of consciousness in which the individual is not aware of current surroundings, similar to "spacing out."

Sexual abuse is more common in school age than in younger children, with about 20% of victims of sexual abuse being of elementary school age. Risk increases when children enter school because the size of their social world expands and exposes children to more danger. Recall that a large proportion of abusers of children are themselves children, although usually several years older than the victim. Behavioral symptoms of sexually abused children at this age include sexualized behavior such as preoccupation with sexual topics, seductive behavior, excessive masturbation, sex play with others, and so on. Elementary age children are

Rationalization: Inventing various explanations to justify situation (while denying feelings).

Blaming: Believing someone other than the self is responsible for a situation.

more likely to use rationalization and blaming as defenses against distress. A child abused at this age may have feelings of guilt, shame, and confusion, particularly if the abuser is a parent whom the child loves. Children may not understand how the same person can be both protector and their abuser. If the child either experienced pleasurable sensations during the abuse or received some other benefit (e.g., increased attention or gifts), the guilt may be particularly strong. Some children will revert to earlier strategies under stress, and thus we observe denial and dissociation in this age group as well. When a child dissociates as a way to cope with the abuse, memories of the event are incomplete or distorted, making it hard for the child to make sense of his or her experience.

Adolescents struggle to define themselves—to decide what kind of a person they want to be. Many teens are preoccupied with sexual themes at this stage. When sexual abuse occurs at this point in development, the adolescent's struggle to establish an identity and build self-esteem can be derailed. It becomes more difficult for the adolescent to explore relationships and sexuality. Abused adolescents are prone to have difficulties forming close and trusting relationships, as their abuser betrayed their trust. They, and younger children to some extent, may believe that the abuse occurred because of some basic flaw in themselves. Some adolescents, to deal with the intense emotional response to the abuse, turn to substance abuse, eating disorders, running away, and sexual acting out.

Most of the investigation of the impact of sexual abuse has concentrated on symptoms of post-traumatic stress disorder (PTSD). Some experts believe a new diagnostic category would be more appropriate for sexually abused children who are unlikely to meet criteria for PTSD. They recommend a diagnosis of disorder of extreme stress, not otherwise specified (DESNOS) to more accurately describe the profile (Courtois, 1995). Young children may exhibit "post-traumatic play" (re-enacting the abuse in play) and a sense of impending doom. The impact of sexual abuse can include such common short-term effects as fearfulness that may be restricted to environments that are reminiscent of the abuse context. For example, sexually abused children may be afraid to go to any park if the abuse occurred in a park, or they may be fearful of individuals who have physical characteristics that resemble the abuser. They may also have stronger fear reactions to news images or television violence. Young children who are abused by primary caregivers are likely to develop insecure attachments that have been associated with other psychological difficulties throughout the lifespan.

The impact of the abuse may disrupt normal development. In young children, abuse can disrupt the important attachment process, particularly if the abuser is a parent. Self-esteem may decrease. Sexually abused children may think their sexualized behavior is an acceptable style for interpersonal interactions. The persistent anxiety experienced by many sexually abused children and adolescents may lead to self-mutilation, eating disorders, or substance abuse, which further derail normal developmental processes.

Cognitive development affects the way in which the abused child understands the abuse. Infants do not have the neurological development required to store specific memories (Alessi & Ballard, 2001). Very young children take their cues from their parents rather than from the event itself. Infants and young children sense when parents are upset and will react to that distress more than to the event that caused it. Young children may be unable to understand that what happened to them is "abuse" or even "wrong," particularly if the abuser is someone they love and trust. The child may be aware of the tension in the family, or the absence of a parent, without understanding the implications of what had occurred. This means that young children may not appear upset about the abuse when it happens, but they may become upset later when they are better able to understand what happened. For example, a young child whose immediate reactions include tantrums and aggression may become depressed as the child matures and is able to understand the abuse.

Although therapists often stress to the child that he/she was not to blame, Finkelhor (1995) talks about two kinds of self-blame: "characterological" and "behavioral" self-blame. When a child is engaged in characterological self-blame, the child believes the abuse happened because of some enduring defect ("I'm a bad child"), which is the kind of thinking that we must help them change. Behavioral blame is situation-focused ("I should have kicked him harder") and could generate a self-protective stance in the future. Females who are close to or post-puberty may understand the implications of sexual abuse in terms of their "reputation," and may view themselves as "damaged goods," leading to social isolation. As boys come to understand the social stigma of homosexuality, their self-esteem may suffer and they may become less likely to disclose the abuse for fear of this label.

The most serious developmental consequences of sexual abuse are likely to occur when the abuse is repetitive, when the abuser is a parent, when the abuse is added to other stressors, and when the abuse occurs at a developmental transition (e.g., a child is abused on a first date) (Finkelhor, 1995).

Assessment

Assessment of sexual abuse is a complex and difficult matter, yet it is absolutely essential for the provision of effective services. Assessment of a child victim after the alleged abuse is a specialized process and only specially trained and highly skilled evaluators should do this. In that situation, the evaluator must determine exactly what occurred and the results of the assessment may lead to legal proceedings. These specialists must also make recommendations regarding the continued safety of the child and the ramifications can be extensive. It is imperative that generalists without special training not attempt to do these evaluations. Those who might be interested in this specialty should consult the website of the American Professional Society on the Abuse of Children (APSAC). Practice Guidelines are available from their website.

Other mental health professionals may be involved in the assessment of the psychological impact of the sexual abuse to provide treatment. Clinicians will want to do a thorough assessment so that an appropriate, individualized treatment plan is developed. In the case of sexual abuse, there are several useful instruments that the clinician might use. The *Child Sexual Behavior Inventory* (Friedrich, 1997) is a checklist completed by a parent or caretaker that identifies behaviors that are frequently associated with sexual abuse. Clinicians may use this when they suspect sexual abuse and want to screen for indicator behaviors. The inventory can help the clinician formulate a treatment plan targeted to the constellation of symptoms presented by a particular client, and is also useful as a way to measure treatment progress.

The *Trauma Symptom Checklist for Children* (Briere, 1996) is a self-report inventory that can be used with children from 8 to 16. It includes several validity scales and provides age and gender specific norms that assist the clinician in interpreting results. For those over 18, there is an adult version by the same author, the *Trauma Symptom Inventory*.

What is crucial to providing professional assessment is that clinicians assess not only the sexual abuse event(s) and its direct consequences, but also evaluate other areas of functioning that will affect decisions about best treatment. The counselor should examine the other problems commonly found in victims of child sexual abuse. To assess more global areas of functioning, the clinician might choose an inventory such as the *Child Behavior Checklist* (Achenbach, 1991). This is an empirically sound instrument, with self-report, parent, and teacher report versions. There is a version for children aged 6 to 18, and another for children 1 to 5 years of age. There are versions in Spanish and English, and translations available for other languages. For adults, there are a number of general adjustment measures available.

While standardized instruments are valuable assessment tools, the clinician will also want to review available records, and informally assess such important variables as the attitude of the caregivers toward the abuse and treatment. The therapist will also want to know about any adjustment problems that existed prior to, or concurrently with, the abuse, as well as client strengths and available resources within and outside the family. A complete assessment should evaluate the levels of fear, anxiety, posttraumatic stress symptoms, depression, self-esteem, trust issues, cognitive distortions, aggression, and socialization difficulties, among others. The relationships of the child to both the offender and non-offending parents are essential to scrutinize because of the impact they have on treatment. The clinician should find out about any disorders in the family, such as substance abuse or mental disorders, to assess how these might influence the treatment. It is important to note that many victims of child sexual abuse will not display any symptoms; one estimate is 40% will not have any evidence of difficulties. However, some children who do not exhibit any of these problems at the time of the event may do so months or years later.

Because of the pervasiveness of this problem, it would be prudent for all clinicians to include sexual abuse in their initial assessment of all clients, regardless of the presenting problem. Overlooking this may result in misdirected treatment that is unlikely to be effective.

Treatment Options and Considerations

As the reader will find with other topics in this book, there are a variety of treatment approaches available for sexual abuse. There are also different strategies for children who are treated as children, and adult survivors of childhood sexual abuse who have never been treated. I will first discuss treatment for children that therapists provide soon after discovery or disclosure, and then review treatment options for adults who experienced sexual abuse as children but who did not receive treatment until many years after the experience.

Treating Children Who Have Been Sexually Abused

Regardless of the treatment strategy employed, it is essential that clinicians keep in mind that children are not able to engage in intensive talk therapy for an entire session. When working with children, it is important to include elements that are fun for the child, and to communicate a warmth and interest in the child apart from the abuse experience.

Experts and researchers sponsored by the National Crime Victims Research and Treatment Center (NCVC) compiled the best available information about twenty-four treatment approaches and evaluated the evidence that supported the effectiveness of these approaches. Such treatment guidelines provide practitioners with a sound basis for selecting interventions that research shows to result in favorable treatment outcomes. Several of the approaches are similar, so I will not review all of the approaches here. Rather, I will describe a few models that represent a variety of theoretical perspectives.

Trauma-Focused Cognitive Behavioral Therapy

Cognitive behavioral therapy is based on the premise that cognition (thoughts), emotions (feelings), and behavior (actions) are interrelated and affect each other, so that a change in one area results in changes in all three. Of the treatment approaches for children evaluated in the NCVC document, trauma-focused cognitive behavioral therapy (TF-CBT) received the highest rating, which means it is a "well-supported, efficacious treatment." A useful manual is available for clinicians using this intervention (Deblinger & Heflin, 1996). This model is designed for treatment with children aged 3 to 13 who exhibit symptoms of PTSD or who have misconceptions about their abuse. Treatment follows a thorough assessment of the child and parent. The role of the therapist is that of advocate, educator, role model, and coach. The approach assumes that the abuse has been substantiated, and is most effective when there is a supportive adult involved in the collaborative treatment. Treatment duration varies from twelve to forty sessions, and involves individual work with the child and the non-offending parent as well as conjoint therapy with the child and parent. This approach includes several components for the child: coping skills training, gradual exposure and cognitive and affective processing, and education; treatment for the parent also includes coping skills training and gradual exposure, and adds behavior management training. The joint sessions again involve coping skills practice, gradual exposure, education, personal safety skills, and family therapy.

Both the child and the parent learn coping skills in their individual therapy sessions. Emotional expression skills provide tools for identifying and communicating about feelings related to the abuse. Cognitive skill training involves recognizing and learning to dispute irrational thoughts, and relaxation training helps with anxiety and tension that often accompany the abuse.

The centerpiece of this approach is the gradual exploration and reprocessing component. Based on the behavioral techniques of systematic desensitization and prolonged exposure, this intervention gradually exposes the client to anxiety-provoking stimuli, with repeated exposure until the anxiety is no longer experienced. This technique often generates increased anxiety at first, but CBT therapists believe that advanced preparation will prepare clients to tolerate the temporary discomfort to obtain the long-term gains. After repeated exposure to the anxiety-provoking thoughts and images, more adaptive reactions—such as feelings of control, bravery, pride—replace the anxiety (Deblinger & Heflin, 1996). Parents also experience this gradual exposure and reprocessing. This prepares them to hear abuse-related material so they can assist the child in coping.

Systematic desensitization: A behavioral technique in which a client is exposed to a threatening situation (usually in imagination) while in a relaxed condition, until the anxiety is no longer experienced.

The "reprocessing segment" is a vehicle for the child to express thoughts and feelings about the sexual abuse episode and the subsequent investigation, and so on. The goal is to help the child reconcile confusing thoughts and feelings. For example, the child will need help in accepting that it is possible to both love the parent/offender and hate the behavior. This segment of treatment also attempts to replace distorted cognitions ("It was my fault," e.g.) with more adaptive and accurate thoughts about the event. This component is also used with parents, who also may experience confusion and dysfunctional thinking when they discover the abuse.

Parents learn behavioral management techniques that will help them deal with the difficult behaviors sometimes exhibited by sexually abused children. They are also encouraged to model effective methods for dealing with the trauma (reporting the offense to authorities, not being angry at the child, talking about feelings) as children will be scrutinizing their behavior for cues. Children and parents are educated about sexual abuse, healthy sexuality, and developmentally appropriate sex education. Children also learn methods for keeping safe in the future.

The final component in this approach employs joint parent–child sessions where the clinician facilitates open communication about the abuse. The gradual exposure process continues, with the parent hopefully modeling successful coping skills. Parent–child sessions reinforce the educational component introduced in the individual sessions.

Trauma-Focused Play Therapy

Play therapy has roots in the psychoanalytic tradition, but is widely used by therapists from all theoretical perspectives. Some therapists view play therapy as a vehicle to form a therapeutic alliance with a child client, whereas others see play as a window into the child's unconscious conflicts. Most would agree that play therapy is a natural way to communicate with children whose verbal skills are unsophisticated and whose usual medium is play rather than sustained conversation. Rated as a "promising and acceptable treatment" by the NCVC, although there is not yet

Therapeutic alliance: A strong emotional connection between therapist and client that facilitates the client's healing.

strong empirical evidence of effectiveness, is an approach to play therapy developed by Eliana Gil (1988) specifically for child trauma victims. Dr. Gil (1988) believes that traumatized children may re-enact the trauma in play and thereby manage and express their feelings and increase their cognitive mastery of the event.

Dr. Gil emphasizes the importance of selecting appropriate toys for play therapy with children who have been sexually abused. In addition to the standard dollhouse and dolls, puppets, and art materials, she recommends telephones, sunglasses, nursing bottles, and story-telling techniques for use with this clientele. She recommends a very individualized approach, with the type of play, pace, and interventions tailored to the particular child. She strongly supports individual therapy for the child, but encourages collateral therapy for parents along with education and support for them. For those interested in exploring play therapy further, Dr. Gil's books on the subject are an excellent starting point.

Art Therapy

Along with play therapy, art therapy helps children express, both symbolically and realistically, emotions and concepts to which they are unable to give voice (Naitove, 1982). Using unfamiliar media (Styrofoam, clay) can help the child get away from preconceived notions of what *art* should look like. Naitove describes various media and their unique properties for art therapy with sexually abused children (p. 281). In addition, the successful completion of a work of art is a positive experience for the child and assists in the development of a strong therapeutic alliance. The skilled clinician will encourage the child to comment on or talk about their productions, eliciting further understanding of the underlying struggles.

Eye Movement Desensitization and Reprocessing

The eye movement desensitization and reprocessing (EMDR) approach to therapy, developed by Dr. Francine Shapiro, is considered to be "supported and acceptable" for sexual abuse. There are training programs available for therapists wishing to become proficient in this treatment, and several books provide detailed descriptions of the approach. If the reader has never observed this treatment, I strongly recommend watching a video demonstration to get a sense of how it works.

EMDR is a highly structured approach and treatment proceeds in a planned sequence of therapeutic interventions. The concept of *dual attention* is the cornerstone of this approach. This means that the client attends to past and present experience while focusing *at the same time* on an external stimulus, which is usually eye movement (following the rapid movement of the therapist's hand) but can also be tapping, tactile stimulation, or auditory tones, depending on the client. During an EMDR session, the therapist repeats a series of brief, directed doses of dual attention many times during a session.

Several controlled studies of this approach have found positive results with traumatized children, and anecdotal evidence abounds. One distinct advantage of

Assimilation: A new experience is incorporated into existing cognitive structures (e.g., a goat is called a "doggie").

Accommodation: Existing cognitive structures are expanded or modified to include new experiences (e.g., a dog is called an "animal").

this approach is its brief duration; there are reports of dramatic positive outcomes in just one session, with two to three sessions as the norm. The exact mechanism by which this treatment effects change is not yet well understood, so skepticism is not uncommon.

This treatment draws from information processing theory and Piaget's concepts of *assimilation* and *accommodation*, and rests on several assumptions:

- Memories of traumatic events are not completely assimilated into the person's cognitive framework, and thus these memories interfere with subsequent information processing tasks.
- Distortions in perception, feeling, and response occur because the trauma disrupts normal psychological and biological processes that are involved in memory processing.
- Individuals have an internal self-healing mechanism that responds to the EMDR procedure.
- Individual self-representations of the trauma memory are unique.
- Clients need skill-building to correct deficits resulting from the trauma.

Here is the recommended format of EMDR treatment that proceeds in a prescribed fashion through the following phases:

- The first of eight phases is a history taking and treatment planning phase. This includes identifying both targets and barriers to EMDR reprocessing, and the treatment plan is developed.
- In the next phase, the client (and caretaker in the case of a child) gets education about this procedure, and learns skills (e.g., relaxation techniques, visualization) to deal with trauma-related material if it should surface outside the session.
- In the third phase, the reprocessing actually begins. The client first identifies a safe place in imagination. The client then identifies the most vivid visual memory of the trauma as well as the related negative thoughts and emotions. The client rates the intensity of the negative emotions on a scale. The client observes where the physical sensations connected to the traumatic memory are located (e.g., upset stomach, headache). The client also generates an alternative positive thought about the trauma that the client rates for validity.
- At this point, the client focuses on the visual image identified earlier while tracking the clinician's fingers moving rapidly back and forth for about 30 seconds. The therapist then tells the client to "let go" of the image and notice what happens. After taking a deep breath, the client describes observed changes in the image, bodily sensations, feelings, or thoughts. The client rates the level of distress related to the memory. This process happens over and over until the client reports no distress associated with the memory.

- Then the clinician asks the client to think of the preferred positive belief identified earlier in the session and repeats the eye movements while the client focuses on the image and the positive belief. This happens until the client rates the validity of the positive belief highly.
- The client then checks for any remaining physical discomfort or tension, and if the client finds any, the eye movements continue while the client focuses on the physical sensations.
- The next phase is closure in which the therapist asks the client to notice (or write in a journal depending on the age) any related image that occurs before the next session.
- The final phase, *re-evaluation*, is used at the beginning of any subsequent sessions. This involves assessing progress toward treatment goals and working with material that has surfaced.

For those interested in EMDR, a book designed for clinicians who use this approach with children is *Small Wonders: Healing Childhood Trauma with EMDR* by Joan Lovett (1999). One of the case examples focuses on a situation involving sexual mistreatment. For readers who would like a very specific guide to using EMDR in treating adults abused as children, I recommend Laurel Parnell's *EMDR in the Treatment of Adults Abused as Children* (1999). Although the book is excellent, I strongly recommend that anyone interested in using this approach obtain training and supervision before using it with clients.

Although there are other approaches to treating children who have been sexually abused, the approaches described in this section are the most commonly employed and have reasonably established efficacy. Readers who choose to provide services to this clientele should obtain specialized training and attend closely to the counselor issues described in the next section of the chapter.

Group Therapy

Group therapy is a standard component of sexual abuse treatment and generally is in addition to individual or family therapy. Children may begin in individual treatment and then add group therapy when the therapist assesses they are ready. The groups might be psychoeducational in nature (providing sex education or safety strategies, for example) or therapy groups where members can focus on deeper emotional issues. Advantages of groups for sexually abused children are the reduction in isolation and withdrawal and self-stigmatizing that often accompany the abuse.

Family Therapy

Sexual abuse has an impact on family members other than the victim. Parents (or the non-offending parent if one is the offender) and siblings experience the trauma and are also often involved in treatment. The nature and format of that treatment varies with the individual circumstances, but often includes the non-offending parent. There are a variety of family interventions described in the literature, but space does not permit a description of all available models. However, regardless of the approach, it is crucial that child safety be the paramount concern. If necessary, the therapist may become an advocate for the removal of the offender from the home instead of removing the child. The family needs to understand the limits of confidentiality in this situation and to recognize that family re-unification is not always possible when sexual abuse has occurred.

Treatment for Boys

Differences related to the abuse event and more general gender differences suggest that treatment approaches that are effective with abused girls may not be useful with boys (Friedrich, 1995). Males are more likely to experience violence in association with the sexual abuse; more likely to externalize (express in aggressive or oppositional behaviors) their distress; and may find less support from mothers. Males are also less proficient in language, more competitive in play, less experienced at identifying and expressing feelings, and less adept at listening than girls. Response to sexual abuse also results in effects that are unique to males: confusion about sexual identity, hyper-masculine behavior to establish masculinity, and recapitulation of their experience as a victim (Friedrich, 1995, p. 13).Treatment approaches must take these differences into account.

Friedrich (1995) has described a treatment program specifically for boys that involves individual, group, and family therapy and incorporates theoretical contributions from attachment theory, dysregulation theory, and self-theory. Interested readers will want to consult Friedrich's book, which includes techniques and clinical examples of his approach.

Treating Adult Victims of Childhood Sexual Abuse

Sometimes, victims become adults before they reveal childhood sexual abuse. Many adults with these histories may not have clear memories of the abuse, but may come to therapy because something triggers an emotional response that they don't understand. They may experience unwanted memories intruding on their thoughts, have sleep disturbances or nightmares and waking flashbacks. Many will come to therapy with histories of substance abuse, depression, self-destructive behaviors, and relationship difficulties. Adult survivors also exhibit varying degrees of resiliency that the clinician will want to emphasize in treatment.

Classen (1995) describes the recovery process for adults abused as children, and by extension the treatment program, as involving three major tasks:

- Establishing a sense of safety
- Remembering and mourning the abuse
- Reconnecting with self and others.

Sgroi (1989), who identifies five stages of recovery from childhood sexual abuse, provides another perspective on the recovery process:

1. Acknowledging the reality of the abuse.
2. Overcoming secondary responses to the abuse (fear, guilt, anger, shame).
3. Forgiving oneself and ending self-punishment.
4. Adopting positive coping behaviors.
5. Relinquishing the "survivor" identity when recovery is complete (p. 111).

Readers are encouraged to consider these two views of the recovery process when reading the following treatment models and when thinking about the case study presented at the beginning of the chapter.

Ecological, Multimodal Treatment

Harvey and Harney (1995) describe an ecological treatment model they recommend for working with adult survivors. This model considers several kinds of variables that affect the person's response to sexual abuse, all of which the clinician will want to assess:

- *Person variables*, such as the individual's age, developmental stage, intelligence, personality, coping style, and more.
- *Event variables*, such as the frequency, duration, severity, level of force, etc.
- *Environmental variables*, such as the home, school, or workplace, community, culture, religion, etc.

Treatment goals are broader than simple symptom reduction. The goals encompass a broader concept of mental health and well-being that includes control of the memory process. This means that the individual recovers important information that she may have been lacking but also is no longer bothered by nightmares, flashbacks, or unwanted thoughts of the abuse. Another goal refers to the emotional arena and seeks a balance between numbness to the memories and being overwhelmed by them. The emotions that are experienced can be identified and tolerated and no longer interfere with the individual's ability to respond emotionally to current stimuli. Symptom reduction is not irrelevant, and medication may be useful to manage related symptoms (e.g., depression, substance abuse). To restore or develop self-esteem, clients reflect on their feelings of guilt, shame, and self-blame to replace them with a more realistic self-evaluation. Clients will value their resiliency and identify the strengths and qualities they have developed in response to the trauma. Clients are encouraged to adopt self-nurturing practices that promote mental and physical health and well-being. As treatment concludes, clients will have made sense of, or found meaning, in the trauma. They may modify or terminate family relationships, may find creative outlets for their experience, or may choose social activism as a vehicle for their energies.

The treatment program consists of three stages. The first stage focuses on the triad of safety, stability, and self-care. The therapist helps the client to establish safety in the present by gaining insight into, and strategies to manage, factors (such as impulses, behaviors, or experiences) that put them at risk. When the client accomplishes these tasks, therapy moves into the next stage, which involves exploring and integrating the sexual abuse experience. The purpose of this is to understand the role that the childhood sexual abuse has in the client's present life. During this stage, group therapy with other survivors of sexual abuse often complements the individual treatment. In stage three, the focus is on building and repairing relationships. Depending on the individual, family therapy sessions focusing on past abuse may be used. Clients may work to increase their capacities for intimacy, sexual and otherwise. Family sessions will target relationships that can be repaired, and encourage the expression of grief and mourning for those relationships that are lost. In this stage, the client learns to respect both the anger and grief that are emotional consequences of the experience.

Group Therapy

Both professional and self-help programs for survivors of childhood sexual abuse recognize the value of group therapy for this clientele, and it is a standard component of most treatment programs for adult survivors. Groups provide unique opportunities for survivors to work on trust issues and feelings of shame and self-blame. This milieu also reduces the feelings of isolation that often accompany a history of sexual abuse. Other survivors can assist the client in discarding their denial and dissociative strategies for dealing with the abuse, and can offer hope that members can make sense of this experience and achieve a sense of overall well-being. A well-designed study by Morgan and Cummings (1999) of group therapy for women survivors of childhood sexual abuse demonstrated significant decreases in depression, social maladjustment, self-blame, and posttraumatic stress symptoms in members of a 20-week therapy group compared to control women who experienced abuse but did not participate in the group. Findings showed positive results regardless of the number of abusers, nature, and duration of abuse.

Ideally, a co-leadership (male/female) model offers the most opportunity for growth in clients. It is also helpful for therapists to have collegial support in working in a difficult arena.

Family and Couples Therapy

Difficulties in intimate relationships are widespread among individuals who experienced childhood sexual abuse. Couples therapy provides an ideal context in which to treat those problems. In some cases, the sexually abused individual may not have disclosed the history to the partner, and this may be a primary task in therapy. Couples therapy will focus on trust, communication, and power in the relationship, the role of the abuse history, the symptoms experienced by the abused partner, and the sexual issues that exist in the relationship. When there are children, parenting issues are also likely to be important. One question that the clinician will have to answer based on the particulars of a given case is "Who will be the therapist for the couple?" In general, one partner's individual therapist does not conduct the couples' therapy. In the case of the sexually abused client, if couples therapy will be supportive of individual therapy, and be brief in duration, the treating clinician may want to provide the therapy. This decision is an important one that the therapist should make after deliberation and, sometimes, consultation.

The use of family therapy with families where sexual abuse has occurred is controversial. In the case of an adult client who was sexually abused as a child, family therapy is less likely to be included as the family unit may not be available. One situation in which experts recommend family involvement in therapy is when the non-offending parent did not protect the child, and the feelings of abandonment and rage continue to affect the client as an adult. It is not unusual to find that clients harbor more anger toward the non-offending parent who did not stop the abuse than toward the perpetrator. One youth wrote, "I told my mother that my father had raped me lots of times. It was hard telling her, because I had kept it a secret for so long. My mother had a strange reaction. She got mad at me and said that my father would never do something like that" (Anonymous, 2004). In such cases, the therapist may have some sessions involving the client, non-offending parent, and any sibling with the goal of facilitating an open and honest discussion of the abuse. Although the client may need to ventilate angry feelings, she is also encouraged to listen to other family members' perceptions, and to recognize the ways in which the family attempted to survive the trauma. The relationships within the family may change in such a way that mutual support is the result (Briere, 1989).

There is controversy around the notion of confrontation of the abuser. Those who believe this is a useful intervention will advocate the opportunity for the client to express directly to the perpetrator how the abuse hurt her, and how she feels toward him now. Advocates of this intervention allude to the need to "break the silence," which typically served to protect the abuser. They also believe that such confrontation may assist the client in attaining a degree of closure on the abuse. Victims may use this opportunity to formally state their intention to sever all contact with the abuser. Opponents of this intervention point to the tendency of many abusers to deny the abuse, rationalize their behaviors, minimize the victims distress, and sometimes even verbally attack the victim ("You know you liked it."). Given the potential benefits and real dangers of such interactions, the therapist must be very careful about the decision to bring the abuser into therapy, and if that is done, to structure and direct the session so that the victim can release pent-up emotions and attain closure. The client must be well prepared prior to the session, and have realistic expectations. It is obviously essential that such a meeting happens only when it is the client's informed desire (rather than the therapist's) to do so.

Self-Help Approaches

I confess to being quite leery of some of the self-help material available for clients who have been sexually abused. However, the series of books by Ellen Bass and Laura Davis, exemplified by *The Courage to Heal*, which has a companion workbook and other volumes, is very popular and many clients have remarked with surprise that they see themselves on every page. I prefer to use this book with adult women who were sexually abused as children in conjunction with other forms of therapy. It is an excellent source of "homework" assignments for clients who wish to continue working outside of therapy sessions. Despite its popularity, the reader must exercise caution when suggesting or using this series. In this book, as in several others discussed later in this chapter, there are statements that suggest that even if a person does not have memories of the sexual abuse, it is likely to have occurred. This is a risky assumption at best, and while it may be a reaction to the long history of discounting children's reports, it may be an example of the pendulum swinging too far in the other direction.

Guidelines for When a Client Discloses Abuse

Regardless of the treatment approach you adopt, it is important to know how to respond when a client first discloses abuse. These strategies are particularly critical with children who report. In a nonjudgmental manner, the counselor should do the following:

- Take the report seriously! Listen carefully, encourage the client to talk freely.
- Reassure the client that telling about the abuse was the right thing to do.
- Emphasize that the client is not to blame for what happened.
- If the client is a child, stress that you will protect them, and that to protect them you will report the abuse to the appropriate agency. Reassure the child of your confidence in the agency, and tell them you will support them through whatever happens.
- If the perpetrator is arrested, the child may assume that he will be sent straight to jail for a very long time, and may find their fears renewed if that is not what happens. Explaining the legal system in simplified terms may help the child realize that justice will be done, but not immediately.

Issues of Diversity

Research consistently finds sexual abuse at similar rates in all racial and ethnic groups, all religious persuasions, and in all social classes. A recent analysis noted minimal differences in rates of childhood sexual abuse, with Whites and Latinos reporting slightly higher rates than African American, Native American, Asian, Asian-Pacific Islander, and mixed race children (Elliott & Urquiza, 2006). These researchers note that conservative cultural norms in several Asian groups, for example, may serve as a protective factor against childhood sexual abuse—or such norms may inhibit Asian children's willingness to report sexual abuse. They also comment on the inconclusive findings of many studies examining racial/ethnic differences in rates of childhood sexual abuse.

There is a small body of literature on racial/ethnic differences in symptom presentation and treatment preference that we should view cautiously due to methodological differences and the recency of this line of research (Cohen, Mannarino, Berliner, & Deblinger, 2000). There is evidence that symptoms are more severe and longer-lasting in minority children than in Caucasian children who were sexually abused. For example, one study found that sexually abused Asian American children displayed less anger and less sexualized behavior than other groups, but more thoughts of suicide. Several studies have found that African American and Hispanic children have more behavioral problems following sexual abuse than other racial groups. However, the absence of strong differences in treatment response by race or ethnicity may be because the experience of sexual abuse has commonalities that transcend demographic differences. This does not mean that counselors do not need to be culturally sensitive. Cohen and her colleagues point out that it is important to consider cultural differences about virginity, sexuality, parent–child relationships, and the like, all of which will affect the child and the treatment. The counselor must understand and respect cultural differences in attitudes about discussing abuse with someone outside the family.

There have been some studies that indicated no differences by race in treatment satisfaction with two types of therapy. There are some data to suggest that in this area, as in general, minority children are less likely to receive mental health services than Caucasian children. The fact that minorities do not use mental health services as much as non-minorities should be a concern for all practitioners. Are mental health services insensitive to the needs of minorities? Do minorities use other resources (e.g., family or church) rather than mental health treatment? Counselors may wish to consider about whether having a counselor of the same background effects the treatment process. There is some evidence that minority clients are more comfortable with counselors of the same ethnicity or race, although the jury is out on whether there are better treatment outcomes in that case.

Two diversity issues we must discuss in more detail are gender and disabilities. Although the vast majority of known victims of sexual abuse are female, the males who are abused are definitely in need of our attention. Due to the way we socialize males in our society, many will not disclose the abuse to avoid the stigmatization. It is also the case that children with disabilities are sexually abused at a rate that has been estimated to be eleven times higher than their non-disabled peers (Manders, 2001). The next sections will review what we know about sexually abused males and those with disabilities.

Sexually Abused Males

Although estimates vary widely, one expert believes as many as one in every six boys is sexually abused before the age of 16. Another puts the rate at 3% of American men, but rates as high as 31% have also been reported (Lab, Fiegenbaum, & De Silva, 2000). In any case, the reluctance to report male sexual abuse means that the actual number is much higher than the number of reported incidents. Another impediment to obtaining accurate data is the attitude or practices of mental health professionals toward sexually abused males. Mental health professionals who routinely inquire about sexual abuse in women often ignore signs and do not ask males about a history of abuse. A fascinating study conducted in England with 179 professionals working in an inpatient psychiatric setting found that most never or only occasionally asked male clients about sexual abuse (Lab et al., 2000). Explanations for this omission included lack of awareness of male sexual abuse, embarrassment about the topic, the belief that clients should be asked only if they first bring the issue forward, difficulty believing women can be sexual abusers, homophobic reactions to the notion of male sexual abuse, and the belief that dominant physically powerful males could not be passive and helpless victims of sexual abuse.

An intriguing study conducted by Holmes and Offen (1996) found professional bias toward male sexual abuse. The researchers presented sixty-one clinical psychologists with two case summaries. Participants listed the clients' primary symptoms and hypotheses about the origin of the problems, which they ranked in order of importance. All participants received the same case summaries, but half were told that client 1 was male and client 2 was female, and the other half were told the opposite regarding gender. Participants hypothesized that sexual abuse was the origin of the problems in female client 2 significantly more often than when client 2 was male.

Although many symptoms associated with childhood sexual abuse are the same for males and females, there is evidence that girls experience more anxiety related to sex while boys described higher levels of eroticism (Feiring, Taska, & Lewis, 1999). Males also are more frequently abused by non-family perpetrators, and the abuse is more often violent with males. While male victims of sexual abuse face the same problems as do females in dealing with this experience, there are some additional challenges for boys and men. Boys tend to act out their distress, in contrast to girls, who tend toward depression. Males are also more likely to contract sexually transmitted diseases as the result of the abuse (Isely, P. J., Busse, W., & Isely, P., 1998). In addition to the risk of HIV or AIDS, male victims may contract other sexually transmitted disease from infected assailants. Men who abuse males are not always homosexual, and may transmit diseases they originally contracted from a woman (Hillman, Tomlinson, McMillan, French, & Harris, 1990).

In males, what professionals recognize as abuse may not be seen as abuse by others. For example, if the abuser is an older female, others may think the male is lucky, rather than abused. If the abuser is a male, the victim must contend with confusion about sexual identity and fears of the label "homosexual" if the abuse is revealed. Lisak (1994) conducted a content analysis of interviews with twenty-six adult males who were sexually abused as children. He found that men abused by females reported more shame and humiliation, whereas those abused by males had more concerns about homosexuality, expressing confusion about their sexuality and questioning what the experience meant regarding sexual orientation. His subjects also struggled to integrate their abuse experience with societal gender norms and expectations. Being a victim is contrary to the stereotypic picture of the strong and dominant male, and gender role prescriptions also influence men's willingness to acknowledge their painful feelings or vulnerability. For many, this translated to feelings of inadequacy about their masculinity.

One of the ways some victims may deal with those issues is to become super-masculine in their dress, activities, language, and so on. They may be promiscuous, having numerous female partners, or victimizing others, to prove their masculinity. Others identify with the abuser and take on that role themselves. Victims often report problems with sexuality. Some men were frightened of sexual intimacy and avoided sexual activity. Others denied their own sexual impulses and attractions.

A disturbing finding in these interviews was that many participants described unsuccessful attempts to obtain help with their problems. It appeared to them that mental health professionals had difficulty believing that males could be victims of sexual abuse, and minimized or rejected the men's concerns. It is imperative that clinicians recognize the extent of this problem and provide competent services to all who need it regardless of gender.

Persons with Disabilities

A definition of *disability* is needed and for the purposes of this book we will use the term as it is used in the Americans with Disabilities Act (42 U.S.C. § 12102(2); 29 C.F.R. § 1630.2(g), 1992). That legislation and subsequent modifications define a disability as "a physical or mental impairment that substantially limits one or more of the major life activities of an individual." That law also includes two other criteria that can be used to classify a person as one with disabilities: a record of an impairment that meets the definition, or having been regarded as having such an impairment.

> **Disability:** A physical or mental impairment that substantially limits one or more of the major activities of an individual.

There is considerable evidence that children and adults with disabilities are at higher risk for sexual abuse than the general population (e.g., Manders, 2001; Sullivan & Knutson, 2000). However, determining rates of sexual abuse (or any abuse) in populations with disabilities is difficult because most states do not record disability status in their abuse records (Sullivan & Knutson, 2000). In an effort to conduct a prevalence study of abuse in children with disabilities, Sullivan and Knutson utilized the data on 40,211 students enrolled in public schools in Omaha, Nebraska. These data were merged with those of public agencies and law enforcement to determine which students had records of some form of maltreatment in at least one of those databases. They then examined the records for special education programs to identify those students with an identified disability. Eleven percent of the school population had been identified as maltreated in one of the databases; school records showed that 8% of children in the schools had an identified disability. Overall analyses revealed that children receiving special education services were more than three times as likely to have been abused than those without a disability. For sexual abuse, children with disability had 3.14 times the sexual abuse rate as their non-disabled peers. Children with visual impairments were at slightly greater risk for sexual abuse, but those with hearing impairments were not an increased risk for sexual abuse. Children with speech and language impairments were three times more likely to have experienced sexual abuse than children without disabilities.

Those persons whose disabilities may be presumed to reduce their credibility (such as blindness, deafness, and mental retardation) may be at even greater risk (Smith, 2002), because the perpetrator may believe that if the victim does report the offense, the victim will not be believed.

It is likely that individuals with intellectual disabilities are sexually abused more often than their non-disabled peers in part because they have difficulty understanding what is happening to them, and may also suffer from communication difficulties that interfere with their ability to report what has happened (Davis, n.d.). On those occasions when the person does report sexual abuse, he or she may not be perceived to be a credible reporter. In addition, workers at agencies who take such reports may be uncomfortable with children with disabilities, may lack the skills to communicate effectively with this population, and thus may be less effective in conducting interviews when sexual abuse is suspected. Workers may not be trained at all to interview nonverbal children (Manders, 2001).

Other individuals with cognitive disabilities may understand that what is happening is assault, but may not realize that the behavior is illegal. Sometimes the abuse is perpetrated by an authority whom the individual has learned not to question. Perhaps most importantly, sex education may be overlooked in this population, which leads to an absence of necessary information.

Those with physical disabilities are vulnerable because they may lack the physical abilities to escape or resist a sexual assault. Another factor that may be involved is that children with disabilities may frequently be subjected to intrusive medical or behavioral interventions, so that the child learns that physical coercion, while unpleasant, may be necessary (Manders, 2001).

Experts recommend that counseling be provided to sexual abuse victims with disabilities by a counselor who has the specialized skills in treating sexual abuse along with expertise in working with those with the particular disability. Such providers are likely to be few and far between, unfortunately. Generalist counselors might assume an advocacy role for this population, raising awareness that sexual abuse *does* occur in this population at higher rates than among the non-disabled. Education programs for students with disabilities, particularly because of their increased vulnerability, should include a strong component of sex education and safety. Counselors, particularly school counselors, can be strong proponents of such programming. They can also be supporters of legislation and regulations that demand adequate background checks for persons who work with persons with disabilities be strictly enforced.

Counselor Issues

Working with victims of sexual abuse is difficult, and the burden of the disclosures can weigh heavily on the clinician. The clinician may feel emotionally overwhelmed by the often horrific events the clients describe. One expert suggests that clinicians who have several victims of sexual abuse in their caseload may experience "PTSD by proxy" (Briere, 1989, p. 169). He describes disturbing nightmares and a hyper-vigilance to danger in some clinicians as examples of this dynamic. The empathy that is necessary to work effectively with these clients may also make the clinician susceptible to trauma reactions, such as anxiety, decreased stress tolerance, irritability, and helplessness. In addition, hearing about such unspeakable offenses, particularly when the victim is a child, can lead to skepticism at best and cynicism and defeatism at worst.

Briere (1989) theorizes that therapists may react to the psychological pressure of working with victims of sexual abuse by either over- or under-investing in their clients.

Those who under-invest become impersonal and detached in their relationship with clients. In so doing, they protect themselves from emotional reactions but deprive clients of an authentic therapeutic alliance. At the other extreme are clinicians who become over-involved with clients by violating the boundaries of client–counselor relationship to rescue or protect the client. For example, these clinicians may allow clients to have additional sessions or to call them at home. Neither of these extreme positions is helpful to either the client or the professional.

Awareness of the potential impact of this work should lead the clinician to take preventive actions. Engaging in personal therapy is helpful for most clinicians, but may be particularly useful for those in this specialty. This is essential if clinicians are also a victim of sexual abuse, however "recovered" they may be. It is too easy for a therapist's personal issues to bleed into the therapy, and for interventions to meet the counselor's needs rather than the client's. Personal therapy can help therapists take care of their own issues in an appropriate milieu.

Another important strategy for clinicians working with this population is to engage in regular consultation or supervision, providing an opportunity to process their work and its impact, and gain essential feedback from other professionals. It is also helpful to limit the number of sexual abuse victims one accepts. Although specializing ensures clients that they will receive quality care, the clinician needs some balance to maintain perspective.

Self-care is important for all clinicians, regardless of their specialty or work setting, and may be particularly so for those who work with this clientele. Having other interests, and being involved with supportive people who do not work with this population, can help counselors disengage and compartmentalize the work so as not to impair their own quality of life.

Briere (1989) suggests a strategy that is noteworthy. As clinicians become aware of the terrible impact of sexual abuse, they may wish to direct some of their energy toward prevention, either by becoming involved in organizations with that goal, or becoming active in political groups that focus on this issue. This allows the clinician to make an impact beyond the clients in their own caseloads, and can help mitigate the discouragement that can arise from dealing with such unacceptable human behavior.

A final issue that counselors must consider is that of the impact of counselor gender on the therapeutic process. There were gender differences in the kinds of behavior and reactions clinicians experienced during therapy with victims of childhood sexual abuse (Little & Hamby, 1996). Other studies have found differences in the frequency of inquiring about sexual abuse between male and female therapists.

Because most victims are female and most perpetrators are male, it seems logical that female clinicians would be preferred and would be more effective with clients who have been sexually abused. Porter and her colleagues (1996) have conducted several studies that found that counselor gender did not affect client response to treatment. In one study, there was no difference in client verbalizations about the abuse to male or female counselors, even though all clients (females aged 7 to 17) had indicated a preference for female counselors. It may be that male counselors need to consider the possible impact of their gender on the process, and be transparent about any concerns that emerge as treatment progresses. It may be therapeutic for the client to realize that not all men are like her abuser. On the other hand, it is important to be respectful of the client's need for privacy and safety, particularly given the violation that has occurred in the abuse. The counselor must be careful not to automatically assume that any reticence is resistance, but rather to honor the client's need to exert control and define boundaries in the sexual arena.

BOX 1.1

A Note to School Counselors

School counselors are not therapists, and definitely do not provide treatment to sexual abuse victims in their schools. However, as the following actual situations illustrate, school counselors may have an important role to play with children who have been sexually abused.

The first case involves mandatory reporting. A child in a kindergarten class told her teacher that she was being sexually abused by her father. The teacher told her colleague, who told the school counselor. Instead of reporting the incident immediately, the counselor told the principal. Two days elapsed before the principal told authorities, and that report was made during an unplanned conversation with a police officer. As it happened, the child was abused in the interval between the time of her disclosure and the time the incident came to the attention of authorities. All four educators were criminally charged with failure to report the abuse. Although the charges against the school counselor were eventually dropped, and she returned to her position, the negative publicity around the incident could not have been easy to withstand. The lesson here is that school counselors MUST report allegations of sexual abuse, and they cannot pass that responsibility along to another. Certainly the principal should be informed, but the counselor cannot assume that anyone else will make the report.

In another case, a girl was sexually molested by her stepfather from age 4 through 12, until she finally revealed the abuse to a mental health counselor. The incident was reported, and the stepfather arrested and charged. He pled not guilty, and the case went to trial, which was a terrible ordeal for the then ninth grade student. The additional harm came at school after her stepfather's conviction and sentencing. Although newspapers do not report names of victims, relatives of the stepfather were aware of the case, and young relatives who attended school with the victim harassed and taunted her to the point that she dropped out of school. Bullying and teasing are areas in which school counselors should be experts, and this behavior should have been stopped.

A final relevant case concerns a child in elementary school who told her mother that she was being sexually abused by a member of their extended family. There were several important roles for the school counselor. First, before the perpetrator was apprehended, the child was extremely fearful that he would find and hurt her because she told. The school counselor was contacted, who provided emotional support at school and helped the student devise a safety plan at school. The second point at which the school counselor was involved was in subsequent months when the child was receiving therapy and being validated for telling someone about the abuse. This positive attention for telling led the child to believe that telling others was a good thing, and she began to tell friends at school. It was necessary for the school counselor to intervene with the friends of the child and the child herself to assist her in practicing appropriate disclosure.

Ethical Concerns

Repressed and Recovered Memories

There are several ethical issues that are unique to working with victims of sexual abuse. The issue of *repressed memories* is a particularly thorny one, and several noted scientists question the very existence of this phenomenon (Loftus, 1993; Neimark, 2004). Repression is a psychological process, first described by Freud, in which memories of traumatic events are forced into the unconscious and away from conscious awareness to avoid the emotional pain such events arouse. Repression is one of several defense mechanisms that protect the self or conscious mind against emotional pain.

In the case of memories of childhood sexual abuse, there has been considerable debate about whether traumatic memories can be repressed and later recovered, whether allegedly recovered memories are accurate, and whether false memories exist. Note that false memories are not lies; they are cases in which a person experiences a memory of something that did not actually happen. In their extensive review of both clinical and experimental reports of these phenomena, Gleaves, Smith, Butler and Spiegel (2004) concluded that both false and genuine recovered memories are possible. They also pointed out that at this point there is no established method for determining whether a given recovered memory is false or real. This creates a significant dilemma for clinicians.

In the early 1990s, there were several high profile cases in which recovered memories resulted in convictions for crimes committed decades earlier. Because recovered memories often first surface in therapy, there were some critics who accused therapists of "implanting" false memories of abuse. While it is certainly possible that an individual can have a false memory (Alessi & Ballard, 2001; Rubin, 1996), it is also possible that real memories are repressed for many years (Williams, 1994). Recent research demonstrated that human memory is not an infallible recording of an event, but an interpretation of an event (Neimark, 2004). Memories of events, traumatic or ordinary, can be distorted or altered over time. In most cases of recovered memories, it is impossible to determine with certainty whether the memory is accurate or false or distorted. What, then, is the ethical therapist to do when presented with a recovered memory of childhood sexual abuse?

The tendency of some clinicians to assume that such memories are always true is a dangerous one. Clinicians may have a perception (or bias) that certain constellations of symptoms are indicative of childhood sexual abuse. While such symptoms may be the result of sexual abuse, there is no symptom or group of symptoms that is definitive, especially when the client does not have any memory of abuse. Abuse may be an underlying cause of many problems, but there is no "litmus test" to determine with certainty that sexual abuse is the ultimate explanation. In inquiring about abuse, it is absolutely critical that the ethical therapist neither suggest nor suppress discussion of possible sexual abuse. I have had clients tell me that they were sexually abused as children although they have no memory or no other information to confirm it. When asked how they know, these clients say a previous therapist told them they were abused because that is the only explanation of their problems. Clients tend to grasp onto such explanations because of their need to locate a source of their distress. However, it is unethical for clinicians to make such assertions. Courtois (1995) expresses this concern very clearly:

> Many issues and symptoms . . . raise the therapist's "index of suspicion" of an abuse history when a client does not know about or discloses such a history. The therapist must be careful, however, not to assume sexual abuse as the only possible explanation of the client's difficulties and must use inquiry techniques that are neutral and non-suggestive. (p. 8)

Mandatory Reporting

When treating a child or adolescent, there is always the possibility that the client may reveal sexual abuse, even if that is not the reason the client came for treatment. Several studies reported by Kennel and Agresti (1995) have documented that mental health professionals do not report all cases of sexual abuse. Although the law considers sexual abuse to be either present or not, clinicians apparently consider a range of severity that influences their decision to report. In their own study, 29% of the sample of psychologists acknowledged they had chosen not to report a case of suspected child abuse when the law would require doing so. Only 62% of the sample had ever reported a case, which is particularly noteworthy given the high prevalence rates of this problem in clinical populations.

The decision to report abuse is a difficult one for clinicians, who may fear damage to the therapeutic relationship, and may be concerned that the safety of the child is at risk. It is important for clinicians to ensure that initial meetings with children and parents include informed consent for treatment that clearly and specifically states that the counselor will report suspected abuse of any kind. It is also good practice, when the information does surface, to remind the child of this requirement, and explain carefully what will happen. It is critical that the therapist not take on the role of investigator, as this will interfere with the investigation by the proper authorities. In these cases, the therapist should acknowledge the child's courage in disclosing this secret and provide support and encouragement for the child as the effects of the disclosure become apparent.

Clinicians with Histories of Sexual Abuse

Mental health professionals are often interested in issues that have been part of their own experience. Data reveal high rates of childhood sexual abuse (CSA) histories among mental health professionals, with rates of 13% in a study of male professionals and 20% among female professionals. Another study found 43% of female clinicians reported childhood sexual abuse (Little & Hamby, 1996). While it is understandable that professionals are interested in helping others with problems they have personally experienced (and hopefully surmounted), there is a concern about objectivity and the ability to maintain a professional perspective when working with such clients. Little and Hamby found numerous difficulties among the professionals with a history of

CSA. Female therapists mentioned these countertransference issues: feeling angry with the perpetrator, feeling deep pain, frequently crying with clients, making boundary mistakes in therapy, feeling deep hopelessness. Male counselors reported feeling sexually aroused and feeling blame toward the victim.

For those counselors who have a history of sexual abuse and who want to treat this clientele, I strongly urge entering therapy to do your own work prior to treating any clients with this problem. In therapy, you will wrestle with the issue of what might constitute appropriate self-disclosure, and the conditions under which that might benefit or harm the client. Further, arranging for ongoing peer consultation and supervision would provide a setting in which to process countertransference reactions. It is also essential to practice positive coping strategies to deal with the emotional responses to this work.

Boundaries of Competence

A final issue to discuss in this section is that of boundaries of competence. There are no certifications for most specialties, and reading, attending workshops, and obtaining consultation and supervision may be the method most clinicians use to become competent in treating a particular type of client. Because clients who have experienced childhood sexual abuse are especially challenging, it is imperative that the mental health professionals treating them be skilled and familiar with the most effective approaches.

Summary

The case of Mark illustrates many of the concepts I have covered in this chapter. He experienced many of the common psychological effects of sexual abuse: depression, social withdrawal and isolation, and sexualized behavior (excessive masturbation). His self-esteem was low and he felt devalued as a person. The effect of the abuse on Mark was exacerbated by his failure to disclose, which meant he lacked support and treatment that he sorely needed.

Mark's borderline intelligence probably contributed to his vulnerability to abuse by the older boy. Even as an adult, he is slow to detect malice in others and continues to be used by people he thinks are his friends. He still struggles with boundaries and tends to do what others want even if the action is not in his best interest. As a male victim, he spent 25 years wondering about, and fearful of expressing, his sexual orientation, and his sense of inadequacy has roots in doubts about his masculinity.

- Sexual abuse is shockingly prevalent, and often undetected. Both males and females are victimized at alarming rates.
- Psychological effects of sexual abuse are many and long-lasting. Sexual abuse appears in the history of many individuals with self-mutilation, substance abuse, and eating disorders.
- For a variety of reasons, children may not report sexual abuse, and when reported it is difficult to substantiate.

- Common effects include fear, depression, PTSD symptoms, and sexualized behavior.
- Memories of sexual abuse are sometimes repressed and may not enter consciousness until many years later, if ever.
- The ramifications of reported sexual abuse (investigation, etc.) can be traumatic for children.
- Various factors tend to moderate the effects of the abuse. The impact is reduced when the perpetrator is not related, and when non-offending parental belief and support are present.
- Trauma-focused cognitive therapy appears to produce positive outcomes.
- Group therapy is often a component of treatment.
- Counselors working with victims of sexual abuse face numerous challenges. For those who have personal sexual abuse histories, I strongly recommended personal therapy, ongoing peer consultation, and supervision.
- Despite mandatory reporting laws, counselors struggle with the decision to report suspected sexual abuse.
- Intake interviews should routinely inquire respectfully about sexual abuse. Counselors often neglect to do so with male clients.
- Several inventories are available to assess for indicators of child sexual abuse.

ADDITIONAL RESOURCES

On the Web for Counselors

- www.jimhopper.com/male.ab A good starting point. Although it specializes in information regarding male victims of sexual abuse, the wealth of information and links (including links to scholarly journals) available on this site make it well worth the time for anyone interested in the field.
- www.gen-assist.com/sasupport Useful information and good links.
- www.calib.com/nccanch/pubs/usermanuals/sexabuse/index.cfm An excellent manual written by Kathleen Faller in 1993 but still very applicable can be downloaded from this site.
- www.acf.hhs.gov/index.html Publications and manuals from the Administration for Children and Families (U.S. Department of Health and Human Services). Many materials are downloadable in PDF format.

On the Web for Clients

- http:sasupport.healthyplace.com Includes personal stories and readings that can be triggering for some clients.
- www.rainn.org Information about a sexual assault hotline.
- http://www.healthyplace.com/Communities/Abuse/safeline/index.html For adult survivors of childhood sexual abuse.

- http://www.sexaa.org/ Clients exhibiting compulsive sexual behavior might consider SA (Sexual Addicts Anonymous), a 12-step self-help organization, as an adjunct to treatment.
- http://www.ppgmv.org/sarc/index.html The Planned Parenthood Sexual Abuse Resource Center includes list of educational videos, as well as a search engine for professionals to search for useful materials. I highly recommend this site for those interested in gathering more information on this topic.

In Print for Counselors

- *Treating Sexualized Behavior in Children: A Treatment Manual,* available from the author William Friedrich at the Mayo Clinic (email: friedrich.william@mayo.edu). This guide involves parents and has useful activities and techniques that are designed specifically for 4- to 12-year-olds of both genders.

In Print for Clients

(Although clients can read many of these books on their own, they are most appropriate when processed with a counselor.)

- *Outgrowing the Pain: A Book For and About Adults Abused as Children* by Eliana Gil. A short, clear, highly readable, and cleverly illustrated book that provides straightforward guidance to the reader. Although it was published in 1983, I still find it one of the best to suggest.
- *The Courage to Heal* (mentioned above) can be an effective adjunct to treatment. An accompanying workbook allows clients to share. Although more recent editions of this classic do make mention of males, it is clearly a book for women.
- *Victims No Longer* by Mike Lew (1988). By and for men. Readers may relate to the many personal stories interspersed with useful information, although others may be put off by the stories.
- *Wounded Boys, Heroic Men* by Daniel Jay Sonkin (1998). A more practical book. Chapters on various approaches to healing are very clear, and clients are likely to find the suggestions helpful.
- A book I would discourage clients from relying on is Engel's *Right to Innocence: Healing the Trauma of Childhood Sexual Abuse* (1990). Although it describes a specific program of recovery, there are several things with which I am uncomfortable, including this statement: "If you have ever had reason to suspect that you may have been sexually abused, even if you have no explicit memory of it, the chances are very high that you were." Given the widespread publicity about sexual abuse, many unhappy individuals may suspect abuse because it would give a reason for their suffering. I believe such a broad statement is dangerous. The author also dwells on the ineffectiveness of many therapists, which may discourage some individuals who could gain from therapy. My final concern is the author's detailed accounting of her own sexual abuse, which blurs the distinction between the personal and the professional. I comment on this book (and others

on other topics) because clients are vulnerable and the effects of such approaches may actually be damaging.

- *I Can't Talk About It*, by Doris Sanford. For "the child who hasn't told . . . yet." The child talks to a dove about her secret and shameful experience with her father, and the dove (identified in the beginning as the spirit of God) provides gentle and wise counsel. Several of my young clients requested their own personal copy of this book.
- *Please Tell: A Child's Story About Sexual Abuse* by Jessie, a nine-year-old survivor of sexual abuse. Illustrated by the author, this beautiful book is one that children can relate to. It may inspire some to tell or draw their own story.
- *Bastard out of Carolina* by Dorothy Allison. An excellent if sometimes disturbing novel about childhood sexual abuse. The story is set in the south in the 1950s and paints a harrowing picture of the physical and sexual abuse the protagonist suffers at the hands of her stepfather.
- *Monkey King* by Patricia Chao (1997). A novel from the perspective of a 28-year-old Chinese American incest victim, hospitalized after a suicide attempt, who reflects on the incest she experienced at the hands of her father, the anger and grief she feels at her mother's refusal to believe her, and her sister's dismissal of her pain.
- *Mouthing the Words* by Camilla Gibb (1999). Set in England, this novel tells the story of Thelma's struggles to integrate her experience of childhood abuse, ultimately requiring hospitalization. In both this and *Monkey King*, the wounded child has a mental breakdown requiring inpatient treatment. Readers should keep in mind that not every victim has a similar outcome.
- *Push* by Sapphire. A very quick and shocking read about an African American victim of sexual abuse. The first sentence, "I was left back when I was twelve because I had a baby for my fahver," sets the stage for this horrifying but enlightening tale.

Film and Television

- *Bastard out of Carolina*. This film is fairly true to the novel and may shock some readers with the degree of violence portrayed. The mother's response to the abuse is a good topic for discussion.
- *Ultimate Betrayal*. An enlightening and powerful film about adults sexually and physically victimized as children, based on actual situations, highlights the ramifications for adults who decide to confront their abusers.

EXERCISES

1. Develop an initial interview protocol that includes non-suggestive, non-suppressive questions about sexual abuse. Consider how and when in the interview you will ask your questions.

2. Assume a child or adolescent you are working with reveals that he or she was sexually abused three years ago by an extended family member. How will you proceed? What will you tell the client about your obligation to report? What will you do if the client says that the perpetrator lives in another state now and is no longer a danger, but the client fears the repercussions on the rest of the family if they find out?

3. Assume you are working with an adult survivor of sexual abuse who has made good progress in therapy and indicates that he/she wants to have a family session that includes the perpetrator. The client wishes to confront the perpetrator in this setting in order to achieve closure on the abuse and to express the feelings to the perpetrator and the rest of the family. How will you decide if this is an appropriate intervention? How will you prepare the client for the session if the decision is to proceed?

4. Assume you are working with an adolescent whose sexual abuse by a step-parent has been substantiated and the offender incarcerated. The client wishes to have a family session in which he/she addresses the lack of protection from the non-offending parent. How will you determine if this is an appropriate intervention?

5. You are working with several adult survivors of childhood sexual abuse, and believe a group would be an excellent adjunct to individual treatment. How will you screen and prepare members for the group?

CHAPTER

2

Self-Mutilation

Few mental health professionals will have careers that do not include at least one client who is a self-mutilator. The goal of this chapter is to provide readers with sufficient information to be able to respond to these clients in a helpful way. For readers who decide not to treat these clients, I hope the increased knowledge will allow them to make referrals without suggesting that clients are hopeless. I will begin with a case study of a self-mutilator to place the concepts in a context.

Case Study

Renee is a 37-year-old black woman who has been self-mutilating for most of the last twenty years. She is one of seven children in a military family that presented a well-functioning face to the community, but whose private world was dysfunctional. Her father was an alcoholic and her mother was highly critical of the children, often making cruel comments and using physical methods of discipline. As a child, Renee was convinced that her mother did not like her.

Like many self-mutilators, Renee has expressed her pain via other symptoms in addition to self-mutilation. She has abused drugs, made several suicide attempts, and has exhibited disordered eating. Also, like many others with this problem, Renee is a victim of childhood sexual abuse. She had repressed her memories of the abuse by her father for many years, but then began having flashbacks and eventually recovered those memories. The abuse occurred when she was very young, and if her mother knew, she did nothing to protect Renee or stop the abuse.

Although she did some scratching of names on her arm as a young teen, Renee's first serious act of self-mutilation occurred when she was a seventeen-year-old inpatient in a psychiatric facility. She felt overwhelmed with anger and rage that she was unable to contain, and needed to do something to relieve the tension. She saw a nail on the floor, and plunged it into her arm. It worked—the tension subsided, which set the stage for a pattern that continued for several decades.

During the worst periods of self-mutilation, Renee would engage in self-mutilating behaviors (SMBs) several times a day. Her preferred method was puncture, using scissors, knives, pens, and pencils, because that would do serious damage and cause more suffering, which she believed she deserved. She mutilated her arms, which allowed her to easily see the scars as a reminder. At times, Renee would conceal the evidence of her behavior under her sleeves, but at other times she would self-mutilate openly, in front of others—friends, therapists, her father. She felt rewarded by their shocked reactions, and also by the solicitous responses that sometimes followed. When her father would learn that she had self-mutilated, he would take her shopping for new clothes; she got a reward for her SMB! Renee used this behavior to express what she was unable at that time to express in words: "I want you to know my pain, how much I hurt."

For Renee, self-mutilating was an attempt to stop feeling intense emotional pain. Physical pain has a known source whereas emotional pain seems endless and hopeless. The sight of blood running down from the wound was reinforcing: she was watching the pain and hurt flow out of her. She felt almost intoxicated by the smell of the blood, which made her want to cut more. Sometimes she would avoid cleaning it up, and when she later would see the stains on the floor, she would want to cut again.

Sometimes, Renee felt "cut off" from herself or numb, and the self-mutilation and bleeding was a way to feel alive. She says she did not feel the pain from the punctures, so she would often leave objects in the open wound (staples, paper clips) so that the wound would become infected—and then she would finally feel the pain. On three occasions, surgery was required to remove the objects from her arm.

Renee has seen many therapists over the years, but credits her current therapist with helping her to finally stop self-mutilating. The clear boundaries that were set in early sessions have removed the rewards for self-mutilating. In the past, therapists would offer extra sessions when she hurt herself, which encouraged the behavior. Her present therapist made it clear that he would not accept emergency calls or have extra sessions in response to SMB. He continues to see her for regularly scheduled appointments, but does not bring his dogs (whom she loves to see) when she has been hurting herself. She finds these behavioral methods to be extremely effective. She also values the list she and her therapist created for alternatives to SMB when she feels the urge to do so. She keeps it with her and can access it when needed. The list includes permission to call the therapist instead of hurting herself, and she has done this with good success. With these strategies to control the SMB, Renee has been able to work in therapy to deal with the many traumas she has experienced and to create hope for her future. Learning to express feelings directly, in words, has been extremely difficult for Renee, but she believes her therapist has encouraged her and supported her efforts to do so. She believes she no longer needs to self-mutilate to express her feelings, and that she will be able to continue to resist the impulse to do so when she notices it.

Definitions and Description of the Problem

Self-mutilation is a baffling behavior because it appears so contrary to the innate human desire to avoid pain. Other terms are sometimes used to describe this behavior (self-injury, self-wounding, and self-harm), but self-mutilation is the most widely used and the most precise. Self-mutilation is not a separate mental disorder, but a symptom of several disorders: borderline personality disorder is probably most commonly diagnosed, but post-traumatic stress disorder and dissociative disorder are also used. This behavior also occurs in individuals with bipolar disorder, major depression, anxiety disorders, and schizophrenia.

Self-mutilation: Self-inflicted bodily harm that is non-lethal and socially unacceptable.

Self-mutilation refers to intentional, non-lethal, repetitive bodily harm or disfigurement that is socially unacceptable. Self-mutilating behaviors include cutting, carving, burning or scalding, preventing the healing of wounds, punching oneself, breaking bones. Self-mutilators often conceal evidence of this activity under clothing, or explain it away ("The dog scratched me, I burned myself while cooking dinner"). It is important to distinguish self-mutilation from related behaviors with which it might be confused. Unlike suicide attempts, the intent of these behaviors is *not* to cause death, although self-mutilators are 100 times more likely to commit suicide within a year of an act of self-harm than the general population (Whotton, 2002). Unlike the widespread practices of tattooing and piercing, self-mutilation is more generally socially unacceptable. Unlike other risky or harmful behaviors such as substance abuse, self-mutilation is intentional and direct self-harm. Self-mutilation usually begins in late childhood or early adolescence, and may continue for ten or fifteen years or more.

Categories of Self-Mutilation

Armando Favazza (1996), a leading expert in this field, describes three types of self-mutilating behavior (SMB).

- *Major* self-mutilation refers to extreme acts that occur suddenly and cause considerable damage. These actions are usually associated with a psychotic state or acute intoxication, and may be a response to religious or sexual delusions or command hallucinations. Readers of the popular novel *I Know This Much is True* (Lamb, 1998) will remember their horror and shock at just such an act. Many readers will be aware of Vincent Van Gogh's well-known act of self-mutilation. Both are examples of this type.
- *Stereotypic* self-mutilation refers to the repetitive, often rhythmic self-injurious behaviors found in autistic and mentally retarded individuals and in about a third of individuals with Tourette's syndrome. This type is usually not secretive, and seems to have a strong biological component. The most common such behavior is head banging.
- *Moderate or superficial* self-mutilation is the type that mental health professionals are most likely to encounter. Behaviors in this category include hair pulling, skin scratching, picking, cutting, burning, and carving. Favazza (1996) further divides this category into three groups: compulsive, episodic, or repetitive.

Compulsive self-mutilation involves repetitive, ritualistic behavior that occurs many times in a day. The two most common forms of this are hair pulling (tricotillomania) and various forms of insults to the skin (scratching, picking, or digging) that are often motivated by attempts to remove imagined blemishes or toxic organisms. Clients who do this will usually be treated by a family physician or dermatologist at first, rather than by a mental health professional.

Tricotillomania: Recurrent pulling of one's own hair that results in hair loss.

Episodic self-mutilation refers to behaviors that occur periodically, but which do not pre-occupy the individual or result in a "cutter" identity. This type of self-mutilation can occur as a symptom or feature of a number of disorders, including anxiety and depression. It appears in clients with personality disorders, most commonly borderline personality disorder.

In contrast, in repetitive self-mutilation, the behavior is a major preoccupation, and the person assumes a self-identity of a "cutter" or "burner." These individuals generally describe their behavior as an addiction that they cannot stop. Favazza (1996) argues that this type of self-mutilation should be a separate mental disorder within the group of impulse control disorders "not otherwise specified." He would call this disorder "repetitive self-mutilation syndrome." This suggested syndrome generally first appears in late childhood or early adolescence, is more common in females, and may persist for many years.

Prevalence

Anecdotal reports from school counselors and other educators strongly suggest that this practice is on the rise, particularly among young adolescents in middle schools. Welsh (2004) called self-mutilation "the next teen disorder" (p. 11A). Several factors that may be related to the perceived increase in self-mutilation in adolescents are the increased public awareness of this behavior, and the dramatic increase in the number of Internet message boards and chat rooms devoted to this topic. According to Adler and Adler (2005), it was around 1996 when self-injury began to appear in the media, and in 2001–2002 when websites on self-injury began to flourish. Message boards and chat rooms may have a particular appeal to adolescents who do not have highly developed social skills as they can practice their skills anonymously in these contexts (Whitlock, Powers, & Eckenrode, 2006). Whitlock and her colleagues completed a content analysis of message board postings on SMB sites from 1998 to 2005. Of the 3,219 postings coded, the most common were those providing support (28%); requesting and sharing techniques of self-mutilation accounted for 6% of posts. Other topics included issues about concealing the behavior or scars, comments about the addictive nature of the behavior, discussions of therapy and medication, and discussion of triggers of the SMB episode.

The frequency of this behavior in the general population is difficult to determine for a number of reasons. Different attempts to determine the prevalence of self-mutilation find different results, due partially to differences in the definition of self-mutilation and how the data are collected. When researchers do not distinguish between self-mutilation per se and suicide attempts that involve self-harm, accurate prevalence rates are impossible to determine (Ross & Heath, 2002). In addition, many, if not most, episodes of self-mutilation will not be noted in medical records, as treatment may not be needed or sought. However, prevalence rates are sometimes calculated from such records.

From the available data it is possible to make some estimates, with the caveat that they are only estimates. Briere and Gil (1998) used data from 927 community subjects who participated in the standardization of a trauma inventory. Self-mutilation was assessed by an item that clearly indicates that suicide was not the intent of the act. Four percent of the participants acknowledged they had engaged in such behavior in the previous six months! At that rate, we would expect eight million Americans to have at least one episode of self-mutilation. Only 0.3% of their sample reported doing such behavior "often." SMB was more likely to occur in subjects who were younger and those who had experienced childhood sexual abuse, but no gender differences were detected in rates of SMB. Rates were somewhat higher in a clinical (people being treated for a mental disorder) population than others in the sample. Favazza's (1996) own research also suggests that the behavior is not uncommon. In a study of university students, he found that 13.8% admitted to at least one act of self-mutilation.

A study of Australian adolescents (Patton et al., 1997, cited in Ross & Heath, 2002), found an overall prevalence rate for 15- and 16-year olds to be 5.1%, with females reporting significantly higher rates than males. In comparison, the rate for suicide attempts was much lower -0.5%. A recent study in the United States surveyed students in an urban and a suburban high school. The urban school was quite diverse in terms of race and ethnicity whereas the suburban school students were largely white upper-middle-class. Data collection included an initial screening questionnaire followed by a semi-structured interview that clarified that the individual met criteria for self-mutilation. Of the 440 participants, 13% of students in the urban school and 14.8% in the suburban school were self-mutilators. The overall prevalence rate was 13.9%, with females significantly more likely to be doing so than males. An online survey of college students in two northeastern universities found that 17% of the 8,300 participants had engaged in a self-injurious behavior in their lifetime, and of those, 75% had done so more than once (Whitlock, Eckenrode, & Silverman, 2006). Additional findings of note were that those who self-injured were more likely to be female, bisexual, or actively questioning their sexual orientation. Further, 36% indicated that they had told no one about this practice.

These researchers also asked the students about specific practices. The most commonly reported method of self-mutilation was skin cutting (41%), followed by self-hitting (32.8%). Another 3.3% favored burning. Another important finding was that 13% of the group reported engaging in this behavior more than once per day, whereas 18% had done so on only one occasion.

There are two environments where self-mutilation occurs at particularly high rates: prisons and inpatient facilities. In prison, self-mutilation may provide secondary gains, over and above the psychological functions it serves. The inmate may feel a measure of control that is lacking in the prison setting. For example, an injured inmate may avoid being moved to a more desirable unit or facility due to the need for medical supervision. It may also provide attention in the form of medical intervention.

Secondary gain: Interpersonal or social advantages that one gets due to an illness.

In inpatient psychiatric settings, contagion may influence the rate of this behavior. Patients may observe that self-mutilators receive attention or medication, and begin self-mutilating to obtain the perceived benefits for themselves. More recently, contagion has been suggested as an explanation for the recent rise in self-mutilation observed in schools (Lieberman & Poland, 2006). Associating with others who engage in SM has been found to increase risk in adolescents. In some settings, there is one powerful individual ("alpha male/female," p. 967) whose behaviors, including SMB, peers imitate.

Contagion: Imitation of behaviors by others in an environment.

Self-mutilation often appears along with other disorders. It is most often associated with eating disorders, substance abuse, and personality disorders. Self-mutilation and eating disorders also may each be replacements for the other (Zila & Kiselica, 2001). These symptoms may represent different ineffective coping strategies.

It would be remiss to discuss self-mutilation without mentioning borderline personality disorder as self-mutilators frequently receive this diagnosis. I want to stress that while this is often the diagnosis, it is not the only correct one for clients who self-mutilate. Also, many self-mutilators are adolescents, and I believe labeling a youth with a personality disorder diagnosis is premature. The *Diagnostic and Statistical Manual of Mental Disorders* (*DSM-IV-TR*) notes that personality disorders can be diagnosed in children or adolescents in certain unusual circumstances (p. 687), and I urge counselors to be very cautious and judicious in making such diagnoses. I have treated adolescents with no other characteristics of borderline personality disorder who confess to briefly experimenting with self-mutilation. It is important to keep in mind the distinction between personality traits, which everyone has, and personality disorders, which are inflexible and enduring patterns of behavior that interfere with one's functioning. Figure 2.1 explains personality disorders for readers who may have not yet studied mental disorders and then lists the criteria for Borderline Personality Disorder (*DSM-IV-TR*; 2000; Morrison, 1995).

Developmental Influences

Self-mutilation often begins in late childhood or early adolescence (Lieberman & Poland, 2006). Experts believe that the roots of this behavior are in early childhood experiences. Some (see Strong, 1998) look to infant attachment disorders as setting the stage for later self-mutilation. Others focus on difficulties encountered by toddlers as they attempt to differentiate from parents and become more independent. Erik Erikson might surmise that self-mutilators did not successfully resolve the developmental crises of earlier stages. Most experts agree that the childhood experiences of self-mutilators were unhappy at best, and often include trauma from sexual abuse, loss of a parent, or illness or surgery.

Walsh and Rosen (1988) found several childhood events and circumstances that were highly correlated with self-mutilation in adolescents. The loss of a parent via divorce or an out-of-home placement was common in self-mutilating adolescents. These authors theorize that loss of a parent in these ways, as opposed to the finality of death, makes it more difficult to heal. A history of serious childhood illness or surgery was also more common among self-mutilators. Medical trauma may lead to hatred of one's body, or alienation from the body. Or, it may be that the child then has a body image of weakness and deformity, so self-harm seems appropriate. Some experts suggest another link between early medical problems and self-mutilation: a child, particularly one who is abused in the home, may experience a secondary gain (attention, regular meals, toys to play with) in the hospital or medical environment, and then come to associate the injury with welcome nurturance. The self-cutting may be an imperfect attempt to recreate the

Erik Erikson (1902–1994) first described his psychosocial theory of lifespan development (The Eight Stages of Man) in his 1950 book *Childhood and Society*. The stages each involve a central "crisis"; the extent to which the person successfully negotiates that crisis affects subsequent development. The stages are:

Trust v Mistrust—infancy

Autonomy v Shame—early childhood

Initiative v Guild—play years

Industry v Inferiority—school years

Identity v Role Confusion—adolescence

Intimacy v Isolation—young adulthood

Generativity v Stagnation—adulthood

Integrity v Despair—older adulthood

FIGURE 2.1   Definition and criteria for diagnosis.

What is a personality disorder? It is:

- An enduring pattern of behavior and inner experience that begins in adolescence or early adulthood.
- A deviation from cultural norms (what is a personality disorder in one culture may be normative, accepted behavior in another).
- An inflexible pattern that is apparent in a variety of situations.
- A pattern that interferes with one's personal, social, or occupational functioning.

How is a personality disorder exhibited? It is manifested in at least two of the following:

- Emotions (appropriateness, intensity, changeability, and range)
- Thoughts (how one interprets and perceives events, people, and the world)
- Behaviors (impulse control)
- Interpersonal relationships

What is Borderline Personality Disorder?   The most obvious characteristics are:

- A pattern of instability
- Frequent crises and mood swings
- Unstable relationships

What are the criteria for a diagnosis of Borderline Personality Disorder? Beginning by early adulthood, the individual exhibits at least five of the following in a variety of situations:

- Desperate attempts to prevent real or imagined abandonment
- Unstable relationships, alternating between putting someone on a pedestal and devaluing the person
- Unstable self-image
- Dangerous impulsiveness (substance abuse, sexual acting out, overspending, excessive risk-taking)
- Self-mutilation or suicide attempts
- Severe mood swings
- Severe problems with anger management
- Brief periods of paranoia or dissociation in stressful situations
- Chronic feelings of emptiness

medical context to gain attention and nurturance. The experience of physical and sexual abuse in childhood often leads victims to believe their bodies are defective or dirty. They may feel betrayed by the body, particularly in the case of sexual abuse. This alienated part of the self then deserves the punishment of self-mutilation. Children who witness family violence are also more likely to self-mutilate than children who do not. Observing impulsive self-destructive behavior may provide an early template for self-mutilation.

While these events in childhood may not lead directly to self-mutilation, the entry into adolescence may intensify these feelings. Puberty brings about changes in the body that the youth may already despise. Now the increase in size and especially the emergence of secondary sex characteristics may increase self-loathing. Pubertal changes may trigger the development of self-mutilation as self-mutilators have been found to have higher rates of eating disorders, high levels of distress about sexual identity, and to be less attentive to personal hygiene and grooming than their non-mutilating peers.

As difficult as it may be to grasp, self-mutilation appears to serve an important function for those who engage in this behavior, and it serves as an effective coping mechanism when other strategies are not present (Alderman, 1997). Self-mutilators typically lack the ability to effectively self-regulate or control their emotions (Lieberman & Poland, 2006). They may discover that cutting serves as a release of pressure (Yip, 2006), akin to bursting a balloon that is stretched too thin. Christina Gonzalez wrote about her first experience cutting her arm. She said, "At first I felt nothing, as usual, then came the pain—like a paper cut—and the feeling that a door had been opened. My heart beat really fast and I felt this rush; I felt powerful, and alive" (Gonzalez, 2004, p.10). In a family environment in which normal emotional expression is discouraged or even punished, children do not learn to develop tolerance for strong emotions. Instead, they learn emotional restraint by observing constricted parents or other adult models. They may even observe others using self-mutilation as a coping technique. In any case, when feeling intense emotions such as isolation, perceived abandonment, discouragement or depression, and the level of tension or anxiety becomes unbearable, cutting relieves the tension. For other self-mutilators, the physical pain of a self-inflicted wound, which has a specific source and is under the control of the individual, is a way to refocus attention away from unbearable emotional pain that seems to be boundless and over which the individual feels a lack of control.

People who are the victims of childhood abuse sometimes learn to dissociate as a way to disconnect from the intense physical or emotional pain they experience. This strategy of dissociating, while useful during abuse, may become frequent and problematic, so that the person feels detached from reality. Self-mutilating serves to increase awareness of and attention to the body, which ends the dissociative experience. Another teen wrote, "No matter how I tried, no matter what I did, cold and empty is all I felt. Then cutting seemed like a way to feel something, anything, again" (Carr, 2004, p. 10).

Self-mutilation may increase the level of endorphins in the system, and this positive state (akin to an opiate "high") can become addictive. Once the person experiences the euphoria that is the effect of endorphins released by the body to ameliorate the pain, they may seek this experience over and over again. For others, cutting and burning are ways to express emotional pain that seems inexpressible in words (Zila & Kiselica, 2001). Expressing pain externally is tangible evidence of the internal suffering. In fact, it may be a way to communicate to others the depths of the suffering. Another perceived benefit of self-mutilating is the self-care that follows.

Endorphin: Hormone found mainly in the brain that reduces the feeling of pain.

For many who feel unloved and isolated, cutting or burning allows them to care for and nurture themselves in ways they do not feel are attainable from others. Others use self-mutilation as a way to establish and express control over their bodies when everything else in their lives appears out of control. For those who were unable to stop the abuse they suffered as young children, the fact that they can stop this abuse may provide a comforting sense of control.

Given the abuse history of many self-mutilators, the acts of self-harm may serve as punishment when they hold the mistaken belief that they somehow caused the abuse, or that they are flawed to a degree that justified the abuse. Others with similar histories may hurt themselves as a way to re-enact the earlier trauma. These individuals will likely have other symptoms of post-traumatic stress disorder as well. For other victims of abuse, self-mutilation is a way to disfigure and make less desirable the body that was appropriated by her abuser.

For some self-mutilators, ritual and symbolism are important elements of the acts. Many explanations given by self-mutilators for their behavior have religious overtones, such as atoning for sins or a ritual for purification. This is not unlike the self-flagellation practiced by some religious sects. Blood also has important symbolic connotations. For some self-mutilators the sight of blood is soothing because it is evidence of being alive. Other cutters find the blood to be symbolic of the "evil" flowing away (as in "bad blood"). The adolescent female may view this blood flow as within her control in contrast to the mysterious and uncontrollable monthly flows she now experiences. Strong (1998) describes a young woman who left the dried blood on her arm as a reminder to herself of her secret act that meant to her that she was in control of this pain.

The purpose of this discussion of the functions of self-mutilation is to impress upon clinicians that despite the apparent dysfunction exhibited in this behavior, counselors need to recognize that to self-mutilators, their actions provide important benefits that they do not know how to obtain any other way. Thus, advising or encouraging someone to give up this behavior before they have developed effective strategies to meet these needs is quite dangerous because there is no replacement strategy for dealing with distress.

Theoretical Views

Different theories seek to explain the origin and dynamics of self-mutilation. At this point, there is no single widely accepted theory that all experts agree upon. Because these theories lead to the treatment approaches described later in the chapter, I will provide an overview here first.

Biological Theories

Biological explanations implicate low levels of serotonin in the brains of self-mutilators. Although the evidence is indirect and hardly conclusive, scientists found that medications that increase serotonin in the brain result in decreases in SMBs (Favazza, 1996).

Endorphins in the brain may also contribute to an understanding of this behavior. Endorphins are neurotransmitters that relieve pain and control emotions. When endorphins are produced, the person experiences pleasurable feelings. When someone is injured (as they are in self-mutilation), endorphins are produced by the brain to reduce the pain. After several such experiences, the person associates cutting or burning with pleasurable sensation that is the result of increased endorphins. This is what is called *classical conditioning*. The expectation of the "high" would encourage the individual to seek out the experience again.

Classical conditioning: The best-known example is Pavlov's dog experiment. When a neutral stimulus (a bell) is repeatedly paired with an unconditioned stimulus (food), the neutral stimulus comes to elicit the unconditioned response (salivating) by itself.

Favazza (1996) noted that one problem with this theory is that the vast majority of self-mutilators report experiencing little or no pain when doing the cutting or burning. Researchers know that abused children, who experience trauma and injury on a regular basis, may actually become less sensitive to pain, due perhaps to the increased production of endorphins. They may become accustomed to these high levels of endorphins in the system; so when they are alone, they may experience a "withdrawal" phenomenon that causes them to self-mutilate to return to the higher level of endorphins. This explanation is consistent with data that show a strong relationship between childhood abuse and self-mutilation.

Psychodynamic Theories

Psychodynamic theories trace their roots to Freud and his followers. Walsh and Rosen (1988) take a psychoanalytic perspective on self-mutilation. Although psychoanalysts interpret self-mutilation in several ways (e.g., the conflict between the life and death instincts, a symbolic castration, an attempt to merge with the menstruating mother), they agree that real or anticipated loss is a significant antecedent to the SMB. These authors describe an episode of self-mutilation as a sequence of events: the experience or perception of loss, the resultant increase in tension that cannot be expressed verbally, a state of dissociation or depersonalization, an irresistible urge to mutilate oneself, the act of mutilation, and the tension relief and return to pre-incident state.

A lesser known developmental theory of Freud's sets the stage for this sequence to occur. The theory proposes three stages in an infant's development: the first, autoeroticism, is the earliest period. In this stage, the infant's sensations and impulses are fragmented and without cohesion or any sense of self. The next is the stage of normal narcissism, in which the infant recognizes that he or she is a unit or distinct identity with impulses, sensations, movements, and so on integrated in one functional organism. The final infant phase is that of object love, when the infant recognizes not only itself as a distinct entity, but also the mother. The infant now possesses the beginning of the ability to form an intimate relationship with another.

When these stages are somehow disrupted, the seeds of the self-mutilative pattern are sown. Psychoanalysts view the mutilation as a regression (return) to the early infant state, which lacks the capacity for object love due to loss or abandonment (real or felt) by the parent. When a person experiences a loss later in life, the loss revisits the pain associated with this early loss and triggers the sequence described by Walsh and

Rosen (1988). The regressive nature of the experience is evident in the inability to verbalize the emotional pain recreated by the present loss. The self-mutilation occurs because the individual reacts to the threat with aggression, which is turned inward. They blame themselves for the loss, and believe they deserve punishment. A further dynamic of this sequence is that when the individual dissociates and experiences the body as alien or fragmented, they may panic because they fear disintegration. Thus, self-mutilation paradoxically assures the individual that the body is one unit. Interestingly, many self-mutilators describe the event as painless, which gives support to the notion of dissociation as a component of the sequence.

Another view from the psychodynamic tradition is that of Connors (2000), who also sees self-mutilation as rooted in childhood trauma and loss. She suggests the skin is a metaphor for the boundary of the self. The process of attachment and separation in early childhood ordinarily results in a child's sense of self, which is usually achieved at age three or four. When there is a trauma or loss at this time, there are long-term consequences to the sense of self. The sense of self depends on a boundary between "me" and "not-me." It allows the individual to discern what are their own thoughts, beliefs, and so on, from those of powerful others. It serves as a kind of "home base," from which the person perceives and relates to the world. Early in the formation of the self, the caregiver (usually mother) regulates emotions for the child. When upset, caregivers soothe and comfort, frequently providing tactile, verbal, and physical reassurance. As the self becomes increasingly defined and bounded, the regulator role is assumed by the individual. Connors (2000) believes this ideally occurs by age 3. As the child continues to develop, he/she gains more practice in self-regulation. When this process does not proceed apace, due to a trauma of some kind, the result may be an inability to self-regulate and a tendency to be overwhelmed by intense emotions along with low frustration tolerance. To compensate for the inadequate self-boundary, the person resorts to cutting the skin, the metaphoric boundary, and that reassures the individual that the boundary is still there.

When a person has a fragile self-boundary, and then feels emotions that are reminiscent of the two-year-old self, he or she may be unable to integrate those feelings with the adult self. Connors thinks a diagnosis of post-traumatic stress disorder is more appropriate than borderline personality disorder because it acknowledges childhood trauma at the root of self-mutilation.

Cognitive Behavioral Theory

Cognitive behavioral theory also offers a way to think about self-mutilation. Cognitive behaviorists see this behavior as a specific symptom and are not concerned with underlying issues. Walsh and Rosen (1988) list four faulty beliefs that lead to SMBs:

- Self-mutilation is acceptable, necessary, or advantageous.
- One's body and self are disgusting and deserving of punishment.
- Some type of physical action is necessary to reduce unpleasant feelings and bring relief.
- Overt action is necessary to communicate feelings to others. If others do not see visible signs, they will not understand how much the individual hurts (p. 156).

These "illogical thoughts" stem from a negative self-image and low self-esteem. Cognitive theorists believe that negative emotional states and self-defeating behaviors are the result of thinking errors that can be corrected. Behaviorists believe that all behavior, including self-mutilation, is learned, and can be unlearned (or extinguished). When an individual associates a pleasurable feeling (relief) with a behavior (cutting or burning) over a period of time, the behavior is conditioned. That is, the person has learned that cutting brings relief from intolerable feelings. Operant conditioning focuses on the manner in which a particular behavior gets reinforced. The release of tension and anxiety that occurs with the self-mutilating act serves as negative reinforcement for the behavior. That is, self-mutilation removes or reduces an unpleasant stimulus (tension and anxiety). This reinforcement strengthens the behavior. In some instances, negative reinforcement can come from others, as when others' anger or rejection stops when they see the self-mutilation. Positive reinforcement may also come from the reaction of others, who may express sympathy or concern, and provide attention. Medical and mental health professionals also provide positive reinforcement via their caring and nurturing behaviors. The fact that both positive and negative reinforcement results from this behavior, from both internal and external sources, suggests that this behavior will be very difficult to eliminate.

Narrative Theory

Miller (1996) bases her theory of self-mutilation on her experience with survivors of childhood trauma. While she accepts that self-mutilation serves important coping functions for the individuals, she focuses on the "physical and psychological *reenactments* of childhood trauma expressed in self-harmful behavior" (p. 214). Miller believes that self-mutilators are reenacting the interpersonal violence they experienced as children, and proving that they are incapable of self-protection because they were not protected as children. Actions committed by self-mutilators are symbolic of what was done to them as children. When the self-harm continues despite intervention, the client and the clinician may both become discouraged, which she believes is yet another replication of harmful childhood dynamics.

According to Miller, four themes are common in those who self-mutilate:

- A hatred of one's own body is central to the self-concept of the individual.
- Secrecy is an organizing principle, as it was in childhood.
- The behavior pattern is rooted in "the inability to self-protect and a fragmented sense of self." The person has not learned how to stay safe, or soothe oneself, and may have used dissociation as a way to manage distress. The *Internalized Abuser* becomes the bad part of oneself, the *Nonprotecting Bystander* is the internalized lack of protection the individual experienced, and the *Victim* is the "wounded child within." The internal dynamic is replayed with every episode of self-harm, and is the internal abuser hurting the victim while the bystander does nothing.
- Relationship problems are frequent as most self-mutilators have a core feeling of loneliness (pp. 217–222).

Treatment Options and Considerations

As theories differ on the causes and function of self-mutilation, they also differ on recommended treatment. In this section, I will review what is currently known about treatment, but caution the reader that there is not unanimity on the best course to take.

There is insufficient research evidence to make any clear judgment about the efficacy of the various treatment approaches (Hawton et al., 1998). Although research is ongoing, it is challenging to compare owing to the different definitions of self-mutilation (most studies include suicide attempters as well) and the differences in outcome measures (repetition of self-harm, elapsed time to self-harm episode, reduction in other symptoms, etc.). It is difficult for researchers to obtain sufficient sample sizes in randomized trials to meet the requirements for many statistical tests. Although readers will note that there is not a shortage of approaches to treatment, there is no one method that has been shown to be superior to any other, leaving the clinician without a standard of practice to adhere to.

The first treatment consideration that clinicians must ponder is whether to make the SMB the focus of treatment. This is a subject of considerable controversy among treatment professionals (Strong, 1998). Temporary increases in the SMB may be a consequence of more intensive therapy that delves into childhood trauma, but this is less likely to happen with short-term cognitive behavioral treatment. However, some clinicians may initially use a cognitive behavioral approach to which they then add more intensive approaches when the client is ready.

In an age of managed care and restricted access to mental health services, long-term intensive psychotherapy is not often available. Residential treatment is also a luxury available to only a few. Self-mutilation is often associated with serious psychological disorders, such as borderline personality disorder or post-traumatic stress disorder, that are not effectively treated with short-term interventions. The clinician may be in a position of choosing the best alternative based on practical issues rather than therapeutic factors.

Another consideration is whether treatment for self-mutilation can be effective when the individual does not want to give up this practice. As noted earlier, this behavior serves a variety of important functions for individuals who do not have other internal resources and then is reinforced with repeated action strengthening the behavior. Clinicians must consider whether working with someone who does not want to change is something they want to do. Favazza (1996), a leading expert on this behavior, cautioned against working with very many of these clients concurrently, as the emotional drain on the clinician is considerable. Given the high incidence of childhood trauma and loss in individuals who self-mutilate, the clinician must be prepared to address those issues in treatment.

Medication

Medication is often used in conjunction with psychological treatment. SSRIs (such as Prozac, Paxil, Luvox, and others) reduce self-mutilation in some clients. Given the

SSRI: (selective-serotonin reuptake inhibitor) A class of drug
that works by making more
serotonin available in the brain.

intractability of this behavior, a referral to a physician or psychiatrist for a trial course of medication would be a reasonable plan.
However, it is important to consider medication as an adjunct to
psychological treatment rather than as a substitute. Favazza (1998)
recommends using medication to quickly reduce the SMB while
other elements of treatment are implemented.

Dialectical Behavioral Therapy

Because self-mutilation is often associated with a diagnosis of borderline personality
disorder, the Dialectical Behavioral Approach developed and popularized by Marsha
Linehan may be useful. Linehan's program is specifically designed for clients who engage
in what she calls "parasuicidal" behavior (self-mutilation and suicide attempts). Research
provides some support for the effectiveness of this approach. However, the research studied women with borderline personality disorder, and there are no data supporting the
efficacy of dialectical behavioral therapy (DBT) in men who self-harm. The underlying
premise of DBT is that self-mutilation is due to a lack of skills for coping with intense
emotion. Typically, the program is delivered on an outpatient basis and includes one hour
weekly of individual therapy, two and a half hours of weekly group therapy, both of which
continue for a year. DBT training includes instruction in mindfulness, interpersonal
effectiveness, emotion regulation, and distress tolerance. Therapy uses a team approach,
and services typically include phone consultation for the client between sessions. Proponents of DBT state that this comprehensive treatment enhances the behavioral repertoire of clients, increases their motivation to change, and ensures that new behaviors are
applied in the clients' world outside treatment. The program is highly structured for both
clients and providers. A manual outlining this approach is available to clinicians, as is
training in this method. The manual (Linehan, 1993) provides lessons, handouts, and
homework assignments for teaching these skills. A series of training videos for use with
clients is available, as are professional development videos on the DBT approach.

Although the DBT approach appears useful, it is also impractical for many
clients due to the intensity of the treatment (Boyce, Oakley-Browne, & Hatcher,
2001). Both finances and time may be a barrier that keeps clients from entering this
type of treatment. Further, this approach is most likely to work with highly motivated
clients, as the guidelines state "Clients who drop out of therapy are out of therapy"
(Linehan, 1993, p. 108). Individuals who self-mutilate are often ambivalent about
treatment, and one study found that borderline patients could manage up to eighteen
sessions with good results. The year-long treatment may not attract the very clients
who need it, so a shorter treatment may be a useful alternative. There are two promising treatments, both developed in the United Kingdom, which are based on this
approach but are briefer, less intensive models. Research to date on these models is
promising, and hopefully U.S. clinicians will become more aware of these approaches.

Manual Assisted Cognitive-Behavior Therapy

Manual-assisted cognitive behavior therapy (MACT) incorporates many of the principles of DBT, but is delivered in a maximum of six sessions (Evans et al., 1999). In fact,

some clients opt to receive the treatment entirely via bibliotherapy (reading the six booklets designed for the program). Participants in a pilot study of this approach were thirty-four patients between 16 and 50, recruited immediately following an episode of self-harm. Of the thirty-four participants, eighteen received the MACT treatment and sixteen received the usual treatment (serving as a comparison group). Patients were not part of the study if their primary diagnosis was organic brain damage, substance dependence, or schizophrenia. Although the numbers were small, results were somewhat encouraging: rate of self-harm at discharge and at follow-up (4–6 months posttreatment) was lower for the MACT group, although the difference was not statistically significant. However, a statistically significant difference was detected between the two groups on depressive symptoms, with the MACT group having fewer symptoms.

Cognitive Analytic Therapy

Another approach developed in England is cognitive analytic therapy (Sheard et al., 2000), designed for use with repeat self-mutilators, and taking into account their ambivalence about therapy. The intervention can be done in one session if necessary, and can be used by counselors without extensive additional training. The essential elements of this approach are a problem-solving focus and analysis of reciprocal role relationships. The intervention includes a Self-harm Self Help file for the client, and an Assessor's Response File for the clinician, both completed prior to the initial session. These assessments provide a structure and focus for the sessions. This model was pilot tested with optimistic results, although the originators of the approach recognize the need for future research to evaluate its effectiveness.

Cowmeadow (1994) outlined the steps of therapy using this approach:

- Assist the client to understand the SMB, so that it makes sense to them and is less shameful.
- Identify the "target problem procedures" (p. 137), the recurrent maladaptive patterns that contribute to the SMB. These include thoughts, emotions, and actions that trigger the episodes.
- The third task is to help the client find alternatives to those maladaptive patterns, using a menu of ways the client might deal with stress other than self-mutilating. This element is a part of many of the approaches covered here.

Both the MACT and CAT approaches have been developed and tested in England. I hope that these theories will be imported and tested in the United States as there is a great need for brief, effective treatment for self-mutilation in this country as well. In an environment in which brief therapy is optimal, both for economic reasons and client compliance, these approaches offer definite advantages.

Narrative Therapy

As Miller sees the origins of the symptoms in childhood trauma, she does not advocate separate approaches for clients with substance abuse, eating disorders, or SMBs. These symptoms are all examples of self-abusive patterns stemming from childhood trauma.

Miller's approach to treatment draws on both narrative theory and DBT. The self-mutilating behavior is an attempt to deal with a negative environment. Symptoms are "stories" in the narrative tradition, in which the problem is located outside the individual. The treatment model proposed by Miller involves three stages, or circles.

The *outer* circle is the focus of the initial stage of treatment. The counselor inquires about the context of the client's life, collecting stories that can be used later to construct a more helpful narrative. During this stage, Miller does not allow the discussion to focus on the trauma or symptoms, including self-mutilation. She believes that it is important to establish a strong therapeutic alliance before such topics come up. In the *middle* stage or circle, the stories more directly consider the trauma and symptoms. In addition, a major effort in this stage is encouraging the client to build a support system. The *inner* stage or circle is focused on identifying, understanding, and integrating the fragmented aspects of self that were internalized as a way to cope with the trauma or abuse. The most important work here, according to Miller, is to help the client replace the Non-Protecting Bystander with a Protective Presence. This process unfolds with the therapist first serving in the role of Protective Presence, with the client gradually incorporating this construct into the self.

Group Therapy

Group therapy is often used in conjunction with individual therapy to treat self-mutilators. Many of the approaches described above incorporate group therapy as part of a broader intervention program. Homogenous groups with self-mutilators provide safety and a sense that the client is not alone in this problem. However, there are some particular challenges in groups that include self-mutilators, which lead Walsh and Rosen (1988) to recommend against homogeneous groups for that population. In groups with members who engage in self-mutilation, there are several potential problems:

- Loss in the group may trigger self-mutilating episodes.
- Self-mutilation may be used as a way to communicate within a group.
- Self-mutilation may be used in a group to manipulate other members or the therapist.
- Members may achieve status in the group, or membership, via their SMBs.

Strategies to minimize these problems include labeling SMB as such and explaining this clearly to the group. This will avoid the life-and-death crisis mentality that could emerge after an episode and inadvertently reinforce the behavior. Others in the group may enjoy the drama and the role of rescuer, so it is essential to correctly characterize SMB and distinguish it from suicidal behavior. Walsh and Rosen (1988) also suggest that therapists, knowing the repetitive nature of this behavior, predict the repetition in advance. This prediction sometimes has a paradoxical intention, but also can enhance the credibility of the therapist if it does occur. The therapist might even predict that some contagion will occur, with other members observing the positive aspects of the behavior and trying it out for themselves. To avoid the manipulative effect of a SMB episode, these experts suggest reframing the "helpful" behaviors of group members (nurturing, attending, etc.) as "harmful" to the person they wish to help.

The potential for group therapy to benefit the self-mutilator are many. The group is an excellent opportunity to teach, model, and reinforce alternative methods of coping with and communicating about distress. Group members can practice skills within the group, try them outside the group, and get feedback from the group on their performance. Preparation for termination is particularly important for self-mutilators, so that they can anticipate and deal with the loss in advance of the actual event.

Inpatient Treatment

In extreme situations, there is one inpatient program that specializes in treatment for self-mutilation. Information about the S.A.F.E. Alternatives program, described by Strong (1998) is at http://selfinjury.com. Such a program is an option if the behavior is escalating and outpatient treatment is not effective.

Do's and Don'ts

Not only is there no consensus on the best method of treating SMB, there is also debate about whether or not to use specific techniques. Of greatest concern are strategies that might be damaging rather than helpful. Solomon and Farrand (1996) emphasized the importance of not demanding that the self-harm stop completely once the client enters therapy. It is important to help the client develop and practice alternative strategies for dealing with impulses to hurt themselves before insisting they stop. Therapy that focuses exclusively on the self-mutilating behavior is unlikely to progress because underlying issues are not addressed. One suggestion is to make an agreement with clients to contact the therapist when they feel the urge to harm themselves. That encourages the client to use an alternative strategy (seeking help or support and verbalizing the pain). The agreement would also restrict contact with the therapist for 24 hours after an event of self-mutilation does occur. The therapist helps clients have a plan for receiving good care for their wounds from medical personnel who are non-judgmental. This strategy stresses the importance of behavior change but does not set up a failure scenario.

As with other issues in treatment of self-mutilation, Conterio and Lader (1998) disagree with this strategy. In their S.A.F.E. program, they require clients to sign a contract that explicitly forbids self-harm while in the program. The consequence of violating the contract is exclusion for the remainder of the current six-week program. Conterio and Lader (1998) describe counseling strategies and techniques that are likely to be harmful or damaging to treatment. However, it is important to remember that there is disagreement about many of these points, with other experts recommending the same interventions. The reader will need to reflect on these ideas and make a personal decision about what is helpful and what is not. Conterio and Lader discourage the following practices:

- Displaying wounds or scars, or encouraging detailed verbal descriptions of the self-mutilating act. They believe such practices serve to glorify the behavior and focus attention away from the underlying painful emotional issues.
- Prescribing substitute behaviors, such as holding ice cubes, writing on arms rather than cutting, breaking eggs on the arm to create the feeling of bleeding.

While behavioral therapists may recommend exactly such techniques, these authors contend that such strategies reinforce the faulty notion that tension must be discharged by "doing" something.

- Anger release techniques, such as punching pillows. They believe the message in such actions is that violent behavior is the only way to discharge feelings of anger, rather than encouraging verbal expression.
- Physical activity. Although counselors often prescribe running or engaging in high levels of exertion as anger management techniques, these authors are concerned that high levels of physical arousal often increase, rather than decrease, the likelihood of self-mutilation.
- Hypnosis. Conterio and Lader are adamantly opposed to this method, and report that clients can suffer serious negative consequences from this treatment.
- Heroic rescue. Therapist behaviors such as taking potentially dangerous objects away from clients, arranging for someone to "babysit" the client, or to respond to self-injurious acts with excessive sympathy and nurturing behaviors actually reinforce the behavior.

On the personal website of a self-mutilator, one client's perception of what is helpful provides a comparison with the professional recommendations described above.

- Show that you are interested in and care about the person behind the self-injury.
- Show concern for the injuries and offer compassion.
- Communicate that you are willing to talk about self-mutilation.
- Help the client recognize and understand the function and origins of the behavior.
- Recognize and acknowledge the ambivalence about stopping the behavior.
- Encourage the client to use the urge to self-mutilate as a signal of difficult and painful feelings, memories, or needs. Help the client learn other ways of expressing these feelings and to ask for support when needed.
- Encourage the client to create and strengthen support systems to reduce the isolation and shame that perpetuates the behavior.
- Recognize that clients can make progress in therapy even if they don't give up the behavior, especially early in therapy. Realize the behavior may even increase as painful issues are talked about.
- Encourage and acknowledge small gains, recognizing that small steps are important and lead to bigger ones.

It is interesting to note that this client does support the use of expressive techniques such as hitting pillows, which is discouraged by Conterio and Lader (1998). This difference of opinion highlights the current state of affairs in which no approach has emerged as superior.

For the clinician faced with a client who self-mutilates, what is the best approach? While DBT may have many positive aspects, the disadvantage is the longtime commitment and the intensity of the program. These disadvantages are particularly problematic in a managed care environment. Clinicians who are interested in working with these clients might do well to utilize elements of DBT (especially the Manual), and to stay abreast of developments of the newer approaches.

It is also important to consider that it may turn out that certain treatment characteristics, rather than the specific model, are the critical elements in effective treatment. Cowmeadow (1994) suggests the following essential ingredients: flexibility to deal with a wide range of client difficulties; relevance to client needs, which encourages compliance; rapid engagement to facilitate the development of a strong therapeutic alliance; and inclusion of a specific problem-solving component.

Issues of Diversity

There is very little about race, ethnicity, or socioeconomic class as they relate to self-mutilation. Lieberman and Poland (2006) assert that the behavior crosses the lines of culture, race, and socioeconomic status. One dissertation study (Mesirow, 1999) found no significant differences by race in incarcerated adult males who self-mutilated and a matched group who did not. Wenz (1977) obtained similar results in a large sample in a northern metropolitan area. However, Wenz included self-mutilation whether or not there was suicidal intent, and Mesirow does not specify her definition.

In the Ross and Heath (2002) study discussed earlier, 77% of the students who were identified as having self-mutilated at least one time were Caucasian, 5% African American, 6.5% Asian, 3.3% Hispanic, and 8.2% were Other Minority. These researchers noted the large percentage of students identified as engaging in self-mutilation were white, even in the urban school that was quite diverse.

Several studies suggest that in terms of gender differences, females self-mutilate at a higher rate than males at all age levels. However, that is not an unequivocal fact, as other studies have found equal rates for males and females (e.g., Briere & Gil, 1998). It may be that females are more likely to seek treatment, and thus there are proportionately more females in samples taken from inpatient or emergency room records. Whitlock, Eckenrode, and Silverman (2006) found that college students who admitted to repeated self-mutilation were more likely to be female, bisexual, or questioning their sexual orientation.

Persons with Disabilities

Self-mutilation, or self-injurious behavior, is a common form of destructive behavior exhibited by individuals with developmental disabilities, found in 2–4% of community-residing adults and as many as 39% with multiple disabilities (cerebral palsy, epilepsy, and learning disabilities) (Martin & Guth, 2005). In this population, the behavior is most often of the *stereotypic* type (Kress, 2003) described earlier in the chapter. The strongest risk factor for self-injurious behavior is the degree of intellectual impairment, with those persons with severe or profound disabilities exhibiting more than four times the SMB than those with mild or moderate disabilities (Oliver, Moss, Petty, Sloneem, Aaron, & Hall, 2003). Studies have found that 13–53% of those with Tourette's syndrome and 3–46% of those with mental retardation or developmental disabilities exhibit these behaviors (Kress, 2003). Oliver and colleagues list the following risk factors for self-injurious behavior: intellectual disability, poor expressive communication skills, and the presence of stereotyped or compulsive behaviors.

Stereotypic behavior: A repetitive, usually rhythmic behavior pattern with no purpose or goal.

Stereotypic SMB is often associated with mental retardation and developmental delays, and appears to have an organic cause. These behaviors can cause tissue damage, ranging from mild to severe. Major SMBs are seen in individuals with severe psychoses, and may be prompted by hallucinations or delusions. People who engage in this type of behavior may report an absence of pain and a feeling of calm associated with the SMB.

Treatment for self-injurious behaviors in persons with disabilities is similar to that used with other populations, although medication and behavior modifications programs may be preferred.

Assessment

There is no assessment test specifically designed to detect self-mutilation. Researchers attempting to define an MMPI-2 scale that would identify self-mutilative behavior were unable to find a particular profile associated with this behavior (Acker, Burck, & Annis, 1995). Many self-report inventories (e.g., Trauma Symptom Inventory) include items that address this concern. Observation and direct questioning about signs may be the most effective way to discover whether self-mutilation is occurring with a particular client, but such strategies are likely to be effective only when there is a solid therapeutic alliance. What is probably more important for the clinician is to remember that when self-mutilation is recognized, it is unlikely to be the only symptom or focus of clinical attention. Thus, given the array of diagnoses and problems that may accompany this behavior, it is essential that the clinician do a thorough assessment to detect any other conditions that may be present. This will provide a basis for a more complete and coherent treatment plan. Kress (2003) emphasizes that inquiring about SMB should be part of initial or intake interviews, and when it is acknowledged, then more in-depth questioning should follow. She also notes that a medical assessment is almost always recommended. In cases of severe SMB, the physician will need to check for infection and other medical consequences. In cases of mild SMB, the medical examination should include advice to avoid sharing blades and other instruments of self-harm to avoid transmitting disease.

Counselor Issues

Probably the most difficult aspect of working with clients who engage in self-mutilation is keeping one's reactions from interfering with the treatment. It is not easy to witness the effects of self-mutilation without having a strong reaction (Kress, 2003). Alderman (1997) described her own intense desire to make a client stop hurting herself, and her frustration at her inability to do so. A counselor needs to remember that this behavior serves important purposes for clients, and they may not be willing or ready to give it up just because they enter treatment. The Counselors must also realize that they do not have the power to change this individual. Professionals must recognize and accept the difficulty of changing this behavior. One needs to somehow avoid open displays of revulsion on seeing the evidence of self-mutilation, or clients will be sure to keep it hidden. Alderman makes an important distinction between sympathy and empathy for these clients; while empathy is helpful, sympathy can be a barrier. Sympathy and excessive concern by a clinician reinforces the behavior and may impede progress. One can empathize with the disappointment, fear, or other precipitating emotion the client experienced as the trigger for self-mutilation, but treating him with solicitous attention because of the wounds is not therapeutic.

Another issue that counselors must recognize is that despite the unpleasant nature of the wounds, self-mutilation does not usually require hospitalization. These wounds are unlikely to be life-threatening, and many do not even require medical attention. It is important that the counselor not overreact and seek unnecessary medical intervention. For one, this kind of attention serves to reinforce the behavior. For another, it may unnecessarily breach confidentiality and undermine the therapeutic alliance. Counselors need to assess suicidal risk and reserve extreme measures for appropriate situations.

Clients who engage in self-mutilation are likely to have frequent crises, and require more "emergency" responses than other clients. This may involve telephone consultation, urgent appointments, and the like. Counselors need to consider whether they are willing to make the kind of commitment that is generally called for in this population.

Some therapists use "no harm contracts" as a way to reduce self-harming behavior. In reality, these contracts are not binding and may put the counselor and the client in a "no-win" situation. What might be more productive is for the counselor to spell out in advance how they will respond to incidents of self-mutilation. Conterio and Lader (1998) address this in their self-help book for self-injurers. They recommend that if a client contacts the counselor following a self-injury episode, the counselor should make an assessment of the client's need for medical intervention. No other interaction should occur outside the session. If a client attends a session with fresh injuries, the counselor should focus on the medical needs, insisting on medical examination in lieu of the therapy session. They believe these behaviors, while not rejecting the client, do not reinforce episodes of self-mutilation.

It is important to recognize when the counselor's frustration and fear becomes an impediment to progress. A website for self-mutilators (http://www.selfinjury.freeserve.co.uk/) included the following comments about therapists:

> I almost lost my first [psychotherapist]. She tried to use my cutting as a boundary. She told me if I cut again she would not see me anymore. She did not see me for a few weeks till I called feeling very out of control. It was out of her frustration with me. (Comment submitted by a female, age 27, 3 years self-injurious behavior).

BOX 2.1
A Note to School Counselors

I have noted earlier in this chapter that self-mutilation is becoming a common adolescent problem (Froeschle & Moyer, 2004; Kress, Drouhard, & Costin, 2006). As such, "self-mutilation is a phenomenon addressed daily by school counselors" (p. 231). While the causes of this behavior are varied and complex, episodes in adolescents are often precipitated by the breakup of romantic relationships or conflict with parents. Regardless of the trigger, school counselors may be the first professionals to discover the behavior, and their actions and decisions are important. Froeschle and Moyer recommend consulting with other professionals and making referrals to community providers when that is indicated.

In addition to educating staff, and providing individual support and group counseling as appropriate, there are difficult ethical issues to be faced (Kress et al., 2006). Probably the most difficult decision the school counselor will make is whether to notify the student's parents once self-mutilation has been detected. The duty to warn when there is the potential for serious harm has been upheld in court, and counselors may be liable if they do not report and the parent later learns that the school counselor withheld this information. There are no specific definitions of what constitutes "serious harm," and the school counselor might well decide that superficial cuts do not qualify. On the other hand, there are arguments to support maintaining confidentiality: the student's feelings of alienation could be exacerbated by breach of confidentiality, and the willingness of students to disclose personal material could be compromised. The best solution, according to Froeschle and Moyer (2004) is to persuade the student of the importance of telling parents, and to offer to be present as a support when the student does so. Kress et al. (2006) recommend that the school counselor conduct a thorough assessment of both self-injury and suicide as a way to decide whether the student is in danger. They also point out that given the increasing frequency of self-mutilation among students, a school policy should be developed that specifies the roles of various personnel (including the school counselors), and includes guidelines for parental notification. Because school counselors, unlike other mental health professionals, have multiple constituencies (students, school administrators, and parents) their roles are quite complex. It might be prudent to consult with legal experts in drafting a policy, and to establish a network of colleagues who agree to stay current and to be available for consultation in challenging cases of self-mutilation in the school.

A 34-year-old female teacher who self-mutilated for 2.5 years posted this observation:

> The first time I cut myself, I called my therapist because I was scared that I couldn't/ wouldn't stop. She seemed ok and calm with the situation that night. I always had difficulty expressing myself and I was totally intimidated by her, so for me to even call her and admit to my foolishness was a big step for me. Unfortunately, she "dumped" me the next evening by saying that she couldn't give me the help she felt I needed. I now know that she was somewhat panic-stricken, but I felt even more worthless than ever . . . I'M SO SCREWED UP THAT EVEN A THERAPIST CAN'T HELP ME! I still feel that she was a coward about the whole thing.

A 39-year-old woman who had been engaging in self-mutilation on and off for 27 years noted:

> Thank God, I found my present therapist 16 years ago and she has been my therapist through periods of self-injury and periods without it (9 years until this one). She would never threaten me or give me an ultimatum over the behavior. MANY previous therapists completely freaked out about it, and ended up traumatizing me one way or another.

One strategy described by Alderman (1997) is to use the frustration as a therapeutic tool. However, it is important for counselors to be self-aware and recognize their own limits and boundaries of competence. It may be that this issue, once known, may be a signal to the counselor that a referral is in order to a counselor who is more prepared to deal with such clients.

Counselors who are not well informed about self-mutilation may not be aware that a client is doing this behavior. They may come for treatment on other issues, often testing the counselor to determine whether the counselor is aware or prepared to address the issue. One way a counselor can indicate to clients that they are knowledgeable about this symptom is to ask about it directly at intake. Although the client may not admit at that point, bringing up the subject gives a message that the counselor is approachable. Counselors providing services to any client should be alert to the possibility of self-mutilation and inquire about bruises, cuts, or burns they notice. Although clients again may not immediately admit the source of the wounds, they are aware of your concern, and if there is repeated new evidence, the counselor has established a foundation from which to discuss the issue.

Ethical Concerns

A mental health professional's ethical obligations regarding suicide, homicide, and child abuse are quite straightforward. Every mental health professional is familiar with the duty to warn and the duty to protect, and clinicians know they must provide informed consent that includes telling potential clients of the limits of confidentiality.

Dealing with self-mutilation is not quite as clear, and therefore may be even more troubling to clinicians who feel ethical and legal guidelines aren't available to guide their decision-making (Alderman, 1997). In one of the few articles that discuss the ethical dilemmas associated with this behavior, Vesper (1996) discusses the question of boundaries of competence. The American Counseling Association standard states: "Counselors practice only within the boundaries of their competence, based on their education, training, supervised experience, state and national professional credentials, and appropriate professional experience." Because there are no empirically validated treatments that are standard practice for treating self-mutilation, many clinicians have developed untested personal theories. Vesper suggests this strategy borders on the unethical, as such treatment might be unhelpful at best, or detrimental in the worst cases. One specific issue she raises is overreaction: because of their own fears, counselors may determine that the very act of self-mutilation is evidence of serious psychopathology and take steps to hospitalize the client who is neither suicidal nor lethal. Some counselors simply refuse to treat clients who self-mutilate, which is unethical unless they make appropriate referrals or assure client safety.

Because self-mutilation can become lethal, Vesper acknowledges that it is important to monitor the client, as would be the case for any client with severe depression or other factors that place them at risk. One potentially difficult situation is that of the client who, perhaps because she is discussing painful issues, begins to self-mutilate (cut or burn) during a session. How should an ethical counselor respond to a client who is scratching or cutting her arm in session, assuming the gesture is not lethal? Vesper points out several inappropriate strategies: to focus on the behavior and discontinue the psychological work is, in her opinion, an impediment to the therapeutic process. However, it is appropriate to acknowledge the behavior but not interrupt without interrupting the work. The counselor might say, "I know this is very painful to talk about, and I notice you are cutting your arm to help you cope." To physically intercede, attempt to remove the instrument of cutting, is to violate the client and perhaps re-enact childhood trauma. Thus, it is ethical to observe the behavior without actively intervening when the action is clearly non-lethal. What if the client's behavior escalates to a level where serious harm is possible? Again, physically intervening is not appropriate, nor is touching the client in this case. Vesper recommends that in this case, the counselor should change the focus of the discussion from the issues to the cutting itself.

Without specific training, what is a well-intentioned counselor to do without going beyond the boundaries of competence? Vesper suggests that an ethical professional will actively seek information and most important, seek supervision and consultation from a colleague who has experience with this issue. Alderman (1997) advises clinicians to distinguish those acts of self-mutilation that are life-threatening from the more commonly encountered acts that may not even require medical attention. Including questions about self-mutilation in intake interviews may alert the counselor to the need for vigilance, and informed consent must be very clear, particularly so with self-mutilating clients. Informed consent should include information about the therapist's competence and willingness to work with clients who self-mutilate. Ultimately, the most ethical course for clinicians who treat this clientele is to stay informed and utilize all available resources to do so.

Summary

- Self-mutilation refers to intentional, non-lethal, repetitive bodily harm or disfigurement that is socially unacceptable.
- Self-mutilators are much more likely to eventually commit suicide than people who do not engage in this behavior.
- As difficult as it may be to grasp, self-mutilation appears to serve an important function for those who engage in this behavior, and serves as an effective coping mechanism when other strategies are not present.
- This behavior is frequently associated with borderline personality disorder, but SMBs exist in adolescents or individuals with other diagnoses too.
- There is no treatment approach that is clearly superior to others for this behavior.

- It is important not to demand that clients give up this behavior before they have learned other coping strategies.
- Dialectical Behavior Therapy is a well-known treatment for this behavior, but it is costly and time-intensive. Briefer therapies are available, along with medication to control the behavior.
- It is important that mental health professionals not directly or indirectly reinforce the behavior.

ADDITIONAL RESOURCES

On the Web

- http://www.behavioraltech.com/index.cfm Information about trainings and videos, as well as concise information for clinicians. Some sections are appropriate to recommend to clients and families, particularly if you are going to be using elements of DBT in your treatment.
- http://www.acat.org.uk/ An outstanding and very complete resource for counselors who are interested in cognitive analytic therapy, with links to many other useful sites, and a list of books and other resources.
- http://www.palace.net/~llama/psych/injury.html The most exhaustive and extensive online site on self-mutilation.

In Print

- *Cut* by Patricia McCormick (2000). Intended for young adults. An excellent opportunity for a clinician unfamiliar with this behavior to get in the head of an adolescent who self-mutilates, without having to respond to a client. A very quick read, and a good first introduction for clinicians.
- *The Scarred Soul* by Tracy Alderman (1997). Useful for both counselors and clients.
- *Bodily Harm* by Karen Conterio and Wendy Lader (1998). Both this and *The Scarred Soul* include sections for therapists.
- *A Bright Red Scream* by M. Strong (1998). Written for the lay audience, this provides excellent, in-depth information about self-mutilation and belongs on every professional's reference shelf.
- *Bodies Under Siege* by A. R. Favazza (1996). The most complete and scholarly coverage of this topic.

EXERCISES

1. After reading *Cut*, advertised as a young adult book, decide if you would recommend or assign it to an adolescent cutter. Explain your decision.

2. A client comes to you for treatment, and you discover early on that the client is a cutter. You feel you are competent to work with this client and arrange for consultation with

a colleague. Given the approaches to therapy described above, decide which approach you think is most appropriate and most compatible with your personal style. Then, develop a conceptualization and treatment plan for the client that is grounded in the theory you selected. Explain your choice, including reasons why you rejected other approaches.

3. Imagine you work with young adolescents in a school or community setting. Discuss the special ethical considerations that you would have to consider if you learned that one of your clients is self-mutilating. Decide how you would resolve the ethical issues, giving reasons for your decisions.

4. Interview a clinician in your area who has worked with self-mutilators. Find out how they take care of themselves when working with this clientele.

5. Termination is particularly important with this clientele. Consider what you might do to prepare and effectively terminate with a client who self-mutilates. Discuss or write about your plan.

CHAPTER

3

Eating Disorders

Health professionals have proclaimed obesity to be a major health problem in the United States. At the same time, the current status of eating disorders has been called "an epidemic" (Croll, Neumark-Sztainer, Story, & Ireland, 2002). And, there are many people who do not meet the diagnostic criteria for these disorders who have problematic eating behaviors. Many of the behaviors that are characteristic of eating disorders are the extremes of a continuum, with most of the behaviors occurring to some degree in the population as a whole (Smolak & Striegel-Moore, 1996). A Canadian study found that many adolescents report purging from time to time; 50% of normal-weight high school girls were dieting, with some using purging as a weight-loss technique (Piran, 2001). Twenty-three percent of 8-year-old girls and 18% of 8-year-old boys reported they "always" wished they were thinner (Shapiro, Newcomb, & Loeb, 1997), with comparable results being found in several countries in the United Kingdom (Littleton & Ollendick, 2003). Among college females, 78% reported binging experiences and 8.2% used self-induced vomiting to control weight. Perhaps most telling are the results of a study conducted in England: 58% of females in a large sample of 12- to 15-year olds listed "appearance" as the biggest concern in their lives (www.anred.com).

Purging: Getting rid of excess calories by self-induced vomiting, misusing laxatives, diuretics, and enemas, or exercising excessively.

Binging: Eating large quantities of food (usually high-calorie) at a time.

These disorders develop in a sociocultural context that is essential to understand. The quest for the ideal body is widespread in Western societies that assume that this ideal is attainable and that those who reach this standard will have a better life (Brownell, 1991). Think for a moment about the ubiquitous symbol of female beauty, Barbie, who has influenced the beliefs of countless little girls since 1939. If Barbie were a real woman, she would be 6 ft. tall and 101 lbs. Her body mass index (BMI) would be 13.7; a person with a BMI below 17.5 is anorexic. Barbie is thinner than female models and anorexics, with extreme measurements at the neck, wrist, waist, and hips (Norton, Olds, Olive, & Dank, 1996). Due to her low percentage of body fat, Barbie would no longer have menstrual periods, nor would department store mannequins on which current fashions are displayed (Rintala & Mustajoki, 1992). The average American girl between 3 and 11 years old owns seven Barbie dolls. What message are they receiving about their appearance? Interestingly, the proportions of the Ken doll are much closer to reality.

Case Study

Maria is one of seven children in a family headed by her Anglo American father and Mexican mother. The family came to the United States when Maria was a toddler, and a sense of fear due to her illegal status pervades her childhood. She observed her mother in a subservient role toward her father. When Maria started school, she attended a school with mostly Anglo peers where she struggled with English and believed she was inferior to her classmates.

The year she was eight, a number of traumatic events occurred. The family was living in a motel managed by her father. They had only two rooms to themselves, and children had to share beds. Her older half-brother sexually molested her during this time. Maria did not tell anyone about this, but her mother once caught her brother fondling her. Although she told him to stop, she did not take any other measures to protect Maria and prevent recurrence. At this same time, Maria's mother had a traumatic late-term miscarriage that made her less available emotionally to the surviving children. Also at this time, Maria began wetting the bed, for which she was shamed and beaten.

Maria's father's unstable employment forced the family to move to another community, where her father was again unable to maintain a job. He decided to move himself to another city across the country seeking work, while Maria's mother and the children remained in the southwest town until he settled in the new location. After her father's departure, Maria's mother began drinking heavily and going out with men. One of her mother's boyfriends also sexually molested Maria. Her mother's abuse, both verbal and physical, increased; Maria believes she was the special target of her mother's abuse because her father always made a point of saying she was the "apple of his eye," incurring the jealousy of both her mother and her siblings. Her father did not send promised funds. The family's economic circumstances were dire, and Maria vividly remembers the crisis when they were evicted from their home. Somehow, they managed to survive, but in very marginal circumstances. Other children teased Maria about living in a shack and wearing Goodwill clothes.

In her family, Maria was "parentified"—given responsibilities that really belonged to a parent. She kept the house and yard clean, cooked meals, and cared for her younger siblings. In reaction to the chaos and upheaval in her childhood, Maria became a perfectionist. She makes sure she is not the inferior being that she believed her childhood self to be. She tends to black and white thinking: Maria has worked hard to discard her belief that her value as a human being is totally dependent on her weight, with thin=good and fat=bad. Maria also has a strong need to control. She is afraid if she doesn't keep everything in control, she will find herself back in the unpredictable state she knows too well from childhood.

Maria had never been told about the facts of life, and when she experienced her first real menstrual period, she was frightened by the blood, thinking something was terribly wrong. When she approached her mother in fear, her mother laughed at her. Mother and siblings began making fun of Maria's body, calling her "fat ass" and a whore. Her mother was always trying to look thin, and was highly critical of women who were "fat." Maria's first diet was at age 12 or 13, using diet pills she stole from a local store.

Maria idolized her distant father. After Maria's 8th grade year, her father went to live in Mexico and took Maria with him. She chose to leave her mother and siblings to live with her father because she anticipated a closer relationship with her "hero," and was surprised when he dropped her off to live with a Mexican family. She attended a private school where most other students were wealthy and "snobby." This time, it was difficult to attend school speaking only Spanish, and she again felt "less than" her peers. Maria lost her virginity at age 15 to the father in that household. At this point, she began restrictive dieting, and also running and exercising to an extreme. After the sexual incident, she moved in with another family that she describes as somewhat better, but she later moved to a border city with her father and his new wife, again hoping for the close relationship that never developed. There she met a 23-year-old man with whom she remained for five years, eventually marrying him. This man was possessive and controlling, and made it very clear that she must be thin, sometime pushing on her stomach to emphasize his point. Maria became pregnant, but had a premature Caesarian delivery, and the baby died within a month.

Maria moved back to a southwestern city when she ended this marriage. She was living alone when she heard from a friend about binging and purging, and decided to try it. She had a boyfriend by then, who always complimented her when she was thin. She began to receive numerous compliments on her appearance when she lost a great deal of weight. This gave her a sense of power, and she would relish the feeling of being the thinnest one in the room. She felt in control. When she binged, she always ate "comfort foods," and felt numb afterwards. When she purged, she would feel euphoric, as though she had gotten rid of difficult feelings. Maria's eating disorder also served to keep her distance from others. She says, "I thought that by looking good on the outside, I could hide my vulnerabilities, secrets, and issues."

When the eating disorder was most severe, Maria would binge and purge three or four times a day. As a result, she began to feel anxious and emotionally distraught, and was perpetually tired and without energy. For brief periods of time, she would stop purging but would start a cycle of over-exercising. Maria describes these behaviors as self-abusive; she was angry with herself and wanted to punish herself.

Maria felt her life was out of control. She was binging and purging all the time. She found a therapist in the phone book, and in the second session, told the therapist about her eating disorder. The therapist became visibly upset, said Maria needed to see someone else who specialized in that disorder, gave her the card of the specialist, and rushed her out the door. Maria describes that interaction: "She acted as though I had told her I had plague." Several days later, she got an appointment with the therapist whom she has been seeing ever since—now eight years. Maria has worked hard in therapy to recover from her eating disorder. She has had relapses, with a major one occurring when her father died in 1995. As a result of therapy, Maria came to understand her mother's behavior, and Maria has now repaired her relationship with her mother.

An essential component of Maria's treatment has been group therapy. Seeing other women with the disorder helped her feel less isolated and alone. Because her secretiveness about her behavior helped her maintain the behavior, exposing it to others in the group was an important step. In the group, Maria could observe something in others—their distorted body image—that she couldn't see at first in herself. She would then realize, "I do that too." In her group, Maria learned that being thin did not equal happiness. For her, the group was an available mini-lab where she could practice new skills before trying them in the real world. She also valued the opportunity to get to know other women. She had always viewed other women as threats, and believes many women see other females as "competition." The group allowed her to form deep relationships with other women that helped her value her own femininity.

An important component of Maria's treatment has been medication, which she has been taking since her therapy began. In individual therapy, Maria has learned a great deal about herself, assisted by the skillful questions posed by her therapist. Homework assignments extended the process beyond the therapy sessions. Maria realizes that her issues encompass more than the eating disorder and values therapy for helping her become more satisfied in all areas of her life. "Exposing these things [my feelings of inferiority, insecurity] with a good therapist made 'looking good' less of an obsession, because I realized that when I start feeling insecure about my body, it is never really about my body, but deeper issues."

The support and encouragement of her therapist gave Maria the motivation to return to school, where she has done very well. Maria has been married for seven years to a man who appreciates and loves her regardless of her weight. Her husband has supported her therapy, even meeting at times with the therapist.

It is still hard to resist the pervasive message that thin is the ideal. Maria, like all of us, receives numerous subtle and not-so-subtle messages about what makes a woman beautiful or valued. She acknowledges that these messages are hard to ignore, but Maria focuses on eating a healthy diet, and exercising reasonably. She is now able to look at her naked body in the mirror without disgust, and she loves her body for its efficient functioning. She thinks of her stomach as her "natural healer," as it alerts her when she is not eating well and taking care of herself.

Maria's therapist is a tall woman with a trim physique. Maria values the honesty of her therapist, who makes it clear to her clients on intake that she herself does not have, and has not had, an eating disorder. She does reveal her humanity to the clients (she is not perfect) and on the rare occasions when she does not eat a healthy diet, she shares that with her clients so that they understand that no one can eat "perfectly" all of the time. She advises clients to "hit the reset button" when that happens, and get back on track. Maria values both her advice and example.

Maria and her therapist have discussed termination of treatment, which Maria approaches with mixed feelings. She knows she has the tools to live a fulfilling life without binging and purging, and has supportive people in her life who accept her unconditionally. She reflects, "I feel confident that I have the skills and knowledge I need to cope with whatever comes my way. I also know that I will not cope with things perfectly all of the time. My recovery is an ongoing learning process and whatever my progress is will be good enough."

Definitions and Description of the Problem

Although eating disorders have existed throughout history, clinical attention to these behaviors has been relatively recent. Physicians first used the term *anorexia nervosa* in 1873. For the first part of the twentieth century, doctors believed this disorder had a biological cause, such as a pituitary deficiency. In the 1930s, attention turned again to the psychological origins of the disorder, and this has remained the focus since then. The term *bulimia nervosa* was coined in 1979, almost a century later than anorexia. This does not mean the disorder did not exist: rather, identification of specific criteria for diagnosis did not happen until that time.

In this chapter, I will often abbreviate the names of the disorders to *anorexia* or *bulimia* in the interest of space. I will also use female pronouns because although there are many males with these disorders, the vast majority of cases are females.

Anorexia Nervosa

Anorexia nervosa has the following characteristics (based on *The Diagnostic and Statistical Manual for Mental Disorders* (DSM-IV-TR)):

- Refusal to maintain body weight above 85% of expected level.
- Intense fear of becoming fat, despite being underweight.
- Body image disturbance: inaccurate perception of weight, self-image based on weight alone, or denial of the seriousness of low body weight.
- The absence of three consecutive menstrual cycles (amenorrhea).

There are two types of anorexia: *restricting type* (body weight attained by restricting intake only) and *binge-eating/purging type*.

Eating disorders often have severe physical consequences. With anorexia, there are numerous potential medical complications that affect the endocrine system, the cardiovascular system, the neurological system, as well as bones and metabolism.

Electrolyte: Substance responsible for moving nutrients into cells and waste products out of cells.

Anorexia often is associated with hair loss and dry skin, and sometimes results in a condition called *lanugo*, which means soft body hair found on the face, arms, and other parts of the body. Electrolyte abnormalities are common and can effect cardiac functioning. Dehydration and constipation are frequently associated with the disorder.

A fascinating study that examined the effects of semi-starvation on adults was conducted in the 1950s by Keys and his colleagues, and described in a series of articles in the late 1940s and early 1950s in the *American Journal of Physiology*. These researchers at the University of Minnesota recruited volunteers to participate in an experiment on the effects of restricted food intake on healthy adult men. The thirty-six healthiest (both physically and psychologically) of the volunteers were enrolled in the study as an alternative to military service. During the first three months of the year-long study, participants ate normally while researchers closely observed their eating habits, general behavior, and personality. For the next six months of the study, the men received half their former food intake. They lost an average of 25% of their previous weight. In the final three months, they were gradually fed and rehabilitated. Keep in mind that the level of food restriction was not as severe as that of many anorectics. These are some of the changes that occurred in the semi-starved men:

- Overwhelming preoccupation with food, with corresponding decreased interest in sex and activity. The men read about, talked about, and dreamed about food. They developed rituals around eating.
- Episodes of binge eating. During the rehabilitation phase, many men ate large quantities of food, and for a few, this persisted for as long as five months after they had free access to food.
- Irritability and anger outbursts were frequent, anxiety increased, apathy was widespread. Two subjects exhibited psychotic symptoms, and most had episodes of depression. For some of the men, the symptoms persisted or even increased

during the period of re-feeding. Participants took a standard personality test prior to and after the experiment, so researchers were able to compare personality profiles before and after semi-starvation. They found serious pathological changes and emotional disturbance after the starvation period.

- Social withdrawal and isolation increased.
- Intelligence testing did not find changes in ability, but participants reported problems with concentration, alertness, comprehension, and judgment during the period of restricted food intake (Garner, 1997).

The implications of these results for individuals with eating disorder are clear: Many of the behaviors associated with anorexia nervosa may be the effect of semi-starvation on the system. The fact that these symptoms continued even when normal feeding resumed suggests that treatment for anorexia needs to continue past the point when the client achieves her weight goals. Healthy and realistic weight goals are established with input from a physician.

Bulimia Nervosa

A diagnosis of bulimia nervosa requires that the following symptoms are present:

- Recurrent episodes of binge eating: eating a large amount of food in a short period of time along with a sense of lack of control during the episode.
- Recurrent inappropriate behavior to prevent weight gain, such as self-induced vomiting, abuse of laxatives or other medication, fasting, or excessive exercise.
- Binging/purging behaviors occur on an average of twice per week for three months.
- Self-evaluation over-emphasizes body weight and shape.
- These behaviors do not occur only during episodes of anorexia nervosa.

There are two types of bulimia: *purging* and *nonpurging*. Nonpurging types use fasting or excessive exercise to control weight.

As with anorexia nervosa, electrolyte abnormalities are common in bulimia, as are dehydration and constipation. For those who purge, erosion of the enamel of the teeth is a potential consequence. I worked with a young woman with bulimia who needed to have very expensive dental work done as her frequent purging had destroyed the enamel on her teeth. In fact, she came for treatment only because her parents had refused to pay for any additional dental work. With bulimia, "Russell's sign" is often an early indicator of the purging behavior: it refers to sores or calluses on the hand caused by using the hand to induce vomiting.

Eating Disorders Not Otherwise Specified (NOS)

This diagnosis refers to behavior that meets most, but not all, criteria for one of the other disorders. For example, the individual may still be menstruating but meet all of the other criteria for anorexia, or the binge–purge cycles do not occur frequently enough to meet the criteria for bulimia. Binge-eating disorder (BED) is included in this category. BED differs from bulimia in that compensatory behaviors such as dieting or over-exercising do not occur regularly, although those behaviors do occur. Clients with BED often eat greater quantities at meals and between meals than equally overweight persons without BED. Because this disorder has some important differences from bulimia, treatment approaches need to be adapted to this clientele (Marcus, 1997).

In contemporary American society, there are many who do not strictly meet all criteria for any of these diagnoses but whose eating patterns and behaviors around food have many characteristics of eating disorders. For example, a study conducted with Minnesota high school students found disordered eating in 30% of the 9th and 12th grade males in their large sample, and 55% of females (Croll et al., 2002). These are shocking figures. Counselors also need to focus on subclinical levels of these behaviors, hopefully preventing the progression to the eating disorders.

Prevalence

Different studies report different rates of these disorders in the population depending on the source of data and the methods used. For adolescent females, eating disorders are the third most common chronic illness, exceeded by only obesity and asthma (Croll et al., 2002). The DSM-IV estimates that 0.5–1% of females meet full diagnostic criteria for anorexia, and 1–3% for bulimia (with males estimated at 5–10% of cases), although rates as high as 5% have been reported (Stock et al., 2002). About one-third of individuals diagnosed with bulimia have previously met the criteria for anorexia. Rates of eating disorders in males seem to be increasing, which may reflect an actual increase or an increase in males seeking treatment (Braun, Sunday, Huang, & Halmi, 1999).

Subclinical: Symptoms that are present but not severe enough to meet diagnostic criteria for a mental disorder.

No prevalence rates are available for eating disorders not otherwise specified (NOS), but logic suggests that it is likely to affect large numbers of adolescents and young adults. Research suggests that full recovery rates for eating disorders are achieved in about 50% of clients, with 30% showing some improvement and 20% making no improvement (Schlozman, 2002). A startling 6–20% of those diagnosed with anorexia die from complications of the disorder (starvation, suicide, heart problems) (Mitchell, Pomeroy, & Adson, 1997).

Populations that are at high risk for eating disorders include those whose activities or careers are believed to be enhanced by a thin physique. These include professional dancers and many athletes. In a study of elite college athletes, none met DSM-IV criteria for anorexia, but almost 3% of female athletes had subclinical symptoms, 2% self-identified as anorectic, and 35% were found to be at-risk. Among the males, none had subclinical symptoms, 1% self-identified as anorectic, and 10% were at risk for this disorder. One percent of females and no males met diagnostic criteria for bulimia, 9% of women and a negligible number of men had subclinical symptoms, 6% of females and almost no men self-identified as bulimic, but 38% of both genders were at risk.

Adolescent and young adult women are the largest group with these disorders, but it is important not to rule out the presence of these problems in males, adult women, and seniors. Eating disorders are in all of these groups, but may be overlooked because of false assumptions that this disorder is limited to young females. Other conditions are frequently associated with eating disorders. Prominent among these are substance abuse, depression, anxiety, and personality disorders. This means that in many cases, treatment must address these comorbid conditions along with the eating disorder.

Developmental Influences

In this section, I will review significant developmental events that contribute to the later emergence of eating disorders. The developmental patterns of the three primary eating disorders are somewhat different. The onset of anorexia is most often in adolescence, whereas bulimia emerges in late adolescence or early adulthood. Binge eating, however, often begins at a very early age. All three disorders are more often found in females, particularly anorexia and bulimia (Smolak & Striegel-Moore, 1996).

Although interest in a biological origin for the disorders diminished after the 1930s, studies that are more recent are exploring the contributions of genetics and biology. Using studies of twins, researchers have discovered that there are genetic risk factors for developing both binge eating and obesity (Bulik, Sullivan, & Kendler, 2003). Genetic factors contribute to 59–83% of the variance in bulimia (Costin, 1999). The increased rates of eating disorders in relatives of eating-disordered patients in treatment are further evidence of a biological influence (Costin). Another twin study found that the genetic mechanisms may not activate until puberty, presumably as a result of the biochemical changes that occur during that process (Klump, McGue, & Ianoco, 2003). The possible link between levels of serotonin, as well as levels of tryptophan (an amino-acid) and eating disorders has received some attention, but so far results do not allow for any firm conclusions about their role (Attia, 2003).

Serotonin: A chemical (neurotransmitter) found in the brain, which is associated with mood regulation.

Psychodynamic theorists emphasize early mother–child relationships in the development of eating disorders, particularly when the mother is ambivalent about the pregnancy (Farrell, 2000). Object relations theories consider food to be equivalent to "mother," and view disordered eating to be a reflection of conflict about separation and individuation.

When an infant is distressed, she feels comfort when fed; not only does the satiation of hunger but also the nurturing, physical warmth, and soothing talk that accompany the food serve to calm the baby. The infant learns that feeding is comforting, and it is not difficult to understand that adults may seek food, which they link with comfort, when upset. This tendency, along with the intense cultural pressure toward thinness, may set the stage for the vulnerable individual to discover the antidote to excessive eating—purging.

Teasing plays a significant role in the development of eating disorders. In one study, individuals with bulimia reported more teasing about weight and size than did those with binge eating disorder. Researchers also found that teasing by significant adult figures (e.g., coaches, instructors) can have a strong influence on later eating-disordered behavior. A former client of mine, a college student, vividly remembers a negative comment about her weight made by a gymnastics coach when she was age eight or nine, and traces the origin of her disordered attitudes about weight and eating to that event. The woman in our case study remembers how hurtful it was to be called "fatso," when she now realizes she was actually at a normal weight. Experts believe that teasing by parents about weight has a profound effect on children, although problems may not emerge until adolescence.

A model developed by Streigel-Moore and Cachelin (1999) proposed two developmental pathways to eating disorders. The first pathway involves the internalization of the pervasive societal messages about thinness as the ideal and the standard of beauty, and the second is the result of inadequate nurturing from parents that leads to low self-esteem. In most cases, both pathways are probably involved.

Littleton and Ollendick (2003) identified the following risk factors in children that may predispose them to eating disorders.

Individual factors:

- Temperament: high levels of negative emotions (irritability, inflexibility) and low levels of cooperativeness were risk factors for disordered eating behaviors.
- Early puberty in girls has been linked to disordered eating, perhaps due to the accumulation of fat that accompanies this developmental process, and the social consequences of early maturity.
- Low self-esteem may include dissatisfaction with one's body image, which in turn leads to disordered eating. Low self-esteem may also involve feelings of ineffectiveness, which results in restrictive eating to enhance feelings of control.

Social factors:

- Exposure to thin media images. The marked rise in eating-disordered behaviors among Fijian teenage girls following the introduction of TV in 1995 illustrates this effect. Fijian TV broadcasts American, British, and Australian programming (Becker, 1995).
- Response to media messages about dieting or exercise products encouraging weight loss.
- Social reinforcement by peers for the thin ideal.

Family factors:

- Disordered eating and dieting behavior in mothers.
- Parental criticism of daughter's weight.

There is a strong association between childhood sexual abuse and eating disorders (Wonderlich et al., 2000). A comparison between a group of girls aged 10 to 15 who had been sexually abused with a matched control group found sexually abused girls were more likely to exhibit weight dissatisfaction, food restriction when upset, and purging behaviors. These girls may dislike their own bodies, and seek to disappear. They may wish to deny their sexuality, so the increased body fat and development of a womanly shape may be particularly frightening and dangerous to a girl who has been sexually abused.

A personality trait observed in childhood that has been linked to eating disorders is *perfectionism*, particularly the tendency to be overly self-critical and to be concerned that making mistakes will result in a loss of others' approval (Bulik et al., 2003). Tyrka et al. (2002) found that perfectionism and low body weight at age 12–16 predicted the development of anorexia in young adulthood, while negative emotional states were associated with young adult development of bulimia. Both studies demonstrated that perfectionism develops prior to the onset of the eating disorder, and is a predictor of later development of the disorder.

Assessment

In this section, I will describe how a professional determines whether a client has eating disorders. For the counselor who does not treat these disorders, he or she may want to make a referral. For the many clients with other disorders in addition to eating disorders, the counselor must consider the best combination of treatment strategies to address the particular constellation of problems the client has.

To decide whether a client meets DSM-IV-TR criteria for eating disorders, a structured clinical interview is often used. However, the clinician will want more information about the client's clinical picture so that she can tailor the treatment to the client's unique profile. Questions regarding weight and body image are very revealing and should be included in the interview. Crowther and Sherwood (1997) recommend getting the highest and lowest weights at current height, range of weight fluctuation, the person's conception of an ideal weight, and their childhood weight (and the presence of obesity and experience of teasing in childhood). Specific information about patterns of binge/purge episodes, dietary "rules," frequency of weighing, and use of compensatory methods to control weight are all important data for the clinician to obtain. Also essential is information about comorbid disorders, previous treatment attempts, and medical status.

Because there is a high rate of comorbidity with eating disorders, the clinicians may wish to administer a general measure to clarify the clinical picture, such as the Minnesota Multiphasic Personality Inventory-2 (MMPI-2) or the Millon Clinical Multiaxial Inventory-III (MCMI-III) (or the Minnesota Multiphasic Personality Inventory-Adolescent [MMPI-A] or the Millon Adolescent Clinical Inventory [MACI]. Because substance abuse is specifically associated with eating disorders, the clinician might be well advised to assess for this problem as well.

There are several formal assessment instruments available to assist clinicians in understanding the various aspects of the eating disorder, and the clinician will select those that are most useful. In considering which assessments to use, clinicians will want to consider whether the sample on which the scale was normed is similar to the clientele with whom they will use it. They will want to examine the subscales to see if information provided is comprehensive. They will want to consider the length and readability of the questionnaire, and the ease and time involved in administration and scoring. For the reader who would like more information on available instruments, an article by Petty, Rosen, and Michaels (2000) reviews nineteen widely used scales and provides excellent comparison information on these assessments.

Self-report questionnaires are useful for initial screening, and structured interviews may add more in-depth data. The Eating Disorder Examination (EDE) is a structured interview protocol that is widely used, and there is also a self-report version of that inventory. A copy of the EDE is in the appendix to Fairburn and Wilson (1993).

Treatment Options and Considerations

In this section, I will discuss in some detail the most empirically supported and widely accepted treatment approaches for eating disorders. Keep in mind that treatment in clinical practice "differs substantially from treatment in research settings with regard to therapist, clients, and treatment components" (Hass & Clopton, 2003, p. 417). Research on the effectiveness of treatment approaches is carefully controlled so that the researchers can be certain that observed differences can be attributed to the type of treatment rather than other factors. That often means that participants with comorbid disorders cannot be participants in the study. Practicing therapists, however, say that most clients with eating disorders have comorbid disorders, so they question the applicability of such research. Further, research participants must receive only the treatment component being studied (e.g., group therapy), but in practice clients may need group and individual therapy, and perhaps medication and other components as well. Clinicians are likely to lack training in using empirically validated treatments. Many therapists depend on reading and occasional continuing education courses for their information, but do not get intensive training. A final concern about implementing these treatment approaches is that the manuals may not be flexible enough to allow for the individual needs of a particular client or of particular settings (Haas & Clopton, 2003).

One way to determine what level of treatment is most appropriate in a particular case is to use the decision tree developed by Garner (Garner & Needleman, 1997). This is a sequential approach to considering the relevant client issues in coming to a treatment decision. Keep in mind that in addition to philosophy and technique, approaches vary in intensity (outpatient, intensive outpatient, and inpatient), intrusiveness, and cost. One should always consider the least intrusive and least costly methods that are appropriate in the situation. The clinician should insist that an evaluation by a physician (if one has not already been done) be included in any treatment plan.

Medication

The mental health professional does not prescribe medication (with the exception of psychologists in a few states), but may recommend that clients seek consultation with a psychiatrist to evaluate the potential usefulness of medication. The clinician will be better able to consult and communicate with prescribing clinicians and clients if they have some familiarity with the use of medication in treating eating disorders.

Although medication may be helpful for many clients with eating disorders, experts caution against relying on it as a first line of defense. Medication alone is almost never an appropriate treatment. In the case of bulimia, evidence is mounting that use of antidepressants along with cognitive-behavioral therapy produces increased benefits. Recent research indicates that the dosage needed of fluoxetine (Prozac) to obtain the desired effects with eating disorders is higher than that typically prescribed for depression (60 mg versus 20 mg). Because anxiety is sometimes a stimulus for the binge/purge cycle, some experts have considered whether anxiolytics (anti-anxiety medication) might be useful. One concern with many medications of this type is their potential for abuse, and as substance abuse is often associated with eating disorders, caution is necessary.

Clients with bulimia may decide to stop taking their medication if side effects are unpleasant, or because their need for control conflicts with the belief that medication can help. Ambivalence about giving up their eating disorders is not unusual, and I have had clients with bulimia panic when they learn that a possible side effect of some antidepressants is weight gain. It makes sense to defer the decision about medication until cognitive-behavioral therapy is attempted. If it is not successful, medication can be added to the treatment plan. Most of these clients benefit from a four- to six-month course of medication, but some will require continued medication to maintain the beneficial effects (Garfinkel & Walsh, 1997).

The use of medication with anorexia nervosa is more controversial. Although symptoms of depression are common in these clients, they may be the effect of semi-starvation, and so it is unclear whether prescribing antidepressants prior to weight gain is advisable. Anxiolytics may help with increased anxiety that accompanies weight-gain strategies, but in these cases, experts recommend a low dose for a limited period of time.

Researchers examined the effect of appetite-enhancing medication for anorexia, and the results have been disappointing. Increased appetite may not be the most useful intervention anyway, as clients with eating disorders did not lose their appetite for food—on the contrary, their disorder involves resisting the impulse to eat despite the presence of a normal (or even increased) appetite.

Another line of inquiry has been the use of estrogen when decreased bone density is a concern, but it appears that it is the weight gain that has the necessary effect on bone density, rather than estrogen therapy. Thus, medication may be helpful as a supplement to other avenues of treatment, and a clinician should be able to discuss these options intelligently with clients and other professionals alike.

Cognitive-Behavioral Therapy

By far, the most widely used treatment for eating disorders is cognitive-behavioral therapy (CBT). The following section describes the approach advocated by Wilson, Fairburn, and Agras (1997). CBT is used for both anorexia and bulimia; research has demonstrated the effectiveness of CBT in the treatment of bulimia, but no such clarity applies to anorexia. Most clients with bulimia are appropriate for this approach, with the exception of those with psychotic symptoms, severely depressed or suicidal clients, and substance abusers. These complicating disorders may prevent them benefiting from this type of treatment.

CBT focuses on the present and future, and the focus is on the specific problem, in this case the eating disorder. CBT sessions have a predictable structure: review of self-monitoring, deciding on an agenda, working on the agenda items, summarizing the session, and assigning homework. CBT therapists recognize the importance of a strong therapeutic alliance, and early stages of treatment concentrate on building that relationship. Initial sessions focus on the client–therapist relationship, explaining this form of therapy to the client, providing information about the effects of the eating disorder, introducing weekly weighing, and teaching the importance of regular meals, healthy food choices, and alternative activities. Clients are likely to be ambivalent about change, with worries about weight gain often predominating over worries about the harmful consequences of the disorder. CBT therapists anticipate this conflict, and use motivational strategies to gain the client's genuine commitment. It is helpful to reassure clients that significant weight gain is unlikely to occur as a result of treatment.

Providing information is an important component of eating disorder treatment. In addition to education within therapy sessions, counselors may require outside reading for additional information. The Additional Resources section later in this chapter will list some of the books you might use for this purpose.

Self-monitoring is an essential technique in this approach. Clients record everything they eat, usually on special forms provided for that purpose. This provides the therapist with detailed information about the eating patterns and situational triggers for disordered behaviors. For the client, this practice increases awareness of patterns and leads to a sense of control. Weekly weighing is a firm requirement. Many eating-disordered clients weigh much too often, and others may refuse to weigh themselves. This weekly strategy allows the client to gauge the effectiveness of the strategies learned in therapy. Clients do not focus on the absolute weight, but on changes they see when they implement the new techniques.

CBT counselors advise eating-disordered clients to eat three healthy meals a day plus two planned snacks every day. This is so that regular eating habits can reduce the urge to binge, and in effect reduce the total number of calories consumed. It may be difficult to get clients to comply with this strategy, but it is essential. A technique to make this plan more manageable is to eliminate binge foods from the house. Another is to ensure that the client prepares a list of alternative behaviors they can fall back on to manage high-risk situations, when they are most likely to purge. Clients also learn problem-solving skills to enable them to cope with difficult situations without resorting to disordered eating.

CBT includes a major emphasis on cognitive restructuring, or changing the faulty thinking patterns that perpetuate the eating disorder. Clients learn to identify irrational or illogical thinking, to bring evidence to evaluate and challenge irrational ideas, and to replace them with more accurate beliefs. For example, individuals with eating disorders tend to think in "black and white" terms, so that fat = bad, which is a notion to challenge. Counselors should help them develop a more accurate definition of *fat*. In the final stages of treatment, time is devoted to planning for the end of treatment by developing plans to maintain gains attained in therapy.

While CBT is effective with bulimia, the jury is still out with respect to this approach to anorexia. Anorexics are difficult to motivate for treatment as their fear of being fat is so intense and ingrained. People with anorexia are often coerced into treatment by significant others, which means they may not be truly motivated to change. Therapists cannot tell them, as they can bulimic clients, that they will not gain weight, as that is the main goal of treatment. Clients with anorexia need to understand the possible medical consequences of the disorder, and need to know that hospitalization will occur if weight falls below a specified minimum. Psychological treatment should always be coordinated with a physician who can assist in evaluating the client's medical status. While CBT treatment for bulimia is relatively brief (twenty sessions), treatment for anorexia should be planned in terms of years rather than months. Initial sessions may be held more often than the once per week format used with bulimia.

Because treatment for this clientele is rarely voluntary, the therapist must concentrate on developing the therapeutic alliance. This may mean stressing that the counselor is not simply following the instructions of whoever initiated treatment. It also means that the therapist must instill hope that this disorder is treatable.

Weight goals are a major focus of treatment, all the more so in the early stages of treatment where the client must gain weight. Each session begins with a weight check, and the results direct the remainder of the session. If the client achieves her weight goals, the counselor and client can address other issues. If not, the weight becomes the focus, with problem solving directed toward resolving the barriers to compliance. As treatment progresses and the client achieves her weight goals, then psychological concerns such as self-esteem, perfectionism, expression of feelings, dealing with conflict, and the like, can occupy more of the treatment time.

There are numerous strategies that assist the client in changing both cognitive and behavioral patterns related to food and eating. The chapter by Garner, Vitousek, and Pike (1997) is an excellent resource for readers who are interested in techniques that are more specific. In fact, the chapter is actually a treatment manual for clinicians, with the caveat that this approach does not have evidence from controlled clinical trials necessary to demonstrate effectiveness. Another treatment manual for CBT is in an appendix to Fairburn and Wilson (1993).

Clinicians have to modify CBT use with clients with BED. Unlike those with bulimia, these clients do not restrict food intake nor do they overvalue thinness as an ideal. Depression is common in this group, and shame and self-consciousness are important themes (Marcus, 1997). Those with other eating disorders often receive praise when they lose weight, while BED clients face scorn and rejection based on their weight. Bulimics over-use exercise to compensate for binge eating, whereas exercise is typically absent in BED.

Some modifications in the CBT approach with BED clients include providing information about obesity, promoting an exercise regimen, extensive nutrition education, and modification of eating habits. While these clients tend not to have distorted body images, they do have "body image disparagement," and will benefit from accepting and caring for a larger-than-average body. CBT treatment tends to be somewhat longer for BED than bulimia, and experts recommend individual as opposed to group treatment formats for most clients.

Interpersonal Therapy

Researchers find improvement in bulimic clients who receive interpersonal therapy (IPT). This approach to the treatment of eating disorders is a modification of the IPT model used for depression. IPT for bulimia was slower than CBT at creating client change, but the changes continued to accrue after termination. A year after treatment ended, IPT had more favorable outcomes than CBT (Fairburn, 1997).

The following overview of this approach describes Fairburn's (1997) model, designed for 15–20 sessions over 4–5 months, and involving three stages. Readers who would like a "cookbook" for this approach will find it in his book.

In the initial stage of treatment, the client becomes familiar with the IPT approach. It is important for the client to realize that the eating disorder per se will *not* be the focus of the therapy; rather, this model emphasizes the primary role of interpersonal relationships in this disorder. Early sessions focus on identifying the client's particular interpersonal problems, by taking extensive histories, assessing the client's current relationships, and determining the interpersonal precipitators of binge/purge behaviors. Problems tend to be in one of four areas: unresolved grief, interpersonal role disputes, role transitions, and interpersonal deficits or difficulty with forming and maintaining relationships.

Once the problems are identified, the therapy moves into the second stage. IPT is a non-directive present-centered approach, with the therapist taking an active role. Sessions focus on interpersonal issues of the client's choice, but the therapist helps the client remain focused on the identified issues, and clarifies and illuminates important points. The therapist provides a summary at the end of each session, and periodically reviews the client's progress. The therapist stresses the importance of change, but the specific changes are the client's choice. In general, IPT counselors avoid behavioral techniques, although some role playing is done to assist the client with interpersonal goals. The final stage of treatment concentrates on preventing relapse, primarily by educating the client about the likely challenges she will face in the recovery process after treatment has concluded.

Fairburn (1997) recommends that CBT be the first choice of approach with eating-disordered clients because of its demonstrated effectiveness. IPT would be a good alternative when CBT does not seem to produce desired results.

Brief Solution-Focused Therapy

Brief solution-focused therapy has gained considerable attention in recent years, initially perhaps because of the influence of managed care. This is probably the least intensive and most cost-effective approach available, using only the minimum number of sessions necessary to accomplish the goals. McFarland (1995) provides excellent guidance for this approach to the treatment of eating disorders.

Brief solution-focused therapy adheres to a set of principles:

- Focusing on the presenting problem;
- Amplifying the solution when it is identified; and
- Not persisting in ineffective interventions.

This is a strengths-based model, believing that the client has the resources to solve her own problems and in fact has already done so in some ways. It is a present- and future-focused model, and does not advocate exploration of past events. The therapeutic relationship is a collaborative one, with the client as the identified expert on her own situation.

In this model, the first session is critical. The counselor needs to learn about previous attempts at treatment and is looking for what worked. Early on, the counselor will pose the standard solution-focused query, called the *miracle question:* "If a miracle happened tonight when you were sleeping that solved the problem, and you didn't know that because you were sleeping, what will be the first thing you'll notice tomorrow that will tell you the problem is solved?" The counselor probes for detail in the responses, which helps in developing specific goals. The next strategy is looking for exceptions, times when the problem was absent or less severe. This allows the therapist to learn about strategies that have already been successful. The therapist asks "scaling questions," such as: "On a scale of 1 to 10, with 10 being the best ever and 1 being the worst, how would you rate the symptoms today?" Or the therapist might ask the client to identify a time when she was a 10, rate today, and inquire about what she needs to get a little closer to the 10. Specific, realistic goals are established. Many solution-focused therapists use a written message to the client from the therapist prepared during a short break in the last few minutes of the session. The message includes appropriate compliments, restatement of counseling goals, and a homework assignment, including the reason for the assignment. Homework is an important component of solution-focused treatment.

In the second session, the counselor assesses the client's motivation to change. The session begins with a question such as, "What is better since our last session?" (McFarland, 1995. p. 128). Subsequent sessions continue to focus on exceptions to the problem, acknowledging the client's efforts and helping the client focus on what is effective.

This approach works in a group context, as well as in individual sessions. McFarland (1995) provides a session-by-session outline for an eight-week psychoeducational body image group. She also advocates the use of aftercare psychotherapy groups for six months following termination from individual therapy.

Self-Help Approaches

In some cases, counselors may use self-help via bibliotherapy if the client's symptoms are not severe. Self-help is unlikely to be useful with anorexics, and is more likely to be an option for clients with bulimia or BED. Self-help is clearly more economical than other forms of treatment, and may provide assistance to clients who cannot or will not enroll in treatment programs. Some of the books available, however, are by authors with dubious credentials in the field of eating disorders and may contain inaccurate information. There have been very few research studies examining the impact of self-help books, but no clear evidence has emerged.

I like the book *Transforming Body Image: Learning to Love the Body You Have* (Hutchinson, 1985) both to recommend to motivated clients, and to use as a source of material and exercises for education and outreach. The author adapted the book from workshops she has taught. Although there are numerous self-help books on the market, and clinicians have their own preferences, the ones I find most useful are: Peter Cooper's *Bulimia Nervosa and Binge Eating* (1993) and Gregory Jantz's *Hope, Help, & Healing for Eating Disorders: A New Approach to Treating Anorexia, Bulimia, & Overeating* (1995). These books are also helpful for parents and family members of clients with eating disorders.

Another self-help approach that is sometimes helpful for bulimia or binge eating disorders is the 12-Step program Overeaters Anonymous. This is a nonprofessional support program led by members and follows the same structure as other 12-Step programs. One of the positive aspects of this approach is the reduction of isolation and the sense of commonality of concerns. Many therapists advocate these self-help strategies in addition to, rather than in place of, professional treatment.

In addition to the approaches described above, which reflect different beliefs about the causes and nature of eating disorders and about the change process, there are several different formats or contexts in which treatment can be provided. The ones most commonly used with eating disorders are individual, group, and family therapy. Because of the complexity of these disorders, a team approach to treatment is often used. I will briefly review each of these modalities as they apply to eating disorders.

Group Therapy

Group therapy is common in treatment for eating disorders, although outcomes seem to be better with bulimia than anorexia. Groups are efficient formats for providing education, which is an essential component of treatment for eating disorders. Using the group format to provide essential information allows individual therapy to focus on more personal, individual concerns.

As with any group, screening and preparing group members will ensure a better-functioning group. Clients who should not be in a group include those with psychotic symptoms, anger management problems, and the like. Setting expectations and formulating goals in pre-session meetings with clients will prepare clients for the experience and reduce uncertainty.

Group therapy might be one component of treatment, usually paired with individual therapy, but it may also at times be the only therapy a client receives. The curative factors that operate in most groups certainly influence eating-disorders groups, but there are several features of the disorder that make groups particularly useful. For eating-disordered clients, for whom secrecy maintains the disorder, disclosing to a supportive, nonjudgmental group is an important step in breaking that pattern of secrecy. Also, because these clients tend to be isolated and socially withdrawn, groups provide an opportunity for interpersonal interaction that may be lacking in their lives.

Groups also demonstrate to clients that they are not alone in their struggle; the shame and secrecy that surround the behavior often keep the client from the awareness that others do this too.

Despite the widespread inclusion of group therapy in treatment programs for eating disorders, experts are not unanimous in their endorsement of this format. Claude-Pierre (1997) worries about *iatrogenic* potential and urges caution about using groups for this population. She points out that the group may become a vehicle for clients to reinforce each others' distorted thinking patterns and promote the tendency to share "trade secrets" about their disordered behaviors. For this reason, she advises against placing eating-disordered clients in groups that are homogenous for that disorder. In an eating-disorders group I co-led, one of the members was a binge-eater who had never purged. Her intense interest in the bulimic behaviors of other members was not a good sign.

Iatrogenic: Negative outcomes caused by treatment.

Counselors need to think about several questions when considering groups for eating disorders. One is whether the groups will include both anorexic and bulimic members. There are valid arguments for both positions. One major concern about groups for only anorexic clients is the tendency for them to imitate and reinforce each other's disorder. With only the leader(s) to model healthy behaviors, the interpersonal power of the group may be detrimental. However, mixed groups also present challenges. Clients may learn weight-loss techniques from each other, and normal-weight bulimics may want to emulate the thinner image of the anorexics. Like other issue-specific groups, there is a danger that clients will see themselves as only able to relate to others with their problem, and this may exacerbate their feelings of social ostracism. Because anorexics tend to require longer term therapy, they are probably not best included in time-limited groups. If they are included in open groups with bulimic clients who exit more quickly, there may be a tendency to see themselves as hopeless. Each therapist will have to decide the heterogeneous versus homogeneous question based on the context of the particular group.

The leaders can structure an eating-disorders group to prevent some of the unwanted behaviors from occurring. It is important to actively work to keep the group from reinforcing or teaching unhealthy behaviors. In setting ground rules, leaders can insist that members do not discuss any specific behaviors in the group. That is, members may not discuss *how* they purge, but should focus on *what* behaviors the member would like to support. For the same reason, discussion of specific weight gains or losses should also be discouraged, as it may engender unwanted competitiveness. Another behavior that should be discouraged is venting without accepting feedback. To keep the group from deteriorating into a litany of complaints, which can be contagious, leaders can model how to frame concerns in a way that will produce growth. For example, instead of saying "Therapy sucks," the therapist can reframe the concern as, "I'm frustrated that I am not making more progress," or "It's hard for me to practice new behaviors and sometimes I wonder if I will ever recover." It is also important not to allow the group to normalize or glamorize the eating disorder (Costin, 1999). Seeing that everyone else in the group has the same behavior may suggest that it is normal, which is something the leader needs to actively guard against. It is also important to keep the group from providing extra attention to the clients with the worst symptoms.

Concerns that are more practical may also drive the composition of the group. Although eating disorders are common in adolescents, they are not exclusive to that age group. A group composed of members with a wide age range and varied life circumstances may have difficulty becoming cohesive. The questions of leadership and open versus closed group may need to defer to circumstance. For example, in some settings with changing populations, such as inpatient facilities, open groups are necessary. Leaders may not always have suitable co-leaders available to work with, and are even less likely to be able to consistently offer a male–female co-leadership model, which is probably ideal.

Family Therapy

A number of pioneers in the field of family therapy did seminal work on families of clients with anorexia, so family therapy has a tradition with eating disorders. Costin (1999) proclaimed that for youthful clients, "family therapy is necessary for recovery" (p. 173). Although the various schools of family therapy differ in some theoretical and technical aspects, there are features that are widely accepted as characteristic of families in which eating disorders emerge: enmeshment, over-protectiveness, rigidity, and absence of conflict resolution. Experts generally believe that the symptoms of the eating-disordered client actually help the family avoid other conflict (Dare & Eisler, 1997).

Enmeshment: An unhealthy extreme of family involvement, characterized by excessive closeness. Boundaries between individuals are blurred and family members are emotionally overreactive to one another.

Family therapists see eating disorders as a symptom of dysfunction in the family system, and so treating the whole system is the logical approach. Family therapists are highly active and directive. The general design of family therapy proceeds in phases: in the first and essential phase, the therapist must gain the family's involvement and cooperation. This is sometimes difficult, because the person with the eating disorder is the "identified patient" and others in the family may resist examining their own role in the problem. Education about the potential medical complications from the disorder may assist in winning the family's participation.

The next phase of family therapy involves assessing the structure and organization of the family, seeking to understand the role of the eating disorder in the system. It is only after these tasks that the family therapist can implement interventions designed to change the system, so that the member with eating disorder can give up the symptom (Agras, 1993).

Family therapy interventions disrupt the dysfunctional organization in the family, and change the structure, often by encouraging a stronger united parental unit with clearer boundaries. One technique is for the therapist to attend a family meal, with the parents encouraged to take charge. Some schools of family therapy favor paradoxical interventions, such as prescribing "no change for now," expecting the family to defy the instructions and change (Dare & Eisler, 1997).

Costin (1999) indicated that in many families in which individuals develop eating disorders, there is a pattern of equating self-worth with achievement. She observed alternating patterns of enmeshment and disengagement in many of the families she has treated. She sees the tasks of family therapy to be: educating the family about the eating disorder, examining the impact of the eating disorder on all family members, reducing blame, understanding parental expectations for the children, elucidating the client's role in the family, addressing any abuse issues, adjusting the structure of the family (by strengthening the parental alliance, for example), and pointing out and changing destructive interaction patterns within the family.

Disengagement: Family members do not show concern for each other and live very separate lives. This is the opposite end of the continuum from *enmeshment*.

Some treatment programs incorporate multifamily therapy groups into the treatment plan. This format provides support for parents, an opportunity to observe how other families respond, and the experience of learning from others.

Multi-Disciplinary Team Approaches

The Best Practice Guidelines published in 2000 by the American Psychiatric Association recommends collaboration by clinicians implementing components of treatment for eating disorders. Given the medical dangers that accompany this disorder, a physician is an important member of the team who can thoroughly assess the client's medical condition and assist in decision making regarding the need for hospitalization. In many cases of bulimia, it will be necessary to have a dental evaluation as well. Because medication may be used along with other therapies, a psychiatrist who can prescribe and monitor the effectiveness of medication is also important. Individual and group therapists are most likely to provide the psychological treatment to the client, but if family therapy is added, treatment outcomes may improve. A nutritionist is an essential member of the team. Nutritional rehabilitation is an essential goal in the treatment of eating disorders, and a specialist in nutrition makes a valuable contribution to the overall treatment program.

Issues of Diversity

At one time, the conventional view of eating disorders was that it is a disease of young white women. We now know that is no longer the case, if it ever was. I will now discuss issues related to males with eating disorders, and then look at racial and ethnic differences, sexual orientation, and disabilities as they relate to this issue.

A *Boston Globe* article (Eating Disorders Emerge, 2001) estimated that males may account for as many as one sixth of individuals in the United States with eating disorders. Men who participate in certain sports where weight is a perceived factor in performance may be especially prone to the disorder. Sports such as gymnastics, swimming, horse racing, running, for example, all promote the notion of low weight as a performance advantage. There are several ways in which experts agree that males differ from females with the disorder: (1) they are less likely to have *anorexia nervosa*, and (2) they are less likely to seek treatment for the disorder, perhaps due to embarrassment at having a "women's disease." Physicians may overlook the possibility of eating disorders in their male patients, while being more alert to the symptoms in females.

Studies have found that men with eating disorders are more likely to have been obese as children, and teased by peers. For example, in Abou-Saleh, Younis, and Karim's (1998) report of five cases of anorexia in Arab clients, both males were adolescent and both had been obese at one time and subject to teasing as a result. The weight of males with eating disorders fluctuates more than the weight of women. Although relatively few men are diagnosed with anorexia, the medical complications tend to be more severe in males. Like many females with eating disorders, males who were sexually abused as children may wish to reverse signs of sexual maturity through weight loss. Decreased levels of testosterone and sexual desire can be the consequences of weight loss in males, equivalent to the cessation of menstrual periods in women. The age of onset of eating disorders seems to be later in males than females; as puberty also occurs later in males, the increased risk at that time period may explain the difference in timing (Braun et al., 1999).

Ethnic and racial differences are difficult to quantify, as different studies use different methods of assessment. Using Caucasian females as the comparison group, researchers found that rates of eating disturbances were similar for Hispanic women, higher among Native American women, and less common in black and Asian American women (Crago & Shisslak, 1996). These researchers also found more eating disorders in minority women who were "younger, heavier, more educated, and more identified with White, middle-class values" (p. 245). An interesting study of college women involving Asian, Hispanic, and white women found that ethnic differences in concern about weight and body shape were related to present body weight and not ethnicity. However, despite similar levels of concern about body image, Whites were more likely to diet in an attempt to lose weight (Arriaza & Mann, 2001). Acculturation patterns may affect rates of eating disorders in minority populations: subclinical levels of eating disorders were related to the level of acculturation in Hispanic college women, but not related in either Asian or European American women (Gowen, Hayward, Killen, Robinson, & Taylor, 1999). Researchers report increased rates of abnormal eating patterns among Hispanic teenagers such that in the seventh grade Hispanic girls reported more frequent weight loss attempts than African American or Caucasian teenagers. These differences disappeared by the tenth grade however, when all groups showed similar rates. In the seventh grade, binge eating was most prevalent among Hispanic girls, but in the tenth grade, Caucasians had the highest rate of this behavior (Shisslak, Crago, Olmsted, & Mays, 2002).

Another study of college women (Mulholland & Mintz, 2001) found the prevalence rates of eating disorders among African American college women to be similar to those of Caucasian college women, although earlier research reported lower rates of bulimia in African American college women than in their Caucasian counterparts. Iyer and Haslam (2003) provide an interesting perspective on the effects of culture on eating disorders. They found that acculturation did not influence disordered eating behavior, but what did have an impact was "hurtful racial teasing," defined as teasing that focuses on the target's "ethnically distinctive attributes." The researchers surmise that racial teasing might encourage individuals to attempt to adopt the body image norms of the dominant society, which include thinness.

Persons who are from non-Westernized cultures may have different cultural practices regarding food and different idealized body images (Abou-Saleh, Younis, & Karim, 1998; Krentz & Arthur, 2001), and therefore eating disorders may be less prevalent.

For example, among some religious groups in Southeast Asia, asceticism (including severe food restriction) is considered to be a route to spiritual growth. The Muslim tradition includes fasting during the holy month of Ramadan, which must not be seen as an example of disordered eating. An interesting observation of the impact of cultural context on eating disorders is found in Abou-Saleh and colleague's report of cases of anorexia nervosa in the United Arab Emirates. These researchers cite the previous work of Nasser, who found disordered eating attitudes in twice as many Arab female students in a London university than in a matched sample attending a Cairo university. They describe five cases of anorexia, three in females and two in males. They speculate that as the country becomes more Westernized, the incidence of the disorder will increase.

Asceticism: Practice of self-discipline and self-denial as a route to spiritual growth.

One study was located that compared body image and attitudes associated with disordered eating in lesbians and heterosexual women (Owens, Hughes, & Owens-Nicholson, 2003). As predicted, lesbians had higher scores on body image and lower scores on attitudes associated with disordered eating than did the heterosexual participants. African Americans also had similar scoring patterns, compared with other races in the sample. The authors caution that although findings were statistically significant, the effects were relatively small. The strongest predictor of both scores was Body Mass Index (BMI); the higher the BMI, the lower the body image and the higher the attitudes associated with disordered eating. The researchers also found that lesbians had significantly higher BMIs than heterosexual women.

Persons with Disabilities

There are few population-based studies that examined the incidence of eating disorders in persons with disabilities. Emerson (2003) analyzed data from 10,438 children aged 5–15 in England, and found no significant differences in the prevalence of eating disorders in children with and without intellectual disabilities. In contrast, Gravestock (2000) reviewed the literature and found studies demonstrating an association between eating disorders and several syndromes and disorders (e.g., Down's, Kleine–Levin, Kluver–Bucy, Turner, and Williams syndromes, phenylketonuria, and autism). Gravestock (2003) observed that due to the complicated diagnostic profiles of both eating disorders and intellectual disabilities, it is likely that many cases of eating disorders are not appropriately diagnosed in this population. The lack of expressive language can interfere with the clinician's attempts to gather the needed information for a diagnosis of eating disorders. Gravestock also noted that when the concept of eating disorder is expanded to include abnormal eating behaviors (AEB), there are many cases of eating disorders in individuals with intellectual impairments. AEB are defined as food faddiness/refusal, rumination/regurgitation, and pica. It is notable that these disorders are diagnosed in infancy or early childhood, but in adults with severe or profound intellectual disabilities, they may emerge or persist.

Abnormal Eating Behaviors:

Pica: Eating non-nutritive substances (such as clay, plaster, sand) on a persistent basis.

Rumination/regurgitation: Repeated regurgitation and re-chewing of food without accompanying nausea or intestinal disorder.

Food faddiness/refusal: An obsession with eating only certain type of food/strict avoidance of certain foods or categories of food.

Some intellectual disabilities are genetic, and may involve biological impairments that manifest as AEBs. In other cases where brain damage exists (including epilepsy), there may be neurological involvement or mineral deficiencies that increase the risk for both AEBs and eating disorders (Gravestock, 2003). Some disabilities have physical complications, such as dental problems, hernias, constipation, or diarrhea, and so on, that can make eating unpleasant or painful, and thus might contribute to eating disorders.

It seems logical that because the development of eating disorders requires a distorted body image, those who do not have the ability to create visual images—those who are blind or visually impaired—would be less likely to develop these disorders (Krentz & Arthur, 2001; van der Wege & Vandereycken, 1995). Research has not supported this position; eating disorders do occur in this population, and a distorted body image is not a prerequisite. Krentz and Arthur suggest that eating disorders may arise from the efforts of blind or visually impaired persons to gain some control in their lives. Among deaf and hearing-impaired persons, binge eating was reported less frequently than by those without hearing impairments, but twice as many deaf women (21%) as deaf men did report disordered eating behaviors. One possible explanation for these findings is that deaf and visually impaired people are aware of cultural ideals of thinness, and attempt to cope with their disabilities by having perfect, unimpaired, bodies. Perhaps future research will investigate this hypothesis.

An additional issue worth mentioning is that many psychoactive medications that are commonly prescribed to persons with intellectual or psychiatric disabilities have side effects of increased appetite and weight gain. This may be an additional risk factor for eating disorders in individuals with disabilities. It is also possible that eating disorders can cause a worsening of visual impairments in some cases (van der Wege & Vandereycken, 1995).

What this information means for the counselor is that when working with clients for disabilities, regardless of the presenting issues, screening and frank discussion of eating disorders will ensure that this problem is not overlooked. In addition, it is helpful for a mental health provider to communicate with physicians who provide care for the disability, to ensure that possible interactions are identified.

Counselor Issues

Counselors' own beliefs and attitudes about a topic, along with their personal experiences, cannot help but affect the way they relate to clients. Eating disorders are not an exception to this challenge. In fact, it is particularly important for counselors to recognize that the same media and societal pressures that affect their clients, affect them as well, and they must be alert to how their own concerns about weight and food affect their clients.

For female therapists in particular, they need to consider the impact of their appearance on clients. What message is your body giving to clients? For the thin or average weight therapist, clients may wonder (and ask) whether you have an eating disorder, or how you keep your weight at that level. If you are overweight, how do you present yourself? Are you confident with a positive self-image, or embarrassed and concerned about your weight? Just as parents' attitudes and behaviors affect children, the modeling by therapists has a considerable impact on clients, particularly those with eating disorders, and the clinician needs to be mindful of this.

A decision about self-disclosure when the therapist does have a history of eating disorders is not an easy one. An interesting article about one clinician's struggle to decide whether or not to disclose to her group and later to an individual client (Bloomgarden, 2000) concludes with some useful questions counselors might ask themselves about self-disclosure that would apply to any issue. Two important ones relate to boundaries: if one withholds relevant personal information, are the boundaries too close so that the therapist is detached from the clients; and if one chooses to self-disclose too easily, are the boundaries too diffuse, so that there is no distinction between therapist and client? What are the risks in telling clients about your history? Readers who are struggling with these concerns may wish to read the article in its entirety.

Clients with anorexia are especially difficult to treat. Their fears of gaining weight are so intense, and their self-image so dependent on their weight, that they are likely to resist the counselors' best efforts to help. Counselors who work with these clients need to consider their own tolerance for frustration, and how they will balance their own need to be helpful against a clientele that does not want to be helped, despite their severe condition. In addition, this disorder has the highest mortality rate of any psychiatric disorder (Eating Disorders Statistics, 2003). Thus, there is the distinct possibility that a counselor will have to deal with the death of a client. Counselors who work with this clientele should seek consultation and supervision from other professionals with whom they can process their own reactions and responses to their work.

BOX 3.1
A Note to School Counselors

What is the best approach for school counselors in addressing this problem? As school leaders, school counselors might begin by assessing the ways in which the school climate promotes an unhealthy emphasis on thinness. Examining the practices related to weight in athletics and cheerleading, taking an active stance against weight- and shape-related teasing, and noting how healthy eating habits are, or are not, promoted in the school are first steps in making positive changes in the overall school climate.

Because school counselors have regular contact with the vulnerable population (young adolescents and adolescents), they are in a position to "identify at-risk individuals, implement effective school-based prevention programs, make appropriate referrals, and provide support for recovering individuals" (Bardick, Bernes, McCulloch, Witko, Spriddle, & Roest, 2004, p. 168). Youth who are close to puberty are prime targets for prevention programming (Omizo & Omizo, 1992). Note that providing treatment is not appropriate or possible in the school setting, but the school counselor may be the first professional to recognize the need for further assessment and treatment, and in so doing may be the first line of defense. Eating disorders, like many of the issues discussed in this book, have the best outcomes when detected and treated early.

Prevention is an important strategy to reduce the harmful consequences of eating disorders. However, Yager and O'Dea (2005) observed that many school counselors lack confidence in their ability to conduct prevention activities related to eating disorders. Research evaluating the effects of prevention programs for eating disorders have found moderate positive effects, but programs that utilize testimonials from recovering celebrities or peers are discouraged, as they may glamorize the behaviors the program hopes to discourage. Likewise, Bardick and colleagues (2004) caution that providing information to students that includes a list of specific eating-disordered behaviors may cause some vulnerable youth to experiment with such behaviors. The experts cited stress the need for school counselors to obtain training to ensure they are well prepared to deliver such programs, and to collaborate with other professional both within the school environment (health instructors, school nurses) and in the community (physicians, nutritionists) to design a prevention strategy.

Identifying at-risk individuals begins with educating all staff about eating disorders and enlisting their cooperation. A brief in-service presentation to faculty and staff, followed by some printed material (such as the Bodywise materials recommended below) can alert them to danger signs. Faculty involved with students in high risk activities (cheerleaders, gymnasts, wrestlers, dancers, etc.) should be particularly vigilant for signs of incipient disordered eating behaviors. Your job is to take a closer look at those children and determine whether further intervention is appropriate.

Once a student has been identified as at-risk, talking with her or him is a first step, but denial of a problem is often the response. The skilled school counselor will use empathy, observation, and skillful questioning to get a sense of whether this student needs further intervention. It is important to share your observations and concerns with the student in an honest, direct, and nonjudgmental manner. If the school counselor believes the concern is warranted, parents must be notified. This, too, is a process that must be handled sensitively; the counselor should express concern for the student's well-being, and suggest that the family seek an assessment from a specialist in eating disorders to evaluate the situation. School counselors are well aware of how referrals to outside agencies must be made to avoid financial liability, but having a list of resources in the community is very helpful.

When students receive outside treatment for eating disorders, the school counselor can provide support at school either during or after treatment. Omizo and Omizo (1992) suggest that support groups at school for students with eating disorders can be very helpful. I urge school counselors who are considering such groups to re-read the section above on group therapy to be aware of the potential pitfalls in such groups.

School counselors, although they do not provide treatment, provide many services that assist students with eating disorders. They are in a unique position, having both contact and awareness, to influence the school climate with respect to the ways in which an emphasis on appearance and bodily perfection may be promoted.

Ethical Concerns

Perhaps the most common dilemma for counselors is that of client competence to consent to treatment. As discussed above, there are cognitive effects of eating disorders that may impair the client's ability to make informed decisions about treatment. However, the clinician should not assume that the client is incompetent to consent to treatment simply by virtue of the diagnosis (Manley, Smye, & Srikameswaran, 2001). Rather, the clinician must carefully assess the client's capacity to understand the nature of the treatment, why it is necessary, and what the consequences might be of not receiving treatment. Unfortunately, there are no clear standards by which to determine this competency, and the clinicians must rely on professional judgment to make these decisions. Informed consent should be an ongoing process, not something only discussed at the beginning of treatment. Client's capacities may improve or deteriorate, circumstances may change, and clients may need frequent reminders of their choices. These decisions are even more complex when the client is a child. Although the parent may give consent, it is essential that the child also understand the decisions to the fullest extent possible.

In addition, there are situations in which the clinician may recommend involuntary treatment or hospitalization, which impinges on client autonomy. Making an ethically sound decision involves considering whether less intrusive methods have been tried, whether there is a medical emergency, and the likely effect on the therapeutic alliance. If the client is at substantial risk and is unwilling to consent to treatment, the clinician may want to involve a treatment team to consider involuntary treatment. Client safety is the most important consideration, and the team should consider and evaluate all possible alternatives. The goal should be to empower the client (Manley et al., 2001) to make informed decisions on his or her own behalf. It is important that decisions regarding involuntary treatment be made compassionately, with concern for the feelings of both the client and significant others, and with the certainty that the decision is made for the client's welfare rather than the convenience of the treatment team or family members. Note that researchers found no significant differences in the short-term response to treatment between voluntary and involuntary patients (Watson, Bower, & Anderson, 2000).

Summary

- Eating disorders are widespread in Western cultures, and are found in males and females from all racial and ethnic groups.
- Three diagnoses are used to describe eating disorders: Anorexia Nervosa, Bulimia Nervosa, and Eating Disorder Not Otherwise Specified, which includes Binge Eating Disorder.
- Although eating disorders are considered mental disorders, there are serious physical and medical complications that may develop.
- Many people who do not meet the criteria for diagnosis engage in disordered eating behaviors.
- Childhood experiences contribute to later development of eating disorders. Perfectionism has been linked to eating disorders, and childhood teasing about weight, especially by parents, is also a common precursor.
- A variety of formal assessment instruments are available for determining if eating disorders are present.
- Cognitive behavioral approaches have the most empirical support for treating eating disorders, but interpersonal therapy and brief solution-focused therapy may also be helpful.
- Treatment includes individual, group, and family therapy. Clinicians should be familiar with advantages and disadvantages of each modality, and know for which clients each is most likely to be helpful.

- A multi-disciplinary team approach to treatment is advised due to the many aspects of these disorders.
- Self-help programs and reading are often useful adjuncts to professional treatment.
- Counselors must be aware of the effect of their own attitudes and appearance on clients with eating disorders.
- This population is difficult to treat, and clinicians need a high frustration tolerance to work with this clientele.
- Ethical concerns about involuntary hospitalization may be confronted, especially with anorexia. Clinicians need clear guidelines for making ethical decisions.

ADDITIONAL RESOURCES

On the Web

- www.eatingdisorderinfo.org has Weekly Updates and a very useful calendar of media events, television programs, and upcoming conferences of interest. The personal stories on the site are also worth looking at.
- www.anred.com (Anorexia Nervosa and Related Eating Disorders, Inc.) has a wealth of excellent information and links. Information is clear and succinct, which makes it a good site to recommend to clients.
- www.EDreferral.com is also one that clients might find helpful. It has good information on research, and even has contact information for clients who might like to be subjects in research studies on eating disorders. There is a listserv one can subscribe to via this site that provides monthly updates on the latest research and events of interest.
- www.altrue.net/site/anadweb/ is the site of the National Association of Anorexia Nervosa and Associated Disorders, and has a variety of information on referrals, including support groups.
- www.nedic.ca is the Canadian National Eating Disorders Information Centre site that has the advantage of having both reading lists and links that include excellent summaries so the user can get an idea of what they will find in those further resources. In addition, this site has an active EDTalk Discussion list, which might be useful for both practitioners and clients.
- www.womenshealth.gov/bodyimage/bodywise/ is an excellent website for school counselors hosted by the U.S. Department of Health and Human Resources that has material the counselor can use immediately and distribute to teachers or parents.
- http://www.eatingdisorderresources.com/ is an excellent source of movies and videos useful for psychoeducational groups and for presentations.

In Print for Counselors

- *Handbook of Treatment for Eating Disorders* by Garner and Garfinkel (1997) is thorough, comprehensive, well researched, and highly readable.

- *Handbook of Eating Disorders* by Brownell and Foreyt (1986) is an excellent edited volume, although it is a little dated. It includes obesity as an eating disorder.
- *The Eating Disorders Sourcebook* (Costin, 1999) is a less technical volume with considerable useful information that is palatable for professionals and consumers alike and may be particularly helpful for family members of clients with eating disorders. The second edition includes detailed information about many treatment programs around the country.
- *When Dieting Becomes Dangerous: A Guide to Understanding and Treating Anorexia and Bulimia* (Michel & Willard, 2003) is very useful and readable for both professionals and family members.
- *The Body Betrayed* by Kathryn Zerbe is less treatment focused but provides an excellent background on all aspects of eating disorders. It is well researched but not dense, so would make a good addition to a clinician's bookshelf.
- *Brief Therapy and Eating Disorders* by McFarland (1995) describes the brief solution-focused approach in cookbook-type fashion for the novice therapist to follow.
- *Practice Guideline for the Treatment of Patients with Eating Disorders* (2nd ed.) published by the American Psychiatric Association (2000) has an extraordinary amount of information in a small volume. It is available in a print version and for download from the association's website. This is an essential reference for any helping professional who provides services for this disorder.

In Print for Clients

- *Overcoming Binge Eating* (Fairburn, 1995) is great for clients with bulimia or BED. The author is a respected expert in the field, and has published empirical support for the approach described in the book. The book is in two parts, with the first providing background information and the second presenting a specific self-help approach to stopping binge eating. It reads easily, and the format is user friendly.
- *Bulimia Nervosa and Binge Eating: A Guide to Recovery* by Peter J. Cooper (1993). The format is similar to that of Fairburn's book, in that Part One provides background information and education about the disorders, while Part Two is a self-help manual complete with useful worksheets and examples.
- *Dying To Be Thin* by Sacker and Zimmer (1987) is quite popular. The strength and weakness of the book are the numerous case histories, which illustrate the points but may take space from the necessary information. It includes advice sections for parents, friends, and teachers of those with eating disorders.
- *Hope, Help, & Healing for Eating Disorders* by Gregory Jantz (1995) is another popular self-book based on what he calls the "whole person" approach that addresses physical, emotional, relational, and spiritual domains. He suggests that the book be used as a companion to therapy. One strong reservation I have is the exclusively Christian interpretation of spirituality. Not all clients will share that perspective.
- *Anorexia Nervosa: A Survival Guide for Families, Friends, and Sufferers* (Treasure, 1997) could be suggested to clients and family members. Given the dangers of anorexia, I am leery of relying on bibliotherapy alone, but do think some reading

can be appropriate in conjunction with treatment. This book offers many specific and practical suggestions for families, and even has sections for teachers and family physicians.

- *Helping Your Teenager Beat an Eating Disorder* by James Lock and Daniel Le Grange (2005) is a recent book to recommend to parents.

Novels for Counselors and Clients

- *The Best Little Girl in the World* by Steven Levenkron (1989) is almost a classic on this topic.
- *Wasted* by Marya Hornbacher (1998) is a memoir of a bright and articulate young woman's struggle with eating disorders. The author is one of the women featured in the video *Perfect Illusions*, recommended below.
- *My Sister's Bones* by Cathi Hanauer (1996) is a novel about two sisters' battles with eating disorders.
- *Second Star to the Right* by Deborah Hautzig (1999) is written from the perspective of the person with an eating disorders, as is
- *Stick Figure* by Lori Gottlieb (2001). These novels also aid the clinician in gaining insight into eating disorders.

Film and Television

A commercial film, *Real Women Have Curves*, is one of the only popular media productions in which a female protagonist has a healthy body image despite immense pressures to be thin. I strongly recommend this film, which would also be wonderful for adolescent girls to view.

A PBS special called *Perfect Illusion: Eating Disorders and the Family* is also an outstanding program for clients and for general presentations where the goal is to raise awareness of eating disorders.

EXERCISES

1. Reflect on your personal body image and level of body satisfaction. Go to http://www. halls.md/body-mass-index/bmi.htm and calculate your BMI. Think about your results, and discuss or write about your reactions. Then consider how your feelings about your own appearance and weight might impact your work with a client with an eating disorder.

2. Assume you have an adult client with anorexia nervosa who needs hospitalization due to her unwillingness to cooperate with weight gain goals. How will you proceed?

3. Assume you have been working with a client with anorexia nervosa. She has attained her weight goal, and has resumed regular menstrual cycles. The client proclaims that she is cured and wishes to terminate treatment. How will you evaluate the appropriateness of termination? If you decide termination is not yet appropriate, how will you present that to the client?

4. Assume you are working with a 10-year-old girl whom you believe is at high risk for later development of an eating disorder. She has been sexually abused, which is the reason for referral. She exhibits many perfectionistic traits. She describes her family as "too busy" to do many things together. How will you attempt to implement preventive strategies to shield her from eating disorders?

5. Assume you accept an invitation to a middle-school class to talk about body image with females. What will you cover? What videos, if any, will you show? What activities might you include?

CHAPTER

4   Sexual Minorities

Sexual minority status is not a disorder, nor is it a problem per se. That sentence could not have been written before 1973, when homosexuality was still listed in *The Diagnostic and Statistical Manual of Mental Disorders* (DSM-II) as a clinical disorder. It was not until 1973 that the Board of Directors of the American Psychiatric Association voted to remove homosexuality from the DSM; in 1974, a vote of the membership supported that decision. However, there continued to be diagnoses that implied that anything other than a heterosexual orientation was pathological. The diagnosis of *egodystonic homosexuality* was included in the DSM-III (published in 1980). This diagnosis pathologized a psychological state that is largely the consequence of the prevailing negative societal attitudes toward sexual minorities. In such a cultural climate, most individuals who become aware of their non-heterosexual orientation experience a period in which their sexual orientation is egodystonic. Finally, in 1986, that diagnosis was deleted from the DSM-III-R, and the American Psychological Association endorsed the change.

Egodystonic: A condition that is unacceptable to the self.

Why then include a chapter on this issue? Perhaps because of the intolerance and discrimination in contemporary society, sexual minority individuals are more likely than their heterosexual peers to seek mental health treatment. In fact, 7% of adults receiving mental health services are gay, lesbian, or bisexual, although current best estimates are that this group represents about 2.5% of the total population (Cochran, Sullivan, & Mays, 2003; Corliss, Cochran, & Mays, 2002). In many ways, the treatment needs of this population are similar to those of other clients, but there is evidence that treatment providers may hold negative stereotypes that interfere with the process. Researchers found that providers had more difficulty recalling information provided by sexual minority clients, avoided topics that were disconcerting for the therapist, and did not accurately assess the relevance of sexual orientation to the client's presenting problem (Cochran, 2001). In addition, sexual minority youth are a particularly vulnerable population, and an awareness of the impact of sexual orientation on adolescents is essential for all counselors. The purpose of this chapter, then, is to inform and sensitize counselors so that they can provide quality services to this clientele.

Case Study

Jerry was raised in a small community where activities revolved around a conservative church. He was the only son in the family, having two older sisters. Throughout school Jerry socialized and dated girls, although he did not enjoy the little physical contact he had with them. He had lots of friends, and often invited them to spend the night. He was aroused by the presence of males, but never acted on his desires. He describes his adolescent thoughts about his homosexual interests as "violent denial." He had repeatedly heard from family, friends, and church sermons about the evils of homosexuality, and he believed that religious fervor was a worthy substitute for sexual passion. In fact, he convinced himself that his chaste behavior with girls was about serving God and remaining pure as he had been taught. He was saving himself for marriage, the only allowable context for sexual behavior.

Jerry remembers learning very early that his homosexual interests were unacceptable when he was discovered at about age six looking at the men's underwear pages in a Sears catalog. He was told that such behavior was "wrong" and that he shouldn't be looking at "such things." He remembers later realizing that it probably would have been okay to be looking at the women's section.

When he was 18 years old, Jerry had his first gay sexual experience. He was so distraught over the incident that he considered killing himself. Instead, he went to the youth pastor of his church and disclosed his fears of being gay. He entered counseling with the pastor's wife with the goal of becoming heterosexual. The counseling had positive benefits, as the focus was on the root causes of the behavior rather than on demonic possession. He had an opportunity to sort out some of his feelings about his relationships with his parents, which he found helpful. In addition, Jerry was instructed by the Bible passages that were believed to condemn homosexuality, and he learned to combat the lustful thoughts with prayer. He was told he could be "cured" by learning to ignore his impure thoughts until they had no influence.

At about this time, the youth pastor took Jerry and several other youth to an "exorcism" in an old church. Jerry understood that the purpose of the ritual was to "cast out demons," which in his case meant his homosexual desires. He was frightened by the behavior of some of the other youth, whose struggle with the demons he witnessed. When it was his turn, however, nothing happened. Jerry's interpretation of this "failure" at the time was that he did not have enough faith, more reason to despise himself.

Jerry moved out of state for a period of time, and then returned to his small community when he was about 20. When he came back, a group of friends invited him to go "gay bashing," at a local park. This actually provided him with important information—a place where gay men could be found. Jerry then began cruising the park on his own, and had sexual encounters with men he found there. He continued to struggle with his identity: being gay meant going to hell, and he did not feel good about who he was. He battled his own homophobia. At one point, he had mononucleosis, and panicked, fearing he had AIDS. He eventually concluded that he would not "win" his struggle against his "animal lust, his dark side," so he gave in to those impulses, and set aside God and church, which he believed were incompatible with his nature.

When Jerry started counseling at age 28, he was still struggling to accept his sexuality. It was difficult for him at first to believe that I did not judge or condemn him. By this time, Jerry had been able to have sexual relationships with men, but they were separate from personal relationships. He had not learned how to integrate his sexual ("dark") side with his non-sexual ("good") side to form meaningful intimate relationships, and this was one of his goals for counseling. By this time, Jerry had already disclosed his sexual orientation to both of his sisters, who took the information well and conveyed that their foremost desire was for Jerry to be happy. In fact, both of them engaged in various matchmaking efforts in an attempt to be helpful.

Early in counseling, Jerry was adamant that he could never tell either of his parents that he is gay. He truly believed that the knowledge that they have a gay son would kill them, and his mother was already in poor health. Several years later, he did come out to his mother, who was in counseling at the time. She was disappointed, but loving nevertheless. She made sure Jerry was on her church's prayer lists. She was welcoming to men with whom her son was in relationships.

Jerry took much longer to tell his father. His step-mother suspected and confronted Jerry, who admitted his orientation to her. She advised him that telling his father would "kill him," so he continued to keep his secret. When Jerry's father finally was told, he was bereft, and focused his anger on Jerry's mother, whom he blamed for this outcome. To this day, although Jerry and his father do communicate, his father never wants information about Jerry's relationships, and has never visited him (although he visits Jerry's sisters, at much greater distance and despite their less-than-perfect behaviors). Jerry accepts that this is his father's problem, and is sad that his father is missing out on knowing his son.

Jerry is now living with his partner in a committed relationship. He misses religion in his life, and thinks he may someday find a church where he feels comfortable. His partner's family is very accepting of him, and he is gratified to be treated as a member of the family rather than as a pariah. He still has challenges related to his sexuality. He has difficulty enjoying sex, and recognizes that the voice of his childhood saying this is evil is still present at some level. Nevertheless, he is more and more comfortable with himself, and is continuing to grow and flourish.

Definitions and Description

The term *sexual minority* is an inclusive term used to refer to individuals who are gay, lesbian, bisexual, transgender, intersex, or questioning their sexual orientation. This group has also been called an *invisible minority* because their minority status may not be obvious or readily apparent. Like other minorities, they comprise a small proportion of the general population, and are subjected to discrimination and oppression based on this status. Unlike most other minorities, sexual minority individuals must decide whether or not to reveal this aspect of their identity (Garnets, 2002). Although the term *sexual minority* will be used generically in this chapter, the reader should be aware that most research has been conducted on gay males, some on lesbians, fewer still on bisexual, and almost none on transsexual, intersex, or questioning individuals. For the purposes of this chapter, the discussion applies to all the groups included in the term *sexual minority* unless otherwise specified, although that is speculation at this point.

Transgendered: Persons whose gender identity (and sometimes their gender expression, e.g., clothing) is not the same as their biological sex.

The question of how one defines homosexuality (gay men or lesbians) is an interesting one. Consensus is lacking regarding relative weight of fantasy, attraction, and behavior in determining sexual orientation. Most agree that a single sexual incident with a same-sex partner does not mean that a person is homosexual. On the other hand, some persons may have strong attractions and fantasies about same sex partners, but resist acting upon them. Most experts rely on the individual's self-identification to categorize individuals. Despite the justified criticisms of many of Kinsey's research findings (1948, 1953), he did contribute a scale of sexual orientation that is still widely used. He proposed that sexuality exists on a continuum from exclusively heterosexual to exclusively homosexual; he developed a 7-point scale to quantify individuals. Scores range from 0 (exclusively heterosexual) to 6 (exclusively homosexual). If this is the case, the following definitions, although widely accepted, are somewhat imprecise.

One's pattern of sexual behavior and sexual attraction is what comprises one's sexual orientation. Homosexuality refers to the "persistent sexual and emotional attraction to members of one's own gender and is part of the continuum of sexual expression" (Ryan & Futterman, 2001, p. 1). The term *gay* refers to males attracted to males, but is also often used inclusively to refer to all sexual minorities. *Lesbian* is the term for females attracted to females and *bisexual* describes the sexual orientation of those attracted to both sexes equally. *Transgendered* persons are those whose gender identity conflicts with their biological or chromosomal gender. *Transsexuals* are those whose gender identity conflict results in behavior to match the psychological identity; some of these individuals choose surgical procedures to align their physical appearance to the gender identity. *Intersex* is a medical condition, often characterized by ambiguous genitalia. *Questioning* individuals are those who are not yet certain of their sexual orientation.

Intersex: A person born with ambiguous genitalia. A variety of conditions can cause this, and there is no precise definition of how variant the genitalia need to be to be considered intersex.

Several other terms are important in this chapter. *Homophobia* refers to an irrational fear of homosexual persons and homosexuality. *Internalized homophobia* is a state in which a homosexual person has incorporated the homophobic attitudes of society into his own psyche. Finally, *heterosexism* is the belief that heterosexuality is the only acceptable sexual orientation.

Prevalence

Research attempting to assess the prevalence of sexual minorities relies on self-disclosure of sexual orientation and behaviors by participants, who may be less than forthcoming given the societal stigma still associated with sexual minority status. The widely cited statistic of 10% of the population being homosexual was based on Kinsey's landmark study of sexual behavior more than 50 years ago. However, Kinsey's participants were not randomly selected, were interviewed face-to-face, and his methods of determining homosexuality are subject to debate. Only recently have studies used general population surveys and anonymous reporting. A range of 3–6% prevalence of homosexuality appears to be widely accepted (Corliss, Cochran, & Mays, 2002).

Developmental Influences

The primary focus of this section is adolescence, as it is the period of life in which sexual orientation and associated challenges are most salient. Adolescence has been defined as the stage of life that marks the transition from childhood to adulthood. The major life tasks at this stage are developing an identity and attaining autonomy, laying the foundation for finding intimacy and a sense of belonging in young adulthood. Sexual minority adolescents are presented with challenges that are different from those experienced by the sexual majority. They must accomplish their developmental tasks while adjusting to a socially stigmatized identity. When these challenges are confronted within a supportive and accepting cultural environment, the deleterious impact of being different can be minimized. Without such support, sexual minority adolescents are vulnerable to internalizing a negative sense of self that has lifelong consequences both for the individual and for our society.

Physical, cognitive, emotional, and social changes are striking during adolescence. During this period, the young adolescent may experience dramatic shifts between the longing to remain close to family, and his or her need for privacy and strivings for autonomy (Marans & Cohen, 1991). As the adolescent disengages from the intensity of relationships within the family, his or her attention and energy is increasingly focused on peer relationships. These changes affect the development of an emerging identity, including sexual identity. This occurs whether the adolescent is among those we refer to as "sexual minority" or not. The aim of this section is not to reiterate "normal" adolescent development, but to focus on those aspects of adolescent development that are particular to sexual minority adolescents.

The developmental tasks of sexual minority adolescents (issues of identity, autonomy, belongingness, and intimacy) are complicated by both intrapsychic and interpersonal factors. Sexual minority adolescents focus their erotic and romantic involvements on members of the same sex. Some become aware of the different-ness of their attractions at a much earlier time in their lives (Tharinger & Wells, 2000); for others this awareness becomes clear only during adolescence or later. Discovering one's same-sex attractions complicates the feelings of estrangement that are typical of adolescence by adding a sense of alienation from peers and family, and feelings of shame and secrecy. ". . . Incorporating into one's own self-image the negative feelings associated with the label 'homosexual' . . . can cripple hopes and dreams for a productive future. Internalized homophobia may also help explain why gay youth are believed to attempt suicide at rates that are much higher than the rates among their heterosexual peers" (Baker, 2002, p. 6). Because of the need for secrecy about their sexual orientation, many sexual minority youth lack contact with peers who are experiencing similar feelings, and they may also lack adult role models, thus increasing the sense of isolation. Unlike the situation with heterosexual adolescents, those in the sexual minority have few socially sanctioned opportunities for dating, for open pair bonding, or for sexual experimentation.

Studies beginning in the 1970s have shown that adolescents are engaging in a greater range of sexual behaviors at younger ages than earlier generations. Self-identification as GLBT also appears to be occurring at younger ages (Wildman, 2000). Intermittent same-sex sexual behaviors between adolescents do not define those individuals as gay, nor do they necessarily lead to a gay identity. To the benefit of those in the sexual minority, cultural barriers against homosexuality have decreased, which allows for achievement of life goals and open social relationships at home, school, and work. This may accelerate the self-identification of sexual minority youth. There also appear to be differences in the timing of these events among ethnic and racial groups, with blacks having developmentally earlier same-sex sexual experiences than whites (Bell & Weinberg, 1978).

Integration of one's sexual identity into all social roles has been conceptualized as the final outcome of identity development for gay and lesbian individuals. It is seen as essential to healthy psychosocial adjustment and psychological well-being (Rostosky & Riggle, 2002). "An individual exploring homosexual interests in adolescence who has a history and repertoire of successful adaptation skills as well as a history of secure attachment will navigate the process—all things being equal—more successfully than the adolescent with a history of poor relational and coping abilities" (Tharinger & Wells, 2000, p. 162). Developmental models of homosexual identity formation have been described by various authors (Cass, 1979; Coleman, 1982; Troiden, 1989), providing a framework for understanding the unique processes experienced by these youths. The disadvantage of these models, however, is the inclination to view them as inflexible, with the expectation that all youth will follow the same linear stages of development. As such, they can be detrimental, just as the assumption of heterosexuality is often detrimental to the developing gay or lesbian child. Further mitigating the usefulness of the developmental models is the fact that some heterosexual youths engage in homosexual behaviors, crushes and affiliations; and some homosexual youths behave in similar heterosexual ways, before their sexual identities have crystallized. With these cautions in mind, Cass' and Troiden's models are outlined below.

The first of stage of Cass' model is *identity confusion*, which is when an individual recognizes his or her thoughts and behaviors as homosexual, and is distressed by that awareness. He or she may seek other explanations or rationalizations for those behaviors, and may begin to seek information on homosexuality. The next stage is *identity comparison*, in which the person accepts the possibility of being homosexual. In this stage, the person may accept that they have engaged in homosexual behaviors while still rejecting a homosexual identity. The third stage is *identity tolerance*, characterized by the individual's understanding that one is probably homosexual. In this stage, the person recognizes that being homosexual involves social and emotional components in addition to sexual desire. Typically, persons actively seek out other sexual minority persons and beings to experience being part of the sexual minority community. In the next stage, *identity acceptance*, people accept that they are homosexual and become increasingly involved with the gay community. This stage is often accompanied by anger toward the anti-gay elements of society and decreasing interaction with heterosexuals. In stage five, individuals often adopt a black-and-white view of society (gay or not-gay) and seek to immerse themselves in the gay community. It is in this stage that disclosure of sexual orientation to family and others occurs. It is often also at this stage that confrontation with heterosexual society takes place. In the final stage, known as *identity synthesis*, the person has integrated his or her sexual minority status with other aspects of identity. Their sexual identity is still important but there is a more balanced approach to relationships.

Troiden (1989) points to the seminal work of Kinsey by acknowledging that the dichotomous labels of "heterosexual" and "homosexual" are artifacts that do not reflect the reality of sexuality for many people. Individuals vary widely in the degree to which they are attracted to the same or to the opposite sex. In that context, Troiden differentiates between the terms "self-concept" and "identity." He defines self-concept as a global term that refers to the mental image that one has of him or herself. Identity, on the other hand, has a situational context: one is a teacher, a garden club member, a criminal, a Sunday school teacher, and so on. "A homosexual identity is a perception of self as homosexual in relation to romantic or sexual situations" (Troiden, 1989, p. 46). He describes three components of homosexual identity: *self-identity* is the view individuals have of themselves as homosexual in relation to romantic or sexual situations; *perceived identity* occurs when the individual believes that others know that he or she is homosexual; and *presented identity* occurs when the individuals announce or present themselves as homosexual. A homosexual identity is most fully realized in situations where these three identities coincide, "where an agreement exists between who people think they are, who they claim they are, and how others view them" (p. 47).

In describing his stage model of homosexual identity formation, Troiden (1989) points out that his postulated stages are general patterns and are not necessarily experienced in a linear fashion. Those people who go through all four stages generally settle into a committed homosexual identity while others may drift away from these stages at any point and ultimately not commit themselves to a homosexual identity.

Stage One: Sensitization begins before puberty when lesbians and gay males have social experiences that give meaning and relevance to their later homosexual identity. They begin to see themselves as different from their peers. For example, boys may feel great anxiety about participating in sports, or girls may feel themselves to be more aggressive or masculine than other girls. During this stage, the experience of being different focuses on social and gender roles, rather than specifically on sexuality. The sensitization stage lays a foundation of meaning for the experiences of later stages, in that the homosexually identified person later reinterprets past experience as early indicators of a homosexual path.

Stage Two: Identity Confusion. In most cases after the onset of puberty, consideration is given to the idea that feelings and behaviors could be regarded as homosexual. No longer able to assume heterosexuality, the individual experiences ambiguity, turmoil, and uncertainty about who he or she is. "By middle or late adolescence, a perception of self as 'probably' homosexual begins to emerge" (Troiden, 1989, p. 53). The stigmatization of homosexuality, along with inaccurate and inadequate information, a lack of role models, and inaccessibility to others with similar feelings all contribute to the confusion of this stage. Genital and emotional experiences lead to a perception of self as sexually different, not just socially different. A variety of defensive "stigma-management" responses typically occur during this stage, such as denial, heterosexual experimentation, psychotherapy to change their orientation, or even taking on anti-gay attitudes and behaviors.

Stage Three: Identity Assumption. Occurring typically during or after late adolescence, identity assumption involves self-definition as homosexual, associating with other homosexuals, sexual experimentation, and involvement in gay culture. For lesbians, this stage is usually arrived at in the context of a love relationship, while for a majority of gay males, it is experienced through sexual contacts with other males. Identity assumption brings on negative aspects of membership in a stigmatized group. This can precipitate defensive strategies such as passing as heterosexual by concealing sexual preferences from others who might be critical or condemning, or adopting stereotyped behaviors that are gender-inappropriate. Affiliating with other gay men and lesbians reduces social isolation and provides opportunities for exposure to positive role models, learning strategies for coping with stigma, and feeling support from others.

Stage Four: Commitment. In this final stage, one realizes that it is less costly to maintain a homosexual identity than to try to hide or change it. This involves self-acceptance and comfort with the role and the identity. Internal indications of this stage are the fusion of sexuality and emotions that allows for entering into love relationships, satisfaction with the homosexual identity, and increased happiness with this self-definition. Externally, this stage is indicated by entrance into a love relationship, disclosure to non-homosexuals, and adopting more effective stigma-management strategies. Cass' and Troiden's stage models are summarized and compared in Table 4.1.

TABLE 4.1   Classic Models of Homosexual Identity Development

Models of Homosexual Identity Formation			
Cass (1979)		**Troiden (1989)**	
Stage	**Description**	**Stage**	**Description**
Identity Confusion	Recognizes one's thoughts, behaviors as homosexual; is distressed by that awareness.	Sensitization	Pre-pubescent social experiences lead to awareness of being different from others of same gender.
Identity Comparison	Accepts possibility of being homosexual, but rejects identity.	Identity Confusion	After puberty, recognizes one's feelings and behaviors are probably homosexual, leading to turmoil and uncertainty.
Identity Tolerance	Accepts probability of being homosexual; broadens understanding.	Identity Assumption	During or after late adolescence, defines self as homosexual, associates with homosexuals, experiments sexually. Experiences being stigmatized.
Identity Acceptance	Accepts homosexual identity, becomes involved in gay community; rejects heterosexual society. Comes out.	Commitment	Accepts and is comfortable with homosexual identity. Fusion of erotic and emotional components; enters love relationship.
Identity Synthesis	Homosexuality integrated with other elements of identity.		

Peer Relationships

It is during early childhood, before understanding what sexual orientation means, that most people begin to sense how society views homosexuality (Baker, 2002). When children are exposed to anti-gay rhetoric, they learn that it is acceptable to harass and vilify those in the sexual minority. As those in the sexual minority gradually become aware that they are different, they learn that this difference is bad and shameful. They become frightened of what their feelings and attractions will mean for their lives and they may begin to hate that part of themselves. Those youth who are able to keep their feelings hidden are less likely to be targets of taunting and victimization. Thus, being "in the closet" often leads to decreased involvement in school and extracurricular activities. Having only a small network of friends while hiding one's sexuality from parents, siblings, teachers, and peers reinforces a sense of being marginalized (Tharinger & Wells, 2000).

In work that seems aptly to describe the negative attitude toward those in the sexual minority, Marsiglio (1993) provided statistical evidence of adolescent heterosexual males' attitudes toward gay male peers. He found that 89% of heterosexual adolescent males feel that sex between two men is "disgusting." Only 12% of these heterosexual youths believed that they could befriend a gay adolescent.

Disclosing one's sexual attractions to others, then, is a very risky business. Particularly during the identity confusion stage, but continuing in later stages as previously explained, many keep their feelings secret to avoid rejection, harassment, and physical abuse by peers and family members. Those who do disclose may choose first to reveal their attractions to a close friend, hoping for understanding and acceptance. Savin-Williams (1998) studied 180 college-aged gay males' recollections of adolescent experiences. He found that a complete 50% first disclosed their sexual attractions to a female friend, while one-third of the group disclosed to a best male friend. The sexual orientation of the male friends varied; some were known or assumed to be heterosexual, while others were gay friends or gay sexual partners. The remaining youths made their first disclosure either to family members or to a supportive adult, such as a therapist.

Intrapsychic Effects

In general, it is believed that theories of development apply to all individuals, regardless of later sexual identity. In looking at the unique challenges to the development of people in the sexual minority, it is useful to consider the impact of early childhood attachment on their ability to integrate a healthy sexual identity. As Tharinger and Wells (2000) point out, there is little evidence to suggest that the quality of the earliest attachment relationships to caregivers differs between gay and non-gay children. As the child grows, and the evidence suggesting same sex attractions mounts, however, there is a potential for disruption of the attachment as both parties (parent and child) come to terms with this emerging stigmatized reality. The ability of a child to adjust to his sexual minority status is influenced by the early attachment experiences. In their provocative work, Tharinger and Wells look at sexual minority individuals who, upon disclosure of their attractions to parents, experienced rejection. Those with secure attachment histories experience the rejection of parents with greater difficulty than those whose attachment experience was insecure. Integrating the new reality (rejection) that is different from their previous secure attachment is difficult. The parental rejection is so upsetting to the previously secure child that future development may be compromised. For those with histories of insecure parental attachment, upon experiencing the rejection of their parents because of their sexual attractions, they integrate the rejection as "more of the same," and they seem not to have as much difficulty with the rejection as their securely attached peers. It may be that those with secure early attachment experiences are more prone to acting out than are those whose attachment was insecure. This appears to be only a temporary phenomenon, however, as there is general agreement that secure attachment is a better foundation for healthy psychological and emotional development than is insecure attachment.

Acting Out

Although many sexual minority youth have fared well and even flourished in school, evidence indicates that, as a group, these students are at higher risk in several important ways. Sexual minority youth who reported high levels of victimization at school had higher levels of substance use, suicidal behaviors, and sexual risk-taking than similarly victimized heterosexual peers (Bontempo & D'Augelli, 2002). Sexual minority youth attempt suicide at a rate that is three times that of their heterosexual peers (Gay Lesbian and Straight Education Network (GLSEN), 2002), and their attempts are more lethal, with three times as many requiring medical intervention. In 1989, suicide was the leading cause of death among sexual minority youth (Besner & Spungin, 1995), and sexual minority youth accounted for up to 30% of all completed adolescent suicides (American Academy of Pediatrics, 1993; Morrison & L'Heureux, 2001; O'Conor, 1994).

Sexual minority students miss school two to four times as often as their heterosexual classmates, often due to fears of harassment and physical harm at school due to their sexual orientation. They also drop out of school at a disproportionate rate (Herr, 1997). Further, these students have been less successful academically compared to heterosexual students (GLSEN, 2002).

The Massachusetts Youth Risk Behavior Survey found significantly higher rates of substance abuse among sexual minority youth compared to other youth (Human Rights Watch, 2001). The survey found that these adolescents were more likely to use drugs prior to the age of 13, and to have a higher lifetime use of illegal drugs (Siecus, 2001). Another high school survey found that the differences between sexual minority youth and heterosexuals in rates of substance abuse were greatest for "hard" drugs (Orenstein, 2001). Risky sexual behavior has also been found to be more prevalent in sexual minority adolescents (HRW, 2001). Extrapolating from data on HIV infection in adult males, and considering the incubation period, estimates are that 20% of HIV-positive adult gay men were infected as adolescents (GLSEN, 2002). The Minnesota study found that lesbian and bisexual females were more likely to become pregnant than their straight classmates, perhaps due to an effort to deny or conceal their homosexuality. Sexual minority youth are over-represented among the homeless, with studies finding 16–40% of homeless youth identifying as sexual minority. These youth are at increased risk for sexually transmitted diseases because many resort to trading sex for survival needs.

Family Issues

Disclosure of sexual orientation to parents and other family members is a significant milestone in the life of sexual minority adolescents, but it is also a major event for parents. Parental reactions to the disclosure vary, from responses that are loving and supportive to those that reject the sexual orientation, or the person. Often the negative responses from parents are rooted in the erroneous belief that they are responsible for their child's sexual attractions. ". . . Families react with shame and guilt to homosexuality in a child partly because of the widespread belief that homosexuality is the result of bad parenting" (Hetrick & Martin, 1987, p. 41). The conflict that results from this belief can be damaging to the youth and to the family, and may become a source of family violence or even ejection of the adolescent from the home. One study (Hunter, 1990) found that more than half (61%) of the violence that all sexual minority youths experience occurs in the home; another (Pilkington & D'Augelli, 1995) found that one-third of their sample of sexual minority youth had been verbally abused because of their sexuality, and 10% physically assaulted, in the home. In her review of this lamentable situation, Morrow (1993) points out that family members, like sexual minority youths themselves, suffer from a lack of accurate information about homosexuality. Furthermore, many family members may experience a normal period of grief over losing the previously presumed heterosexuality of their child. Given time, these families can learn better coping skills in dealing with their child's homosexuality.

In his proposals for family therapy as a modality to assist in the coming out process, Lasala (2000) reiterates that it is considered psychologically healthy for sexual minority youths to come out of the closet. He also notes the shock, disappointment, and shame that many parents feel when they learn of a son or daughter's sexual orientation. Disclosure often precipitates a painful family crisis, which can lead to serious disruption of relationships among family members. Parents must grieve what many parents experiences as the loss of their hopes for their child, and obtain accurate information about gay lifestyles. Lesbians and gay men need support as they struggle to cope with their parents' negative reactions. Lasala suggests that during family therapy, family members should be coached to maintain non-combative communication following the disclosure, even if contacts are initially brief and superficial.

Sexual Minority Adults

This discussion of adulthood for sexual minorities must be read cautiously, as most of the scant research has been done with white, educated samples, and the conclusions drawn from that research may or may not apply to ethnic minorities. Like their heterosexual peers, adulthood for sexual minorities is usually focused on work and family, and balancing the two. For gay men and lesbians, the issues they may face in adulthood are very much a function of the historical period in which they developed. To Kimmel and Sang (1995), the impact of the demonstrations at the Stonewall bar in 1969 and the later AIDS epidemic were profound. Stonewall "began to change the social construction of homosexuality from a personal pathology to minority group membership" (p. 190). Some gay men and lesbians did not come out until middle adulthood, and may have been in heterosexual marriages. Their adult experience will be different from those of adults who came out in adolescence and early adulthood and have lived their lives as sexual minorities. Those who do not disclose their homosexuality until middle adulthood may feel the need to learn new social skills and may face turmoil from the effects of the disclosure on family members.

Stonewall Riots: On June 27, 1969, police raided a popular gay bar (Stonewall Inn) in New York City. Patrons resisted, and a "riot" ensued. This event marked the beginning of the "gay liberation movement."

For lesbians, midlife may be less momentous than for heterosexual females. While many heterosexual women may be returning to the workforce after an interruption to raise children, they may be more susceptible to concerns about the youthful standard of beauty prevalent in society. However, most lesbians have worked throughout adult life. As a result, their major challenge might be balancing the needs of career and family or relationships, which is particularly salient for those lesbians in committed relationships.

There is a popular perception that gay men are more highly educated and earn higher incomes than their heterosexual peers. Although the data on that are mixed, it has been suggested that because most gay men are denied the opportunity to invest in family roles such as fatherhood, their energies are more focused on careers. However, other gay men who were not out in their workplace may have turned down promotions that involved relocation because of the impact on partners. Because they did not feel safe to explain their decision, such workers may be seen as lacking ambition and may in fact be passed up for future promotion opportunities.

For midlife lesbians and gay men, social support and a sense of belonging is likely to come from friends and the sexual minority community to a greater degree than from family. Even for those who have been out to their families for years, there may be a sense that they cannot be fully understood or be fully themselves except when with others like themselves.

Parenting

In the 2000 U.S. census, there were 163,879 households identified as headed by same-sex couples, and an unknown number headed by a single gay parent (Dingfelder, 2005). Only in recent years has parenting been an option for sexual minority individuals and couples. Previously, parenthood was considered the domain of heterosexuals. Gay men and lesbian couples who were parents generally had children from previous heterosexual relationships, or had become single parents by choice. Gay families were often subject to discrimination, ranging from unkind remarks to loss of legal custody. Adoption by sexual minorities was rarely allowed. Now, some gay men and lesbians opt to have children in the context of homosexual relationships. While society has not yet advanced to full acceptance of alternative models of the family, there are more and more sexual minorities who choose to raise children. This section will present some of the unique challenges faced by those individuals, some of which may bring them to the counselor's office.

First, it is important to address the widespread misconceptions about sexual minority parents. A body of research has consistently found that children of gay and lesbian parents have no more mental health problems than children raised by heterosexual parents. What has been found is that it is the warm relationship with parents (or lack thereof) that affects a child's adjustment, not the sexual orientation of the parents. In addition, children of same-sex parents are no more likely to be homosexual or bisexual than children from heterosexual families (Wainright, Russell, & Patterson, 2004).

Different issues emerge in families depending on the way children came into the family. Some families headed by same-sex parents were created when a sexual minority person had children in a previous heterosexual relationship or marriage, and then formed a new relationship with a same-sex partner. In other cases, gay men or lesbians become parents via artificial insemination, surrogacy, or adoption. Because families with sexual minority parents are still stigmatized, not least by the lack of legal recognition of their status as a family, gay men or lesbian parents may be less confident in the role of parents, particularly when they are not the child's biological parent. The non-biological parent, who does not have legal parental status, may be reluctant to invest fully in the parental role, fearing they will lose the child if the relationship ends or the biological parent dies (Martin, 1998). This emotional distance is likely to have an effect on children, and may create problems in the relationship as well.

In families where children were born in the context of a heterosexual marriage, the challenge, in addition to the task of helping the child deal with parental divorce, may be in telling the child in an age-appropriate manner that the parent is homosexual. The parent may fear rejection by their children if they tell them about their sexual orientation. If this disclosure comes closely upon the announcement about a divorce or separation, the children may feel emotionally overwhelmed. Depending on the age of the children, they may be aware of the social stigma of being a sexual minority, and may fear the consequences for their own social relationships. How and when to come out to children is a delicate decision, and Martin (1998) advocates that disclosure wait until custody arrangements are secure and the parent is able to present the information about his or her sexuality in a positive way.

For those who chose parenting via donor insemination, surrogacy, or adoption, there are unique issues to be addressed. Aware of the numerous decisions to be made in these situations, some may seek assistance from a counselor. For couples who elect to have a child via insemination or surrogacy, there are numerous decisions about the identity of the donor and to whom that should be revealed. If the sperm donor is known to the couple, his role with respect to the child must be defined. If the donor is anonymous, the developing child will not have access to answers about his or her biological father. In the case of a surrogate mother, she cannot be anonymous, and her role must also be defined. For sexual minority individuals who choose adoption, finding an adoption agency that is knowledgeable about this population is essential. In some states, both parents may not be legally recognized, which can create a new set of challenges. Counselors can help clients work through the decision-making processes and the feelings associated with all these concerns.

It is also important for counselors to remember that when the child of a same-sex couple is referred for counseling, the sexual orientation of the parents may not be a central issue (Martin, 1998). Although it is important for the counselor to pay attention to how the family configuration may be related to the presenting issue, it is also important to avoid assuming that whatever problem there is must be caused by the sexual orientation of the parents.

Sexual Minority Elderly

Older adults often feel that ageism is commonplace, and that elders are devalued in American society. So it is with sexual minorities, so that for the older sexual minority person, the discrimination and prejudice has dual sources. As with sexual minority persons in middle adulthood, the issues for sexual minority adults will vary with the historical context in which they have lived. Prior to the Stonewall riots in 1969, there was a social climate that stigmatized gays and lesbians as perverted and evil, and forced them to conceal their identity or contend with prevalent discrimination. Recall that until 1973, homosexuality was listed as a psychiatric disorder!

The coming out process can be seen as a major developmental transition (Reid, 1973) that provides inner resources and develops strength that can then be utilized to adapt to other challenges, such as those associated with aging. Friend (1991) has proposed a theory of successful aging for gay men and lesbians, in which achieving a positive identity as an openly gay man or lesbian provides an advantage for adaptation to the physical, psychological, and social changes that are inherent in the aging process. He suggests that because the social environment for older gay men and lesbians was one of negative evaluation, those individuals who were able to reject that evaluation and create a positive personal identity as gay or lesbian have strength of character and self-esteem that transfers to other life challenges. Friend calls those who have achieved this positive personal identity "affirmative" individuals, because they have adjusted well despite a less than supportive social context. For those older gay men and lesbians who accepted the negative evaluation promoted by the social environment, Friend posits two outcomes: keeping one's sexual identity a secret and living with internalized homophobia and self-hate; and those who attempt to live their lives as heterosexuals.

Research has found that older gay men and lesbians vary in their adaptation to aging as do their heterosexual contemporaries. There are, however, several unique aspects of aging that confront older gay men. The gay subculture often idolized youth (Reid, 1995), so that older gay men see themselves as old at a younger age than do their straight peers. If sexual minority elders never had children, they may miss the support and assistance that children often provide aging parents. They may have to confront the archaic policies of hospitals and nursing homes that do not consider them to be family, and the absence of legal status may marginalize their role in end-of-life decision-making for partners.

Gutièrrez (1992) suggested that counselors keep a developmental perspective in mind when working with older gay men. The counselor must consider the individual developmental stage (e.g., Erikson's integrity versus despair), the developmental stage of a couple for the partnered gay client, and any discrepancies between the developmental stages of a couple. Considering these aspects of development would be useful for working with any older client, but are particularly important with aging gay men.

Loneliness is an issue for many older adults as friends and partners die. Sang (1992) points out that older lesbian women often prefer to socialize with other lesbians, and may not have access to that social group. Sang recommends that the counselor explore with the older lesbian client who is lonely whether she is isolated because of real circumstances or because she fears exploring new relationships due to fears of rejection or limited social skills.

Assessment

Because sexual minority status is not a disorder, assessment is not an issue. Any assessment the counselor might use would relate to the reason the person is seeking treatment. However, the clinician must be alert to the impact of sexual orientation on the presenting problem. One must also be sensitive to subtle ways in which assessment forms may reflect heterosexism; forms that ask for the name of the spouse convey the message that marriage is the only acceptable form of coupleship, thereby discounting the gay clientele. Checking assessment forms and other documents for discriminatory wording is essential to convey a message of acceptance.

Treatment Options

There are a number of treatment options, including controversial approaches like *conversion therapy* and *reparative therapy* (to both of which I am personally strongly opposed), as well as therapies specific to bisexual clients. In this section, you will find guidelines for effective treatment of sexual minority clients, as well as suggested ways in which the counselor may convey a sense of safety and approachability for sexual minority clients.

Conversion or Reparative Therapy

Conversion or reparative therapy is an intervention with the goal of changing a homosexual orientation to a heterosexual one. A coalition of ten organizations, including the American Counseling Association, the American Psychological Association, the American Academy of Pediatrics, and several educational professional organizations published a fact sheet (APA Online, 2005) in response to the promotion of conversion or reparative therapies. The publication includes this statement: ". . . health and mental health professional organizations do not support efforts to change young people's sexual orientation through 'reparative therapy' and have raised serious concerns about its potential to do harm" (p. 6). Despite this and similar statements by mental health organizations representing 477,000 health and mental health professionals, there are counselors who continue to provide such "treatment." Given that sexual minority status is not a mental disorder, the goal of "curing" someone of this affliction is in contradiction to the current knowledge of professionals.

Why do some gay or lesbian individuals enter this type of treatment? Some gays and lesbians feel disconnected to other gay men and lesbians, and seek to belong to a community. They may believe that being homosexual is the cause of their alienation from others, and seek treatment that will reinforce that belief. Others seek this kind of therapy because of religious guilt or fear or eternal damnation. Some may have been rejected by their religious congregation because of their homosexuality, and seek a way to reconcile their life and their religious beliefs. Others come for therapy to save a heterosexual marriage or keep their children. Some clients who become involved in this type of therapy originally sought therapy for other issues; when they disclosed their sexual orientation, the therapist told them that their problems could not be addressed until they had undergone this treatment (Shidlo & Schroeder, 2002).

Techniques used by these approaches often come from a cognitive behavioral repertoire and include the following: cognitive reframing of homosexual impulses as symptoms of psychological distress; covert sensitization: imagining a negative consequence when experiencing same-sex arousal; opposite sex partners as replacement for desired same-sex partners; and strategies to displace sexual energy such as playing sports, working, praying, and reading the Bible.

In their survey of 202 persons who had experienced conversion therapy, Shidlo and Schroeder (2002) noted that 87% reported having "failed" in this approach. Study participants reported some positive effects: feeling a sense of community in their ex-gay groups, improved self-esteem, increased hope, and increased understanding of their parents. An interesting phenomenon was that for some who "failed" this treatment, the treatment confirmed for them that sexual orientation could not be altered, and so they experienced relief from pressure to change.

The harmful effects included increased depression, suicidal ideation and attempts, even among those without a prior history of such symptoms. Other participants experienced decreased self-esteem and increase in internalized homophobia as a result of the therapist's devaluing of their sexual orientation and providing negative information about sexual minority individuals. Sexual dysfunction, including intrusive imagery, was reported by participants as a consequence of the aversive conditioning. Some participants reported damage to parental relationships as a result of attributing their homosexuality to poor parenting. Other participants reported the loss of important relationships and social support, and many found that their religious faith was compromised by this treatment.

If a sexual minority client inquires about this approach to therapy, informed consent is mandatory. That includes information that professional organizations oppose this form of therapy, that there might be negative consequences of this approach, and that homosexuality is not a disorder. Further, be prepared to provide accurate information about sexual minorities, and be familiar with the many referral sources that can help the client make an informed decision.

A Model for Counseling Bisexual Clients

Some bisexual individuals may seek counseling because of a belief that one must be either heterosexual or homosexual. They may even experience rejection by the GLB community, who may believe that those who identify as bisexual are not courageous enough to affirm their identity as a homosexual. Wolf (1992) proposes a model for intervention with such clients, described by the acronym PLISSIT. The strategies are employed in sequence, as the client may profit sufficiently from the first steps to terminate counseling.

- The initial intervention is *Permission*, which refers to granting the person the freedom to explore their bisexuality. To do this effectively, the counselor must accept that this is a real orientation and refrain from mirroring the social stigmatization of the larger society. For some clients, this intervention is all that is required. For others, the next step is needed.
- This step, *Limited Information*, involves providing references in the form of readings, information about organizations, and sometimes information about how to meet other bisexual people. In this way, the permission to explore is validated by external sources. Again, counseling may no longer be needed after this step.
- For other clients, the next phase, *Specific Suggestions*, is recommended. In this phase of counseling, the counselor may provide guidelines for such important decisions about who to tell about the bisexuality, how to develop a support system, and how to deal with bisexual feelings within a relationship. Consistent with all counseling approaches, such suggestions are carefully presented as alternatives rather than dictates. For the few clients for whom the previous three steps did not resolve the problems, *Intensive Therapy* may be indicated
- In *Intensive Therapy*, the underlying concerns (depression, substance abuse, etc.) can be addressed, along with couples or family therapy when necessary.

Guidelines for Effective Treatment of Sexual Minority Clients

Division 44 of the American Psychological Association published guidelines that provide a context and information for providing services to sexual minority clients (Division 44, 2000). These guidelines are consistent with ethical principles of counselors and with the policies of other mental health professional organizations. The counselor or social worker who follows these guidelines is assured of ethical practice with this clientele. I have left the word "psychologists" used in the guidelines as authored, but the reader can easily substitute the word "counselor" or "helping professional" and find them applicable. The Guidelines are as follows:

1. Psychologists understand that homosexuality and bisexuality are not indicative of mental illness.
2. Psychologists are encouraged to recognize how their attitudes and knowledge about lesbian, gay, and bisexual issues may be relevant to assessment and treatment and seek consultation and make appropriate referrals when needed.
3. Psychologists strive to understand the ways in which social stigmatization (i.e., prejudice, discrimination, and violence) poses risks to the mental health and well-being of lesbian, gay, and bisexual clients.

4. Psychologists strive to understand how inaccurate or prejudicial views of homosexuality or bisexuality may affect the client's presentation in treatment and the therapeutic process.

5. Psychologists strive to be knowledgeable about and respect the importance of lesbian, gay, and bisexual relationships.

6. Psychologists strive to understand the particular circumstances and challenges faced by lesbian, gay, and bisexual parents.

7. Psychologists recognize that the families of lesbian, gay, and bisexual people may include people who are not legally or biologically related.

8. Psychologists strive to understand how a person's homosexual or bisexual orientation may have an impact on his or her family of origin and the relationship to that family of origin.

9. Psychologists are encouraged to recognize the particular life issues or challenges that are related to multiple and often conflicting cultural norms, values, and beliefs that lesbian, gay, and bisexual members of racial and ethnic minorities face.

10. Psychologists are encouraged to recognize the particular challenges that bisexual individuals experience.

11. Psychologists strive to understand the special problems and risks that exist for lesbian, gay, and bisexual youth.

12. Psychologists consider generational differences with lesbian, gay, and bisexual populations and the particular challenges that lesbian, gay, and bisexual older adults may experience.

13. Psychologists are encouraged to recognize the particular challenges that lesbian, gay, and bisexual individuals experience with physical, sensory, and cognitive-emotional difficulties.

14. Psychologists support the provision of professional education and training on lesbian, gay, and bisexual issues.

15. Psychologists are encouraged to increase their knowledge and understanding of homosexuality and bisexuality through continuing education, training, supervision, and consultation.

16. Psychologists make reasonable efforts to familiarize themselves with relevant mental health, educational, and community resources for lesbian, gay, and bisexual people (Division 44, 2000, pp. 1441–1448).

Welcoming Sexual Minority Clients

Sexual minority individuals are likely to be cautious about revealing their sexual orientation to a counselor for fear they will be rejected or judged. They may be uncertain about the counselor's commitment to confidentiality. To avert some of the fear associated with disclosing their sexual orientation, the counselor may wish to provide evidence of his or her openness to discussion. One way to do this is to include posters or other material that proclaim one's commitment to diversity, including sexual orientation. Reading materials and literature, when available, should include content that addresses this clientele. The counselor's professional disclosure statement should be written so as to make it clear that the counselor is willing to work with clients of all diverse groups.

Clients will be alert to the subtle ways in which the counselor may communicate heterosexism. For example, in an initial interview, counselors may inquire about romantic relationships. Asking a female client about a "boyfriend" or a male about a "girlfriend" conveys the assumption that same-gender relationships are not acceptable. The counselor can avoid that perception by referring to "romantic interests" or "significant other" in questions about this area of functioning.

Issues of Diversity

Cultural attitudes regarding sexual minorities are important considerations when working with individuals with diverse cultural backgrounds. Remember that individuals within a culture vary widely in their identification with the cultural beliefs and practices so counselors must avoid making any assumptions based solely on the culture of an individual. Knowing about cultural differences does allow the counselor to inquire sensitively about how cultural factors may be involved.

Ethnic Minorities and Sexual Minorities

Ethnic minority sexual minority persons are "minorities within minorities" (Greene, 1997, p. 232). For some, their experience in coping with racism and discrimination as a person of color may have provided skills with which to manage the additional burden of sexual minority status. On the other hand, they may find themselves the victims of racism within the sexual minority community and homophobia within the cultural community, essentially limiting their ability to experience a secure sense of belonging to either group.

Native Americans. Native American conceptions of homosexuality are quite different from those of the majority culture. These differences are reflected in the 168 native languages currently spoken in the United States that have words for people who are neither male nor female (Tafoya, 1997). Because the native terms were not directly translatable into English, the term *two-spirited* is now used by many to describe those who have both male and female spirits (Jacobs, Thomas, & Lang, 1997). In most native cultures, two-spiritedness is not solely a function of sexual orientation, but it also includes one's social and spiritual identity. Those native youth who are in contact with or influenced by the dominant culture may feel forced to decide if they are either homosexual or heterosexual. In fact, Tafoya notes that, perhaps as a reflection of the more fluid concepts of sexuality and relationships, there is a higher reported rate of heterosexual experience in Native American gays and lesbians than in other ethnic groups.

Tafoya (1997) also notes that in pre-Columbian times, two-spirited people were highly valued in many native tribes and were accorded positions of high status. With the advent of European culture and values, many of which were inculcated in vulnerable youth via the federal boarding school system, some tribes have adopted the homophobic attitudes of the dominant culture.

African Americans. In African American communities, family ties are typically strong and extensive, as the notion of family includes aunts, uncles, grandparents, and so on, to a greater degree than in some other groups. In addition, gender roles have been quite flexible, perhaps as a legacy of the more egalitarian African cultures, and also as a response to racism which made it difficult for African American males to find employment and take on the stereotypical role of provider in the dominant European culture (Greene, 1997). Religion plays a large role in the lives of many African Americans.

Greene (1997) reported that African American gays and lesbians view that community as very homophobic. One explanation for that attitude is the strong influence of Christian religious groups that use selective Biblical references to justify this position. In addition, the perceived shortage of potential African American marriageable males may support a bias against gays, while the importance of bearing children would mitigate against lesbians.

These negative attitudes toward sexual minority individuals in the African American community discourages many from coming out to their African American families and friends, thus depriving them of important sources of support. Because their allegiance to the African American community is primary for many, they may be reluctant to identify with the sexual minority community, thus lacking support there as well. Interestingly, in their study of intimate relationships in African Americans lesbians and gay males, Peplau, Cochran, and Mays (1997) found that one-third of their participants were in interracial relationships, with gay men more likely to be in interracial relationships than lesbian women, and that such relationships are more common among homosexual than heterosexual African Americans. These researchers speculate that when gay or lesbian African Americans move into urban areas with more active sexual minority communities, they are more likely to meet and form partnerships with those of other races.

Latino/a Americans. In addition to differences in country of origin, Latino/as in the United States differ on the degree of acculturation to the majority culture. Thus, readers must be cautious about making assumptions based on these generalizations.

Two characteristics of Latino/a culture bear on the current issue: the centrality of family and the relatively rigid gender roles. One clue to the cultural attitudes toward sexual minority status is found in the language. There are no words for lesbian or gay men that do not have pejorative implications. According to Greene (1997), same-sex sexual contact, especially among males, is not always met with disapproval, but overt expression of a gay or lesbian identity is unacceptable.

Some experts believe that homophobia in the Latino/a community is stronger than that in the dominant culture. For some Latinos/as, being openly gay or lesbian is seen as a betrayal of the family and the culture. On the other hand, families often tolerate a family member who is gay or lesbian, allowing them to maintain family ties, without acknowledging or accepting their sexual minority identity. The fear of being ostracized from family and culture can coexist with a desire to express one's sexual identity, causing significant stress for such individuals.

Morales (1992) describes *states* (as opposed to stages, which imply an orderly and linear progression) experienced by Latino/a sexual minorities as they attempt to resolve their multiple identities. These states are:

- *Denial of Conflicts:* The individual minimizes or denies the discrimination they experience as a dual minority (ethnic and sexual). In this state, they may have an idealized picture of an accepting society in which they are welcome. For those who seek counseling in this state, Morales (1992) recommends helping the client create a more realistic picture of their position in society, and helping them re-frame their multiple identities as assets.
- *Bisexual versus Gay or Lesbian:* In this state, some Latino/a sexual minority persons choose to identify as bisexual, believing that this identity is less negatively treated. Some also view sexuality more broadly than behavior, and may consider themselves as bisexual even though all their partners have been of their own sex. A further reason for identification as bisexual is that the gay and lesbian community may be seen as racist. A counselor can assist clients in this state by helping them recognize the depression and hopelessness inherent in this state, and by helping them find a supportive community where they can feel safe as both a sexual and ethnic minority.
- *Conflicts in Allegiances:* When uncertain about whether one can integrate ethnic and sexual minority identities, one strategy is to attempt to separate the two to avoid anxiety. The tension that accompanies this conflict can be debilitating, so the counselor working with clients in this state will want to help them see a multicultural perspective in which they can operate from the identity that best fits the given situation and context.
- The next state is *Establishing Priorities in Allegiances:* In this state, sexual minority Latino/as' primary identity is their ethnic identity. Typically, they express anger at rejection by the GLB community because of their ethnicity. When a client is in this state, the counselor might focus on how the person identifies him or herself, encouraging Latino/a rather than "minority," which suggests oppression. The counselor might also encourage developing a social network with other Latino/a gays and lesbians, and seeking support from others.
- The fifth state is *Integrating the Various Communities:* In this state, the focus is on how to integrate the multiple identities into a multicultural perspective. For some GLB Latinos/as, the risk of coming out and revealing yet another status that may result in mistreatment or rejection is a major one. The counselor can validate clients' skill in making judgments about where, when, and to whom to come out, while also encouraging clients to rely on the support systems they have created.

Morales (1992) stressed that individuals may revisit these states multiple times, and may in fact present elements of more than one trait at any given time.

Asian Americans. Most of what has been discussed in the literature about sexual minority Asian Americans is based on those with Chinese or Japanese ancestry. Applicability to other Asian groups is uncertain. In traditional Asian cultures, obedience to family, respect for elders, clear gender and generational distinctions, are important cultural features. Men pass on the family name by marrying and having children, and women are identified with their roles of daughter, wife, and mother. Sex is a taboo topic, and is not discussed openly. Although men may have sexual relations with other men, they are not necessarily considered gay. A gay or lesbian identity is viewed as a threat to traditional values and roles. Bringing shame to the family is to be avoided at all costs (Greene, 1997). Therefore, a gay or lesbian Asian American would likely struggle with the conflicts inherent in being both Asian American and a sexual minority.

Chan (1995) emphasizes the distinction between public and private selves, which is an important feature of Chinese culture. The public self is prescribed by one's roles within the family. Interestingly, in the two main Chinese languages, individual names are rarely used. People are referred to by the family role: first daughter, third son, little sister. In the same vein, there is no concept of sexual identity in traditional Chinese culture, where sex is part of the private self. One's sexuality must not interfere with one's prescribed role in the family.

As a result of these values, Chan (1995) believes, Asian American gays and lesbians are more likely to come out to non-Asians. In her study, many participants had not come out to their parents although they had been out to others for an average of six years.

Jewish Americans.   Jews and sexual minorities have several commonalities, the most obvious of which is their physical invisibility. That is, neither is readily identifiable, which provides the option to "pass." The ability brings with it an internal struggle over whether to proclaim one's identity (either cultural or sexual) publicly and risk the racism and discrimination, or to avoid discrimination by denying one's identity. As Dworkin (1997) so aptly put it, "A Jew struggles with the Christian assumptions of society and a lesbian struggles with the heterosexual assumptions of society. Jews experience oppression at the hands of the dominant culture, and so do lesbians" (p. 75).

Religious (Orthodox) Jews condemn homosexuality, but the more liberal traditions (Conservative and Reform) often welcome sexual minority congregants although they may be excluded from important roles in the synagogue. One reason for the opposition to homosexuality is the strong need to increase the community and bear children, which gays and lesbians are assumed not to do. There are now gay and lesbian synagogues that integrate new prayers with the traditional liturgy. These prayers acknowledge that gays and lesbians also died in the Holocaust, and also acknowledge the loss of life to AIDS.

Persons with Disabilities

It is essential to keep in mind several factors when thinking about or working with sexual minority persons with disabilities. First, neither of these statuses (ability or sexual orientation) is a psychological disorder. Second, the focus of counseling for these persons may be neither the disability nor the sexual orientation. Although both disability and sexual minority status are often misunderstood and both may be the target of discrimination and stigmatization, it is essential not to make assumptions when such a client comes for counseling. Finally, while both of these statuses may be invisible, it is also possible that one is apparent and the other not, so it is important to inquire about all potentially relevant information when conducting intake interviews with all clients.

Much of the scant literature addressing sexual minority individuals with disabilities focuses on a specific subgroup, for example, lesbians with physical disabilities, or deaf gay men. Most of the implications for counselors apply across disabilities, so in the interest of space, my discussion will be mostly quite general in this regard. I will include some useful references in that section at the end of the chapter.

From their in-depth interviews with twenty-five white lesbian women with physical disabilities, Hunt, Matthews, Milsom, and Lammel (2006) learned about their experiences with counseling. While some reported experiences were positive and others negative, themes were extracted that inform counselors about what factors were important to this clientele. First, the overall counseling skills of the clinician were of central importance. The cultural sensitivity of counselors was noted by many participants, who desired to be completely understood by the counselor, and to feel confident that the counselor could be helpful. Several of the participants had experiences with counselors who seemed to hold stereotypical views of lesbians or people with disabilities, and other counselors did not appear to have the needed information. Other clients arrived at first appointments to find information forms that subtly reflected assumptions of heterosexuality that offended the participants.

One theme expressed by participants I think is particularly important for counselors to heed. They did not expect counselors to be knowledgeable about every disability—there are simply too many—but they did value an overall appreciation of how disabilities affect individuals, and most of all a willingness to learn on the part of the counselor. Participants did not want to spend their counseling sessions educating clinicians about their disabilities, but they expected the counselor to read or consult once the disability was identified. I have learned a great deal about working with traumatic brain injuries (TBI) from a referral by a case manager. The presenting issue was not the TBI, but that was an important part of understanding this client. The case manager appreciated my other skills and experiences, and provided me with several readings on TBI that were extremely helpful as I worked with this and later other clients. Another behavior that was highly valued by participants in the Hunt et al. (2006) study was a willingness to advocate for lesbian clients with disabilities, and to teach clients how to advocate for themselves. Also important for counselors to know is that although some participants found the counselor's sexual orientation or disability status to be important, most did not mention it. It appeared that their acceptance of these clients was what mattered more.

In terms of identified problems, sometimes offices were not user-friendly, either in terms of accessibility or written materials (for visually impaired clients), and assessment procedures that were not applicable to persons with disabilities. Finally, because many individuals with disabilities have limited incomes, adjustments in fees were greatly appreciated.

Boden (1992) also worked with lesbians with disabilities, and provides insight about dynamics that are unique to sexual minorities whose disabilities were either congenital or evident in early childhood. When the person with disabilities was grow-ing up, she developed a sense of being different as a result of her disability. This sense of being different sometimes was internalized to mean being defective. When the developing person then realizes she is a lesbian, feelings around the earlier awareness of how others responded to the disability may be reawakened.

Another aspect of disabilities of importance to sexual minority individuals is the reduced number of potential life partners (Lawson, 2005). Lawson observes that having an autistic spectrum disorder and being a lesbian does not have to be a problem, but "it might present us with extra difficulties that require some navigation" (p. 83).

Persons whose disabilities are developmental and cognitive in nature are often excluded from the discourse on disabilities: "Theories about *disability* are really theo-ries about *physical disability*" (Thompson, Bryson, & De Castell, 2001, p. 55). These authors contend that people with developmental disabilities are generally not accepted by either the community with disabilities or the sexual minority community, depriving them of much needed support. They also are not provided with adequate and accurate sexual information, which is sorely needed. The absence of appropriate sex education is also a problem for deaf individuals, some of whom are sexual minorities. Swartz (1993) found that sex knowledge of deaf college freshmen was less than that of the hearing peers, consistent with the alleged absence of sex education for this population.

There appears to be a commonly held myth that persons with disabilities are asex-ual and certainly cannot be homosexual (O'Toole & Bregante, 1992; Shakespeare, 1999; Thompson et al., 2001). In fact, Appleby (1994) was critical of the lesbian community, which she believed was not inclusive of lesbians with disabilities, due in part to the acceptance of this myth. Partners of persons with disabilities are often assumed to be caretakers. This assumption of asexuality often means that sexual minority persons with disabilities do not receive important and needed information about sexuality from medical providers. Shakespeare (1999) observed that individual gays and lesbians with disabilities varied in the salience of each status in their self-image. In general, the stronger identity was with the status that appeared earlier in life, so that if the person was disabled as a child, the person was more likely to be identified as one with disabilities, but if the disability emerged after the sexual identity had been disclosed to others, the sexual minority status was likely to be more prominent in the individual's self-identity. For some, having dealt with one difference was helpful in facing another. Many of his partic-ipants (twenty-two gay men and lesbians with disabilities) observed that the sexual minority community is not particularly welcoming to those with disabilities. That posi-tion is supported by Nora Rae Bednarski, who is wheelchair-bound (Hays, 2001), who has personally experienced the insensitivity and inaccessibility of sexual minority events. Further, many people with disabilities do not reveal their sexual orientation because of fears about the effect of the disclosure on caregivers or residential institutions on which they depend.

Asexual: Sexless, lacking sex-ual desire, having no interest in sex.

One last concern must be mentioned. Because marriage is not legally sanctioned in almost all places for same-sex couples, medical crises can create difficulties for the life partner of the person with disabilities to be recognized by the medical community as a sanctioned decision-maker (O'Toole & Brigante, 1992). The case of Sharon Kowalski and Karen Thompson is often cited as an example of the way same-sex partners can be denied a role in medical situations. Both women were non-disabled, and had been living together as a committed couple for four years prior to the accident that severely disabled Sharon. Her parents did not want to allow Karen to be Sharon's guardian, and although the legal case was eventually resolved in Karen's favor, the litigation continued for a decade. Counselors should inquire of partnered sexual minority clients whether they have made legal arrangements to ensure that their role in each other's lives will be respected in all situations. This may be especially important for HIV-positive clients, but this case illustrates that such a situation can be completely unanticipated, and all sexual minority clients, with or without disabilities, should think about the potential consequences.

Counselor Issues

In a sincere effort to be inclusive and nonjudgmental, counselors may take the position that since sexual minority status is neither a disorder nor a problem, they should not inquire about sexual orientation, nor focus on it in counseling. While such a position is understandable, it can also be shortsighted and harmful to the client. Many other issues (family relationships, depression, abuse, even career concerns) should be addressed in context, and sexual minority status is part of the context. As long as this remains a stigmatized attribute, counselors will do their clients a disservice if they do not examine the impact of sexual minority status on other aspects of client functioning.

Most identity development models describe the coming out process as an essential task in reaching the most integrated developmental stages. It may follow that counselors, then, would encourage clients to take that important step. It is absolutely crucial that clients not feel pressured to come out before they are ready and prepared for the consequences. First, clients should feel clear about their sexual identity before coming out, particularly to those whose possible rejection would be traumatic. Clients also need help in finding the optimal time and situations in which to make this disclosure. Despite its importance to the sexual minority individual, the client should assess the receptiveness of the persons to whom he or she is disclosing (avoiding times of high stress, poor health, etc.). Clients need to be well prepared for possible anger and distress from loved ones, particularly following an initial disclosure. What is critical here is that the counselor self-monitors to be sure that it is the client's needs and agenda that drive the decision, not the counselor's.

As with all the other issues in the book, counselors who are a sexual minority themselves must be conscious of how that affects their reactions to clients, and must be clear that they are not imposing their own agenda on others. When disclosing their sexual minority status to clients, counselors must be sure that the disclosure is appropriate, for the client's benefit, and not the focus of clinical attention. I strongly recommend that all counselors seek supervision, but particularly when they work with clients whose issues have a personal meaning for the counselor.

BOX 4.1

A Note to School Counselors

While protection of rights is an important element of the role of schools with sexual minority adolescents, school counselors are in a position to make a significant contribution to the welfare of these students. In fact, school counselors may be the first school person to be approached by sexual minority youth (HRW, 2001). This section will discuss the special responsibilities of school counselors to this group of their constituents.

As student advocates and mental health professionals, school counselors should be at the forefront of promoting acceptance of diversity in schools, and are in a unique position to take the leadership in promoting a safe and supportive school climate for sexual minority students (Bauman & Sachs-Kapp, 1998; Monier & Lewis, 2000). Counselors have a number of avenues by which they can positively impact the school experience of sexual minority youth, and by extension, of all students (Anderson, 1994; Reynolds & Koski, 1994; Besner & Spungin, 1995). Counselors are leaders in staff development and training and student wellness promotion, are strong student advocates, and provide direct services to students and parents. These tasks can all be successfully employed in the service of sexual minority students.

Two studies examined the role of school counselors with sexual minority youth. Price and Telljohann (1991) found that 71% of their sample had counseled at least one gay or lesbian student, with more experienced counselors having had more contact with sexual minority youth, as expected. Fontaine (1998) surveyed school counselors in Pennsylvania and found that 56% of secondary school counselors had worked with students who were questioning their sexual identity, and 42% had worked with students who identified as gay or lesbian. The most common issues counselors addressed with these students were related to a negative self-concept and fears related to their sexual identity.

School counselors are already in the role of consultant to teachers and administrators. In this capacity, they can assist teachers in developing lessons and strategies that are more inclusive of sexual minorities, and in devising classroom management approaches to deal with unacceptable behavior toward these students. As student advocates, counselors must insist that discriminatory behavior toward any student, including sexual minority students, be confronted and disciplinary action taken. They must insist that all students' rights are respected and their welfare promoted, and they must intervene when this does not happen.

Counselors could be proponents of, and leaders in providing in-service training to teachers and staff to raise awareness, provide information, and dispel misinformation. This training can be an opportunity to sensitize the adults in the school about the impact of language. Evidence is accumulating to support the benefits of staff training. A study by Laura Szalacha (Sadowski, 2001) found that more than twice as many students perceived that sexual minority students had faculty support in schools where staff training had been provided than in schools where it had not been offered. Counselors must work with administrators to ensure that such training be required, so that staff who attend do not fear being labeled, and so that those most in need of the training must participate. Excellent resources are available for counselors to use in designing staff training (e.g., Besner & Spungin, 1995).

School counselors can also be leaders in diversity training and programming for students within the school, and can promote the value of including sexual minority issues in such training (Bauman & Sachs-Kapp, 1998). Bauman and Sachs-Kapp describe a powerful workshop conducted for and by students on this important topic. Experiential exercises were included along with informational presentations so that students were engaged and involved. Anecdotal comments by student participants revealed that the workshop had a significant impact.

In their consultant role, counselors can initiate task forces within their schools to focus on these issues, and should be actively and visibly involved in efforts to improve climate for sexual minority students, including publishing clear policies of non-discrimination. Counselors can speak out when they become aware of incidents or policies that are detrimental to sexual minority youth. Due to their professional training and sensitivity, counselors may be alert to the more subtle cues that exclude sexual minorities, and can be vigilant and assertive in raising awareness of the negative consequences of such practices. Students who see that counselors take an active and visible stance regarding sexual minority students are more likely to approach them for assistance.

Counselors are not always seen by sexual minority youth as advocates or sources of support. A student interviewed by Herr (1997) described her experience with a school counselor that revealed the counselor's insensitivity, misinformation, and lack of preparedness to deal with concerns. Sears (1992) found that sexual minority high school students did not see their counselors as approachable regarding this issue, and some youth perceive that their counselors are uncomfortable or misinformed about their concerns (Pennington, 2002). In Price and Telljohann's (1991) survey of school counselors, 70% of respondents believed that the school counselor should provide counseling for sexual minority students only if the student requested it. Contact with sexual minority youth was only infrequently reported by school counselors in Monier and Lewis' (2000) study. One researcher found that only 15% of his sexual minority adolescent sample believe that school counselors could be helpful to them, and even more alarming, 46% believed that their school counselors would be "unhelpful" (Berger, 1989, cited in Muller & Hartman, 1998). Sexual minority students may fear negative judgments from their counselors. Confidentiality and privacy concerns must be explicitly addressed if sexual minority youth are to feel safe approaching school counselors with these issues. Two actions are important for counselors to take with respect to confidentiality: informing students of any limits to student–counselor confidentiality, and advocating strongly for explicit policies that prohibit disclosure of students' sexual orientation or gender identity (HRW, 2001). Counselors need to make it clear that they are willing and able to work with sexual minority youth, by having visible indicators prominently displayed that convey their openness to diversity in general and sexual minority issues in particular. Their offices make statements about their openness, and if posters and symbols reflect acceptance of sexual minority students, these will be recognized. Unfortunately, in Monier and Lewis' (2000) sample of members of the Washington School Counselor Association, only 50% of high school counselors and 24% of middle school counselors indicated that they had displayed books, posters, and symbols, while 19% and 30% respectively believed they would not be allowed to do so.

In addition to individual counseling that allows sexual minority students to discuss their concerns with a nonjudgmental professional, group counseling can be a very effective format for working with students. In-school support groups provide a safe and supportive environment within the school for discussion of the particular issues that arise in the school setting (Muller & Hartman, 1998). The discovery that they are not alone can be a very healing experience for all students, but particularly for sexual minority youth who often feel isolated within the school milieu. An extremely small percentage (6% at high school and 3% at middle school) of the counselors in Monier and Lewis' study had started such support groups, and approximately half at each level indicated they do not plan to do so. In addition to group counseling, gay–straight alliances (GSAs) have been found to be important in changing school climate. Counselors should be advocates for gay–straight alliances in schools, and can take comfort in Laura Szalacha's finding (Sadowski, 2001) that schools with GSAs were considered safe for sexual minority students by three times as many students as those without such groups.

(continued)

BOX 4.1   **Continued**

To provide effective services to sexual minority students, school counselors must be well informed and connected to community resources to which students can be referred. Monier and Lewis (2000) found that only 15% of middle and high school counselors had assembled a resource packet, and that 28% of high school and 15% of middle school counselors did not plan to do so. Referrals are most effective when they include more than just a telephone number. Offering information about organizations and services conveys to the youth that the counselor is personally interested enough to seek out this information.

While school counselors cannot provide ongoing family therapy to families of sexual minority students, they can utilize their knowledge of family issues to assist interested parents in obtaining information and support, and recommending family therapy when indicated. Talking with parents about their distress and fears, and normalizing them, can be an important contribution. It is essential that school counselors have information readily available about Parents and Friends of Lesbians and Gays (PFLAG) and other resources that are appropriate for parents, including family therapists with expertise in helping families through this adjustment.

The importance of school counselors' role in working with sexual minority youth is obvious, but lack of training and skill may inhibit counselors from taking this responsibility (Monier & Lewis, 2000; Sears, 1992). School counselors (Fontaine, 1998) answered questions related to their competence in working with sexual minority students. Only 8% rated themselves as highly competent, the same percentage that rated themselves as not at all competent. A positive discovery was that 89% of the counselors indicated at least some level of interest in further training in counseling sexual minority youth. However, only 2% of respondents reported having received in-service training on this topic. Graduate training programs for school counselors do not seem to be providing sufficient training in working with sexual minority youth, and many counselors receive the majority of their training at seminars and workshops (Monier & Lewis, 2000). Reynolds and Koski (1994) lament the lack of training for school counselors in working with this population, and the Human Rights Watch report stresses the importance of specialized training for counselors in addition to training for teachers and administrators and other school staff (HRW, 2001). Counselors can take the initiative in insisting that such training be provided by professional organizations and their local districts, and actively soliciting such training.

In the absence of training, the sources of information for working with sexual minority youth currently used by counselors in Fontaine's (1998) study included, in order of frequency: professional journals, mass media, gay and lesbian individuals, workshops and conferences, and textbooks. An examination of all the articles published in journals dedicated specifically to school counseling through 2000 (i.e., *Elementary School Guidance and Counseling*, *School Counselor*, and *Professional School Counselor*) revealed that with the exception of a special issue in 1998 devoted to this topic, only four other articles discussed working with sexual minority students. In response to questions related to counselor's beliefs about the causes of homosexuality, the most often selected contributing factor was "choice as a lifestyle." If school counselors believe that sexual minority status is a choice, the implication is that one can be persuaded to choose differently. While this was not an explicit finding, the possibility is alarming. One must hope that effective training will enlighten counselors about sexual orientation.

We have not addressed the particular issues of sexual minority youth of color, who have "double minority" status. One would expect that these youth would experience increased risk and negative outcomes as a result of experiencing discrimination on more than one dimension of identity. However, a study of sexual minority youth of color found that while they earned lower grades than their heterosexual counterparts, the difference in grades was significant only for white youth (Russell & Truong, 2001).

The researchers speculate that minority youth of color may have more experience with prejudice and discrimination than white youth, and that this prior experience serves to inoculate them against the toxic effects of added discrimination. White youth may be experiencing minority status for the first time, and their negative school outcomes may reflect the absence of coping strategies for dealing with discrimination.

If the mission of school counselors is to contribute to the academic, personal, and career successes of all students in the schools, it is imperative that they accept and exercise their responsibility for working with and for sexual minority youth. This responsibility extends to taking leadership in promoting an inclusive school climate in which acceptance of differences is the norm, and in assuring that sexual minority youth are protected and welcomed in the schools that are such an influential social environment for developing adolescents. This responsibility is a weighty one. From comments supplied by some respondents in Monier and Lewis' (2000) survey, it is clear that some counselors fear the reactions of parents and other educators should they take visible actions on behalf of sexual minority students. They perceive the larger social context to be unsupportive of sexual minorities in general, and critical of any efforts by school personnel, including counselors, to support this population. Hopefully, school counselors are strongly rooted in their professional codes of ethics and their primary commitment to student welfare, and will accept their responsibilities to sexual minority students.

Ethical Concerns

One of the most challenging ethical dilemmas that a counselor may face is more likely to arise when working with sexual minority clients. I refer here to the ACA Ethical Code (ACA, 2005), principle B.2.b.

B.2.b. Contagious, Life-Threatening Diseases

When clients disclose that they have a disease commonly known to be both communicable and life threatening, counselors may be justified in disclosing information to identifiable third parties, if they are known to be at demonstrable and high risk of contracting the disease. Prior to making a disclosure, counselors confirm that there is such a diagnosis and assess the intent of clients to inform the third parties about their disease or to engage in any behaviors that may be harmful to an identifiable third party. (p. 7)

If a client were to disclose that he or she is HIV positive, and having unprotected sexual relations with a partner who does not know of the HIV status, what does this ethical code say? First, it may be the case that the role of the counselor is to assist the client in telling the partner. It has been my experience that clients do not feel good about keeping this secret; they are terrified of losing the relationship and fear that will happen. In many cases, with support (and perhaps rehearsal) the client will make the disclosure, and the counselor will not need to break confidentiality.

In the event that does not happen, the counselor must confirm the diagnosis before taking any further steps. It is possible that the client may believe he/she is HIV positive but has never been tested. In that case, the counselor must urge the client to get accurate test results. In other cases, the diagnosis is confirmed. If the client agrees to use effective protection, is the counselor obligated to take any further steps? The use of the term "high risk" in the ethical code suggests that if the counselor is certain that the client will not engage in unprotected sex, the counselor does not have to inform the partner. However, in such a situation, it is absolutely essential that the counselor seek consultation. In fact, most professional organizations offer free consultation on ethical matters, and this would certainly be a situation in which to take advantage of that service.

Summary

- Sexuality minority status is not a disorder, which is important for counselors to remember. However, despite advances in public awareness, sexual minority individuals continue to experience discrimination.
- Sexual minority clients seek counseling for a variety of reasons; the counselor must be sensitive to ways in which their sexual orientation impacts other areas. At the same time, the counselor must not assume that sexual orientation will be the focus of counseling.
- Development of sexual identity and the coming out process is a major developmental milestone for many sexual minority clients. Counselors must be aware that particularly for adolescents, support and acceptance are critical. Screening for such disorders as depression and substance abuse is prudent with adolescents who struggle to navigate this process.
- Issues for adults and older adults vary with the historical context. For many, the absence of legal status as a couple creates challenges in parenting and end of life issues. The counselor can serve as a support and a resource for essential information.
- For ethnic minority gays, lesbians, and bisexuals, there may be some conflict around identifying as a dual minority, and a sense that the GLB community is not accepting of ethnic minorities. Morales provides a model to help conceptualize these challenges.
- Reparation or conversion therapy exists despite the lack of professional support. The counselor must be familiar with this approach to provide accurate information to clients. Some clients seek counseling from other therapists after such therapy, and the counselor must understand the ways in which such treatment may have been harmful.
- Guidelines for effective therapy with sexual minority clients are available and the ethical counselor will be cognizant of these principles.

ADDITIONAL RESOURCES

On the Web

- http://www.pflag.org/ is the site for Parents and Friends of Lesbians and Gays (PFLAG).

- http://www.glsen.org/cgi-bin/iowa/home.html Gay Lesbian and Straight Education Network (GLSEN) has excellent information on topics of importance, as well as information about starting chapters (Gay Straight Alliances) in schools.
- www.deafqueer.org A website for deaf gay men has links to resources, a chat, and other features that might be of interest to deaf gay clients.

In Print for Counselors

- *Counseling Gay Men and Lesbians: Journey to the End of the Rainbow* by S. H. Dworkin & F. J. Gutièrrez (Eds.). Although it is a 1992 edition, the variety of specialized topics covered in the book is valuable to the counselor.
- *Homosexuality and the Family* edited by Frederick Bozett (1989) has good information for anyone working with gay fathers.
- *The Sharon Kowalski Case: Lesbian and Gay Rights on Trial.* Casey Charles (2003), an HIV positive gay lawyer and English professor, has written a very thorough account.
- *Why Can't Sharon Kowalski Come Home?* is Karen Thompson's story of this case.

In Print for Clients

- *GLBTQ**, by Kelly Huegel (2003) is written from the perspective of one who struggled personally with this issue at that age. It is a handbook, written in a frank and conversational voice that speaks to many of the questions youth may have.
- *Gay Relationships* by Tina Tessina (1989), addresses many of the specific questions that may be important to a client newly out.
- *The Best Little Boy in the World* was published by John Reid in 1973. He later revealed he was actually Andrew Tobias, a well-known financial guru. The book tells the story of a boy coming to terms with being gay, and is an insightful personal account of one person's struggle.
- *The Best Little Boy in the World Grows Up* by A. Tobias (1998) describes the personal and political aspects of life as a gay man in America.
- *Becoming a Man: Half a Life Story* by Paul Monette is another memoir of the struggle to accept oneself as gay that won the National Book Award in 1992.
- *A Face in the Crowd: Expressions of Gay Life in America*, edited by John Peterson and Martin Bedogne (2002) is a lovely photo-essay book, written after the death of Matthew Shepard, which has moving photos and brief stories.
- *Quee Crips: Disabled Gay Men and Their Stories* (2004) by Bob Guter and John R. Killacky provides personal perspectives on this experience.
- *Sex, Sexuality and the Autistic Spectrum* by Wendy Lawson (2005) is also a personal account.
- *School Experiences of Gay and Lesbian Youth: The Invisible Minority* (Harris, 1997). I strongly recommend this book for school counselors, in which the school experiences of sexual minority youth are described in an excellent collection of articles.

Films and Television

- *Philadelphia* (1993), starring Tom Hanks, is a mainstream film that broached the difficult subject of AIDS. The issues are still current and the treatment is timeless.
- *Laramie Project* is about the horrific murder of Mathew Shepard in 1998 that shocked the nation. With actors playing the roles of various townspeople, this film highlights both the tragedy and the increased awareness that resulted from this terrible crime.
- *Brokeback Mountain* has raised the public consciousness of what has been a painful secret for many gay people, and hopefully has helped normalize sexual minorities. It is well worth watching.
- *Transamerica* and *Boys Don't Cry* portray the marginalized transgender group and are both extremely well done.

EXERCISES

1. Attend an event or visit the local chapter of PFLAG or another local organization that supports sexual minority individuals and their families. Write a brief paper describing what you learned.

2. Imagine a client comes to see you wanting conversion therapy. What would you say? How might you explore with the client their motivation in seeking such therapy?

3. Describe how you will make it clear to potential clients and referral sources that you are open to working with clients of minority sexual orientations.

4. Imagine you have an adult client who learns that his/her child is gay or lesbian. List some possible goals for the counseling.

5. Assume you are working with adolescents who recognize they are gay or lesbian and want your help telling their parents. How would you work with these clients?

CHAPTER

5

Substance Abuse

Substance abuse is the number one health problem in the United States, causing more deaths, illnesses, and disabilities than any other preventable condition (Robert Wood Johnson Foundation, 2001). In addition to the human cost, the economic cost is also great, with a national price tag of 484 billion dollars per year (Hanson & Li, 2003; National Institute of Drug Abuse (NIDA), 2005) for health care costs, lost income, and the costs of crime and accidents associated with substance abuse.

Many problems linked to substance abuse may come to the attention of a counselor. In addition to treatment for substance abuse, there are many other psychological disorders that are frequently diagnosed along with substance abuse—eating disorders, depression, abuse, family and relationship problems, to name only a few. Many family members of substance abusers seek counseling for help in dealing with the substance abuser's behaviors. In fact, substance abuse has been called a family disease, as the problem has such a great impact on family members. So, as is the case with many of the topics in this book, counselors will surely have clients with problems directly or indirectly connected to substance abuse whether or not they specialize in services for this clientele. Many graduate programs in counseling offer courses in substance abuse counseling, but such courses are rarely required in a general counseling program. CACREP (The Council for Accreditation of Counseling and Related Educational Programs) does not require a specific substance abuse course in their guidelines for training programs. Consequently, there will be many readers who have no formal training in this area, and this chapter will provide an overview of important concepts. Treatment for substance abuse is gradually expanding beyond the purview of specialists and more clinicians are choosing to include substance abusers in their general practices (Berg & Miller, 1992).

Most people are familiar with the disease model of alcoholism and the 12-Step philosophy of treatment. These models have been applied to other substances as well, and have been the prevailing models for decades. I hope that by the end of this chapter, readers will be aware of many more options for working with

Disease model: Considers alcoholism to be a chronic, progressive, and potentially fatal disease, characterized by tolerance and withdrawal, loss of control, and an inability to abstain. This term was popularized by Dr. Elvinn Jellinek in 1960, although the concept of alcoholism as a disease was proposed in the United States by Dr. Benjamin Rush in 1784. The American Medical Association endorsed the disease model in 1987.

12-step model: This is the approach that originated in the formation of Alcoholics Anonymous (AA) in the 1930s. Proponents believe that to gain sobriety, individuals must work through each of the 12 steps outlined.

clients with substance abuse problems, and will be able to either treat or make referrals with a greater awareness. In this chapter, substance abuse is used as an inclusive term. I will not review each of the many substances that are sometimes abused, as this chapter will be more general. References for such information will be suggested.

Case Study

Hector is a handsome, well-dressed, and carefully groomed 52-year-old man who works as a counselor at a large public mental health center. He sees his conquest of his substance abuse problem as a miracle—he was someone everyone expected to be dead by now.

Hector was the sixth of eight children, and believes he was the "unwanted" child, being the only one who was raised apart from the family. At a very early age, he was sent to be raised by an aunt and uncle, already in their 50s. The neighborhood in which he lived was poor and crime-ridden. He describes his "parents" as old-fashioned, and unsure of how to deal with the behavior problems he began exhibiting early in elementary school. Hector's introduction to substances occurred when he was in 7th grade, when he began smoking marijuana and drinking beer to fit in with the neighborhood kids. He said he "felt normal" when he was using, and also felt more accepted and part of the peer group. Later on in school, Hector discovered that his classmates were great sources for new drugs, and he tried everything that he could get, including a variety of pills and LSD. He did not do well academically, but he continued to be passed, which he believes was because the teachers feared having him again if he had to repeat a class or grade. His parents were blind to his drug use, and while still in school, he kept a low profile.

At age 16, Hector had a fight at school and was told he was expelled. His aunt and uncle did not see this as too serious, as Hector promised to get a job and contribute to the family income. He continued to get into minor trouble for such behaviors as curfew violations. When he was first caught with drugs, the police called his aunt and uncle, with a warning and advice to deal with the problem. Within six months of that event, Hector was found with a jar of reds (pills) and placed in juvenile detention until he was 18. While he was incarcerated, he stayed away from drugs at first, and followed the rules. This led to weekend passes. At that time, there were no UAs [urinanalyses] or searches when he returned, and he began carrying and selling drugs to other inmates.

When he was released, he met a woman whom he married when he was 20. They were divorced when he was 22, after they had a daughter together. This woman was not a drug user, and got tired of his frequent stays in the county jail and his inability to hold a job. It was at age 19 that Hector met the "love of his life" – heroin. He said his first experience was an unbelievable high. He felt as though he was "The Man." At first, he used only once a week or so, but he was never able to duplicate that first intense high—not for lack of trying. At first he used it as a way to party; then it became a habit, and finally using was a matter of survival. By the time he was 21, heroin was the only thing that mattered to him. His wife didn't matter, his child didn't matter, and money didn't matter. His wife left when he was serving a one-year sentence in the county jail for burglary and selling drugs.

When he was released, he didn't miss a beat. He was back in prison within a year, this time with a sentence of five years to life. He got out in three years, with three years of parole ahead. He was "in the spoon by noon," picked up by a friend who provided the first high as a welcome home gift. He kept using "until the wheels fell off." The pattern continued: he violated parole within 60 days, and got another year in prison. He continued his old behaviors, doing robberies and selling drugs, ending up in prison. Although he used in prison, he saw that as a more controlled environment where he had access but not as consistently as in the community. On one of his times in the community, Hector was introduced to speedballs (combined cocaine and heroin, which he injected). This became his drug of choice.

The revolving door into prison became a pattern that continued until he met a woman (another addict) who encouraged him to move to another state, where her parents provided an apartment in which he lived. They both got into a methadone clinic, and Hector got a job. However, it didn't take long before he was back to his criminal activity and speedball use. He was using so much that he was having hallucinations and lost so much weight that he "looked like a skeleton, like walking death." He was arrested on a domestic violence charge and went to prison for another ten years. He realized that he was comfortable and at home in prison, that he had become "institutionalized." He always spent a lot of time in solitary confinement when in prison, which he preferred. Someone noticed this, and took enough interest to refer Hector to the prison psychiatrist. Then began a series of diagnoses, medications, and new treatment providers.

This time, when he was released he had no notice, no plan for housing, and was dropped off at a parole office on the outskirts of a medium-sized city. He walked downtown and began asking the "street people" about where he could sleep and eat. One of them gave him the number of an outreach program, which he called. He talked to a counselor who told him to come in the next morning, which he did after spending the night on the street. He enrolled in a treatment program for the first time in his life, and was given assistance with housing, and a psychiatrist whom Hector says was patient and understanding. Despite his difficulty trusting, he could see the people at the center were caring and understanding, and he kept his agreement to show up every day. The staff introduced him to Narcotics Anonymous (NA), and extended themselves to help him. He was attending a computer course half days to get a skill.

Despite all the progress, Hector relapsed during the holidays. By then, he knew how to "beat UAs" and continued to use for several months. In the spring, Hector overdosed three times in one month. The last time, the nurse who attended him observed that he was lucky to be alive. He called his counselor, confessed his use and his lies and manipulation. He expected to be returned to prison. However, the parole officer noticed that he had never been sent to a substance abuse rehab program, and sent him to one. At first, he didn't want to be there, but after 60 days when he could have been released, he opted to stay for another four months to complete the program. He became involved in NA and found fellowship there. He attributes his sobriety to his Higher Power, from whom he gets strength and wisdom and help with difficult decisions.

He has been clean and sober for two years, the longest period in his adult life. He now has a job, is attending junior college, has his own apartment and his own car. He is extremely proud of his accomplishment, and is grateful to the programs that helped him.

Definitions and Description of the Problem

First, the term *substance* is used to include the variety of matter used for mood-altering purposes, including alcohol, illegal drugs, prescription drugs used for non-medical purposes, and inhalants and other chemical products when used to produce intoxication. *Substance abuse* refers to patterns of continued use despite problems in personal, social, educational, or vocational functioning. A more colloquial definition considers substance abuse to be a pattern of harmful use. *Substance dependence* is what is commonly known as addiction: a chronic disease characterized by *tolerance* and *withdrawal*. Physical dependence refers to the body's adaptation to the presence of the substance, so that the substance becomes necessary for normal functioning. Substance dependence is usually accompanied by considerable functional impairment in several areas of life. In *The Diagnostic and Statistical Manual of Mental Disorders* (DSM-IV-TR), tolerance and dependence are not required for a diagnosis of dependence, but they are often present. The focus for diagnosis is on behavioral symptoms (loss of control over use, and interference with normal functioning), but tolerance and physical dependence must be addressed in treatment when they are present.

> **Tolerance:** A need for increasing amounts of substance to obtain the same effect.
>
> **Withdrawal:** A physiological reaction when the substance is not present in the body.

Prevalence

Eighteen percent of the U.S. population will meet the diagnostic criteria for a substance use disorder at some time during their life. More than a third of psychiatric inpatients and one in five patients in medical hospitals have substance abuse disorders, for which they may or may not be treated (Galanter & Kleber, 2004). Other statistics also illustrate the magnitude of the problem: 15.9 million Americans over age 12 reported using an illegal drug within the previous month (Office of National Drug Control Policy (ONDCP), 2003) and 15.1 million Americans abused prescription drugs in 2003. Lifetime use of marijuana was reported by 37% of the population, with 12.3% reporting lifetime use of cocaine and 12.5% reporting lifetime use of hallucinogens. Recent data reveal that 13% of children live with adults who use illegal drugs and 24% live with an adult who is a binge or heavy drinker. In addition, almost 20% of alcohol in the United States is consumed by underage drinkers (Foster, Vaughan, Foster, & Califano, 2003) although around 90% of young people with drug problems have not received treatment (Anthony & Chen, 2004). Numerous similar figures could be presented, but it already seems clear that substance abuse is a major health problem in this county.

Developmental Influences

Before discussing the unique aspects of substance abuse at different points in development, it is important to review what is known about the causes of the problem. Considerable research has accumulated evidence of a genetic component to substance abuse. Twin and adoption studies have contributed a great deal to this line of inquiry, and findings suggest that the contribution of genes to the development of substance abuse is somewhere between 25% and 65% (Anthony & Chen, 2004). The greatest genetic influences in substance abuse are via the genes that initiate drug use (Cloninger, 2004). The evidence suggests that this influence is nonspecific as to drug, but is a more general predisposition to substance problems. Environmental factors, such as availability of specific substances, are influential in determining which substances will be used. Certain personality traits with strong genetic links are also influential: high novelty-seeking (impulsivity) and low harm-avoidance (risk-taking), along with early antisocial characteristics, are predictors of early onset substance abuse.

Some scientists, while not discounting the genetic predisposition in some individuals, focus on the learning model, and refer to research with other animals as evidence that most humans can become addicted (Higgins & Heil, 2004). Operant conditioning theory posits that we repeat behaviors when they are positively reinforced. Laboratory animals have used lethal doses of some drugs, or used drugs while neglecting food, because the drug is self-reinforcing. Environmental stimuli can also become associated with the reinforcement, so that when a certain setting and pleasurable consequences (intoxication) are paired often enough, the setting alone will produce the desire for the drug. Social learning theory would emphasize that we learn by modeling. Those who grow up in families with substance abuse observe many instances of that behavior, which may be a partial explanation of the high rates of addiction in children of addicted parents.

Operant conditioning: Modifying behavior by using rewards (positive reinforcement) and punishment (negative reinforcement). Positive reinforcement increases a behavior, while negative reinforcement decreases it.

Fetuses and Neonates

When women use substances during pregnancy, the developing child is affected. At least 20% of unborn children are exposed to legal substances (including alcohol and tobacco) and 10% to illegal drugs (King, 1997). Alcohol is a *teratogen*, an external agent that causes birth defects. The most severe damage occurs during the first three months of pregnancy; the effects are intensified if poor nutrition is also present. The most well-known negative outcome is *fetal alcohol syndrome* (FAS), which is characterized by slow growth (before and after birth), facial deformities, and central nervous system disorders. FAS is the most common cause of mental retardation. However, the syndrome does not invariably occur when alcohol has been used, and rates of FAS babies vary among chronic alcoholics from 6% to 50%. A less severe consequence is *fetal alcohol effect*, in which only the central nervous system problems are detected. This condition affects three times the number of children than does FAS. Problems that appear in the later stages of development include hyperactivity, incoordination, language problems, impulsivity, poor judgment, learning problems, seizures, and distractibility (Jacobson & Jacobson, 2003). In some neonates exposed to alcohol before birth, withdrawal symptoms may be observed: hyperactivity, crying, irritability, poor sleeping patterns, excessive eating, and excessive perspiring. These symptoms may persist until the child is 18 months old.

Teratogen: A chemical that can cause birth defects.

Crack (a form of cocaine) babies received considerable media attention when it became clear that children could be born with addictions. In some cases, use of crack and cocaine causes spontaneous abortion and death in utero. Birth weight tends to be low, and there is an increase in reports of micrencephaly in these babies. Newborns may experience the equivalent of withdrawal symptoms in adults, with shaking or tremors, irritability, vomiting and diarrhea, high-pitched crying, seizures,

Micrencephaly: Having an abnormally small brain.

and problems in sucking frequently observed. As they develop, these babies may exhibit cognitive and neurological problems as well. Neonatal withdrawal symptoms are found in 60% of fetuses exposed to drugs in utero.

There is also evidence that prenatal exposure to drugs leads to difficulties with emotional and behavioral self-control as children grow up. Complicating the picture is the fact that in many cases where prenatal substance abuse occurs, ongoing substance use by caregivers may lead to neglect, inadequate health care and nutrition, and generally ineffective parenting beyond the perinatal period.

Tarter (2002) points out that the deficiencies in cognitive and behavioral skills associated with the prenatal exposure to substances increases the likelihood that the child will be vulnerable to substance use in childhood and adolescence. In addition, temperament in infancy is known to influence the quality of caregiver's parenting, and infants experiencing withdrawal are less likely to receive parental investment. It is also the case that those children who are maltreated in early childhood are at higher risk for developing substance abuse problems later. De Bellis (1999) describes the physiological changes that occur in major biological stress response systems of abused children, and links these changes to increased risk of later substance abuse. It is conceivable that infants who are difficult to soothe because of symptoms of intrauterine substance use may also be prone to child maltreatment, increasing the odds that they will later develop substance abuse problems.

Children

Although substance abuse typically emerges in adolescence, there are some indicators in childhood that portend increased risk for later substance abuse. In addition to child abuse, mentioned above, temper tantrums and noncompliance in early childhood are risk factors, as is non-criminal antisocial conduct during childhood (Conger, 1997; Greene et al., 1999). Additional risks factors are alienation from school and school truancy (especially when accompanied by inadequate parental supervision), and affiliation with deviant peers. Awareness of risk factors is important for counselors who have the opportunity to intervene early to deflect some of these effects. Some children do begin to experiment with substances before adolescence: Substance Abuse and Mental Health Services Administration (SAMHSA) data revealed that of the 74% of people over 21 who reported starting to drink alcohol before age 21, 4% started drinking before age 12. In that same study, 16% of those who started drinking before age 12 reported substance abuse or dependence in the past year compared to only 2.6% of those who started drinking after age 21. It is clear that early use of alcohol (and most likely other drugs) increase the likelihood that substance abuse or dependence will develop.

Inhalants   Inhalants, one category of substances abused by children, are often the first psychoactive drug children use. Inhalant use appears to be on the increase, despite a recent decline in the use of many other substances. In addition, the proportion of 8th graders who think inhalants are dangerous has declined in each of the last three years.

More than 25% of sixth graders (and 3% of fourth graders) have used inhalants at least once, and use in children as young as six to eight is not unheard of. The peak age of inhalant abuse is in middle school (ages 14 to 15) with use typically diminishing by age 19 or so. Continued use beyond this age is more common in males than females. One reason for the young age of users is availability: inhalants are readily available in stores in the community. Recall that inhalants are not illegal—they are substances used for psychoactive effects that are intended for other purposes.

Inhalant: A substance or chemical in vapor or aerosol form that is inhaled.

There are four general categories of inhalants: *solvents* (liquids that vaporize at room temperatures, such as paint thinner, gasoline, and correction fluid), *aerosols* (which contain solvents and propellants, including spray paint and hair spray), *gases* (such as anesthetics, octane boosters, butane lighters, refrigerants), and *nitrites*, used as sexual enhancers (video head cleaner, leather cleaner). Inhalant users have many ways to ingest these substances: sniffing or snorting the fumes from containers, spraying aerosols directly into nose or mouth, inhaling fumes from inhalants placed in plastic bags, inhaling from a rag soaked in inhalants, and inhaling from balloons filled with nitrous oxide. The "high" is short-lived, prompting users to inhale repeatedly over a span of hours. Inhalants operate by depressing the central nervous system and activating the brain's dopamine system (the pleasure response). Nitrites operate differently, by relaxing blood vessels.

Inhalant intoxication is similar to alcohol intoxication. With increased consumption, solvents and gases produce anesthesia and a loss of sensation, occasionally unconsciousness. Some long-term users experience compulsive use and may experience withdrawal symptoms. Medical consequences can be very serious in heavy users: widespread and long-lasting brain damage and central nervous system damage is one toxic effect of chronic use. Mild impairment of cognitive abilities can occur, as can severe dementia. Coordination problems, loss of hearing and vision, heart damage, lung, liver, and kidney damage are all possible in chronic users. Decreased brain mass can be seen on CT scans and MRIs. Solvents actually dissolve brain cells, which have high fat concentrations. There is a syndrome, "sudden sniffing death," that can happen in even one session of inhalant use. It is most often associated with use of butane, propane, and aerosols. These substances can cause irregular and rapid heartbeat, with heart failure and death following within minutes. Sudden sniffing death usually occurs when the user is startled during inhalation as a result of the increase in adrenaline. Of those deaths attributed to this condition, 22% had no prior history of inhalant abuse. Death from inhalant use is also caused by asphyxiation, suffocation, convulsions, choking, and injuries sustained while intoxicated on inhalants.

It is obvious that inhalant use is extremely harmful, and because of the availability to youthful users, is a major concern. Experts recommend prevention efforts beginning in kindergarten, along with research to identify what interventions and programs are most effective. Counselors who notice (or hear from parents) about unusual changes in a child's behavior (drunk or disoriented, slurred speech, lack of coordination, loss of appetite, and especially chemical odors or other evidence of stains or empty containers) should investigate whether the child might be using inhalants.

Adolescents

One reason for focused attention on adolescent substance abuse is that substance use is only rarely initiated either before or after this development period (Schulenberg, Maggs, Steinman, & Zucker, 2001). Among adolescents in the United States, substance abuse is the most prevalent cause of mortality, with death resulting from motor vehicle accidents, suicide, violence, and unprotected sexual activity. Consequences of adolescent substance abuse include academic problems, family disruption, and legal problems. It has been estimated that 1.4 million adolescents aged 12–17 have current substance abuse problems, and that only 10% of those receive treatment (Brannigan, Schackman, Falco, & Millman, 2004).

Recent research has increased our understanding of brain development during adolescence. We now know that the brain undergoes major changes, forming new connections among neurons and pruning existing connections. The changes affect planning, decision making, impulse control, voluntary movement, memory, and speech production. In addition, the parts of the brain that control the way a person responds to psychoactive substances also undergo change, and thus adolescents appear to be affected differently than adults (Spear, 2000). For example, it appears that alcohol may affect memory more in adolescents than in adults, and the changes may be longer-lasting (Watkins, Ellickson, Vaiana, & Hiromoto, 2006). Alcohol has been found to reduce the size of the hippocampus, a brain structure associated with memory and learning (Butler, 2006; DeBellis et al., 2000). Adolescents may also be less sensitive than adults to some of the effects produced by alcohol consumption. While this line of research is in the early stages, results suggest that adolescents may be able to stay awake and be mobile with higher concentrations of alcohol in their system than adults (National Institute of Alcohol Abuse (NIAA), 2003). This accumulating evidence points to an increased vulnerability to addiction during adolescence (Watkins et al., 2006).

Although some people view any adolescent use of substances, including tobacco, as abuse because they are not of legal age to use these substances, most experts agree that some use of alcohol and tobacco can be considered normative (Kaminer & Tarter, 2004). By the age of 18, approximately 80% of American youth have drunk alcohol and 4% drink regularly. Interestingly, only 66% have used tobacco by that age. In addition, 8% have used cocaine, 15% have used inhalants, stimulants, or hallucinogens. It is important to note that most adolescents who use substances do not develop substance use disorders, and that for many individuals, heavy substance use is limited to this period of life (Kaminer & Tarter).

There are several approaches to understanding why some youth do develop substance abuse problem during adolescence. Keep in mind that adolescence is a time of numerous transitions. Some readily apparent changes are puberty and the move into middle school or junior high. Other changes include cognitive maturation (adolescents enter Piaget's formal operations stage and are able to think abstractly and hypothetically), increased independence and separation from parents with a focus on peer relationships, and identity development, which is a primary development task of this period.

When adolescents move to middle school and high school, they typically have increased exposure to older teens, who may influence them to use substances

(Tarter, 2002). Early maturing females are at particular risk in this regard, as they may be attracted to and interested in older males who use substances. They also may have increased access to social and other peer activities in which substances are used. An additional factor for many teens is the opportunity to find employment, increasing the availability of discretionary funds. Teens who work learn many useful skills and values, but also have increased financial resources at a time when they do not have increased financial obligations. Some teens will find that obtaining substances is facilitated by their financial status.

One model seeking to explain adolescent substance abuse focuses on the overload some adolescents experience during this transition. When the transitions exceed the current coping capacity of an adolescent, the youth may utilize less effective coping strategies such as substance use to manage stress (Schulenberg et al., 2001). Another perspective considers the influence of a developmental mismatch, which occurs when the developmental needs of the individual are in conflict with the context or setting in which the adolescent must function. When the adolescent needs more independence and opportunities for exploration and finds that parents and school personnel provide close monitoring and supervision, some of them will use substances in an effort to exert independence.

Another approach is the "pathways" perspective that suggests that the adolescent transition is more difficult for those who have struggled in previous developmental stages. Recall the overview of Erikson's psychosocial theory of development discussed early in this book. For adolescents who have already developed self-defeating thoughts about themselves and their place in the world, and who have found support from deviant peers who engage in risky behaviors, substance abuse in the adolescent stage is more likely. Note that a certain degree of risk-taking is a normal part of adolescent identity exploration, and substance use may be part of that normal experimentation. Another view suggests that in times of increased change, people in transition may be more open to trying novel experiences, such as substance use, as part of exploring their new contexts.

Researchers have attempted to define the differences between early adolescents (7th to 9th graders) who abstain from substances and those who experiment. They found significant differences in levels of stress (experimenters reported higher levels), levels of parental support (experimenters reported lower levels), coping strategies (experimenters' strategies were less adaptive) and deviance-prone attitudes (experimenters' attitudes were more deviant) (Wills, McNamara, Vaccaro, & Hirky, 1997). Other researchers have identified certain characteristics that influence the age at which persons begin using substances, how much and often they use, and the degree of negative consequences they experience. Behavioral characteristics include impulsivity, aggression, difficulty delaying gratification, and high levels of risk taking. In addition, the presence of psychiatric disorders, especially conduct disorder, greatly increases the risk for substance abuse in adolescence. There are also characteristics of the environment that affect substance use patterns in adolescents. When there are stressful events, an absence of parental support, easy availability of drugs, and social and peer values that accept drug use, the adolescent is at higher risk for substance abuse. Obviously these behavioral and environmental risk factors are additive and interactive, so that the more of these factors that are present, the greater the risk for substance abuse.

It is important to mention the widely known "gateway hypothesis," proposed by Kandel. She noted that there is a progression in drug use behavior that is common. The progression goes from beer or wine to cigarettes or hard liquor to marijuana to other illegal drugs. Kandel (2002) says, "Entry into a particular stage is a common and perhaps even a necessary step but is not a sufficient prerequisite for entry into the next higher stage. Many youths stop at a particular stage without progressing further" (p. 4). One study cited by Kandel found that of those youth who used alcohol and tobacco, about half progressed to other illegal drugs.

Gateway hypothesis: Kandel's theory that an introduction to drug use via tobacco, alcohol, and marijuana is related to later use of other illegal drugs.

Knight (1997) proposed a cycle of adolescent substance use, which begins with abstinence. Many teens then move to experimental use, which typically involves friends (both as sources of the substance and co-users). During the period of experimental use, substance use produces a mild euphoria, and a return to baseline levels of mood and functioning follows use. For some experimenters, serious consequences can ensue from consuming too much of the substance (alcohol poisoning or drug overdose, automobile accidents). Some teens then progress to the stage of regular use, which in adolescents often means frequent binge drinking (defined as more than five drinks consumed at one sitting). Regular use moves to problem use when negative consequences accumulate (school failure, interpersonal problems, legal problems) although the adolescent does not see the relationship between these problems and his/her substance use. Although the euphoria of intoxication is still associated with intoxication, problem users may not return to the baseline mood after using. They may experience anxiety and guilt feelings after bouts of substance use. It is in this stage that Knight theorizes that some adolescents will increase their patterns of use (more quantity and/or frequency) and possibly move on to harder drugs. At this point, most adolescents are still able to stop using or reduce their use to earlier levels with little intervention, but others move on to the stages of substance abuse and dependence, which usually require professional intervention and treatment. Characteristics of effective treatment for adolescents will be discussed later in this chapter.

Trends in drug use and preferences in adolescence are followed closely by various agencies, and the Monitoring the Future (MTF) Survey is often examined for changes over time. One substance that has gradually gained popularity over the last 15 years is sedatives, which reached a high in 2005, with 7.2% of high school seniors reporting having used them for nonmedical purposes (NIDA, 2006). Steroid use declined for high school seniors from 2.5% in 2004 to 1.5% in 2005. Steroid use did not change in that period for 8th or 10th graders. Steroid use is a concern because some of the physiological changes may be permanent, and risk is elevated for liver and heart disease, stroke, aggression, and depression in users of both sexes (Volkow, 2006). A third substance that is increasing among adolescence is opiates, including heroin, and the prescription drugs OxyContin and Vicodin. Heroin use has doubled in 10 years, and the use of prescription opioids has increased even more (Zickler, 2006). The use of cold medicine and cough syrup as intoxicants has also shown an increase among youth (Associated Press, 2006). Counselors need to be alert to current trends, and be sure to inquire about all substances that may be abused by adolescent clients (Watkins et al., 2006).

College Students

Although most college students are technically still adolescents and are subject to many of the same factors described above, there are additional pressures that increase the risk of substance use in this segment of the population. The problem is most severe during the freshman year, when students are adjusting to the new environment (Dimeff, Baer, Kivlahan, & Marlatt, 1999). For many youth, the freshman year of college is their first experience of independence and living away from family. Deaths (1,400 per year) from alcohol-related injuries, assaults, and unsafe sexual encounters are unfortunate consequences of the increased use of substances in college students. In addition, academic problems and health problems also are associated with this behavior. Knight, Wechsler, Kuo, Seibring, Weitzman, and Schuckit (2002) reported an alarming rate of 31% of college students who met the criteria for alcohol abuse and 6% who met the criteria for alcohol dependence in the previous year.

College students report they drink to get drunk and commonly engage in binge drinking. These behaviors are more likely among sports fans (Nelson & Wechsler, 2003). Among other reasons, alcohol is promoted at sports events, and sporting events may be viewed at bars, which further encourage increased use by offering special promotions during sporting events. In areas close to many colleges and universities, numerous establishments selling alcohol rely on college students for their business. College students find themselves in a context in which drinking is entrenched and customary. In a time when some are dealing with the adjustment of being away from family, there may be increased vulnerability to messages promoting alcohol as a route to social acceptance.

Although colleges and universities are well aware of the problem, and have expended considerable effort in attempting to prevent substance abuse, the problem persists. Treatment strategies for this subgroup of adolescents must take the context into account.

Adults

Young adults are at greatest risk for developing an alcohol problem in their early 20s, but most heavy drinkers change their patterns of use by their late 20s. Most adults with substance abuse disorders begin to use substances in early developmental stages, but treatment may not occur until adulthood. Adults with chronic substance abuse are likely to have difficulty maintaining obligations to family, job, and community, and it is often the case that failure to maintain responsibilities is the precipitant to seeking treatment. They are also likely to have other psychiatric disorders as well, with one study finding 45% of individuals with an alcohol use disorder and 72% of those with a drug use disorder had at least one other psychiatric diagnosis (Brady & Malcolm, 2004). Treatment programs generally were designed for adults, and these will be discussed below.

The Elderly

Some experts believe that substance abuse among the elderly (those over age 65) has reached epidemic proportions (Elderly Alcohol and Substance Abuse, 2005; Gfroerer, Penne, Pemberton, & Folsom, 2002; McGrath, Crome, & Crome, 2007; Onen, Onen,

Mangeon, Abidi, Courpron, & Schmidt, 2005; Widlitz & Marin, 2000), but at the same time, problems in this group are least likely to be noticed or treated. One study reported a prevalence of substance use disorders in the elderly to be 20% (Widlitz & Marin). Elderly individuals may not be routinely screened for substance abuse problems, and problems that are caused by substance abuse (such as cognitive impairment) may be incorrectly attributed to other causes (Whelan, 2003). In addition, substance use in the elderly is often complicated by the use of prescription and over-the-counter medication.

At present, the vast majority of elderly substance abusers use alcohol (Gfroerer, 2004). However, as the baby boomers age, the rate of substance abuse in that group is expected to increase overall, with a notable increase in illicit drugs. The population of those over age 50 is projected to increase by 50% from 2000 to 2020, with an accompanying increase of 70% in rates of substance abuse in that group, and an increase in the number of substance abusing or dependent older adults expected to increase by 150%! This means that primary care physicians and mental health professionals should be prepared to screen for and treat these problems.

While some elderly substance abusers have abused substances throughout their lives, there are some who do not initiate this behavior until their senior years. These patterns are known as *hardy survivors* (early onset) and *late onset*, respectively (Benshoff, Harrawood, & Koch, 2003), although others refer to these patterns as *chronic* versus *situational*. Estimates are that two-thirds of those elderly persons with alcohol problems are early onset drinkers. Almost all late onset substance abusers use alcohol rather than other drugs. However, abuse of prescription drugs, benzodiazepines (prescribed for insomnia, anxiety, pain) in particular, is also a serious problem and should not be ignored. There is speculation that the baby boomer generation may use substances after age 65 at a higher rate than previous generations.

There are several factors that complicate substance abuse in the elderly. Regarding alcohol, metabolism of alcohol slows with age, and so alcohol use is likely to cause more damage in an elderly person than in a younger person, given the same level of consumption. They have increased sensitivity to the effects of alcohol and decreased tolerance, which may be a function of the loss of body mass, a by-product of the aging process. In this age group, falls result in serious consequences, and there is a correlation between falling and the use of psychoactive substances. In addition, mood and anxiety disorders in this age group are exacerbated by the use of alcohol and other drugs.

Many assessment procedures will not be applicable to elderly clients, but there are several new approaches for this group that will be discussed below.

Assessment

Effective treatment of substance use disorders depends on an accurate assessment. In this section, I will review common assessment approaches that practitioners might use in a general practice. Given the prevalence of substance disorders in all groups, it makes sense to have procedures in place to screen clients for this widespread problem. I have had several clients come for counseling for other problems, and only later did I realize that substance abuse was involved and needed clinical attention. Certainly asking about substance abuse should be part of all routine initial interviews, so that the counselor can determine whether a more in-depth assessment is appropriate. Counselors should keep in mind that clients who do not meet DSM-IV-TR criteria for a substance abuse or dependence disorder may nevertheless exhibit harmful or risky behaviors with substances that should be addressed as part of treatment.

There are a great many instruments for assessing substance abuse problems, and I will not list all of them here. I will discuss several commonly used instruments that have no cost to counselors, and a few instruments that do require a cost but which have particular interest. There are several publications and websites, listed under Additional Resources, which have lists and sources of the most available instruments. The counselor can review those if a specific need arises.

There are a number of short screening instruments that can be employed by most counselors without specialized training in substance abuse. Some counselors who do not specialize in substance abuse may be reluctant to broach this topic. A useful way to frame any assessment is to tell clients in initial interviews that you believe it is important to do a thorough assessment to avoid overlooking something that could be important. If you stress that you want to provide the best possible services, and that in your experience many areas of a person's life may be affected by the presenting problem, most clients appreciate the attention to their case.

You will note that there are more instruments that focus on alcohol than those that include drugs. I will review some of the most widely used assessments next, and then discuss those instruments designed for specific age groups. Many of these assessments are in the public domain, which means there is no permission necessary and no cost for using them. Instruments vary in their sensitivity (ability to detect substance abuse when it exists) and specificity (ability to correctly identify non-abusers), and the clinician considering an instrument for use should always check these rates. For example, an instrument can have 100% sensitivity by classifying everyone as a substance abuser; all substance abusers would be correctly identified. It is therefore essential to be certain that sensitivity is not attained at the expense of specificity.

The CAGE

The CAGE (Ewing, 1984) is a four-question assessment for alcohol disorders (the CAGE-AID was developed later to include drugs in addition to alcohol) that is widely used because it is easy to remember and very quick to administer (see Figure 5.1). It has been translated into several languages. The questions usually asked are related to lifetime use (e.g., "Have you ever . . ."), but can be more focused. This instrument is more likely to identify alcohol-dependent persons, but may miss those who binge drink. It has

FIGURE 5.1   The CAGE.

1. Have you felt the need to **C**ut down on your drinking?
2. Do you feel **A**nnoyed by people complaining about your drinking?
3. Do you ever feel **G**uilty about your drinking?
4. Do you ever drink an **E**ye-opener in the morning to relieve the shakes?

been found to be less sensitive for women. A score of 2 or more indicates the need for further evaluation; a cutoff score of 1 has been found to result in 47% of false positives.

The Michigan Alcoholism Screening Test

The Michigan Alcoholism Screening Test (MAST; Selzer, 1971) is another well-known instrument that is in the public domain and easy to use (Figure 5.2). The twenty-five items can be administered as a paper-and-pencil test or in an interview format. There are also short (13-item) and brief (10-item) versions available as well. The MAST can be administered in about eight minutes and scored in five minutes. It can be found online,

FIGURE 5.2   Michigan Alcoholism Screening Test (MAST).

Item	Pts			
1.	2	YES	NO	Do you feel you are a normal drinker?
2.	2	YES	NO	Have you ever awakened the morning after some drinking the night before and found that you could not remember part of the evening before?
3.	2	YES	NO	Does your wife (husband, parents) ever worry or complain about your drinking?
4.	2	YES	NO	Can you stop drinking without a struggle after one or two drinks?
5.	1	YES	NO	Do you ever feel bad about your drinking?
6.	2	YES	NO	Do friends or relatives think you are a normal drinker?
7.	2	YES	NO	Do you ever try to limit your drinking to certain times of the day or to certain places?
8.	2	YES	NO	Are you always able to stop drinking when you want to?
9.	5	YES	NO	Have you ever attended a meeting of AA?
10.	1	YES	NO	Have you gotten into fights when drinking?
11.	2	YES	NO	Has drinking ever created problems w/ you and your wife (husband)?
12.	2	YES	NO	Has your wife (husband, family members) ever gone to anyone for help about your drinking?
13.	2	YES	NO	Have you ever lost friends, girlfriends/ boyfriends because of your drinking?
14.	2	YES	NO	Have you ever gotten into trouble at work because of drinking?
15.	2	YES	NO	Have you ever lost a job because of drinking?

16.	2	YES	NO	Have you ever neglected your obligations, your family, or your work for 2 or more days in a row because you were drinking?
17.	1	YES	NO	Do you ever drink before noon?
18.	2	YES	NO	Have you ever been told you have liver trouble?
19.	2	YES	NO	Have you ever had delirium tremens, severe shaking, heard voices, or seen things that weren't really there after heavy drinking?
20.	5	YES	NO	Have you ever gone to anyone for help about your drinking?
21.	5	YES	NO	Have you ever been hospitalized because of your drinking?
22.	2	YES	NO	Have you ever been a patient in a psychiatric hospital or on a psychiatric ward of a general hospital where drinking was part of the problem?
23.	2	YES	NO	Have you ever been seen at a mental health clinic (gone to a doctor, social worker, clergyman) for help with emotional problems in which drinking has played a part?
24.	2	YES	NO	Have you ever been arrested, even for a few hours, because of drunk behavior?
25.	2	YES	NO	Have you ever been arrested for drunk driving or driving after drinking?

SCORING: A score of three points or less is considered non-alcoholic, four points is suggestive of alcoholism, a score of five points or more indicates alcoholism.

with immediate feedback to the client. The MAST does not assess for problem use of drugs other than alcohol, and has a tendency to produce false positives. There is a modified MAST/AD (Westermeyer, Yargic, & Thuras, 2004) that includes drugs in each of the twenty-four questions. Thus, clinicians should not rely on this test for anything other than initial screening. There is a version of the MAST specifically for the elderly population with twenty-four items (MAST-G), which has acceptable reliability and validity data.

The AUDIT

The AUDIT (Babor et al., 1992) is a 10-item screening questionnaire that can be administered in less than two minutes (see Figure 5.3). It was developed for the World Health Organization. It is also in the public domain so there is no fee associated with use of this questionnaire. A training module is available for a fee.

FIGURE 5.3   Alcohol Use Disorders Identification Test.

AUDIT

Please circle the answer that is correct for you

1. How often do you have a drink containing alcohol?

    Never

    Monthly or less

    Two to four times a month

    Two to three times per week

    Four or more times a week

2. How many drinks containing alcohol do you have on a typical day when you are drinking?

    1 or 2

    3 or 4

    5 or 6

    7 to 9

    10 or more

3. How often do you have six or more drinks on one occasion?

    Never

    Less than monthly

    Monthly

    Two to three times per week

    Four or more times a week

4. How often during the last year have you found that you were not able to stop drinking once you had started?

    Never

    Less than monthly

    Monthly

    Two to three times per week

    Four or more times a week

5. How often during the last year have you failed to do what was normally expected from you because of drinking?

    Never

    Less than monthly

    Monthly

    Two to three times per week

    Four or more times a week

6. How often during the last year have you needed a first drink in the morning to get yourself going after a heavy drinking session?

   Never

   Less than monthly

   Monthly

   Two to three times per week

   Four or more times a week

7. How often during the last year have you had a feeling of guilt or remorse after drinking?

   Never

   Less than monthly

   Monthly

   Two to three times per week

   Four or more times a week

8. How often during the last year have you been unable to remember what happened the night before because you had been drinking?

   Never

   Less than monthly

   Monthly

   Two to three times per week

   Four or more times a week

9. Have you or someone else been injured as a result of your drinking?

   No

   Yes, but not in the last year

   Yes, during the last year

10. Has a relative or friend, or a doctor or other health worker been concerned about your drinking or suggested you cut down?

   No

   Yes, but not in the last year

   Yes, during the last year

Procedure for Scoring AUDIT – Questions 1–8 are scored 0, 1, 2, 3 or 4. Questions 9 and 10 are scored 0, 2 or 4 only. The response is as follows:

   0

   1

   2

   3

   4

(*continued*)

FIGURE 5.3   Continued

Question 1

   Never

   Monthly or less

   Two to four times per month

   Two to three times per week

   Four or more times per week

Question 2

   1 or 2

   3 or 4

   5 or 6

   7 to 9

   10 or more

Questions 3–8

   Never

   Less than monthly

   Monthly

   Weekly

   Daily or almost daily

Questions 9–10

   No

   Yes, but not in the last year

   Yes, during the last year

The minimum score (for non-drinkers) is 0 and the maximum possible score is 40. A score of 8 or more indicates a strong likelihood of hazardous or harmful alcohol consumption.

The Addiction Severity Index

The Addiction Severity Index, 5th edition (ASI; McLellan, Luborsky, O'Brien, & Woody, 1980; McLellan et al., 1992), is widely used but is probably best reserved for counseling that is more focused on substance abuse issues, as it is more detailed than instruments that are designed for screening purposes. It is useful for treatment planning and for outcome evaluation. It is a semi-structured interview format that includes 200 items and can take an hour to administer, and thus is unlikely to be used unless there is already sufficient information to suggest a serious problem with substances. It does address both alcohol and drugs, has adequate psychometric properties, and has norms for a variety of populations. It is in the public domain, and can be obtained at http://www.tresearch.org/resources/instruments/ASI_5th_Ed.pdf.

The Substance Abuse Subtle Screening Inventory—II

The Substance Abuse Subtle Screening Inventory—II (Miller, 1999) is different from the instruments above in several ways. First, it does include both alcohol and other drugs. Second, it was developed to detect substance abuse problems even when the person is trying to conceal them. Third, it is not in the public domain and must be purchased. It is available in several formats including computerized versions. There are both adult and adolescent versions and there is a Spanish version of the adult form available as well. The tests take clients about 15–20 minutes at most to complete (there are audiotapes available if literacy is a problem). In addition to an indication about substance abuse disorders, the profile provides additional clinical information that the counselor may find quite useful. Although special training is not required, it is available and can be quite helpful. The authors report excellent reliability and validity, but I have some concerns about their conclusions. You can read my detailed review of the revised adolescent version at http://aac.ncat.edu/newsnotes/y02win.html.

The Drug Use Screening Inventory

Another instrument that does evaluate both drug and alcohol concerns is the Drug Use Screening Inventory (DUSI; Tarter, 1990), which was designed for adolescents but now has an adult version as well. This inventory assesses problems in ten areas, of which one is substance abuse. Scores are given both as relative severity of these areas, as well as absolute severity in each area. As these areas are often related, the information is important for treatment planning. There are several formats, including computerized formats and interview formats. It is a bit longer than the Substance Abuse Subtle Screening Inventory (SASSI), and takes about 20–40 minutes to administer.

The SOCRATES

The Stages of Change Readiness and Treatment Eagerness Scale (SOCRATES) (Miller & Tonigan, 1996) is designed to determine how the clients' readiness to make changes in their drinking or drug use compares to clients already seeking treatment for those problems. There are separate versions for alcohol and other drugs. Results provide information about whether the testee is high or low on Problem Recognition, Ambivalence, and Taking Steps. This assessment is related to Motivational Interviewing, one of the treatment approaches described below.

This list of available assessment tools is hardly exhaustive, and has focused on screening instruments that can be used by generalist clinicians who do not specialize in substance abuse treatment. See other resources for more extensive lists of assessment tools.

The CRAFFT

The CRAFFT (Knight, Sherritt, Shrier, Harris, & Chang, 2002) is a screening test with good psychometric properties designed specifically for adolescents. Questions include both alcohol and other drugs. This screening test was validated on a diverse

C Have you ever ridden in a *car* driven by someone (including yourself) who was "high" or had been using alcohol or drugs?

R Do you ever use alcohol or drugs to *relax*, feel better about yourself, or fit in?

A Do you ever use alcohol or drugs when you are by yourself, *alone?*

F Do you ever *forget* things you did while using alcohol or drugs?

F Do your family or *friends* ever tell you that you should cut down on your drinking or drug use?

T Have you ever gotten into *trouble* while you were using alcohol or drugs?

© Children's Hospital Boston, 2001
Reproduced with permission from the Center for Adolescent
Substance Abuse Research, CeASAR, Children's Hospital Boston.
For more information, contact info@CRAFFT.org,
or visit www.crafft.org

group of 14- to 18-year-olds seeking routine health care. Authors recommend a cut-off score of 2 as indicative of a need for further assessment of possible substance abuse, and a score of 4 for further assessment of substance dependence. This brief screening would be especially useful for school counselors concerned about identifying youth who may need intervention for substance abuse concerns (Burke, DaSilva, Vaughn, & Knight, 2005). The questionnaire is administered orally; the client responds "yes" or "no"; each "yes" answer scores one point.

Treatment Options

In the United States on any day, there are more than 700,000 people being treated for alcohol dependence, and a large number in drug treatment. Most people think of 12-Step groups (e.g., AA, NA) when they think about treatment for substance abuse. In reality, this is only one of a number of approaches available. It is important for clinicians who do not specialize in substance abuse to recognize the range of options available, and to help the client who is uncertain about what to do to make the most suitable choice for that client, increasing the odds that the person will follow through.

In this field, we do not have to guess about what treatments are most effective. William Miller and his colleagues (Miller, Wilbourne, & Hettema, 2003) have done extensive reviews of published outcome studies, and have created a Cumulative Evidence Score (CES) that takes into account the methodology of the study and the strength of the outcome findings. Table 5.1 lists the most and least effective approaches based on their research. Keep in mind that effectiveness cannot be demonstrated without research, and some approaches have not generated enough research (three studies were the minimum to be included) to be on the list. An overview of the most widely used of these approaches will be included later in this chapter.

For drug abuse, there are less specific data on which approaches are the most effective (Gerstein, 2004). Some of the approaches (12-Step and Oxford House) do not provide sufficient data for analysis. Detoxification as a stand-alone treatment (rather

TABLE 5.1   Most and Least Effective Treatments for Alcohol Abuse and Dependence

Most Effective Treatments	Least Effective Treatments
Brief interventions	Hypnosis
Motivational enhancement therapy	Psychedelic medication
GABA agonist therapy	Alcohol sensitizing agents (Antabuse or Temposil)
Community reinforcement	Non-SSRI antidepressant therapy
Bibliotherapy	Standard treatment
Naltrexone therapy	12-Step facilitation
Behavioral self-control training	Milieu therapy
Social skills training	Anti-anxiety medication therapy
Behavioral marital therapy	Mandated attendance at AA meetings
Nausea aversion therapy	Relaxation therapy
Case management	Confrontational therapy

than as a first phase of a treatment program) has been found to have no effect on future use of substances, and has no documented advantage over untreated withdrawal.

Methadone Maintenance

Among the other approaches that have been evaluated, *methadone maintenance* (for narcotics, especially heroin) has been well studied. Research has consistently demonstrated that clients on methadone maintenance remain voluntarily in treatment longer and show a greater sustained decrease in criminal behavior than those who do not receive methadone maintenance.

Methadone is a synthetic narcotic, taken orally, that occupies the opioid receptors in the brain, reducing cravings while blocking the "high" of narcotic drugs of abuse. It produces a fairly even effect over a 24-hour period, unlike the shorter duration and more intense highs and lows of other opioids. Not all methadone maintenance programs offer the same services, and the one variable that has been found to make a difference in effectiveness is dosage: 60–120 mg/day have the best results, but some programs will prescribe 30–50 mg/day. Lower doses have been associated with poorer outcomes.

Residential Treatment

Long-term residential treatment is another approach to drug abuse. Long-term residential treatment for drug abuse is virtually synonymous with therapeutic communities, which were originally designed to treat severe heroin-dependent clients. Currently, younger cocaine-dependent clients are the majority of the clients in such programs. Length of treatment has decreased significantly from the early (1960s) programs (now typically 6–12 months followed by gradual re-entry into society), and 12-Step programs are often incorporated into the treatment plan. The wide use of group therapy promotes a simulated family, based on the premise that many clients lacked a functional family structure at critical developmental periods. Research on long-term residential treatment has lacked randomized clinical trials necessary to evaluate effectiveness. The limited data available suggest that increased length of treatment is associated with better outcomes such as reduced consumption of illegal drugs and alcohol, reduced criminal activity, and reduced unemployment. One reason for the variation in outcome results is that programs vary considerably on many components, including policies, staff training, and overall design.

Short-term residential treatment programs were designed to treat individuals with alcohol problems, but they now serve those with drug problems as well. These programs tend to be utilized by clients with medical insurance that covers the cost. These programs are known as the Minnesota model or Hazelden-type programs, which are infused with the 12-Step approach. Length of stay is generally three to six weeks. Typical components include in-depth initial evaluation, development of a recovery plan based on the 12-Step model, attendance at educational sessions in which the "disease concept" of chemical dependency is taught and the negative psychological and medical consequences of addiction are stressed. Programs also include family education and therapy. Aftercare is strongly recommended, but is the least developed component in most cases. There are no data about the effectiveness of these programs, despite their widespread popularity.

Guidelines for Effective Treatment of Substance Abuse

NIDA (1999) has developed a set of general principles for effective treatment of drug abuse that are important considerations regardless of the specific approach:

1. No one approach is best. Treatment should be matched to individual needs.
2. Treatment should be accessible and available.
3. Treatment should address not only the individual's substance abuse, but also other problems.
4. Treatment should be flexible and be modified as client needs change.
5. An adequate duration of treatment increases effectiveness. For most clients, three months is the minimum time necessary.
6. Counseling and therapy are important components of treatment.
7. Medication is helpful for many clients.
8. When a substance abuser has other psychiatric diagnoses, both should be treated in a coordinated fashion.
9. Medical detoxification is not a treatment, but may be a first step for treatment in some cases.
10. Involuntary treatment can be effective.
11. Treatment should monitor drug use during treatment.

12. Assessment for HIV/AIDS, hepatitis, and other infectious diseases should be conducted in conjunction with drug abuse treatment.
13. Multiple courses of treatment may be necessary. Follow-up support after treatment can increase success.

A list of components of effective substance abuse treatment for adolescents was generated by Brannigan et al. (2004), who interviewed twenty-two treatment experts. The key elements are as follows:

1. Treatment should be linked to thorough assessment and matched to the individual's needs.
2. Treatment should address other areas of life in addition to substance abuse.
3. Including parents in treatment improves outcomes.
4. Adolescent programs should be geared to that developmental level.
5. In order to engage adolescents, a trusting therapeutic alliance between client and counselor should be developed.
6. Staff delivering treatment programs to adolescents should be qualified and trained.
7. Treatment should reflect awareness of gender and cultural differences.
8. Treatment should include planning for post-treatment needs and services.
9. Treatment programs must evaluate outcomes and use findings to improve treatment services.

In their national survey of 144 highly regarded adolescent treatment programs, Brannigan and colleagues found that most programs fell short: the mean score was 23.8 out of 45 components, with 44% of programs satisfying less than half the components. The element with the highest score overall was "qualified staff," while the lowest scores were obtained on evaluating treatment outcomes, attending to gender and cultural differences, and assessment and matching treatment to client needs. This finding is particularly disturbing as the programs surveyed were considered to be the best in their states.

Medication

Several pharmacological treatments are available for substance abuse. They are generally best employed as adjuncts to a psychosocial approach. Medication can be useful in several situations: if the substance abuser has co-occurring psychiatric disorders that improve with medication, to reduce symptoms of withdrawal, and to reduce cravings and interfere with the intoxicating effects of the drug of choice. In addition, some medications help keep the person in treatment and create an opportunity for psychosocial interventions to be delivered, and reduce the level of criminal activity. As the medication for other psychiatric disorders will vary with the condition, I will discuss only medication used specifically for substance abuse treatment. Note that there are some in the treatment community who oppose the use of any psychotropic medication for addiction treatment.

The first drug to be approved to treat alcoholism was Antabuse (disulfuram) in 1948. This medication interferes with the metabolism of alcohol in the body so that the person will experience extremely unpleasant (sometimes deadly) side effects, including nausea and vomiting, when alcohol is ingested. The intensity of the reaction is related to the amount of Antabuse and the amount of alcohol in the system. The use of this medication requires that the client take it on a daily basis. To ensure compliance, many programs require that the medication be taken in the presence of a counselor, and that the client remain in the presence of the counselor for a long enough period to ensure that the client has actually swallowed the medication. There are some medical conditions that preclude the use of this drug, which must be prescribed by a physician. It is typically used to establish a period of sobriety, after which the psychosocial treatments continue. However, in some cases, Antabuse can be continued indefinitely.

Naltrexone was approved in 1994 for substance abuse treatment. It operates very differently from Antabuse, in that it does not interact with alcohol or affect alcohol metabolism, nor does it produce tolerance or dependence. It is an *antagonist* that works by blocking brain receptors for endorphins (naturally produced opiate-like chemicals that create the "high") so that the desirable effects of alcohol or opiates are not experienced. It is usually taken daily, and is used to treat alcoholism as well as problems with opiates.

Heroin and other opiates cause an excess of the neurotransmitter dopamine to be released in the body, so that users eventually need opiates to constantly occupy the opioid receptors in the brain. *Agonists*, such as methadone, are synthetic narcotics that activate (rather than block) these receptors in the brain. When methadone is taken orally on a daily basis, it keeps the person from experiencing withdrawal symptoms for 24–36 hours. It also decreases cravings and blocks the "high" from heroin. Methadone users do not experience the fluctuating highs and lows of heroin, which acts quickly but then produces extreme lows that cause the user to need another dose. Methadone users are dependent on this drug, but are able to stabilize their lives and reduce criminal activity associated with heroin use.

Several other medications are used in some clients to treat alcoholism or opiate addiction. Levo-alpha-acetyl methadol (LAMM) received FDA approval in 1994 for treatment of opioid dependence. It is similar to naltrexone but works for a longer period of time, so a client needs to take it only three times per week. However, several serious side effects were reported and several manufacturers stopped selling this medication. Buprenorphine is another (partial) agonist that allows those addicted to opiates to stop using heroin without experiencing withdrawal. It has fewer side effects than opioid agonists. A recent random-controlled study found that adolescents who took buprenorphine had better attendance in outpatient counseling sessions than peers who took clonodine, had higher rates of treatment completion, and greater willingness to enroll in continued treatment (Zickler, 2006).

Even when these medications are used, psychosocial treatments and counseling are recommended. It is believed by those who promote their use that these medications assist the client in abstaining from their addictive drugs and alcohol, and allows the client to benefit from other elements of treatment and to be more compliant with treatment.

Brief Therapies

Brief therapies for substance abuse initially gained attention because they are less costly than more extensive approaches to treatment. However, studies have determined that these approaches are also effective, and can be provided in less restrictive settings than many longer-term approaches. Of the brief approaches, I will describe three: solution-focused, motivational interviewing, and brief cognitive-behavioral treatment. These approaches have several things in common in addition to brevity: they focus on the symptom rather than underlying causes, they work toward specific goals, they utilize active therapeutic techniques. These approaches also enhance the client's self-efficacy for change, and believe that the responsibility for change remains with the client.

Solution-Focused Treatment for Substance Abuse. Brief solution-focused treatment for substance abuse is an application of the more general solution-focused approach. In this approach, the focus is on client successes and strengths. In addition, the frame of reference and goals for treatment are the client's, not the therapist's. This means that if the client's goal is reduced use of substances rather than abstinence, the therapist accepts that goal. The client's solution is sought, not the therapist's. This is markedly different from more well-known approaches in which abstinence is the only acceptable goal and the therapist takes the position of expert. Small changes are seen as having a snowball effect, and as such are to be encouraged. Treatment seeks to identify what the client is already doing to reduce or eliminate the problem behavior, and support the client in implementing what has already been found to work. The client–counselor relationship is a cooperative one, and much attention is given to generating goals that are important to the client. Goals should be small, concrete, and specific; behavioral goals should be expressed in positive terms (what will be done rather than what will not be done). They must also be realistic and achievable with appropriate effort.

There are a number of techniques that brief solution-focused therapists use to promote change. The first is to highlight any changes the client makes between setting the appointment with the counselor and the first meeting. The counselor asks the client to describe any changes that have occurred in that pre-session time period. The counselor then seeks exceptions to the problem. In the case of substance abuse, the counselor asks about times when the client has used less often or been abstinent. The "miracle question" is a technique to help the client envision life after the goals have been met. The client is asked to imagine that a miracle happened during the night, and the problem was solved, but the client did not know about this miracle. The client is asked to note the first indication that the problem is solved. This focuses the client on what life will be like without the problem behavior, and gives him an image of positive benefits of change.

Solution-focused therapists also use scaling questions to put a numerical value on the problem. For example, the counselor might ask, "If 10 refers to your life without the problem, and 1 stands for the worst the problem could possible be, what number would describe the problem for you today." Once the client has placed the problem on the scale, the client can be asked what would need to happen to make a small improvement (from 3 to 4 for example). This scaling technique can be used in many ways to help the client reflect on improvement and identify small steps to take. An additional question is the "how do you manage to cope" with life with this problem. This helps clients identify their own resources and validate their strengths. Solution-focused treatment for substance abuse generally involves one to twelve sessions over a three-to-four month period.

Although there are other interventions a solution-focused substance abuse counselor might use, the essential flavor of the approach is captured in the description above. There are treatment manuals and video demonstrations available for the counselor interested in finding out more about this approach.

Motivational Interviewing. Motivational Interviewing is a treatment strategy developed by Miller and Rollnick (1991). The purpose is to assist clients in resolving their ambivalence about quitting and to enhance the client's own motivation to change. This approach is based on a trans-theoretical model of the stages of change that was first proposed by Prochaska and DiClemente in 1983. Treatment typically consists of one to four sessions, with the goal of strengthening the client's commitment to change. According to this theory, behavior change unfolds in a series of stages and effective interventions are targeted to the client's current stage in the process. Motivation is seen as a state that can be influenced by the counselor using supportive and client-centered strategies. The stages of change are shown in Table 5.2.

In contrast to other approaches, client resistance is seen as the counselor's problem rather than the client's. That is, if the client is resisting, the therapist is not matching the intervention to the client's stage of readiness to change. Confrontation is also discouraged in this approach, as it tends to solidify the client's defenses against the counselor's assault. Ambivalence, or uncertainty about change, is viewed as normative, and the client's point of view is accepted rather than challenged. Open-ended questions are used to elicit self-motivating statements from the client. For example, when the results of an assessment are presented objectively (including giving the client's personal score and the "normal" range), the counselor may say, "What do you make of this?" The skill of summarizing is used to condense the client's position: "You are troubled by this DWI and wonder if you are drinking too much, but you are not sure whether you should just be more careful or whether you should stop drinking all together. Is that right?"

TABLE 5.2   Stage of Change

Stage	Client Characteristics
Pre-contemplation	Client does not see a problem, not interested in changing
Contemplation	Client recognizes the problem and is considering whether to change
Preparation	Client is making specific plans to change in the near future
Action	The client is taking steps to change the problem behavior
Maintenance	Client is using strategies to maintain the changes

A signature feature of this approach is the initial assessment. The first session provides feedback on the assessment, and is designed to generate a discussion of the client's use of substances to elicit statements of motivation to change from the client. The main counselor techniques used are expressing empathy, developing discrepancy (between current behavior with substances and future goals), avoiding argument, and "rolling with resistance" (seeing it as part of the process of change rather than blocking change). There are a number of acronyms counselors learn to capture the essential elements of motivational interviewing. Table 5.3 presents the FRAMES mnemonic with the key principles of the theory.

Although this approach is highly individualized to the client's needs and stage of change, it can also be delivered in a group format. A manual for group treatment based on this model is listed in the resources section. A useful discussion of this approach with adolescents can be found in Knight (1997).

A recent research discovery may be very applicable to this approach (Mason, 2007). Bartsch et al. (2007) built on the work of previous research, using sophisticated technology and strict criteria for participation, and concluded that, "remarkable morphological, metabolic, and functional brain regeneration is not just feigned by rehydration and can be attained rapidly by abstinence" (p. 44). In their study, uncomplicated alcoholics were assessed at enrollment in the program, and again between 35 and 42 days later. These findings can be explained to clients, says Mason, which might encourage them to get and stay sober. Some persons with long-term alcoholism believe that the damage to their bodies is irreversible, which reduces their motivation to participate in treatment programs. Mason suggests that the findings in this field of research can be used as a motivation tool to promote the benefits of sobriety.

Brief Cognitive-Behavioral Therapy. Cognitive-Behavioral Therapy (CBT) as applied to substance abuse treatment focuses on helping clients recognize the situations in which they are most likely to use substances, teaching ways to avoid these

TABLE 5.3   Frames

Provide **FEEDBACK** of personal risk or impairment based on initial assessment	Based on objective information, given in non-judgmental manner, with concern
Emphasize personal **RESPONSIBILITY** for change	"You'll have to decide what to do about this."
Give clear **ADVICE** for change	"I hope you decide to do something about this." If asked what to do, "I know what I would do, but I don't know if that would work for you."
Offer a **MENU** of alternative options	Abstinence, vacation from drinking, self-help groups, etc.
Express **EMPATHY**	Role is supportive companion plus consultant
Facilitate client **SELF-EFFICACY** for change, and optimism about success	Reinforce positives in person's efforts, affirm ability to change

high-risk situations, and providing coping skills to manage problems associated with substance abuse. CBT is an educative, directive approach that seeks to help the client alter learned behavior patterns and replace those with more adaptive behaviors. For example, clients are taught how to manage cravings using specific techniques. They are coached in identifying and changing the thinking patterns that maintain the substance use. They learn how small decisions can lead to larger consequences, and are helped to develop problem-solving skills that can be applied to substance related problems. In many cases, assertiveness skills are practiced so that the client is able to avoid high-risk situations.

Unlike the other brief approaches, CBT is highly structured and of longer duration (12–24 weeks), with the therapist taking a very active and directive stance. For those clients who respond well to CBT treatment, a self-help program called Rational Recovery (RR) may be a useful adjunct to treatment. Unlike Alcoholics Anonymous (AA), however, RR groups are not as universally available. One study found that cocaine abusers who receive CBT were more likely to be drug-free four weeks post-treatment than clients who received 12-Step facilitation therapy. Further investigation revealed that CBT was more effective than 12-Step facilitation for those clients who scored higher on a pre-test of abstract reasoning (Maude-Griffin et al., 1998). RR is a self-help program based on the principles of cognitive therapy.

Other Approaches

The Minnesota Model.   The Minnesota Model of treatment developed by Hazelden (a private, non-profit group of treatment centers) subscribes to the disease view of addiction and relies heavily on the 12-Step approach. It is usually a 22–28 day residential treatment program with a goal of lifelong abstinence from psychoactive substances. The client is expected to accept the need for lifelong sobriety and to recognize that the 12-Step program is the only way to accomplish this. Treatment begins with a thorough assessment, from which treatment goals are generated. Most therapy occurs in a group format, with individual sessions used to review and integrate various aspects of the program. This model prefers that the counselor be recovering from substance addiction using a 12-Step approach, but does hire some non-recovering counselors. There is a perception that this model employs harsh confrontational methods, but the program insists this is not the case. Family members are involved in the assessment process, and are invited to educational programs to familiarize them with the disease model of addiction. Family members are urged to become involved in Al-Anon, a 12-Step program for those affected by others' addictions.

Twelve-Step Facilitation.   In this approach, based on the Minnesota model, the client works individually with a counselor, but the 12-Step group is where the real work is done. The program is a highly structured individual outpatient treatment protocol, and is delivered over twelve sessions in twelve weeks. The approach subscribes to the "disease model" of alcoholism and views AA groups as the primary change agent in treatment. In this model, it is necessary that clients accept that they are alcoholic (have the disease of alcoholism, which is progressive and incurable), and that to "recover" from this illness the client must acknowledge their loss of control over alcohol and that a Higher Power can help them recover. This model was developed for alcoholism, but can be applied to other drugs as well. Abstinence is the only acceptable goal.

Clients are expected to attend several 12-Step meetings per week, and to read the "Big Book" of AA. Counselor self-disclosure of recovery status is encouraged, and if the counselor is not in recovery, thorough familiarity with 12-Step philosophy and practice is essential. Counselors who use this approach must have attended many AA meetings themselves (open meetings can be attended by anyone) and have read the AA literature. The role of the therapist is to support the client's involvement in AA, to discuss the client's journal entries, to assign and discuss readings from AA literature.

Relapse Prevention. Because there is strong evidence that relapse (return to substance abuse) is common among substance abusers, Relapse Prevention (RP) Therapy (Marlatt & Gordon, 1985) was designed to prepare clients for high-risk situations that have been found to precipitate a return to substance use. RP views addictions as collections of maladaptive habit patterns that can be changed. This approach, which emphasizes self-management, has been used as a follow-up to other forms of treatment, as an adjunct to other approaches, and as a stand-alone treatment approach. It has been found to be particularly effective with cocaine abusers, for whom treatment has often had disappointing outcomes.

In RP, clients are taught to recognize high-risk situations and practice strategies for dealing with those situations. An analysis of relapse found three common triggers for relapse: negative emotional states, interpersonal conflict, and social pressure. Clients are taught strategies to manage these situations, which increases their confidence for handling these predictable events. Clients also learn how to deal with cravings and how to recognize when life pressures are likely to increase the likelihood of a return to substance abusing behaviors. An important element of RP is responding to a "lapse," or an incident of substance use. The aim is to prevent a lapse from becoming a relapse (returning to former patterns of use and abuse) by framing the lapse as a learning opportunity by which the client can recognize the triggers and renew their skills to respond to such circumstances.

RP employs several interventions to prepare clients to anticipate and prevent relapse: coping skills training is a cornerstone of the approach, along with cognitive therapy (e.g., reframing lapses as learning opportunities), and lifestyle modification. Lifestyle modification encourages positive practices that will strengthen the client's internal coping resources, and include meditation, exercise, and spiritual practices.

There is some evidence that clients who receive RP have lower relapse levels at later times after treatment, suggesting that clients may become better at using this approach with practice. With respect to adolescents, Bell (1990) makes an interesting point: actual relapse rates may not be as high as they appear. The real problem is that many adolescents do not respond to treatment and are discharged without having attained sobriety. They demonstrate pseudo-compliance while in treatment to satisfy adults, but do not internalize the need to change. Bell's book reviews relapse prevention in adolescents, and discusses the specific treatment needs of adolescents with their developmental level in mind.

Harm Reduction.   Harm reduction approaches to substance abuse differ from all other approaches in its de-emphasis of abstinence as the only acceptable goal. Abstinence may not be the most realistic goal for some clients, particularly in the short term (Riley & O'Hare, 2000). Harm reduction does not disparage the value of abstinence, but the emphasis is on reducing harmful effects of the problem behavior. This approach views addiction as "maladaptive coping responses" (Marlatt, 2000), rather than as a disease or as a moral deficiency. Practitioners of harm reduction favor a multifaceted view of the etiology of addictions, recognizing that there are biological, psychological, and social factors that contribute to the development of substance abuse problems. The central principles (Harm reduction defined, n.d.) are:

- Harm reduction is pragmatic, and recognizes that use of drugs and alcohol is a reality.
- Harm reduction avoids moral judgments about the user.
- Harm reduction promotes services that are accessible and user-friendly.
- Harm reduction teaches clients how to reduce risk and harm from using substances.
- Harm reduction neither promotes nor discourages abstinence as a goal.
- Harm reduction helps clients weigh the costs and benefits of using or reducing use of substances.

Typically, harm reduction uses an interactive model in which education is active and clients are encouraged to discuss both abstinence and substance use and to weigh the pros and cons of each. Personal choice and responsibility are emphasized. Role plays are widely used to practice responses to high-risk situations, and moderation skills may be taught. The goal of treatment is to keep the behavior from getting worse, and then reducing the harmful consequences.

Some examples of interventions supported by a harm reduction approach are needle exchange programs (which reduce harm from HIV infection), methadone maintenance, and moderate drinking strategies (including labeling the amount of alcohol in standard serving units, and training alcohol servers in recognizing impaired customers), free transportation services for impaired drivers, and so on. Moderation Management is a self-help program for those consistent with a harm reduction approach.

Brief Alcohol Screening and Intervention for College Students (BASICS; Dimeff et al., 1999) is a harm reduction approach for college students that incorporates the basic principles of harm reduction using cognitive behavioral and motivational interviewing techniques. It is similar to relapse prevention models in terms of the skills taught, but is considered a primary intervention rather than a treatment. Components of the program include:

- Identification of high-risk situations
- Providing accurate information about alcohol
- Identifying personal risk factors for developing alcohol problems
- Challenging myths and positive alcohol expectancies
- Establishing appropriate and safe drinking goals

- Managing high-risk situations
- Learning from mistakes
- Increasing self-efficacy
- Attaining life style balance.

As college students are at elevated risk for harm from alcohol use, this program, which has been adopted on many college campuses around the country, is an effort to avert problems with early information in a format that can be accepted by the target population.

There are numerous other approaches to substance abuse treatment, and a discussion of all of those is beyond the scope of this book. The additional resources section will include information about some of these models that might be suitable for specific clients.

The Matrix Model.   A relatively newer approach to the increase in need for effective treatment for methamphetamine addiction is the Matrix model, which is an intensive outpatient program. Federal agencies are currently studying this approach and are gathering data on the effectiveness of treatment. The Matrix model was originally developed to provide treatment for cocaine addiction, and has been modified to address the increased demand for efficient, effective treatment for methamphetamine addiction (Obert et al., 2000).

The program is delivered over sixteen weeks in a three times per week format based on behavioral, educational, and 12-Step methods. Most sessions use a group format, although individual or couple sessions are sometimes incorporated to address specific individual situations. The Matrix model often utilizes a technique known as *contingency management*, which rewards clients for drug-free urine samples, often with vouchers for groceries, and the like. In some programs, the value of the rewards increases with successive drug-free urine. A major research study recently found that programs using rewards for abstinence were effective in increasing rates of treatment completion, increasing the number of counseling sessions attended, and in the duration of abstinence (Whitten, 2006). The program also includes family participation and relapse prevention components, along with a weekly social support group. Participation in 12-Step programs is emphasized.

Adolescent Models of Treatment

There are some professionals who consider any use of alcohol or other substances by adolescents to be abuse because such use is illegal. This belief results in referring for treatment adolescents who have minimal or experimental use of substances. Such placements are inappropriate, in my opinion. Treatment intensity should be matched to the severity of the problem; adolescents who abstain or experiment are likely to benefit from a proactive educational program rather than treatment.

Although most adolescent treatment programs use the treatment approaches described above and rely heavily on 12-Step programs, many do incorporate adaptations to the developmental needs of this clientele. For example, there is an adaptation of the 12 Steps for adolescents that reduces much of the resistance to the traditional

12 Steps. One version of the modified 12 Steps can be found at http://www.cmcsb. com/12%20Steps%20for%20Teens.html. I do want to mention one approach that has been designed with the developmental needs of adolescents in mind.

Multidimensional Family Therapy.   Multidimensional Family Therapy (MDFT; Athealth, 2001) has been subjected to rigorous scientific studies and has demonstrated *efficacy*—(evidence that the treatment can be effective when administered under controlled conditions). (Note: *Effectiveness* means that a treatment typically has favorable outcomes in actual clinical practice.) The program is manualized to ensure that clinicians provide the treatment in the approved manner. The approach is an out-patient family-based program that has been used with white, African American, and Hispanic teens from inner-city locations. The goal of the approach is to promote positive functioning in many areas of the adolescent's life including peer relationships, school, and age-appropriate identity formation and autonomy. Parents are involved and taught communication strategies and parenting skills.

MDFT takes into account the interconnected systems (individual, family, friends, and community) that influence the adolescent. The approach is built upon knowledge of healthy development. Sessions may be individual, family, or multi-family, and may be held in a treatment facility, in the home, or in locations in the community such as the school or court. Individual sessions with the adolescent focus on skill development in areas such as decision making, communicating about emotional issues, and managing stress. Career and job skills are also included.

When MDFT is delivered as originally designed, it would involve sixteen to twenty-five sessions over four to six months, with sessions sometimes occurring more than once per week. The program is organized around five modules: (1) Interventions with the adolescent; (2) Interventions with the parent; (3) Interventions to change the parent–adolescent interaction; (4) Interventions with other family members; and (5) Interventions with systems external to the family (Center for Treatment Research on Adolescent Drug Use, 2002). A modification of this approach has been developed for use with teens who abuse marijuana (Liddle, 2002).

Issues of Diversity

Gender

Research has identified some important differences between males and females regarding substance abuse, both in terms of how the two sexes respond to substances and their patterns of use and abuse. Regarding alcohol, the metabolism and absorption of alcohol is different in women from these processes in men. A woman who has consumed the same amount of alcohol as a man of the same weight will have a higher blood alcohol concentration than the man. There are two biological reasons for this: women have a smaller proportion of body water than men (so the alcohol is more concentrated rather than diluted). They also have less of the chemical metabolizing enzyme ADH (alcohol dehydrogenase) in the stomach, which allows more of the alcohol to remain in the blood. Hormonal fluctuations in women may also affect blood alcohol concentrations, as estrogen is believed to slow alcohol metabolism (Dimeff et al., 1999). Women appear to be more vulnerable than men to negative health consequences of heavy drinking, including liver and heart diseases.

Advances in neuroimaging technology have allowed scientists to study gender differences more precisely. Researchers using these techniques have learned that the differences in brain volume between alcoholic and nonalcoholic women are greater than the differences between alcoholic and nonalcoholic men, even though the women had fewer years of alcoholism (Hommer, Momenon, Kaiser, & Rawlings, 2001). This finding suggests that women progress more quickly to dependence on alcohol than males, and that the negative effects on the brain occur sooner after the onset of heavy drinking. A more recent, carefully controlled study was able to determine that brain atrophy was reversible with a relative brief (4 week) period of total abstinence (Mann, Ackermann, Croissant, Mundle, Nakovics, & Diehl, 2005).

Atrophy: Decrease in size; wasting away.

A large-scale study by the Center for Addiction and Substance Abuse (CASA) at Columbia University examined gender differences in young persons' (ages 8–22) use and abuse of substances. The three-year study found important differences between males and females. Girls who abuse substances are more likely than boys to be depressed and suicidal, a known risk for substance abuse. They are also more likely than boys to have eating disorders, and to have been physically or sexually abused, both of which are associated with increased risk for substance use disorders. Early-maturing girls use substances earlier and more often than girls who mature later.

In addition to differences in use and risk factors, girls also react differently to substances. They progress more quickly from use to abuse than males, are more likely as teenagers to become addicted to cocaine than their male peers, and have higher susceptibility to medical problems from alcohol (brain damage, liver disease, and heart disease) than males. Increased rates of brain damage from Ecstasy are found in females when compared to males.

Treatment needs may be different for men and women. For example, women may need more emphasis on relapse prevention using social support, leisure activities, and resource acquisition (Walton, Blow, & Booth, 2001). Substance use for women is more often initiated and maintained by an intimate partner or family member, and women are more likely to use substances alone, so developing social support and leisure activities outside this circle is essential. There are several variations of the 12 Principles of AA created specifically for women: The Feminist Twelve Steps can be found at http://www.religion-online.org/showarticle.asp?title=923, and the Sixteen Steps are included in Kasl's *Many Roads, One Journey* (1992), listed in the references for this chapter.

Race and Ethnicity

There are differences in the rates and patterns of substance abuse problems among racial and ethnic groups; there are also cultural factors that affect approaches to treatment. The following discussion is intended to raise counselor awareness of general concerns linked to diversity, not to provide definitive or descriptive information about any client or group of clients. It is essential to remember that there is considerable within-group variation, and that information presented here describes generalities rather than specifics.

Experts generally agree that culturally competent substance abuse treatment involves several strategies: racial/ethnic matching between clients and staff, language matching, and cultural competency training for staff. Data from 618 outpatient programs revealed that 42% of programs allowed clients to select staff from a racially similar group, 10% offered single race therapy groups, 11% had bilingual staff, and 57% reported that staff received cultural competency training.

Of the 1.7 million Americans who were admitted to publicly funded substance abuse treatment programs in 2003, 62% were white, 24% African American, 13% Hispanic/Latino, 2.3% Native American/Alaska Native, 1.1% Asian American/Pacific Islander. The remainder were unknown or other. The greatest number of admissions (23%) was for treatment of alcohol problems, with 15% for marijuana and 14% for heroin.

African Americans.   Although data have consistently found that African Americans report lower rates of use of alcohol and illegal drugs than whites, the consequences of substance use and abuse appear to be more pronounced in this population. They are more likely to be victimized by drug-related crimes, more likely to contract HIV/AIDS, more likely to develop alcohol-related problems, and more likely to die than those of other racial groups (Virginia Department of Mental Health, Mental Retardation and Substance Abuse Services, 2003). They are also more likely to be incarcerated for drug-related crimes than others. Marijuana is the most common drug for those who use, and more African American marijuana users move on to heroin than those of other groups. Among those who enter treatment, alcohol accounts for the most admissions among African American males, followed by cocaine and marijuana.

Minority clients, including African Americans, are under-represented in treatment programs, and have higher rates of non-completion and lower rates of success than those in other groups (Campbell & Alexander, 2002). Studies have found that African Americans may be averse to treatment services because they are perceived as an instrument of the system of oppression they have experienced. Treatment programs may not be sensitive to the cultural factors in African American clients, and may not address the client's reactions to a counselor from a different background. Important aspects of many African American clients that must be addressed in treatment include the role of extended family, the role of the church, and the role of racism (Department of Mental Health, Mental Retardation, and Substance Abuse Services, 2003). Harm reduction approaches have not been well received in many African American communities (Loue, 2003; Woods, 1998), which may be because of the devastating consequences of substance abuse in many African American communities. Marlatt (2000) recommends that any harm reduction programs should be developed within and by the black community to acknowledge the importance of self-determination.

Native Americans.   Alcohol was initially introduced to the Native Americans by the U.S. government, and it became a strategy for subjugating the native population.

There have been laws prohibiting consumption of alcohol by Indians since 1832. Such laws promoted the binging pattern of drinking which is problematic (Daisy, Thomas, & Worley, 1998).

Native Americans have the highest rates of substance abuse among all racial ethnic groups (Substance Abuse, n.d.; U.S. Department of Health and Human Services, 2003; Wallace et al., 2003), and the problem appears to affect both sexes equally. Indian adolescents also use substances at a rate higher than their non-Indian peers (Beauvais & Oetting, Wolfe, & Edwards, 1989). Substance abuse results in death and disability among native people, which may reflect the lack of prevention and treatment opportunities on many remote reservations. Alcohol is by far the most problematic substance, with a rate of 49.3 alcohol-related deaths per 100,000 people in 2003, more than the combined death rates for firearms and drugs. As many as 90% of homicides involving Native Americans are associated with alcohol, as are many suicides and vehicular accidents. In recent years, methamphetamine use has increased, leading to a ban on the substance in 2005 by the Navajo Nation. Among Indian clients of behavioral health services in Arizona, a state with a large native population, substance abuse was the most common presenting problem (Gerard, 2005).

Some experts find that treatment programs that are culturally specific may be more effective with native clients. Programs may be specific to individual tribes, and incorporate traditional practices such as purification sweats, vision quests, and the Sun Dance. In addition, there are AA programs specific to Native American clients (AI-AA) in many areas of the country that use a 12-Step approach that has been revised to reflect native values and beliefs. For this population, outpatient programs must provide child care, and transportation services may be needed. For adolescent clients, family involvement in treatment is essential, as is aftercare with stable living situations. Counselors in adolescent programs must be trained to deal with trauma, violence, and abuse that may be revealed during treatment (Daisy et al., 1998). Gender-specific, all-native programs are recommended.

Because many treatment approaches have not been effective with native clients, Daisy et al. suggest that harm reduction approaches might engage more native clients and their families in treatment. Harm reduction programs can also incorporate local control, cultural sensitivity, and use of traditional practices, which have been found to increase success rates.

Asian Americans/Pacific Islanders.   This group includes many different ethnic groups, and large variations exist among those groups. In general, however, Asian Americans have very low rates of substance abuse. Some interesting patterns have been identified, however. Although rates of alcohol use are very low, among those who do drink, the daily consumption is the highest of any ethnic group. Marijuana use among Asian youth declined from 1999 to 2000 more than any other group, but Filipino youth have the highest rate among all groups, and among those over 26, the rate of current marijuana use among Vietnamese Americans is almost equal to the rate among whites. Another variation is reflected in the comparison of Southeast Asians, who have the highest rates among Asian Americans for use of cocaine and amphetamines, and Pacific Islanders, who have the lowest rates of those drugs but are high in use of marijuana and inhalants.

Thus, any generalization about Asian Americans must be considered in light of these large inter-group differences (Drug and Alcohol Services Information System, 2005).

Despite the increased overall low rate of substance use, admissions to treatment programs have been increasing for Asian Americans, and cultural sensitivity is no less important with this clientele. The Asian concept of family is much broader than the Western view, and family includes both past and future generations. Asians consider mental health problems to be genetic and thus a threat to future generations; such problems may be concealed outside the family. Thus, seeking treatment for mental health, and perhaps substance abuse, problems is not widespread, and prevention or early treatment is often absent. There are also religious beliefs, such as *karma* (current troubles are the result of misbehavior in earlier lives) that make the Western notion of treatment unsuitable. Education in this community to create awareness of substance abuse problems, and acknowledgement of the primacy of the family, might be worthwhile goals with this population.

Hispanic/Latinos.   This ethnic group contains several distinct subgroups, depending on the country of ancestry, and rates of substance use vary among the groups. Among Hispanics who were admitted for substance abuse treatment in 2003, the most common drug-of-choice was alcohol, followed by opiates and marijuana. Hispanics had higher rates of opiate abuse than non-Hispanics and lower rates of alcohol abuse (Drug and Alcohol Services Information System, 2005). Puerto Ricans reported their primary substance was most often opiates, whereas for Mexicans and Cubans, alcohol was most often the primary substance of abuse. Men comprised 78% of admissions, compared to 68% among non-Hispanics. For males, alcohol was the most commonly reported substance of abuse, whereas for females, opiates and alcohol were equally common. Hispanic adolescents use substances at a rate below that of whites, but above that of other minority groups. Hispanic eighth graders have the highest rates of substance abuse in the nation, but that declines to the level of whites thereafter (De La Rosa, Holleran, Rugh, & MacMaster, 2005).

Hispanics seem to have more severe consequences than whites from substance abuse. They are more likely to die of cirrhosis of the liver than whites, although they drink at lower rates. Hispanics have higher rates of infection of Hepatitis C, which raises the risk of cirrhosis in drinkers (Health problems, n.d.).

Machismo: Sense of masculinity stressing physical courage and prowess, virility, aggressiveness, and domination of women.

Marianismo: Sense of femininity associated with sexual purity and passivity, valued for her nurturing qualities and deference to men.

Culturally appropriate treatment for Hispanics must take acculturation levels and language use into account. Increased use of substances is associated with acculturation to the majority culture (Franklin & Markarian, 2005). In addition, the role of the family is central, and family values must be respected. Gender role expectations, such as *machismo* and *marianismo*, may be in conflict with traditional approaches to substance abuse treatment. Loue (2003) notes that strong family bonds should be considered strengths to be recognized in treatment. Traditionally, older individuals are considered wise and their advice valuable, while the father is the authority or head of household, and the mother is esteemed for her devotion to the family. Loue also observes that warm, friendly relationships are highly valued, and a treatment setting that is cold or clinical may be aversive to this population. The practice of aggressive confrontation utilized in some treatment programs might be considered disrespectful and could result in premature termination.

Persons with Coexisting Disabilities

Substance abuse affects individuals of all races, ethnicities, genders, ages, and disabilities (Koch, Nelipovich, & Sneed, 2002). The Americans with Disabilities Act of 1990 legislated equal access to all people regardless of disability. The description of conditions that are considered disabilities under this law includes substance use disorders. Hence the title of this section, as I will discuss issues related to substance abuse in individuals with other disabilities. I will first provide an overview of substance abuse in persons with coexisting disabilities, followed by some issues related to specific disabilities.

Substance use disorders are found at higher rates in persons with physical and cognitive disabilities, but effective treatment is less likely for those individuals (Koch et al., 2002; Substance Abuse and Mental Health Services Administration, 1998). Barriers to effective treatment include "attitudinal barriers; discriminatory policies, practices, and procedures; communications barriers, and architectural barriers" (p. 5). The consensus panel that authored the Treatment Improvement Protocol cited here stresses the need for addressing these barriers, either by modifying existing programs or finding alternative methods to deliver services. In addition, the panel advocates for staff training to address attitudinal barriers to effective treatment, and recommends that all programs screen for disabilities, which are not always obvious, so those with coexisting disorders are identified and their needs assessed.

In their attempt to understand the high rates of substance abuse in persons with disabilities, Li and Moore (2001) surveyed 1,876 individuals with disabilities who were receiving vocational rehabilitation services in three states, of whom 304 admitted to using illicit drugs. These researchers examined the relationship between substance abuse and perceived discrimination of the basis of disability and their self-acceptance of their disability. They proposed that some persons with disabilities develop an "attitude of entitlement" (p. 9) that reflects a belief that persons with disabilities have more reasons to use and misuse substances than those without disabilities. Their findings revealed that perceived discrimination was the most influential factor in the individual's self-acceptance of the disability. They also discovered that substance abuse was associated with male gender, multiple disabilities, and attitude of entitlement.

Self-acceptance of disability: The individual views his or her disability as "non-devaluating" (Li & Moore, 2001, p. 9).

Some experts suggest that a categorization developed by the Substance Abuse Resources Disability Issues project (SARDI) is useful in working with individuals with substance abuse and coexisting disabilities (Koch et al., 2002). There are three categories proposed, each with specific challenges for treatment. Although the focus of their work has been individuals with blindness or visual impairments, this categorization could be applied to most coexisting disorders.

- Type I: Substance abuse exists before blindness or visual impairment.
- Type II: Blindness or visual impairment present before onset of substance abuse.
- Type III: Substance abuse and blindness/visual impairment occur simultaneously.

Those in the Type I group may find that the pre-existing problems created by the substance abuse make it more difficult to face the challenges of adjusting to a visual impairment or blindness. Those in Type II have likely adjusted to the disability, but may be using substances as a method of coping with grief, anger, and frustration related to the disability. A concern is that continued substance use might erode the skills previously acquired. Those who fall in the Type III group may be using substances to deal with the emotional consequences of having the disability. However, the substance abuse may complicate the adjustment and make living with the disability more difficult.

Blind or Visually Impaired. Koch and his colleagues (2002) reported that as many as half of the population in the United States with visual impairments could have substance abuse disorders serious enough to require treatment. These authors express concern that substance use may be overlooked or ignored as issues related to the visual disabilities assume prominence. SARDI suggests that significant people in the person's life may also ignore the signs of substance abuse because of their understandable focus on the disability. The effect of this lack of attention to substance abuse is not only psychological, but can be physical as well. Several progressive visual impairments (e.g., glaucoma) can be worsened by even moderate consumption of alcohol (SARDI, n.d.) Further, the absence of a case manager or coordinator of services may hinder the needed cooperation between the various treatment providers involved with the client. Lack of training or qualifications to work with visually handicapped clients may interfere with these clients getting needed services. Professionals who work with blind and visually impaired clients may not know to whom they can refer for appropriate services. In addition, physicians may prescribe psychotropic medication without screening for substance abuse, unintentionally contributing to the problem.

Psychotropic: Medication affecting mental processes or mood.

The issue of accessible services goes beyond architectural features of a facility. Substance abuse programs often use printed materials for educating clients, and these are frequently unavailable in another format (audiotapes, Braille, large print) (Koch et al., 2002). SARDI suggests that substance abuse treatment providers learn how to assist visually impaired clients with such tasks as navigating the facility, and how to respond to guide dogs.

Deaf/Hearing Impaired. Although blindness and deafness are both sensory disabilities, deafness and hearing impairments affect communication, which is the basis of therapy. In fact, these communication barriers contribute to a lack of awareness about substance abuse problems within the deaf community (Guthmann & Blozis, 2001). Although most readers will not be serving this population, it is important to be informed so that you can advocate for appropriate services for this population.

The greatest barrier to effective treatment is language; most deaf persons communicate via American Sign Language (ASL) and require an interpreter to communicate with those who do not speak ASL (Guthmann & Blozis, 2001). This creates several barriers: certified interpreters must be hired, which adds to the cost, and confidentiality is compromised by having an interpreter present. In addition, interpreting is very tiring, and if sessions are to be longer, there will be a need for a second interpreter to relieve the person. Eye muscles are easily fatigued, so hours of therapy (as is common in residential programs) are overwhelming and exhausting to the deaf client (Whitehouse, Sherman, & Kozlowski, 1991). There are very few treatment programs that have the staff and materials that are specialized for this population (e.g., having all visual materials available with captioning or signing, having flashing light signals in addition to sounds, having TTY access for telephones, etc.). A list of available programs can be found on the SADI website.

Because there are so few programs, deaf persons seeking treatment often go to distant locations to obtain appropriate services (Guthmann & Blozis, 2001). When they return home afterward, they are likely to find few support and self-help programs available (Rendon, 1992; personal communication, January 2, 2007), and may need to arrange for an interpreter for each meeting they attend. Substance abuse treatment programs often stress that recovering persons will need to change their social environment to maintain sobriety. Given that the deaf population in most areas is not large, asking someone to change friends is tantamount to prescribing social isolation. Groups (the most widely used format for substance abuse treatment) are particularly challenging, as members often speak over each other, and the interpreter can only sign one person's comments at a time. Group members who are not familiar with deaf culture may look at the interpreter rather than the deaf person, which is discourteous.

Persons with Multiple Sclerosis. This disability is an example of another condition for which substance abuse treatment poses particular challenges. Bombardier and colleagues (2004) cited prior research that found almost 14% of patients with multiple sclerosis (MS) had a history of problems with alcohol, and 23% were described as heavy drinkers. These authors point out that the dangers of alcohol and drug abuse are quite serious for those with this progressive disease. First, tolerance for alcohol may be reduced as the disease progresses, so individuals will feel the effects with fewer drinks than before. As a result, their difficulties with balance and coordination that are symptoms of the disease may be exacerbated by alcohol, and put the person at risk for injury.

Spasmolytic: Drug to reduce or prevent muscle spasms.

Because the central nervous system is the site of the disease process, alcohol and other drugs may cause further neurological damage. Many persons with MS take spasmolytic medications, which may interact negatively with alcohol and illegal drugs. Finally, it is possible that heavy alcohol use might magnify the subtle cognitive problems associated with the disease.

Bombarier et al. (2004) also found high rates of depression to be associated with self-reported abuse of alcohol. This was true for drug abuse as well. The researchers recommend screening for both depression and substance abuse in patients with MS, and urge physicians to urge MS patients to reduce their use of substances. They note that people may reduce substance use when medical status changes, so there may be opportune moments in treatment when this kind of intervention will produce good outcomes.

Counselor Issues

Many counselors come to substance abuse treatment via personal experience. That is, they describe themselves as "recovering" addicts or alcoholics. Recall Hector in the case study for this chapter. It is important to consider whether this personal experience increases the counselor's effectiveness. Also, it is likely that most counselors will have some personal relationships that have been affected by substance abuse, which means separating one's personal history from professional perspectives will be a challenge for many.

In my experience, counselors who are themselves recovering from addictions tend to believe strongly in the method by which they achieved sobriety. While this is understandable, it may compromise their objectivity in employing or recommending the approach to treatment best suited to the individual client. It is also important for the recovering counselor to maintain the focus on the client. One may rationalize that telling the client about one's own experience is for the purpose of providing a model to the client, but it also may be that the greater benefit is derived by the counselor.

Another issue is that of training. Can a generalist counselor treat clients with substance abuse problems, or is this the province of a specialist? There is much debate on this topic, and I weigh in with those who believe that a generalist who is well informed and who has obtained some training can provide treatment. Training in the motivational interviewing approach, for example, can be obtained in a workshop setting lasting from three to five days. As with any new skill, I advise supervision by a more experienced colleague.

Regardless of one's belief about the 12-Step approach, any counselor who encounters clients who may be referred for treatment needs to understand this model, as it is still widely used, and is also readily available and free. Attending several meetings is a good way to experience the approach, and allows the counselor to provide accurate information to clients who inquire about this.

BOX 5.1

A Note to School Counselors

Substance abuse among children and adolescents is a serious problem that must be addressed at family, community, and national levels. While schools and school counselors can make important contributions toward this effort, they cannot make a difference without collaborating with other entities in the community. The school counselor is most likely to have relationships with those external resources, and most equipped by training to engage in productive consultations with families, treatment providers, public organizations, and other involved parties.

School counselors are often the designated person to coordinate the school's efforts to prevent and reduce substance use and abuse among students. Elementary counselors contribute to that effort by presenting classroom guidance and curricula designed to develop social skills, problem-solving and decision-making skills, and skills to resist peer pressure (Coll, 1995; McLaughlin & Vacha, 1993; Why elementary counselors, n.d.). Such skills are believed to be increasingly important as children have more opportunities to experiment with and abuse substances. In some cases, the school counselor will deliver a curriculum to provide information about the effects of substances on the body and life of users, whereas other schools may bring in outside experts to teach those lessons. The school counselor should oversee whatever curriculum is used to ensure it is current, and appropriate for the age and community served by the school.

Watkins and her colleagues (2006) have based their middle school curriculum (Project ALERT: see Resources section for information) on a sound theoretical understanding of how people change. They have learned that adolescents (and presumably children even more so) do not take in all the information about specific drugs, but respond best to messages that apply to all drugs. Messages about how one's use of drugs would affect others they care about made a strong impression, and apply to all drugs. However, the school counselor should have accurate and current information about how specific drugs might affect students so that they are able to answer student questions and dispel misinformation. For example, school counselors need to be aware of the dangers of *pharming*, and be able to explain those to vulnerable teens. These researchers believe the school counselor is the best person to deliver these messages because they have established a trusting relationship with students, and because they are trained to be nonjudgmental and non-threatening, and can deliver the information in that manner.

Pharming: Mixing up an assortment of pills gathered from medicine cabinets and friends in a bowl, reaching in to get a few, and swallowing them.

School counselors also need to respond to the children in their schools whose families are involved in substance abuse. With their knowledge of both child development and substance abuse, school counselors must provide help and support to students who come from such difficult family situations (Gerler, 1991). Many elementary school counselors offer support groups for children from substance abusing families.

School counselors can assist with early identification of substance use problems in vulnerable students. Referrals can come from teachers, other staff, parents, and sometimes friends. The school counselor then determines whether substance abuse exists, and if so, how serious the problem is. The assessment tools described earlier in this chapter will be useful for school counselors. If the school counselor determines that substance abuse is an issue for a particular student, what options are there for intervention?

In some cases, in-school counseling groups may be appropriate. Groups may be offered to students from substance abusing families, those who are at risk for developing substance abuse problems themselves, and those who have received treatment and wish support in the school setting to maintain sobriety. In many cases, treatment provided outside the school setting, either outpatient or inpatient, will be indicated. In that case, the school counselor must confer with the student and parents to discuss this suggestion and to provide a list of possible treatment providers. If a student is to attend outpatient treatment, the school counselor may assist the family in making arrangements for schoolwork to be continued during treatment, and will surely assist the student in the transition back to school when treatment is completed.

One ethical issue is often raised by school counselors who conduct these types of groups. Schools may have policies requiring all personnel to inform the administration if they are aware that a student is using substances. If a school counselor learns in a counseling group that a student has used, and informs the administration, students will quickly learn that they cannot be honest in such groups. The other dilemma relates to mandated counseling when there has been an infraction. When the school counselor does not have an opportunity to screen students who will be in a group, there is

(*continued*)

BOX 5.1   Continued

less likelihood that the student will be committed to the process. In addition, such groups often serve to bring together peers who have similar attitudes, and so on, which can have the opposite effect than intended. In fact, after extensive research, Poulin, Dishion, and Burraston (2001) recommend that groups composed of children and adolescents with problem behaviors are likely to increase those behaviors, especially in those with the lowest levels of the behavior at the outset of the intervention. Also see Dishion, McCord, and Poulin (1999) for an excellent discussion of this problem. It is essential that school counselors use their expertise to advocate strongly for using other types of consequences for students who are having substance abuse problems and who have not sought help.

Ethical Concerns

There is an important issue that is not often discussed that I think raises ethical questions for counselors, and that is the reliance on AA and 12-Step approaches to treatment. Given the nature of the program, there is a lack of research evidence of effectiveness (Le, Ingvarson, & Page, 1995), but it is nevertheless used by the vast majority of substance abuse treatment programs. As many as 80% of AA members were referred to the program by professional treatment programs or counselors. In addition to the absence of empirical support, there are also aspects of the program that conflict with most contemporary counseling approaches. I will summarize some of the most salient differences in the hope that readers will reflect on these to clarify their own thinking on this question.

Lê, Ingvarson, and Page (1995) examined each of the 12 steps and compared them with what counselors typically espouse. For example, the first step begins with an admission of powerlessness. Counselors promote client empowerment and self-responsibility, and this crucial first step is in direct contradiction to that belief. Further, for women and minority clients who may struggle to overcome the effects of oppression and discrimination, accepting one's powerlessness may be a dangerous endeavor. These authors propose a reworded Step 1: I realize that I am not in control of my use of alcohol (p. 604). Note the change in the personal pronoun; we frequently ask clients to speak in the first person to help them own their thoughts and feelings, yet the 12 steps are all expressed in the plural, and the past tense, which implies a completed action rather than an ongoing process. The steps focus on deficits (e.g., Step 6, We were entirely ready to have God remove all these defects of character), which the authors point out is contrary to the emphasis on developing human potential that is basic to most counseling perspectives. There is also a passive reliance on external agents for change (Step 7: We humbly asked Him to remove our shortcomings) rather than support for developing internal strengths.

While this is not the place to review each of the steps, it is important to decide as a counselor if you subscribe to the principles promoted by AA and other 12-Step programs, and if not, whether you will refer clients to this widely available free resource.

The fellowship aspect of AA can provide much needed social support, particularly in times of crisis. Nevertheless, AA's steps revolve around themes of powerlessness, dependency, and humility. AA members are encouraged to relinquish self-direction and self-responsibility and to turn their lives over to the care of a power outside of themselves. The steps emphasize removing character defects and personal shortcomings, rather than developing strengths and abilities (Lê & Ingvarson, 1995, p. 609).

Summary

- Substance abuse is a serious disorder that is often found along with other issues discussed in this book. It is sometimes overlooked by counselors when the other problems are the presenting issue. Counselors need to include screening for substance abuse problems in their initial information gathering about clients.
- Substance abuse often begins in adolescence but is not confined to this age group. College students are at high risk for substance abuse, and older adults are at risk for substance abuse problems that may not be detected or treated.
- There are numerous assessment and screening strategies and instruments that are available to the general counselor who can then refer the client for more specialized assessment when necessary. There are also numerous options for treatment, although many of those incorporate 12-Step involvement. There are variations on the 12-Step philosophy for women and adolescents. There are some professionals who find the 12-Step philosophy to be in conflict with the principles of counseling, but the reality is that it is widely available, free, and provides an opportunity for clients to meet others who are struggling with the same problem.
- Diverse groups are affected by substance abuse, and treatment must be sensitive to cultural differences and needs. It is also essential that counselors remember that there are more differences within groups than there are between groups, so it is imperative not to make assumptions about a client's needs based solely on their race or ethnicity.
- Some counselors who specialize in substance abuse treatment are recovering addicts, which can be either a benefit or barrier depending on how their personal experience is used.

ADDITIONAL RESOURCES

On the Web for Counselors and Clients

- http://www.projectalert.best.org/Default.asp?bhcp=1 School counselors interested in Project ALERT, a substance abuse curriculum with a strong research base and many resources for the counselor, can begin their investigation here.
- http://www.alcoholics-anonymous.org Alcoholics Anonymous
- http://www.al-anon.alateen.org/ Al-Anon and Alateen

- http://www.womenforsobriety.org/ Women for Sobriety
- http://www.charlottekasl.com/16steps.htm Sixteen Steps
- http://www.moderation.org/ Moderation Management
- http://www.secularsobriety.org/ Secular Organizations for Sobriety
- http://www.nida.nih.gov/TXManuals/CRA/CRA1.html Community Reinforcement Approach
- http://www.rational.org/ Rational Recovery
- http://www.whitebison.org/home.html Native American treatment approach
- http://teens.drugabuse.gov NIDA has developed this website specifically for teens. It has a great deal of useful information presented in a way that is palatable for this population.
- http://www.med.wright.edu/citar/sardi/index.html Substance Abuse and Resource Disability Issues (SARDI). This site has a wealth of information about working with substance abusing clients with coexisting disabilities, including resources and publications that are free or inexpensive, some of which can be downloaded. It has an up-to-date list of research in this area and links to related sites.

Web Sources of Free Print Materials

- http://alt.samhsa.gov/communication/pubs.asp You can obtain treatment guides, assessment protocol, and materials for prevention.
- http://www.nida.nih.gov/PubCat/PubsIndex.html offers free or very inexpensive materials for clinicians
- http://www.niaaa.nih.gov/Publications/EducationTrainingMaterials/default.htm National Institute of Alcohol Abuse and Alcoholism also provides useful materials
- http://depts.washington.edu/adai/ click on Publications. This is the library of the Alcohol and Drug Abuse Institute at the University of Washington and is a tremendous source of materials. They have available for download many assessment instruments that are in the public domain.

In Print for Counselors

- *Addictions Counseling* by Dianne Doyle Pita (1994). A unique aspect of this book is the use of Erikson's stages of development as a framework for helping addictions. This model does rely on the 12-Step approach.
- *Alternatives to Abstinence* by Heather Ogilvie (2001) explains the perspective of professionals who challenge the disease model and the 12-Step approach. I think it is important to know these arguments, whether or not you agree with them.
- *The Small Book* by Jack Trimpey (1995) is no longer the mainstay of Rational Recovery; it is of interest to those who favor a cognitive behavioral approach.
- *Rational Recovery: The New Cure for Substance Addiction* by Jack Trimpey (1996) is the currently recommended guide for the RR program.
- *When AA Doesn't Work for You: Rational Steps to Quitting Alcohol* by Albert Ellis (1992) is also another guide for using the cognitive behavioral model.

- *Sober for Good: New Solutions for Drinking Problems—Advice from Those Who Have Succeeded* by Anne M. Fletcher (2001) is an overview of different strategies for attaining sobriety. It is an excellent review for counselors, and can be recommended to clients as well. It is written by a journalist and is useful for its objective descriptions.

Books for Clients

- *Changing for Good* by Prochaska, Norcross, and DiClemente (1995) is a self-help book based on the transtheoretical model of behavior change. This book can be used by clients alone or as an adjunct to counseling.
- *The Miracle Method: A Radically New Approach to Problem Drinking* by Scott Miller and Insoo Kim Berg (1995) takes a brief solution-focused approach to self-help and can be useful for clients.
- *Controlling Your Drinking: Tools to Make Moderation Work for You* by Miller and Muñoz (2005) is a good resource for people who want to moderate their drinking. For clients who are resistant to abstinence as a goal, this strategy is worth attempting.
- *Over the Influence* by Denning, Little, and Glickman (2004) is on harm reduction and is both thorough and very specific. Although it is written for clients to use independently, it is an excellent resource for counselors as well.
- *Big Book* of Alcoholics Anonymous (2002) is the foundation of the 12-Step approach. It is even available to read online: http://www.aa.org/bigbookonline/
- *It Will Never Happen to Me* by Claudia Black (1981) is a classic for children of alcoholics. Many who have grown up in homes with an alcoholic parent relate to this book and see how the family is affected by a parent's addiction.
- *Another Chance: Hope and Health for the Alcoholic Family* by Sharon Wegscheider-Cruse (1989) is another book on families with alcoholism.
- *Adult Children: The Secrets of Dysfunctional Families* by John and Linda Friel (1988) is another popular title. These last three titles can be found used for minimal cost.

Film and Television

- *Days of Wine and Roses* (the portrayal of the delirium tremens in an alcoholic is still shocking).
- *The Man with a Golden Arm* (the struggle of a heroin addict).
- *The Lost Weekend* (an epic binge).
- *I'll Cry Tomorrow* (the story of Lillian Roth's descent into alcoholism).
- *Clean and Sober* has a realistic account of a cocaine addict's experience.
- *When a Man Loves a Woman* for its portrayal of substance abuse in relationships.
- *Leaving Las Vegas* is another source of understanding of the depths to which substance abuse can lead.
- *My Name is Bill W.*, a made-for-TV movie about the beginning of Alcoholics Anonymous.
- *Trainspotting* is a shockingly realistic film about heroin addicts—but I found the dialog hard to understand.

EXERCISES

1. Any counselor who is going to treat or refer clients for substance abuse treatment should get first-hand knowledge of 12-Step programs. Thus, attend at least five different meetings of AA, NA, or another 12-Step group, and discuss your experience with your class or in a paper.

2. Review and select at least three assessment instruments you think you might use. Administer them to individuals (real or role playing), interpret the results, and indicate what you would recommend to the client.

3. Read the article by Lê, Ingvarson, and Page (1995) and write a brief paper in which you agree or disagree with their position.

4. Assume you have an adolescent client whose parent has a substance abuse problem. How would you help the client understand and cope with the situation? What resources might you recommend in addition to counseling?

5. Assume that Hector's young wife comes to you for help. She tells you she is depressed and angry at her husband's behavior, and is ashamed to admit that her family was right about him. What goals might you have for counseling with this client? What referrals will you consider?

6 Suicide

Suicide is the most frequent crisis situation for counselors in all settings. It is also one of the most challenging and disturbing situations a counselor ever faces, regardless of how much experience and training the counselor has. In my career as a counselor, I have intervened many times with individuals contemplating suicide. Several former students and clients who are now leading satisfying and productive lives at one time needed to be hospitalized for serious and lethal attempts to take their lives. I am gratified to know my professional skills allowed me to intervene successfully in so many cases. There was also a time when I was unable to prevent a suicide, and that story will be the case study for this chapter. I share the story because I hope by doing so others can learn from my disastrous experience.

Case Study

There have been many situations over the years when I have intervened with a suicidal client, and all had a positive outcome, with the client safe and obtaining help—except one. I tell the painful story of this situation because it illustrates every counselor's worst nightmare. It is a difficult story for me to tell. I have changed some details to protect the privacy of others, but the essential information is unfortunately accurate.

Although this event occurred over twenty years ago, I remember it clearly. I was working as a counselor in high school where the admission process included an initial interview by a counselor with each potential student. Students completed an application form and a problem checklist, which were reviewed during the interview. Most students checked a fair number of problems on the checklist of 240 issues often reported by adolescents, and one thing that stood out about John, age 17, was that he checked only two. John's response to my expression of surprise at the small number of concerns, and to my inquiries about many items that other students often checked, made it clear that he was very invested in being "normal," and being able to handle difficult situations, including his parents' divorce and other stressors. At the time of this initial contact, John was living away from home and working to support himself, and he expressed a desire to earn his high school diploma. With my assistance, he selected his classes and enrolled.

Attendance was a requirement of the school, and students who exceeded a specified number of absences were dropped from the program, with the option to re-enroll when their circumstances (internal or external) would allow them to attend regularly. John was quickly dropped from the program his first term due to absences. At the next opportunity to enroll, he applied for re-admission. We met again, and talked about what had interfered with his attendance the previous term (including difficulties with his work schedule), and he insisted he now had everything under control and was ready to commit to school. Nevertheless, his lack of attendance again quickly resulted in his second dismissal from the program. Other students mentioned him occasionally in conversation, often referring to his reckless driving behavior.

When he came to see me for the third time about re-entering, I pointed out that when students had been dismissed three times, they were considered a low priority for available openings, and that it was therefore important that he consider whether this was the best time to try again. He considered the obstacles, but appeared determined to be successful this time. I encouraged him to come to see me so that I could support his efforts to stay in school and assist him if problems arose. He agreed to do so. The second day of the new term, he telephoned me to say he would be absent but that he would communicate with me and come to see me the next day. He did so, and said his relationship with his girlfriend was not going well, and that their late-night arguments had resulted in his oversleeping and missing school. He reported that the previous evening their conversation had been very productive and she agreed that his education was a priority. He attended an entire day of school and stopped by before leaving to say his day had gone well.

The next morning, I was in my office meeting with a student in crisis. The secretary always honored my request not to interrupt such sessions, so I was quite surprised when the intercom buzzed. She said I had a call that she thought I should take, because the student had been calling every few minutes for the last hour. It was John, of course, and I answered, intending to say I would call him back when I was free. The quality of his voice when he answered made it obvious he was in distress. Mindful of the other upset student in my office, who could hear my end of the conversation, I said he sounded distressed, and he replied, "Yes." I said something about being glad he called and that I was with another student right then, and would be glad to call him or meet with him later in the morning. I could tell he was crying and I said something like, "I'm worried that you are thinking of hurting yourself." He responded with more sobs. I asked if he would come to school and meet with me. When he declined, I assumed he did not want to risk being seen by other students in his emotional state, so I said I would meet him at a local coffee shop close by if he preferred. He declined again, and I assumed the same reason was involved. I foolishly said I would come to his home, and he thanked me, said that would be much better, and he then provided directions to his rural address. I explained that I would need some time to finish my current session, and then I would leave. I told him approximately when to expect me.

As soon as the other student left my office, I attempted to call John back and confirm the appointment and let him know I was on my way. When there was no answer, I became alarmed and rushed out the door. My fear was that he would have driven his car dangerously on a mountain road, perhaps after drinking alcohol, and killed himself. In my panic, I hurriedly told the secretary where I was going and left. She handed me one of the earlier phone messages he had left, which I stuffed in my pocket. I read it later: the message was that he wanted to thank me for all my help. My alarm escalated, and I drove to his home.

When I approached John's rural home, I noted with relief that his car was there. I knocked on the door, and was answered only by the dog's barks. I remember still the terrible sense of dread I felt, and I ran across a field to the closest neighbor to call the police. It turned out that the neighbor was a relative of the young man, and was certain my fear was unfounded. She reported that John frequently listened to loud music in his room using headphones and would not hear the door. I repeated my wish to call the police but she insisted she accompany me back to his home. The door was unlocked, and the aunt walked to his room, with me following. I could hear her cry and saw only the legs on the bed when I realized what had happened.

I called the police, who arrived about 15 minutes later to this rural home. I also called the school, told the principal what was happening, requested that a faculty meeting be scheduled for late that afternoon, and that the district's crisis response team be contacted and asked to send representatives.

The aftermath included meetings with the police, the family, and staff at the school, and the next day meeting with groups of distressed students. In a small school, news travels quickly and news of this kind brings up many issues in students, both those who knew and those who did not know the deceased. In meeting with the police and the family, I learned that four notes had been left (although I was not privy to the contents), that John had told his brother earlier in the morning that he was going to kill himself and the brother told him to call his counselor. The lethal method was a gunshot to the head.

I know some of my colleagues both in the school and in the community believed I was responsible for the suicide, and that I could have prevented it had I responded more appropriately and effectively. Although I will never know if that is the case, guilt and self-doubt plagued me for a long time. It may be that John pulled the trigger as soon as he hung up the telephone and that the police would only have found his body. It may be that if I had asked the other student to leave, I could have kept him on the phone and provided other options. That I think is more likely. I didn't think quickly enough, and the one mistake for which I hold myself most culpable is not staying on the phone when I realized John's level of distress. I could have signaled the other student to wait outside, and been able to assess the situation more directly. I don't know if that would have changed the outcome, but it is the professional response I wish I had made. My assumption about his refusal to meet anywhere but at his home was faulty, and this was not a time for assumptions.

My own help and support came from the members of the school district's crisis response team, who listened to my story as often as I needed to repeat it, who assured me that I was not responsible for the death, and encouraged me to continue doing this work. They also provided direct assistance in managing the students who needed support and assistance in the days following the suicide. I definitely needed the support; rumors quickly spread about what had occurred, and what my involvement had been. In fact, I still remember the sick feeling in my stomach when, not very long after this incident, I was in a district-wide meeting of counselors. Someone introduced the story with something like, "I heard that a [irresponsible—I don't remember the word used, but I know it was not supportive . . .] counselor . . ." When the person finished, I said, "That was me." The silence that followed was not a comfortable one, to say the least.

Personally, I struggled with guilt and self-doubt, and wondered if I should leave the profession. I did not. I know I did not cause the suicide. I will never know if any of the things I wish I had done and said would have prevented it, but I have come to accept the uncertainty. There was also definitely a long-term impact on my professional behavior; I know that I am now hyper-vigilant when there was the slightest hint of suicidal ideation, but I also developed strategies for consultation and collaboration so that I never made decisions in isolation again. Although I can't say for sure, I don't think I've avoided dealing with suicidal individuals, but I have definitely been overly cautious in responding to individuals who express any level of suicidal ideation. If I were to make another error of judgment with a client, it would be to over-react in a case of low lethality.

Definitions and Description of the Problem

Definitions of suicide convey the harsh reality of this behavior: Self-murder, self-inflicted death, deliberate self-annihilation, self-destructive act with intent to die: these are among the definitions found in the literature. Suicide is usually a conscious, planned, and premeditated act, but can also be impulsive and unplanned (particularly in adolescents), a desperate attempt to end unbearable pain. A suicidal event (thought, gesture, attempt, threat) may be what brings the person to see a counselor, but it is often the case that the reason for seeking help is something other than suicidal thinking. Counselors may also work with survivors of suicide (friends and loved ones of someone who completes an act of suicide), and when a client completes a suicide, professionals must cope with their own survivor issues.

Graduate training programs are inconsistent about training students in the management of suicidal clients, so many readers may have had only perfunctory coverage of this topic in their coursework. While this chapter does not pretend to be a comprehensive manual on suicide, readers will gain an awareness of the issue and how they might respond in their work setting. Experts recommend that counselors need information about suicide risk assessment and treatment of suicidal clients (Foster & McAdams, 1999) along with clinical training and preparation for the possibility of a client suicide. I will address each of those topics in the chapter. Please note that the content of this chapter overlaps that of chapter I authored elsewhere, which is listed in the References section.

A word about terminology: I strongly object to the phrase *successful suicide* to describe someone whose suicidal act is fatal. I use the term *completed suicide* to avoid the connotation that suicide is a successful solution to a problem. Suicidal *ideation* refers to thoughts of suicide that are nonspecific as to plan or timing ("Sometimes I think I'd be better off dead"). I use the term *gesture* to refer to an act that is meant to imply suicidal intent but which is of very low lethality (e.g., making a very superficial cut on the wrist, taking five aspirins) and is intended to be a cry for help. A suicidal *attempt* is more lethal (e.g., taking a bottle of sleeping pills), and implies that the person believed their action would result in death (even if that belief was based on inaccurate information) and, if the individual survives, it is because someone intervened or interrupted the act. *Suicidal behaviors* refer to all of the above.

Prevalence

In 2001, suicide was ranked eleventh among the causes of death in the United States, accounting for 30,000 deaths or a rate of 10.8 per 100,000 people. Suicide deaths occur more often than homicides, at a ratio of 5:3 (NIMH, 2003), and this rate has been fairly stable over time (American Association of Suicidology (AAS), n.d.). There are undoubtedly some suicides that are incorrectly classified (particularly as accidents), so the true figure is somewhat higher. In addition to completed suicide, there are many more cases of suicide attempts; the figure of ten attempts per completed suicide is widely quoted (e.g., Mann, 2002). Among adolescents, however, the ratio is 100–200:1!

While the overall suicide rate is sufficient cause for concern, these rates vary sharply by age and race/ethnicity. Death rates have been reported by states since 1933, and for each year since, adults over age 65 have maintained the highest suicide rates among all age groups. Males over age 65 have the highest rates in the population, with those aged 85+ committing suicide at a rate of 54.5 per 100,000. Among Americans aged 15–24, suicide is the third leading cause of death (www.cdc.gov/factsheets). This rate has increased threefold since the 1950s, and this has generated high levels of concern among the public and mental health professionals.

Across age groups, firearms are the most frequently used method of suicide. In 2000, 65.5% of all suicides were accomplished using guns. Suffocation (including hanging) was the next most common method, accounting for 19.4%, followed by poisoning (including drug overdoses) with 16.6% of suicides. Rates varied somewhat by age, with 28% of suicides among those aged 15–24 being the result of suffocation, and 7.6% due to poisoning. The only age group for which firearms were not the most common method was age 10–14, in which suffocation accounted for 56% of suicide deaths and firearms 36.7%.

Data from a large study of a nationally representative sample of 15–54-year-olds found that 13.5% had thoughts of suicide in their lifetime, 3.9% had made plans to commit suicide, and 4.6% had made attempts. That means more than one in five people have at least thought about suicide at some time! Of those who had made attempts, 39% said the attempt was serious and that it was only luck that prevented their death. Another 13% said the attempt was serious, but they knew the method was not foolproof. Forty-seven percent said they did not want to die, but wanted help (Kessler, Borges, & Walters, 1999).

Men commit suicide at four times the rate of women, but women attempt suicide at three to nine times the rate of men. College students commit suicide at a lower rate than their non-student peers. Although there have been many attempts to explain this difference, the one factor that has been reported consistently is the reduced availability of firearms, the most lethal method of suicide. The highest rates of suicide are among white males over age 65. The rates increase with age, so that white men 85 years and older have the highest suicide rate of all demographic groups. Among the elderly, suicide attempts are more often fatal than in any other group.

Other demographic variables have been found to increase the risk for suicide. For example, single individuals commit suicide at a higher rate than married people, with the highest rates found among formerly married persons (widows, widowers, and divorced persons). Catholics have been found to commit suicide less often than Protestants and Jews. People in high status occupations (e.g., physicians) have higher rates of suicide than those in lower status positions; a decrease in status also increases risk. A serious, chronic physical illness is also associated with increased risk for suicide (Kaplan & Saddock, 1994), especially in the elderly.

A Model of the Path to Suicide

The Suicide Trajectory model proposed by Stillion, McDowell, and May (1989, cited in Stillion & McDowell, 1996) is based on the premise that a combination of biological, cognitive, psychological, and environmental risk factors interact to bring the individual to consider suicide (suicidal ideation). This model applies across the life span and may be useful to keep in mind as a framework for understanding suicidal clients. Suicidal ideation begins when the combined pressure from the four risk factors overtaxes the individual's coping skills. Once suicidal ideation has occurred, if a triggering event ("last straw") is added to the mix, the individual engages in suicidal behavior. From this perspective, *biological factors* include male gender and a genetic predisposition to depression. *Cognitive factors* include rigid, inflexible thinking patterns, and the presence of certain cognitive distortions. Depression, hopelessness and helplessness, low self-esteem, and inadequate coping skills are *psychological factors*, and loss, negative family experiences and life events, and availability of lethal means are *environmental factors*. Stillion and McDowell discuss how this model applies to individuals at various life stages, including children and adolescents. In children, impulsivity (considered a biological factor) is more prominent than at other life stages. In the psychological domain, a sense of inferiority and the *expendable child syndrome* (belief that they are unworthy and their death would not be a loss to anyone) are risk factors particular to this age group. Cognitive risk factors at this age include immature understanding of death and the concreteness that is characteristic of children's thinking at this age, whereas environmental factors focus on the home environment. In adolescents, the biological factor includes puberty, the psychological factor focuses on identity development, and the cognitive factor includes the disillusionment that may come from the newly emerged ability to think hypothetically (about such things as an idealized world). In the environmental factor, conflicts in the family are risk factors, as is abuse.

Developmental Issues and Risk Factors

Suicide occurs throughout the life span. Some individuals are more likely than others to contemplate or commit suicide, due to the presence of risk factors that render them more vulnerable to this behavior. Being aware of these developmental and risk factors helps the counselor direct prevention and intervention efforts where they are most needed.

The most important predictor of suicide potential is a history of previous attempts. The more prior attempts, and the more lethal those attempts, the greater the current risk of suicide. Gathering such information is essential in any evaluation of suicide risk. It is important to keep in mind, however, that over-relying on this risk factor is dangerous, as more than two-thirds of suicides occur with the first attempt (Mann, 2002).

There are other known risk factors that can be grouped into those that predispose an individual to suicide or increase their vulnerability (chronic factors and traits), and those more immediate situational factors that may impel the individual to act (Haley, 2004). The following is an overview of those factors.

There is ample evidence that suicide is associated with the presence of psychiatric disorders, diagnosed or not. Over 90% of suicide victims have a psychiatric disorder (often undiagnosed), most often a mood disorder such as bipolar disorder or depression (Mann, 2002). When these disorders are combined with either a personality disorder or substance abuse, the risk is substantially elevated. Again, although this is a well-known risk factor, it is important to keep in mind that most people with psychiatric disorders do not commit suicide. The implications for mental health professionals are twofold: the importance of correctly diagnosing and treating mood disorders, and the need for ongoing monitoring of suicide risk in clients with mood disorders.

Substance abuse, particularly alcohol, is a potent risk factor. In fact, in those with a history of attempts, alcohol abuse is the strongest predictor of a subsequent suicide. In addition, for children and adolescents, parental alcoholism elevates their risk for suicide. Experts theorize that alcohol use in a depressed person leads to suicide by acting as a depressant (which alcohol is) and by reducing impulse control. Individuals, particularly those who are dually diagnosed with a mood disorder and substance abuse, require close monitoring. In adolescents, acting out behaviors may mask underlying depression, and it is important to be thorough in evaluating younger clients for both disorders. There are prevention programs in schools that include a screening for depression for all students.

There are also genetic factors in suicide, meaning that the tendency toward suicidal behaviors and thoughts is, at least in part, inherited. Evidence of genetic influence has been found in twin and adoption studies, which show a greater incidence of suicide in those whose biological parents have committed suicide, and greater similarity between identical than fraternal siblings. The genetic influence in suicide is about the same as heritability of major psychiatric disorders, such as bipolar disorder and schizophrenia.

A history of suicide of a close family member increases the risk. In adolescents, the suicide of a friend or family member elevates the risk of suicide. Other conditions that are risk factors for suicide include physical or sexual abuse in childhood, head injury or neurological disorder (e.g., epilepsy), and cigarette smoking. In children, witnessing the abuse of another elevates their risk for suicide. Those individuals who lack problem-solving skills and who have difficulty coping with stress are more vulnerable to suicidal thinking and actions. Problems in the family system may exacerbate these existing skill deficits, leading to a desperate act. The old adage, "Suicide is a permanent solution to a temporary problem," seems apropos to such circumstances.

An important risk factor, particularly in adolescents, is sexual minority status. Numerous studies have found higher rates of suicide ideation, attempts, and suicides among gay, lesbian, bisexual, and transgendered adolescents and young adults than in the general population. That risk factor is reduced when the individual has a supportive family and social group (Ryan & Futterman, 1998).

Environmental variables that increase the risk of suicide are living in a rural area, access to guns, poverty and unemployment, and social isolation. Researchers found that 50% of people who committed suicide did not have a single close friend. The presence of a serious medical illness or condition may elevate suicide risk. This may explain, in part, the high rate of suicide in the elderly, whose health status may be a factor, along with social isolation. Across age groups, people with HIV/AIDS commit suicide at much higher rates than the general population.

In addition to these risk factors, there is often a precipitant—an event close in time to the suicide that was the "last straw" in the life of a vulnerable individual. In children and adolescents, the precipitant is often the loss of an important relationship via death, break-up of a romantic relationship, relocation. In the elderly, concerns about medical conditions are often a precipitant. Protective factors include the absence of risk factors, a sense of hopefulness, having the responsibility for children, having strong social support, and having access to mental health care.

A model that attempts to describe the vulnerability to suicide is useful, particularly when viewed as a formula shown this way:

> Long-term predisposing risk factors (such as genetics or biology, and personality traits such as rigid thinking, perfectionism, hopelessness, impulsivity)
>
> + Short-term risk factors, including environmental factors (unemployment, change in marital status) and a psychiatric diagnosis
>
> − Protective Factors + Precipitating Factors (immediate factors such as legal problems, experience of humiliation, recent loss or separation, unwanted pregnancy)
>
> = Risk.

> (Matthews & Paxton, 2001)

Thinking of suicide in this way reminds us that suicide has multiple causes, and the counselor's role, once the immediate crisis has passed and the client's safety is assured, is to assist the client in addressing all of the factors involved.

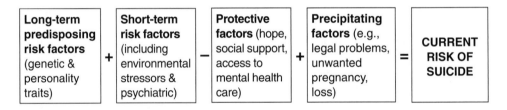

Assessment

When a mental health professional suspects or believes that a client is considering suicide, an immediate assessment of risk is in order. Unlike other types of assessment, in which care is taken to include a variety of measures and sources of information to assist in decision making about an individual, suicide assessment must be done immediately and accurately. The goal of a suicide assessment is to determine the client's level of current risk so that the counselor can take appropriate action. This aspect of suicide assessment engenders understandable anxiety in counselors, both experienced and neophyte, because the consequences of making an error are so serious.

I will describe in some detail several widely used assessment approaches. Some readers may already be familiar with these, but in the event they are not, I want to be sure the reader has some basic tools available. There are both formal and informal assessment tools. Informal tools do not have norms or guidelines for interpretation, nor are there psychometric data on their reliability and validity. There are two widely used informal assessment tools that can be quite useful in determining the level of risk for suicide, although I have been unable to find the original source of these methods. Each uses an acronym to help the clinician remember to inquire about all pertinent issues.

FIGURE 6.1   The SLAP Method of Suicide Assessment.

S = How SPECIFIC is the plan? Has the client thought about details? Does the client have a time frame? Has the client made special arrangements to make sure the plan works? A client whose plan is more specific is at higher risk. For example, a client who says "I'm going to take some pills" is at lower risk than one who says "I'm going to pick up a refill on my prescription for Valium, and take them all with a stiff Bloody Mary."

L = How LETHAL is the plan? Firearms are the most lethal, along with jumping from high places or jumping in front of moving cars. Hanging, overdose, and cutting can also be lethal, but can more easily be reversed if the person has second thoughts, and are also more easily interrupted by others. The more lethal the plan, the higher the risk.

A = How AVAILABLE is the method? If the client intends to shoot himself in the head, does he have a gun, or does he plan to go to a store and buy one? Does the client who intends to overdose on barbiturates already have them, or will she have to make an appointment and request a prescription? Does the client who intends to use a knife have a knife selected? The more available the means, the higher the risk.

P = Are others in close PROXIMITY? Are there significant others who could interrupt or interfere with the plan? Are there others whose help can be enlisted (e.g., to remove firearms from the home, flush medication, remain with the client, etc.)? The greater the distance and isolation of the client, the higher the risk.

The SLAP method in Figure 6.1 is used when the clinician learns of a client's suicidal ideation.

One potent risk factor for suicide is a previous attempt. When the clinician learns that there has been such an attempt, the DIRT method, shown in Figure 6.2, is a useful tool to assess the seriousness of that attempt.

Another scale that utilizes an acronym as a mnemonic device for clinicians is the SAD PERSONS scale (Patterson, Dohn, Bird, & Patterson, 1983). This scale has also been adapted for use with children and adolescents (Juhnke, 1996). This scale is more formal, in that there are guidelines for interpretation. The scale has demonstrated usefulness in accurately evaluating suicide risk. This method is easily learned and used, and is a systematic approach that the counselor can use in a crisis situation. The scale and interpretation are described in Figure 6.3. Note that reliability and validity of suicide assessments are problematic for ethical reasons. No researcher would choose not to intervene in the case of a client assessed at high risk for suicide to test the validity of the scale.

Juhnke (1996) noted that some modifications would make this scale more appropriate for use with children; his modified version is the Adapted Sad Persons Scale (ASPS). Goldston (2003) noted that there is no research providing data on reliability of the validity of this measure, but there are few measures that do have such data. Juhnke's modifications include revised scoring for several letters in the acronym: age (adolescents

FIGURE 6.2   The DIRT Method of Assessing the Severity of an Attempt.

D = How DANGEROUS was the attempt, or how lethal was the method used?

I = What was the client's IMPRESSION of the lethality? In this case, the clinician wants to know how lethal the client believed the method to be. For example, taking ten Tylenol may not be highly lethal from a medical perspective, but if the client *believed* he would die, that is more important in assessing the seriousness of the attempt.

R = What was the probability of RESCUE? Did the client take pills when others were at home? Did the client expect a friend to arrive? Did client announce his plan to others? Did she choose a public place (e.g., a school restroom) where she was likely to be observed and stopped?

T = What was the TIME frame of the most recent suicide attempt? The more recent the attempt, the higher the current risk.

FIGURE 6.3   The SAD PERSONS Scale for Assessing Suicide Risk.

Scoring: 1 if present, 0 if not present

S = Sex	Score if the person is male
A = Age	Score if the person is under 25 or over 45
D = Depression	Score if there are signs of depression
P = Previous attempt	Score if there was a previous suicide attempt
E = Ethanol (Alcohol)	Score if there are symptoms of substance abuse
R = Rational Thinking loss	Score if person is psychotic, disoriented, has bizarre thoughts, is confused, irrational, etc.
S = Social Support loss	Score if person has lost (via death, break-up) a close relationship recently
O = Organized Plan	Score if the person has a fairly detailed plan that is lethal
N = No lover, mate, spouse	Score if person does not have a committed relationship
S = Sickness	Does person have a chronic, serious or terminal illness?

Intervention

0–2	Send home with follow-up appointment
3–4	Close follow-up, consider hospitalization
5–6	Strongly consider hospitalizing, depending on follow-up arrangements
7–10	Hospitalize or commit involuntarily

15 or older are scored, whereas younger children are not scored on this item). Social support is scored 1 if the child has no close friends. "N" signifies negligent parenting, family stressors, or suicidal modeling by parents or siblings, and the final "S" = school problems. In addition, Juhnke recommends scoring each factor on a scale from 1 to 10 (except sex), and offers recommendations based on scores:

0–29   Encourage counseling services

30–49   Strongly recommend counseling and follow-up services, contact parent or guardian, get "no-suicide" contract

50–69   Have formal evaluation for hospitalization unless follow-up arrangements and counseling plan are highly reliable

70+   Arrange for immediate hospitalization

An unpublished instrument for the assessment of suicidality in high-risk prisoners (Giles, 1997) contains one item that I have not seen elsewhere, and that I now ask routinely as part of a suicide assessment: "What is one thing that could happen to you that would push you to actually try to hurt yourself?" The response gives important information to the clinician. The person may deny current suicidal plans or intent, but reveal that "if my boyfriend left me," or "if something happened to my mother," the equation could change very quickly. Such a response alerts the counselor that the person has not ruled out suicide as an option, and provides clues to the type of stressors the person does not feel capable of managing. Sometimes individuals say something like, "Nothing, I would never consider taking my life no matter how bad things get," which is important to know in planning treatment. Another useful question is "What would stop you from killing yourself?" which may indirectly identify the precipitant or stressor, and give an indication of the protective factors the client may have.

When there has been a suicide attempt, a scale available online for assessing the risk of repetition can be quite useful, although there are no psychometric data available. The scale can be obtained at www.wellclosesquare.co.uk/protocol/psych/suicide.htm.

An assessment designed for college students with good psychometric properties and items that relate to the consequences of alcohol abuse in that setting is the Young Adult Alcohol Problems Screening Test (YAAPST; Hurlbut & Sher, 1992; personal communication, July 17, 2003). Since the initial article, the authors have added several useful items that can be obtained by contacting Dr. Sher.

There is an eventuality in suicide assessment that calls for advance planning. If you have a suicidal person in your office, and you believe they need either hospitalization or close monitoring by family members along with counseling, how do you manage to make arrangements and consult with colleagues without leaving the person alone? One should absolutely not leave a client alone, even for a few minutes, if there is any chance the client will panic and leave. I once was called to the emergency room to assist the family of a client because the family was too distressed to provide needed information. The doctor left the bedside to consult with me, and while he was doing so, the student (who had taken medication with alcohol and was barely conscious) managed to disappear! Security was called and there was high drama until she was located. At that moment, she wanted to die and did not want anyone to stop her. (She is now a professional adult with her own family.)

So how do you remain with the client, and contact parents/hospital/police, inform your supervisor, or consult with colleagues? One way that works well (in the absence of "panic buttons") is to pre-arrange a code with someone in the office. The code might be a fictitious doctor's name. Then, you can tell the client that you will need to cancel an appointment with your doctor to continue your meeting. When you call your own office, you say, "Would you please cancel my appointment with Dr. Tarasoff? I'm with a client and can't leave right now." This is a signal to the person on the phone that you have a difficult situation and need your supervisor or colleague to knock on the door. When she does so, you can tell the client you'd like to invite this person in because you trust her and you would like her help. You can then discuss your concerns in brief, and ask this person to make the phone calls, and so on.

Readers who are interested in technical information and psychometric properties of suicide assessment measures for children and adolescents will find the new book by the American Psychiatric Association (Goldston, 2003) to be a good reference.

Treatment Options and Considerations

While the first consideration is always to provide for the client's safety and prevent suicide, once that goal has been accomplished, it is important to address underlying issues so that the risk of future attempts is reduced. There are three essential components of suicide intervention: assessment of risk, removal of means of suicide (e.g., guns, medications) and diagnosis and treatment of the psychiatric disorder. Risk assessment was discussed in the previous section. One strategy, often used in conjunction with the assessment process, is the "no suicide contract." This technique is controversial, and I will focus on it in the next session.

The need to remove means of suicide (firearms, medications, etc.) is obvious, but accomplishing this requires the cooperation of others. The counselor must evaluate the level of cooperation and reliability of family members or whoever will provide safety monitoring in the crisis period. For example, are parents or family members willing to remove all firearms and knives from the home? Are they willing to remove all medications (prescription or no) to a locked cabinet, and dispense only the necessary dosage to the client? If there is resistance, or claims of inconvenience, and so on, the individual might need to be hospitalized for safety reasons. Are family members willing and able to take time from work during the acute period to ensure the client is not left alone? How seriously do family members consider the attempt or threat to be? If the counselor has misgivings about the family's ability to provide close monitoring and follow-up services, hospitalization is a reasonable consideration.

There are clients who threaten suicide unless certain conditions are met ("If you don't . . . I'll kill myself"). Such demands can be seen as manipulative behavior, and may engender negative reactions on the part of clinicians and family members. Although such behavior may in fact *be* manipulative, one must realize that the individuals do not believe their needs would be met unless the response is coerced. Dr. Motto (1999) recommends that even if the client is being manipulative, if the demand is realistic and feasible, it can be met and later explored with the client (e.g., "How have you come to believe that others will not respond to your requests without being coerced?"). If the demand cannot be met, it is suggested that the reasons for refusal be made clear, and in response to the threat, the message should convey that ultimately, suicide is an individual's decision, and that if the person does choose to end his or her life, you will be sad, but not guilty. Motto suggests that by making clear that others will not feel guilty, one possible motivation for suicide (to punish others) may be removed.

Some mental health professionals use no-suicide contracts with clients as a strategy to manage risk. Such contracts are typically used in acute crisis situations, when there is elevated risk for suicide, and usually include two elements: a commitment from the client not to act on suicidal impulses, and an agreement from the client to contact the clinician if the urges to suicide become difficult to resist. Although this technique is widely used, there is little research on its efficacy. A critical element in deciding whether a no-suicide contract is appropriate to a particular case is the strength of the therapeutic relationship. If the client and counselor have a positive and strong bond, the client is more likely to take the contract seriously. If the client has no investment in the relationship, he or she may say or sign anything in order to avoid more intrusive interventions, and may have no commitment to adhere to the agreement. I remember a student who came to school one day with hospital bandages on his wrists. When I inquired, he told me he had made a serious suicide attempt, and that he had been hospitalized the night before. I expressed surprise that he had been released, considering the severity of the injuries, and he told me he had signed a no-suicide contract in order to be released. When I asked if he intended to uphold the agreement, he said something like, "What can they do to me if I violate the agreement and kill myself? Sue me?" This comment made a strong impression on me, and I am very cautious about relying on such contracts to ensure client safety.

A major disadvantage of this contract is that the counselor may consider this to be the extent of risk management with suicidal clients. At best, a contract can be one component of a much larger safety plan involving significant others and removal of means, and the like. Further, such a contract may inadvertently restrict the client's expression of suicidal thoughts and impulses, fearing that such revelations will be seen as a violation of the contract that will result in hospitalization. Some clients may see the contract as an effort on the part of the clinician to cover themselves to avoid legal ramifications should the client eventually commit suicide—which they may interpret as the counselor being more concerned with self than with the client. The clinician will have to weigh all these factors in the decision to use a no-harm contract or not.

Once the suicidal crisis has been managed, it is necessary to diagnose and treat any psychiatric disorders, and in the case of clients who are already diagnosed, to re-evaluate the treatment plan.

Children

Thankfully, the rate of suicide in pre-pubertal children is low, but it is the fifth leading cause of death in children 5–14 years old. Chances are good that many child suicides are not so designated; it is difficult to get a ruling of suicide in a child's death, with investigators more likely to assume accidental causes (e.g., gunshot or poisoning) due to lack of evidence of intent (Davis, 2004).

The lower rates for this age group can be explained by a number of factors, most important of which is their limited cognitive ability for planning and carrying out a suicide. In addition, thinking at this age is primarily concrete, and thinking about the future (which, when bleak, may influence suicidal thinking in adolescents and adults) is not well developed, which serves as a protection from hopelessness. Young children have more limited information and access about lethal methods of suicide, and are less likely to have problems with depression or substance abuse, which elevate risk in older individuals (Goldman & Beardslee, 1999).

Assessment of suicidal thoughts is difficult with young children. First, they are likely to be uncomfortable talking to a "stranger" about personal material. Second, their verbal abilities and vocabulary may not be sufficient to express these ideas. Skillful use of play and art therapy approaches may allow a clinician to detect suicidal thinking in a child. Children who are questioned about suicidal ideation or attempts may also deny such ideas for fear they will get in trouble if they tell the truth.

When children are diagnosed with a depressive disorder, medication is one of the options. With increasing publicity about increases in suicidal behavior in children taking antidepressants, physicians are more cautious about prescribing these drugs. The use of medication to treat depression in children and adolescents has received a great deal of publicity, much of it misleading. The National Institute of Mental Health (NIMH) weighs in on the debate on their website, stating that selective serotonin reuptake inhibitors (SSRIs) "have been shown to be of benefit to adolescents with major depressive disorder" (NIMH, 2005). The site acknowledges that more research is needed to increase knowledge about the use of antidepressants with youth. In an FDA review, 2,000 children treated with SSRIs were studied, and no completed suicides occurred. However, the rate for other suicidal behaviors (including attempts) was 4% for those treated with SSRIs and 2% for those who received placebos. They caution that any child or adolescent taking antidepressant medication should be closely monitored. In clinical trials, one in ten children experienced adverse side effects. NIMH warns that a *small subset of adolescents* [italics in the original] may have an increase in suicidal behaviors when taking fluoxetine (Prozac), and there is no way to determine in advance who will have such reactions.

In their review of the research on the use of medication for depression in children and adolescents, Emslie and Mayes (2001) noted that research has examined effectiveness at different points in treatment. For acute treatment, tricyclic antidepressants were not found to have a clinically significant effect over a placebo. However, all but one study found a substantial effect for fluoxetine (Prozac) at this stage of treatment, with more subjects recovered using fluoxetine than a placebo and no difference in response between children and adolescents. Because children and adolescents have a high rate of recurrence of depression after recovery, it is important to examine the effects of continuation of medication beyond the point at which symptoms are no longer present. Only one study of continuing medication was reported, and findings demonstrated effectiveness of fluoxetine over placebo for preventing relapse and increasing the amount of time before relapse occurred. There was no information available on the effect of long-term treatment with medication in children and adolescents.

SSRIs are used with children and adolescents because they have fewer side effects than older tricyclic antidepressants, and are less toxic in an overdose. Fluoxetine is the only antidepressant that has received FDA approval for use in children aged 8 and older, but physicians can prescribe other medications in what is known as "off-label use." Whereas Prozac contains a warning for use with children, another SSRI (paroxetine a.k.a. Paxil) was specifically advised against by the FDA. Research is likely to increase in the future, as the FDA Modernization Act of 1977 required manufacturers of certain medications approved for adults but used with children to conduct studies on children (Emslie & Mayes, 2001). Even when medication is utilized, it should not be the only treatment.

Adolescents

Since about 30% of adolescent suicides are repeat attempts, follow-up after the initial assessment and treatment intervention with a suicidal teen are particularly critical. In a large majority of cases, those who eventually commit suicide will die by the same method used in their first attempt, and the first few months following the initial attempt are the time of greatest risk (Spirito, Boergers, & Donaldson, 2000). Among suicide attempters, substance-abusing teenage males have the highest risk for eventually completing suicide. The best predictor of additional attempts is the lethality of the initial attempt; the presence of a mood disorder, and/or ongoing conduct and behavior problems are additional predictors. Adolescent suicide attempters are also at greater risk for death by other means, including vehicle accidents, homicide, and overdose.

A major concern with adolescents is that there is often poor compliance with outpatient treatment. Researchers have been unable to identify factors that contribute to better compliance, but there is some evidence that the type of treatment may be important. In one study, the best rates of compliance were with medication, followed by individual therapy, with poorest compliance for family therapy. Given the importance of follow-up with this age group of suicide attempters, there are some strategies that may improve involvement in treatment following a suicide attempt. First, when an assessment or hospitalization is completed, a specific appointment for counseling should be set. At this time, the adolescent and his or her parents or guardians should be given information about therapy, and the importance of restricting access to lethal means should be emphasized. They need to understand that not only firearms, but medication, toxic household chemicals, cars, belts, and shoelaces, and the like, can all be used for suicide, and they must be highly vigilant during and following the acute crisis. Phone numbers to use in emergencies should be provided (with 24-hour coverage), and some potential stressors should be identified and possible coping strategies discussed. For example, if the adolescent has been hospitalized and has missed school, he or she should anticipate that friends and classmates may ask where she or he has been. An answer that is acceptable to the client should be planned and rehearsed. Any barriers to involvement in treatment should be discussed (e.g., transportation) and strategies devised to ensure participation. Phone reminders the day before appointments may be helpful. Finally, suggesting brief therapy (six sessions, e.g.) may counter the client's or family's belief that treatment is endless.

What kind of treatment is effective? While empirical studies are few, there are clinical suggestions that are useful to consider in treatment planning. First, the motivation for the suicide needs to be explored, so that alternative strategies and more effective ways of coping with the underlying issues can be generated. For example, if the adolescent attempted suicide because of perceived alienation from friends and family, they can be helped to develop more effective social and communication skills to increase social support. They also will need to accept the reality that not everyone will like them. Other cognitive techniques may help adolescents more realistically assess the nature and severity of their problems (to counter the tendency to catastrophize), and to generate alternatives for resolving problems. For many adolescents, learning to manage intense emotion (such as anger) will be useful, as will modifying negative self-talk and learning relaxation methods.

Because depression is so strongly linked to suicide, it is useful to know something about treatment approaches found to be effective with this disorder.

Interpersonal Therapy for Adolescents

In addition to medication, a form of therapy has been found to be effective for depressed adolescents—interpersonal psychotherapy (IPT-A). IPT is a brief treatment with the dual goals of identifying and treating depression first, and then identifying and treating the interpersonal problem areas related to the depression. The problem areas are grief, personal role disputes, role transitions, and interpersonal deficits. For adolescents, an additional problem area is single-parent families. The focus in this approach is on the present, rather than the past (Harrington, Whittaker, & Shoebridge, 1998). Curry (2001) utilized criteria for considering treatment to be efficacious: it proved superior to placebo or other treatment in a randomized, controlled trial, and the research design included a treatment manual, a defined population, reliable and valid outcome measures, and appropriate statistical analysis. When the criteria have been met in more than one research setting, the treatment is considered "well established." IPT-A is considered "possibly efficacious" because only one research group meets the criteria. Mufson, Weissman, Moreau, and Garfinkel (1999) found that following a twelve-week IPT-A treatment program, the treatment group reported fewer depressive symptoms than the control group, were rated as significantly less depressed by clinicians, reported significantly better functioning with friends and dating relationships than the controls, and showed better problem-solving skills than controls.

One other study compared IPT with CBT (cognitive-behavioral therapy) and wait-list controls with Puerto Rican adolescents, and reported a significant impact on self-reported symptoms of depression as well as improved self-esteem and social adaptation with IPT (Rossello & Bernal, 1999). Unlike the Mufson et al. (1999), study, these researchers did not measure diagnostic status after treatment, nor did they utilize the Mufson et al. modification of the problem areas. Hollon, Thase, and Markowitz (2002) noted that previous studies found both IPT and CBT to be more effective at reducing depressive symptoms than the control condition, with IPT having a greater effect. The additional benefit of improved self-esteem and social adaptation was found in the IPT group only.

Cognitive-Behavioral Therapy.   Cognitive-behavioral therapy is based on the notion that depression is associated with faulty cognitions or maladaptive coping behaviors

(Curry, 2001). CBT treatment differs in emphasis according to development, with children receiving more behavioral interventions and the focus in adolescents on cognitive strategies (Holland, Thase, & Markowitz, 2002). All of the six controlled studies of CBT with children prior to 2001 were conducted in the school setting and examined self-reported depressive symptoms. Nine controlled studies investigated the effectiveness of CBT with adolescents, most using an experimental design with subjects randomly assigned to groups. Curry concluded that in children with severe depression, CBT has demonstrated efficacy in symptom reduction. Other researchers found CBT more effective than systematic behavioral family therapy or nondirective supportive therapy (Holland, Thase, & Markowitz).

Combined Treatment. What does research suggest is the best treatment for depression in children and adolescents? Recent clinical trials with 439 adolescents aged 12–17 at thirteen sites around the country found that fluoxetine (Prozac) in combination with CBT was superior to either the medication or therapy alone and a placebo alone (March et al., 2004). A positive response to treatment for those participants who received the combined fluoxetine and therapy was 71%; for fluoxetine alone, 61%; for therapy alone, 43%; and for the placebo group, 35%. Regarding suicidal behaviors, the rates in the fluoxetine alone and the placebo alone were similar. However, there were more suicidal behaviors in the therapy plus medicine group, which the research team found confusing. They speculated this may relate to the small number of cases.

In a critique of recent research on the controversy regarding the use of medication with children and adolescents with depression, Dubicka and Goodyer (2005) concluded that basic psychoeducation should be the first effort at treating the problem. If the depression does not remit, and is mild, CBT should be provided; if it is severe, then fluoxetine and CBT should be used together. They add that if there is no response in a reasonable time period to the combined treatment, alternative SSRIs should be considered. Interestingly, these authors comment that adverse effects of medication must be documented, but there is no requirement to record information about adverse effects of therapy, which they believe could also occur.

While family problems may underlie the suicide attempt, the clinician might want to defer family therapy until the adolescent is more stable and has acquired some skills to communicate effectively. In fact, it may work best to consider the adolescent the client, and to invite family members as "consultants" at some point in the treatment program.

College Students

The comparatively low rate of suicide among college students does not mean counselors working with this population should be any less vigilant about suicide than those working with other groups. Suicide is still the second leading cause of death in this group (Ellen, 2002). A survey of a nationally representative sample of college students found that 10% had seriously considered suicide in the previous year. It is likely that college students who engage in suicidal behavior have not met developmental challenges earlier in life, so are not equipped with the necessary coping skills (Schwartz & Whittaker, 1990). Surveys of college students who attempted suicide reveal that there are particular issues that are mentioned often as the precipitant: grade problems, loneliness, money problems, and problems in romantic relationships. In addition to these precipitants, other risk factors included legal problems, parent problems, and hopelessness and helplessness. Substance use elevated the risk for suicidal behavior, and joining a sorority or fraternity served as a protective factor.

A major concern with this group is that they tend not to seek counseling services, and thus problems that could lead to suicidal behaviors continue unresolved when treatment could be a great benefit. Outreach to college students is an important component of counseling this population. In one study, only 12% of students reported receiving any suicide awareness at their institution. There are some aspects of college life that may push a vulnerable student to suicide: leaving home (and social support networks), facing new academic and social pressures, and sleep deprivation. In addition, several serious psychiatric disorders, such as schizophrenia and bipolar disorder, begin to appear in this age group, adding to the risk factors. The prevalence of substance abuse on many campuses is an additional complication for many students.

Some colleges have begun to utilize screening for depression and suicide and other mental health problems, in some cases using online surveys that students can take in their own homes. It has been suggested that a freshman survey on an intake form would help identify students at risk, and a follow-up could inform them of available services. It has been reported that college students who commit suicide are 150 times more likely to have a psychotic disorder than their peers. Screening to identify such students would allow for early intervention and treatment. Because of the relationships between substance abuse and suicide, substance abuse screening can be an important element of a suicide prevention plan for college students.

Several groups of students are an elevated risk. Foreign students, who may be struggling with separation from family and adjusting to a new culture in addition to any risk factors they already have are particularly vulnerable. Other students who come from communities that are markedly different from the university setting are also at risk, as social isolation and a new setting add to the pressure of increased academic expectations compared to their high school experiences. Programs on campus that help introduce freshmen to campus would benefit from the inclusion of campus counselors and community resources on the program.

Because many students, particularly freshmen, live in residence halls, resident assistants and hall directors need to be well trained in identifying students at risk for suicide, and in intervention and referral techniques. In one university, the counselors from the campus counseling center are assigned to each residence hall, and form relationships through workshops and other programming for both students and staff. With such an arrangement, if students need to be referred for services, the counselor will be more familiar and less threatening to students than if they had never met.

Adults

As with other age groups, the presence of risk factors is the backdrop for suicidal behavior. Adulthood is characterized by starting families and establishing careers. Young adulthood is a time of peak mental and physical performance, and for many this is the time in which their roles as partners, parents, and workers are defined. In Erikson's terms, early adulthood is focused on achieving intimacy, and in those who do not accomplish this task successfully, the outcome may be isolation. In middle adulthood, persons are concerned with generativity (or leaving something behind for future generations); when this does not occur, the individual experiences stagnation. In this period of life, most adults experience increased responsibilities as well as opportunities to make significant contributions to work and family. Many adults begin to reflect and evaluate the course of their lives (the "midlife crisis"). For some midlife adults, changes such as launching of the last child may precipitate a feeling of loss along with a heightened awareness of their own mortality. These tasks of adulthood may generate the precipitating events for suicide in vulnerable persons.

Working with suicidal adults requires the same skills for working with suicidal individuals at other stages of life. Recognition of risk factors, assessment of the ability to cope with stressful life events, assessing for substance abuse and mental disorders (particularly mood disorders) provides the counselor with basic information about how vulnerable the individual might be to suicidal behaviors. With adults, it is always important to be sure clients have had recent complete physical examinations, as some psychological symptoms (e.g., depression) can be linked to physical conditions (e.g., thyroid function). Because adults will have had more life experience than younger clients, they may benefit from attention to how they have coped with stress before, with a focus on enhancing coping skills. It is important to assess the level of social support, which is a protective factor against suicide. In America today, there is much mobility, and the availability of family is often compromised as a result. Clients may need assistance in establishing new networks of support, and so the counselor must be aware of community resources that clients may be encouraged to access. Researchers found that the mobility factor most closely associated with nearly lethal suicide attempts is the number of moves in the previous year (Potter et al., 2001).

Treatment for suicidal adults follows the same model as treatment at other ages. Research has found cognitive behavioral treatment and medication to be the most effective, with interpersonal therapy for depression also showing positive results. Because of the central role of family in the lives of most adults, involving family members in treatment and/or using some strategies from family therapy is generally helpful. Simon (2004) stresses the importance of acknowledging the adult's status when working with potentially suicidal individuals: refer to them by their last name, inform them immediately about issues of confidentiality, and involving spouses or other family members in safety plans. Assessing the likelihood of compliance with treatment is important, as the best plans will not be effective if not followed. It is essential to inquire about substance use and abuse, as this elevates suicide risk and may require targeted treatment once the suicidal crisis is stabilized.

The Elderly

Erikson described the task of older adults as seeking integrity, a sense that one's life had purpose; the opposite pole is despair. Physically and cognitively, many older adults must face loss of physical abilities, sensory acuity, and intellectual facility as aging increases sensory loss (hearing declines, vision deteriorates), more frequent and serious medical illness, and some cognitive slowing. These developmental characteristics may be a factor in the high suicide rates observed in this age group.

Given the relatively high rates of suicide in the elderly (especially elderly males), this is an important population to discuss. Older Americans who commit suicide are less likely than younger people to signal their intent or provide clues to their plans, and are less often to use suicidal behaviors to cry for help. They are more likely to make lethal attempts and to plan carefully to avoid surviving the attempt. Additional risk factors that appear in this age group may alert counselors that suicide is a possibility. Losing a spouse increases the risk for suicide, with the greatest risk being in the first year following the death (Osgood & Thielman, 1990). Social isolation also increases risk, particularly if the elderly person also is depressed or has another serious mental disorder. The single most common reason for suicide given by the elderly (when a reason is known) is health status, with as high as 35% of suicides in this group being associated with a physical illness (Conwell, 1997). The increasing number and seriousness of health problems creates many stressors for the elderly, such as concerns about access to health care and medication, inability to manage ordinary daily tasks, and reduction in activities. If an elderly person has also made a suicide attempt earlier in life, they are twenty times more likely to commit suicide than those who had made no previous attempt.

Depression may not be diagnosed in the elderly, who can be successfully treated. Mental health professionals working with an elderly clientele need to take a careful history to determine the presence of chronic risk factors, and to get an accurate picture of their current status. Asking about suicide is an important part of history-taking, and this should not be overlooked in this population.

Counselors can also serve as advocates for better vigilance on the part of physicians. While many elderly may not seek mental health treatment, they are likely to see a physician. Most elderly people who commit suicide have seen a physician within thirty days of their death, and some within a week. If primary care physicians are most likely to see elderly clients, they need to be educated about the risk of suicide. There are numerous treatment options for this group, including medication, psychotherapy and counseling, electroconvulsive therapy, life review therapy, supportive group therapy, and environmental changes. It is essential that access to lethal means be prevented. One expert suggested that elderly people need to have three things in their environments: connectedness, effectance (a sense of control over one's life and the ability to make choices), and identity. Living conditions, whether at home or in an institution, need to provide for these needs, and counselors again can be advocates for these conditions. Dr. William Thomas has taken these needs into account in designing a unique nursing home. His ideas are applied in the Green House Project. Readers can learn more about this by visiting this website http://www.npr.org/templates/story/story.php?storyId=4713566, or reading his book.

A final word on counseling geriatric clients: as suicide is more prevalent in this group than any other, and because there are so many unique stressors for this age group, the effective counselor will need to involve a multidisciplinary team, including medical doctors, to be successful in preventing suicide in this clientele.

Survivors of Suicide

A completed suicide affects a wide range of people—friends, family, and counselors among them. Although grief and bereavement will be covered in a separate chapter, there are unique aspects to this process when the deceased died by suicide. Several former clients come to mind. One young woman, aged 16, had been romantically involved with a talented and popular young man for about a year, and the relationship was becoming very serious. The girl decided that they were too young to be so serious, and told the young man she thought they should date others. He hung himself that evening. She was devastated, both by the loss and by the reactions of peers, many of whom were quite vocal about how she had "killed" her boyfriend. Instead of being supported in her grief, she was taunted by the comments of others, and eventually had to change schools in an effort to get beyond this terrible period in her life.

Another young man, aged 15, shared that his mother had committed suicide when he was nine years old. He had found her body when he arrived home from school. Although he had a very loving and supportive father and grandparents, he suffered from chronic depression. He was tormented by questions: "Why did she not want to see me grow up?" "She must have known I'd be the one to find her. Didn't she care what that would do to me?" "Didn't she love me?" Every significant event in his life—positive or negative—brought those questions to the forefront. There were times when he entertained suicidal thoughts himself, and needed to be closely monitored by his father (who clearly had his own struggles with his wife's death). At one point, he visited his mother's grave and left some poetry he had written to express his feelings, in the hopes that this act might relieve some of his pain. I suspect this incident will resurface at various times in this young man's life, with variations on the questions taking new meaning as he reaches milestones in his own life.

In addition to the emotional impact of the suicide, there are elements of this kind of death that add stress for family members. Death by suicide generally involves investigations by police, and may result in attention from the media. Each of these procedures is difficult to cope with at a time of tragic and unexpected loss. In addition, some religious denominations have restrictions on the rites available to those who die by suicide, and planning for services may be complicated. The assistance of a family friend or pastor with managing these intrusions can lessen the burden for the family.

Survivors of a death by suicide generally struggle to make sense of the death. Questions of "Why?" trouble survivors, and the fact that the answer may never be known is particularly difficult. Even when there is a suicide note, the content often raises more questions than it answers, and survivors ultimately must accept that their questions will remain unanswered. An additional burden for survivors is often guilt. They may blame themselves for acts they perceive contributed to the decision to suicide ("If only I had not said such mean things to him"), or feel responsible because they did not recognize the signs or intervene to prevent the suicide ("If I had come home earlier, I could have stopped her"). Emotionally, it is confusing to survivors who feel rejected or abandoned by the deceased, ("I must not have been very important to her") and at the same time experience anger ("How could you do this to me?").

Among adolescents, I have noticed that when there is a peer death (accident or suicide being the most common cause of death), there is a tendency for many students to describe themselves as "best friends" of the deceased. Whether or not this is fact, it makes sense for counselors to respond to their grief. The loss of a peer at this age makes their own mortality apparent, and youth may appear to experience exaggerated bereavement when in fact they are grieving both the loss of the person and the loss of the illusion that they will live forever.

These emotional reactions may be experienced in a context (real or imagined) of isolation or stigmatization by others. Survivors may believe others hold them responsible or have other negative beliefs, and they may feel a lack of social support at a time when such support is very much needed. Because family relationships may be strained at such a time, individual survivors may feel they cannot talk about the suicide or their feelings in the family. In fact, family members themselves are at elevated risk for suicide.

What might be helpful to survivors of suicide? Counseling may be offered, and sometimes is accepted. However, in those cases in which the deceased was receiving counseling and then completed the suicide, the survivors may feel anger and distrust of counselors, who were unable to prevent their loss. In these cases, groups of suicide survivors receive support from others who had a similar experience. Hospice groups in many communities offer special support groups for survivors of suicide. For others, who are reluctant to engage in any social networks, bibliotherapy may provide some helpful information. Helpful books will be listed in the Resources section at the end of the chapter.

Screening for Depression

In elementary age children, depression is often expressed as bodily complaints. Frequent stomachaches and headaches are observed. Anxiety about school (not wanting to go to school, excessive worrying about school performance) is another way depression is exhibited in children of this age. They may be extremely fearful of being separated from parents, and may develop temper tantrums and behavioral problems, and be irritable or agitated. Such symptoms may not raise a red flag to the uninformed observer, and such children are often treated as discipline problems. Underlying sadness and hopelessness may not be easily detected, and poor self-esteem and expression of guilt may not be associated with possible depression. The counselor may be the only person who is aware of the link between such a pattern and possible depression, and as such has an opportunity to intervene and refer the child for further evaluation.

In adolescents, the sadness and hopelessness may be more obvious, and withdrawal from friends and previously enjoyed activities is another sign. Changes in eating and sleeping patterns, poor school performance, and low energy are other signals. The challenge with adolescents is that many teenagers experience these symptoms on occasion, and adults may dismiss them as "just being a teenager." In adolescents, we are more likely to find drug and alcohol abuse (which may be initiated as a kind of self-medication of unpleasant feelings) and suicidal thoughts and behavior, so identifying untreated depression is particularly important.

Children and adolescents may mask their feelings, and may have difficulty verbalizing what they are experiencing. The observant counselor can pay attention to other means of expression that provide clues to the inner world of the child. Play, art, and writing are activities that may reveal clues to a depressed child. Drawings that look sad and morose, or contain damaged or morbid images and gloomy colors, may signal sadness or preoccupation with fears and death. Stories and other writings, particularly in adolescence, may reveal thoughts and feelings that are not openly talked about. Adolescents may appear angry rather than sad.

Various behaviors might also lead a counselor to wonder about possible depression. When a child suddenly develops behavior problems, or seems unusually (for that child) irritable, distractible, and easily frustrated, depression may be behind the behaviors. Disciplinary referrals are likely to increase, and the counselor should make note of this. In addition, unexpected changes in grades and school performance may be more than laziness or lack of interest; sleeping in class may also signal underlying mood problems.

Children who exhibit one or more of the symptoms described above should be screened for depression. It is important to clarify what is meant by screening. Screening is *not* diagnosing. Screening is a way to learn whether symptoms are present and how severe they are. Students who score above the cutoff should be referred for a more thorough evaluation by a physician or psychologist. The referral to a physician is important because there are some medical conditions that will produce symptoms similar to depression, and those should be ruled out or treated. There are several well-researched screening tools that are available and easy to use in the school setting; these are described in Table 6.1. All are self-report measures. I encourage you to contact publishers or go to publishers' websites for further information. Counselors may wish to compare costs, ease of scoring, and psychometric properties in deciding which inventory would be most useful in their setting.

Issues of Diversity

Members of diverse groups experience additional risk factors not present in Caucasians. Counselors must be sensitive to these differences, and work to provide treatment that is responsive to the needs of all clients. Ideally, we would have a more diverse population of counselors; in locales where that is not the case, counselors would do well to create collaborative relationships with diverse professionals who work in other settings whom they can call upon when needed.

Gender

Suicide at all ages is 5.8 times as common in males as in females (www.postsecondary.org), but females attempt suicide at a higher rate (Moscicki, 1997). Eighty percent of those who commit suicide are male, but the majority of suicide attempts are found in women aged 25–44 (Gliatto & Rai, 1999). Clinicians should routinely ask about suicidal thoughts and past attempts in initial contact with male clients, who may not mention these things without prompting.

Age

A cause for alarm is the rate of suicide in children 10–14 years old, which increased 109% from 1980 to 1997. While the absolute number is relatively small (300 in 2000),

TABLE 6.1 Screening Instruments for Depression

Instrument	Appropriate for	Written at Reading Level	Number of Items	Comments
Children's Depression Inventory (CDI)	Ages 7–17	1st grade	27 items in the regular form. Also available in a 10-item brief form of the most important items.	This screening inventory has three statements after each stem, and the child marks the one that is most like him/her. Quick to administer and score. Available in Spanish.
Reynolds Child Depression Scale (RCDS)	Ages 8–12	2nd grade	30 items	Easy to administer and score. Available in Spanish.
Reynolds Adolescent Depression Scale (RADS)	Ages 13–18	3rd grade	30 items	Easy to administer and score.
The Beck Depression Inventory for Youth (BDI-Y)	Ages 7–14	2nd grade	20 items	Students respond to statements by indicating how frequently a statement is true for them. No Spanish version available.
Center for Epidemiological Studies—Depression Scale for Children (CES-DC)	Ages 12–18	6th grade	20 items	Scoring is straightforward.

the fact that any suicides occur in this age group is particularly disconcerting. Within this age group, suicide rates increased 233% among African Americans. Firearms were used in 69% of suicides among African American males aged 15–19. The greatest increase in this group was found in the Southern part of the United States. In rural areas, guns may be used for subsistence hunting, but the availability of lethal means increases the risk, so counselors working with depressed African American males may want to gather information about the accessibility of firearms.

Race and Ethnicity

African Americans. In their study of ethnic differences in patterns of suicide over the life span, Garlow, Purselle, and Heninger (2005) examined records of suicides in Fulton County, Georgia from 1994 through 2002, and found that rates and patterns mirrored those reported in national samples. As in other studies, African Americans commit suicide at lower rates than whites, and females had the lowest rates of all groups. Among victims younger than 20, significantly fewer African Americans tested positive for substances at the time of death than did whites in the same age group. In attempting to account for their findings, these researchers noted that although the rates of psychiatric disorders (including depression) have been found to be similar in both groups, the availability of mental health treatment for African Americans is limited, and of lesser quality. Perhaps as a consequence, young African Americans may be reluctant to seek treatment. Counselors must conduct outreach with this population, and provide culturally sensitive and culturally compatible treatment for depression and other disorders that are linked to suicidal behaviors.

On the other hand, African American culture may mitigate against suicide. The protective factors of family support and religiosity are suggested to explain the overall low rates of suicide in this group, and the widely held attitude among African Americans that suicide is not acceptable may also serve as a protection. Counselors need to access community support, and in an intervention, it would be advisable to consider including extended family members as well as clergy. Based on this study, the best prevention strategies would be those that serve to strengthen the protective factors (and those that include screening for depression).

A recent study (Joe, Baser, Breeden, Neighbors, & Jackson, 2006) demonstrated that blacks are not a homogenous group. They discovered that black men of Caribbean birth or ancestry had the highest rate of suicide attempts compared to other black men and women. They also found that the highest rate of suicidal behaviors occurred in the late teens and early 20s. Suicidal behaviors in this age group were more impulsive than those at later ages, which tended to be more planned. The highest risk for progression from suicide ideation to planning to attempts was in the first year after the onset of ideation, so this is a crucial period for intervention. As in other groups, those with suicide ideation who had a psychiatric disorder were significantly more likely to attempt suicide than those without such a disorder.

Hispanics/Latinos.   Although Latino youth in the United States commit suicide at lower rates than other ethnic groups, they are much more likely (particularly females) to make suicide attempts (Canino & Roberts, 2001). The Latino or Hispanic group is not homogeneous, and although the following discussion will generalize some concepts, there are intra-group differences depending on country of origin. Suicide ideation and attempts of Latino-American youth (Mexican American, Puerto Rican, and Dominican American) are higher than rates among comparable youth in their country of origin. This fact may provide some insight into the increased ideation and attempts: acculturative stress. A detailed discussion of that concept is beyond the scope of this chapter, but acculturative stress refers to a number of stressors such as conflicts in values between cultures, perceived discrimination, language difficulties, and perceived poor opportunities. Family support and positive expectations about the future appeared to protect against acculturative stress and thus protect against suicidal behaviors. Counselors would be wise to consider acculturation factors in planning suicidal prevention, intervention, and postvention. The protective factor of family support is important, but many counselors face a language barrier when communicating with Spanish-dominant or monolingual Spanish-speaking clients. Parent training and education programs are usually presented in English, excluding those parents who are not fluent in the language. The need for more bilingual and bicultural counselors to serve this group is critical.

Native Americans.   Native American youth have the highest rate of suicide among all groups. These youth experience many of the risk factors as other groups, but also have added risk factors unique to this group: social disintegration and cultural conflict (Webb & Metha, 1996). While some tribes have maintained their separate cultural identities, others have integrated with the majority culture. For many Native American youth, adopting the majority cultural values means a loss of pride in their culture and decreased self-esteem. High rates of alcoholism and suicide may be the effect of "social alienation, social confusion, and self-hate," (p. 25).

Gary, Baker, and Grandbois (2005) believe that suicide among Native Americans is a fatalistic suicide, a reaction to the historical regulation by the dominant culture, including loss of their land, exploitation of natural resources, forced relocation, and forced assimilation. These experiences have led to pessimism about the future, and suicide may be the result. Living conditions on many reservations are substandard, with high unemployment and inadequate health and education facilities and services. In addition to the high rates of suicide, these authors point out that Native American youth die at high rates from preventable injuries, some of which may actually be suicides. Previous research found that for a large sample of Navajo adolescents in grades 6–12, risk factors for suicidal behavior included feelings of alienation from family and community, having a friend who made a suicide attempt, and use of alcohol on a regular basis. Family history of suicide, a history of physical abuse and violence in the family, and sexual abuse were additional risk factors. Protective factors were also detected. Girls were protected by attention in the family, positive feelings about school, and caring by family and other adults. For boys, positive experiences at school, participating in traditional activities, good academic performance, and caring by family and other adults were the most prominent protective factors. For both boys and girls, support and caring by tribal leaders was a protective factor. Another previous study on Northern Plains reservations found that commitment to cultural spirituality was associated with reduced suicidal behaviors. In addition to common risk factors, an additional risk is the presence of guns in the homes. As many Native Americans hunt for food, guns are among the basic tools found in the homes of many families.

Metha and Webb (1996) cite LaFramboise and Bigfoot, who observed that the governmental pressures to assimilate (via boarding schools and prohibition of native language use in government schools for many years) may have created only one road to freedom: suicide. Further, some cultural attitudes may make suicide a more viable option to at-risk individuals. The self-control that is admired in the culture may cause some youth who are experiencing psychological problems to internalize those problems. In some tribes, death is not as feared as it might be in other cultures, and the belief in ongoing contact between the human and spirit world may diminish the fear as well.

In some tribes, large ceremonies (sometimes involving giveaways) that occur after a death, including a suicide, may be attractive to vulnerable youth.

Implications for counselors include the high need for suicide awareness programs for Native Americans in schools and communities (Metha & Webb, 1996). Parent education is also crucial, and often difficult to implement. Outreach should be ongoing, and personal visits and tribal liaison personnel must be used to encourage involvement in programs and activities. To increase attendance at programs for suicide awareness, counselors can encourage the use of raffles and food as an incentive for attendance, and support the use of tribal members as speakers. Finally, staff training in suicide awareness for all professionals working with Native Americans should be mandatory, and should include follow-up sessions on a regular basis.

In addition, intervention strategies should employ traditional native practices (such as the healing circle and the medicine wheel), and the role of the counselor might be to refer to tribal sources for these practices. When the only mental health providers are non-Indians, the use of traditional healers is especially important to avoid conflicts with cultural beliefs. Involving family when a person is at imminent risk, and bringing members of the extended family into the consultation may increase the effectiveness of the intervention. As involvement in traditional cultural practices is a protective factor, encouraging and supporting that involvement is a useful preventive effort (Gary, Baker, & Grandbois, 2005).

Asian Americans/Pacific Islanders.   Although no literature speaks to specific risks for suicide in Asian Americans/Pacific Islanders, suicide is the third leading cause of death in youth in this group aged 10–24; this group should not be ignored in efforts to reduce suicide. Suicide is also the eighth highest cause of death among Asian and Pacific Islander males of all ages. Chung (2002) noted that Asian American youth are considered to be prone to depression. She cites racism, the absence of Asian teachers and professionals in the school system, conflict with parents (students are likely to be more acculturated than parents), and parental emotional unavailability as unique risk factors for this group.

Sexual Minorities

Sexual minority youth are also at higher risk for suicide than their heterosexual peers (Russell, 2003). For this group, an additional risk factor is the possibility of abuse from relatives and family members who reject the child's sexual orientation. These students are often victims of violence and bullying at school as well. The adolescent task of identity formation may be difficult for sexual minority youth because of societal attitudes (Kirk, 1993). Social support from other LGB peers, family support, and self-acceptance of the sexual minority identity are protective factors. School counselors must be available to these students and be an advocate for measures to protect them in the school environment. Further, with student consent, school counselors can provide parents with information about community resources that might be helpful as they adjust to their child's sexual orientation.

Overall, members of these diverse groups experience additional risk factors not present in Caucasian students. School counselors must be sensitive to these differences, and work to provide programming that is responsive to the needs of all students. Ideally, we would have a more diverse population of school counselors; school counselors would do well to create collaborative relationships with diverse professionals who work in other settings whom they can call upon when needed.

Persons with Disabilities

There is strong evidence that having any disability increases risk for suicide (Charlifue & Gerhart, 1991; Hartkopp, Brønnum-Hansen, Seidenschnur, & Biering-Sørensen, 1998; World Health Organization, 2000). I will provide an overview of what is known about the relationship of some types of disability and suicide, but it is far from inclusive. I recommend that mental health professionals carefully assess for suicide in all clients, particularly those with disabilities.

Hartokopp and colleagues (1998) examined the records of 888 men and women with spinal cord injuries. The rate of suicide was higher than that in the general population (also found by Charlifue & Gerhart, 1991), but the rate declined over time. The highest rates were immediately following the injury. Poisoning was the method in 48% of the suicides. Risk factors were previous psychiatric diagnoses and previous attempts. In fact, 22% of those who committed suicide sustained their spinal cord injury in a suicide attempt, and two of those eventually committed suicide using the same method. These researchers made several surprising discoveries in the data. First, rates of suicide were higher in those patients who had almost complete physical recovery from the spinal cord injury. They theorize that it may be easier to adjust to an extreme loss (total paralysis) that is clear and definite than from a condition that is less certain. They also suggest that perhaps less support is provided to these individuals because their prognosis is so much better. An additional surprise in the findings is that the rate of suicide was higher for women than for men. The authors speculate that women's self-image is more often tied to their physical appearance, making it more difficult to cope with physical disabilities. For older women who have been caretakers in marriage, the reversal in roles necessitated by the disability might be intolerable. The final important point is that even those who are quadriplegic are able to commit suicide (via poisoning).

Charlifue and Gerhart's study of suicide in individuals with spinal cord injuries compared those who committed suicide with a matched control group. The most important factors were identified: family disruption prior to the injury and depression, alcohol abuse, apathy or withdrawal, weight loss, anger, and destructive behavior after the injury. This combination of factors was found to predict suicides with 80% accuracy. This suggests that these factors are signals that should alert providers that intervention by mental health professionals would be helpful.

Patients with traumatic brain injury (TBI) are also at high risk for suicide, with a rate of four times that in the general population (Simpson & Tate, 2005). León-Carrión and colleagues (2001) found that clinical depression, known to be associated with suicide in the general population, is associated with suicidal ideation in TBI patients, even after more than eighteen months following discharge from the hospital. Of the TBI patients in their study with depression, 65% were found to have suicidal tendencies. These patients needed more emotional support than they were receiving because they had difficulty coping with stress, dealing with complex situations, and using abstract reasoning. The authors recommended against using exclusively cognitive approaches treatment with this group, who needed assistance managing emotions and needed instruction in social skills. Graham and Tate found elevated risk in those clients with a history of psychiatric or emotional disturbances after the injury, substance dependence, or both. They also found that those who made repeated attempts did so within a circumscribed period of time, suggesting a need for close monitoring for up to a year after the initial attempt. They found that the most effective method for preventing suicide was limiting the availability of methods (medications, sharp objects, etc.).

Persons with epilepsy have a risk for suicide that is five to ten times that of the general population (Nowack, 2006). Sander and Bell (2004) report a rate three times the general population, with higher rates for those with temporal lobe epilepsy. These authors suggest that cooperation between medical providers and mental health providers would be helpful for this population.

Another disability that appears to be associated with an increased suicide risk is an HIV-positive diagnosis (Kalichman, Heckman, Kochman, Sikkema, & Bergholte, 2000). Among those at greatest risk are those HIV-positive persons who also abuse drugs, are socially isolated, and lack social support. The risk appears to be greatest soon after the positive diagnosis is confirmed, suggesting that suicidal thoughts may diminish with time after the diagnosis. However, it is possible that there will be an increased risk when AIDS symptoms appear. In their diverse sample, the presence of suicidal ideation was highest among white gay men who were currently experiencing symptoms. The researchers were surprised to find that suicidal ideation was higher among those who had disclosed their HIV-positive status to close friends and family. They speculated that when such disclosures are met with rejection, the consequence is psychologically devastating.

Multiple sclerosis (MS) is also associated with higher rates of suicide (Feinstein, 2002). Men who were diagnosed prior to age 30 were at higher risk. In his comparison of suicidal and non-suicidal MS patients, Feinstein found that living alone, having severe depression, and a lifetime diagnosis of an alcohol abuse disorder predicted increased suicide risk in the MS patients. Perhaps the most important finding of this research was that many of the suicidal and depressed patients had not been treated for their mental health issues, despite the efficacy of both medication and psychotherapy for depression in MS patients.

Persons with sensory disabilities (blindness, deafness), like the disabilities described above, have increased risk for suicide. It is important for mental health practitioners to keep in mind that the rate of disabilities increases with age, so that the elderly, particularly those with visual impairment, neurological disorders, and malignant diseases are especially vulnerable, and should be assessed (Waern, Rubenowitz, Runeson, Skoop, Wilhelmson, & Allebeck, 2002). Half of deaf respondents to a survey conducted by a charity in Glasgow, Scotland, reported they had considered suicide, with those who became deaf having greater risk than those who were born deaf (Henderson, 2006). Those with low vision, in contrast to those with complete blindness, demonstrate more depression, hostility, and anger (Kaldenberg, 2005). Those who become blind later in life experience grief at the loss of their sight that sometimes becomes severe enough to precipitate suicide or attempts (DeLeo, Hickey, Meneghel, & Cantor, 1999). Those persons who had progressive diseases that lead to blindness had the greatest risk of suicide, greater than those with complete blindness. That is, the risk of suicide in those with visual impairments is greatest when sight remains but the prognosis is blindness. These authors also report that adults who had procedures resulting in the restoration of sight were at elevated risk for suicide, perhaps due to the unanticipated impact of the change.

In summary, I reiterate that clients with disabilities are vulnerable to suicidal ideation, and clinicians need to be sure to assess for suicide in these clients. Perhaps more important, I would hope that mental health practitioners advocate for more collaboration between the medical community that provides treatment for the physical aspects of disabilities and the mental health providers who can address the very important psychological consequences of these disabilities. The research described above is strong evidence of a need for mental health services to clients with disabilities. Physicians treating these disabilities must be educated about the importance of referring clients to mental health professionals to address the serious risk of suicide.

Counselor Issues

There is no doubt that working with suicidal clients is demanding and at times overwhelming. A counselor's skills are tested and counselors fear any mistake can have disastrous consequences. It is absolutely essential that counselors have their own support systems available to debrief these situations, provide professional consultation, and assist in managing their own emotional response.

In situations of such high stress, counselors must not overlook the basic qualities that make them effective in all situations. In their own anxiety, counselors may inadvertently communicate to the client that their interest in the client is only to prevent the suicide, rather than a concern for the client's overall well-being (Hanna & Green, 2004). The counselor must communicate empathy for the client; a deep understanding of why this person considered taking his or her life. The client must believe that he is worthy of the compassion and support of the counselor, and this requires empathy on the part of the counselor. Counselors also must continually monitor their reactions to the client and be sure that any negative feelings are kept in check (and processed with colleagues or in supervision) so that these issues do not interfere with their relationship with this fragile client. Counselors need to explore their own beliefs and fears about suicide and death, and be able to separate those needs from those of the client. Counselors who have experienced a suicide in their own families must be acutely aware of the tendency to be emotionally raw, and recognize their own limitations for working with suicidal clients. Counselors must be aware of the ethical principle not to abandon clients, but referring clients to a more specialized professional may be in the best interest of the client when the referral is made skillfully and at the appropriate time (Remley, 2004).

Record keeping and documentation become even more important in the case of a suicidal client. Documenting all aspects of the case is absolutely necessary. Documentation should include any consultations with other professionals (dates, times, nature of contact). Records should clearly indicate steps that were taken to ensure the client's safety and to notify appropriate persons of the danger. When the counselor makes an assessment of suicidal risk, notes should indicate not only the method of assessment but the rationale for all decisions made in the case. Some experts suggest that the no-suicide contract is helpful for documentation, but if this strategy is used, it is important to note how and why the counselor believed this was appropriate.

BOX 6.1

A Note to School Counselors[1]

School counselors may be involved in all aspects of suicide from prevention programs and activities to intervention with suicidal students, and unfortunately, with response services to students following a completed suicide. School counselors are resources for students and educators, administrators, and family members who seek the advice and expertise of the counselor for addressing this challenge. "Counselors are on the front line for identification, prevention, intervention, and postvention of suicidal behavior. As oppressive as that may feel to counselors, it is nonetheless a fact" (Stefanowski-Harding, 1990, p. 334).

Despite their crucial role, specific training for the school counselors' role in dealing with suicide is lacking in most graduate training programs (Foster & McAdams, 1999). The Council for Accreditation of Counseling and Related Educational Programs (CACREP) guidelines does not require training for suicide response, and most programs, even those not accredited, follow CACREP guidelines in designing their curricula. If an elective course in crisis intervention or suicide is available, not all students will have that training. Thus, most school counselors rely on general counseling skills and techniques, and professional training workshops and other sources, for their skill development. I hope this chapter will provide additional knowledge and resources.

While the roles in prevention, intervention, and postvention are similar at elementary and secondary levels, there are some important differences. Curriculum approaches to suicide awareness are not recommended for elementary students, but classroom guidance lessons that address many of the risk factors for suicide are typically conducted by the counselor. At these times, the counselor needs to be alert to students whose reactions suggest they need further assessment. Although rare, suicides in elementary students do occur, and any mention of suicidal thoughts or behaviors should be taken seriously regardless of the age of the child. Elementary counselors usually provide group counseling and guidance to students, and grief groups are not uncommon. Parental contact tends to be more frequent at the elementary level, so counselors may have more information about family climate and changes in

[1] Some of the material in this chapter, and in this section particularly, was also used for my chapter, *Suicide Prevention, Intervention, and Postvention* in H. L. K. Coleman & C. J. Yeh (Eds.), *Handbook of School Counseling*. Mahwah, NJ: Lawrence Erlbaum Associates, Inc.

(*continued*)

BOX 6.1   **Continued**

the family than do secondary counselors. Secondary school counselors with large caseloads may not have the opportunity to get to know each student well, and thus may not have had the opportunity to build a trusting relationship with the student who is referred for suicidal concerns. Despite these differences, the roles of school counselors at all levels are much more similar than different.

The concepts of primary, secondary, and tertiary prevention are useful frames for the schools' role in suicide reduction (Poland, 1989). Primary prevention efforts target the general population (all students) and have as a goal increasing awareness and knowledge of suicide along with enhancing resilience in students in order to prevent suicidal ideation from emerging. Primary prevention programs are usually components of the curriculum (e.g., health) delivered by teachers or school counselors in a classroom setting. Some programs include a screening component, by which students at risk for developing suicidal behaviors are identified, either by the staff or by students themselves. These students are encouraged to seek assistance to prevent the emergence of suicidal behaviors. One of the resources for help for students at risk is the school counselor.

Secondary prevention efforts target those who are known or believed to be at risk for developing suicidal behaviors. These students may be identified by screening procedures, may be referred by self or others (parents, teachers, administrators), or by contact from outside agencies (police, health providers). Services to these students may take the form of support groups, other counseling groups (e.g., self-esteem building), monitoring, and programs designed to address other risk factors (e.g., substance abuse) and thus indirectly impact the risk for suicide. Even programs (such as buddy systems) for new students can be considered secondary prevention of suicide, as transitions are known stressors that increase risk for suicide in vulnerable students. These prevention efforts are often provided, initiated, and monitored by the school counselor.

Tertiary prevention involves actions directed at those who have already been affected by a suicide, including students who have made an attempt and return to school, and students who have been exposed to the suicide of a friend or family member. The goal of tertiary prevention is to reduce the level of distress and assist students in returning to their former level of functioning. This includes monitoring for signs of increased suicidal ideation, as loss is frequently a precipitant of suicidal behavior. Again, it is the school counselor who is largely responsible for providing these services.

The role of the school becomes one of intervention when a student has been identified as suicidal. The student is provided with support while the counselor assesses the lethality of the student's suicidal behaviors. The assessment strategies described in this chapter are useful for this purpose. The tools for screening for depression in children and adolescents are also helpful in this regard. At this point, it is important to note that the school counselor has a responsibility to notify the parents or guardians and assist them in obtaining appropriate services for the student, from outpatient counseling to hospitalization. The school counselor must also notify the administration according to established procedures.

One of the most difficult aspects of dealing with suicide in the school is responding to the suicide of a student. It is important to recognize that there is a fine line to walk between ignoring and glamorizing a suicide while providing support to those students who are most affected. In addition, a topic that receives too little attention is that of the impact of a student suicide on the school counselor, who may be providing support for students, family, and teachers, and whose own needs are often given short shrift.

For school counselors interested in implementing a suicide prevention and intervention program, there are clearly a number of models from which to choose. They vary in the degree of empirical support for effectiveness, and also in target populations (staff, parents, students, community resources), and other components, so that counselors can determine the best fit for their environments—and they do not have to re-invent the wheel!

Ethical Concerns

There are a number of ethical standards that apply to the school counselor dealing with suicidal students. The Code of Ethics of the American Counseling Association is clear about the counselor's duty to warn in the case of imminent danger. That section of the code also mentions the importance of consulting with others when there is any uncertainty. Another section of the code emphasizes that the limits of confidentiality should be discussed with all clients at the beginning, so the need to break confidentiality in the case of a suicidal client should not be a complete surprise. Figure 6.4 contains the relevant sections of the ethical code.

The other ethical issue related to suicide is that of boundaries of competence. Counselors are expected to practice only in areas in which they have sufficient training. As suicidal clients may be found on any counselor's caseload, regardless of specialty, it is essential that all counselors obtain and advocate for training in suicide prevention, intervention, and postvention. That section of the code is given in Figure 6.5.

FIGURE 6.4   Sections of the *ACA Ethical Code*.

B.1. Right to Privacy

Respect for Privacy. Counselors respect their clients' right to privacy and avoid illegal and unwarranted disclosures of confidential information. (See A.3.a. and B.6.a.)

Client Waiver. The right to privacy may be waived by the client or his or her legally recognized representative.

Exceptions. The general requirement that counselors keep information confidential does not apply when disclosure is required to prevent clear and imminent danger to the client or others or when legal requirements demand that confidential information be revealed. Counselors consult with other professionals when in doubt as to the validity of an exception.

Explanation of Limitations. When counseling is initiated and throughout the counseling process as necessary, counselors inform clients of the limitations of confidentiality and identify foreseeable situations in which confidentiality must be breached. (See G.2.a.)

FIGURE 6.5   Sections of the *ACA Ethical Code*.

C.2. Professional Competence

Boundaries of Competence. Counselors practice only within the boundaries of their competence, based on their education, training, supervised experience, state and national professional credentials, and appropriate professional experience. Counselors will demonstrate a commitment to gain knowledge, personal awareness, sensitivity, and skills pertinent to working with a diverse client population.

While this chapter is not a substitute for such training, it is a good first step to meeting the requirement of competence to treat suicidal individuals and to do so with respect for the many aspects of diversity that may affect their needs and responses.

Summary

1. Suicide is a problem for all age groups, with white males over age 65 having the highest rates of all groups.
2. The most frequent method of suicide in all age groups (with the exception of ages 10–14) is firearms. Restricting access to guns is an important prevention and intervention strategy.
3. Researchers have identified factors, known as risk factors, that elevate a person's risk for suicidal behavior. The more risk factors present, the higher the risk for suicide.
4. Among risk factors, a previous attempt is the strongest predictor of future suicide. Also highly correlated with suicidal behavior are depression and substance abuse. Thus, methods to reduce those problems will reduce suicidal behavior.
5. There are a variety of suicide assessment tools available, from formal standardized instruments (such as the Beck inventories) to informal methods using acronyms. The most important assessment method is the careful clinical interview, gathering information about thoughts, plans, and lethality.
6. No-suicide contracts are widely used, but the counselor must not rely on these as the sole method of suicide prevention.
7. Counselors must break confidentiality to ensure the safety of a suicidal client. Informing all clients of limits to confidentiality at the beginning of counseling makes this easier for clients to accept.
8. Research to date suggests that medication, medication and cognitive-behavioral therapy combined, cognitive-behavioral therapy, and interpersonal therapy for depression, are useful approaches for treatment.
9. Counselor self-care takes on particular importance when working with suicidal clients.

ADDITIONAL RESOURCES

On the Web

- http://www.suicidology.org/ American Association of Suicidology. The links to other resources on this site are exceptionally thorough and include resources for specific groups (e.g., suicide of a sibling).
- http://www.afsp.org/ American Foundation for Suicide Prevention.

In Print for Counselors

- *Suicide Across the Lifespan: Premature Exits* by Judith Stillion and Eugene McDowell (1996).

- *Suicide Across the Lifespan: Implications for Counselors* by David Capuzzi (2004).
- *How to Prepare for and Respond to a Crisis* (2nd ed.) by David Schonfeld, Robert Lichtenstein, Marsha Kline Pruett, and Dee Speese-Linehan is a brief book with step-by-step information that includes many sample documents that a team would find helpful.
- *Suicide Prevention in the Schools: Guidelines for Middle and High School Settings* by David Capuzzi (1994) provides sound information and many handouts that could be used in prevention programming.
- *Night Falls Fast: Understanding Suicide* by Kay Redfield Jamison has the unique quality of having been written by a psychiatrist who has made a suicide attempt herself.
- *No Time to Say Goodbye: Surviving the Suicide of a Loved One* by Carla Fine, is a very helpful perspective on the experience of survivors written by one whose husband committed suicide.
- *Ordinary People*, a novel by Judith Guest presents the serious suicide attempt by an adolescent in a gripping and complex portrayal that helps dispel many of the myths about suicide.

Film and Television

- *Remembering Tom* focuses on the survivors of an adolescent suicide—his parents and two siblings. What is so helpful about this video is that we see how differently each of the family members responds to the loss, and how differently they grieve. Their process of coming to grips with the suicide includes counseling, and counselors can see what was effective.
- *Choice of a Lifetime* profiles a number of individuals who came very close to committing suicide, but did not. Each talks about what led them to that point, what stopped them (in some cases, others intervened), and how they have lived their lives differently since that time. The video includes representatives of a number of high-risk groups, including the elderly, sexual minority, Native American, and other minority group members. Counselors can learn a great deal from listening to these honest and self-aware individuals describe their experiences with suicide.

EXERCISES

1. Counselors need ongoing practice doing a suicide assessment. Assume you are working with a client who experiences a significant loss (e.g., romantic breakup), and you are aware that there are several risk factors present. Role play the interview in which you assess for current suicide risk.

2. Assume you conclude that this client is at imminent risk for suicide. How will you notify family members? What will you recommend? Assume the family members arrive in your office. Role play your session with the family.

3. If you are a school counselor in training, consider that you have a student who you have determined is at high risk for suicide, and that the stressor is conflict with parents. How will you handle informing these parents, and how will you ensure that doing so does not increase tension at home?

4. Watch the movie *Harold and Maude* or *Ordinary People*—what risk factors were present in Harold and Conrad's cases? How does their recovery fit with your understanding of protective factors and treatment?

5. Watch the video *Fatal Mistakes: Families Shattered by Suicide* and discuss the feelings experienced by counselors. Although this video, available from the American Society for Suicide Prevention, weaves factual information with personal testimony of survivors of suicide, the vignettes may evoke emotions that counselors should explore as a vehicle to understanding their own reactions to suicide. One concern with both this video, and another video available from AFSP (*The Suicidal Patient*), is that counseling is not mentioned as a source of help to clients. Write a letter to the producer of the movie discussing your concern about this omission, and explain how counselors can be effective helpers for suicidal individuals.

CHAPTER

7

Trauma and Violence

If one reads a newspaper or watches television, it may seem as though trauma and violence are constants in our lives. We are bombarded by information about natural disasters, war, and deliberate acts of violence. Terrorism, a word now commonplace in daily vocabulary, is an undertone of daily existence. Ten months after Hurricane Katrina devastated the Gulf Coast:

> New Orleans is experiencing what appears to be a near epidemic of depression and post-traumatic stress disorders, one that mental health experts say is of an intensity rarely seen in this country. It is contributing to a suicide rate that state and local officials describe as close to triple what it was before Hurricane Katrina struck and the levees broke 10 months ago. (Saulny, 2006)

Despite the seemingly ubiquitous nature of trauma, its hallmark is its ability to overwhelm our adaptive capacities. It was only in 1980 that the condition, *post-traumatic stress disorder* (PTSD) received a place in the *Diagnostic and Statistical Manual* (DSM); clearly, trauma did not begin so recently. Mental health professionals finally recognized that there was an identifiable cluster of symptoms in some people who had been exposed to all manner of traumatic events, and the inclusion of this diagnosis was an important acknowledgement of the long-term psychological consequences such events can initiate.

Most people (94%) who experience a trauma will have symptoms of psychological disorders (including PTSD and depression) immediately following the trauma, but in most cases these symptoms are no longer present six months later. However, for those who develop PTSD, about 30% still have the disorder after ten years. To reflect these phenomena, PTSD has been described as a "disorder of 'non-recovery' from trauma exposure" (Monson & Friedman, 2006, p. 6).

Helping professionals must understand the nature of trauma, and the ways in which people react and recover from traumatic experiences. Counselors may be part of response teams for events that affect large numbers of people, but they also will work with individuals whose lives have been scarred by more personal traumas. Even the clinician who does not become a trauma specialist may encounter trauma in their workplace, or a disaster in the community (e.g., New Orleans since Katrina, September 11). I conducted several groups during the week of September 11 that were far from the site of the attacks, but all my clients, regardless of their reason for being in counseling, were distressed in varying degrees, and I needed to have sufficient information to help them deal with their reactions and make referrals if needed.

Whether or not you will work with trauma survivors as a specialist, this chapter is important to read. Making appropriate referrals requires considerable knowledge about the effects of trauma, how to assess whether a person is experiencing trauma-related symptoms, and which treatments have been shown to be effective. Only then can an appropriate referral be made. And, given the prevalence of traumatic events in our world, it is likely that in the course of your career, at least one client receiving services for a different issue will experience a traumatic incident while they are in treatment. Responding effectively requires a degree of understanding that this chapter will provide.

Case Study

Jane was starting out on a road trip to introduce a foreign friend to the American desert when the excursion was abruptly terminated. At 30 years old, Jane had been driving for fourteen years. She had been a passenger in two minor fender-benders in her lifetime, neither of which involved injuries. During high school, she had been treated for bulimia, but had been symptom-free for many years.

On this day, she and her friend, both wearing seat belts, were about an hour and a half into the eight-hour planned journey on a divided interstate highway. There were two lanes in each direction, and Jane had set the car's cruise control to travel a mile or two above the posted speed limit. She passed some cars traveling slowly in the right hand lane when she suddenly had to apply the brakes behind a semi-trailer traveling below the speed limit in the left lane. She was uncomfortable traveling for any distance in the left lane, and returned to the right lane where she gradually built up speed to the previous level. She was slightly ahead of the semi when she heard a loud noise and lost control of the vehicle.

Jane realized that the semi had hit her car on the rear driver's side. "Oh God" and "I could die" were her thoughts as the accident seemed to happen in slow motion. She was watching out the windshield, terrified and helpless, as the vehicle spun and flipped and somersaulted along an embankment. She felt as though they were in a clothes dryer being tossed about. At impact, she watched the windshield cracking as the car finally came to a stop, landing on the car's roof, with both Jane and her friend hanging upside down by their seat belts. She was completely disoriented, and could not free herself from the seat belt. She felt the weight of her body on her neck. She heard her friend's voice saying "Are you okay?" and saw that her friend had managed to free herself from the seat belt. At the same time, she heard voices outside the car and saw feet and heard someone say, "Don't move, the car is unstable." She saw blood dripping, and knew it was her own. She was also shaking uncontrollably, and felt desperate to get out of the vehicle. She asked people to clear a space so she could see out the window.

An off-duty firefighter was among those who stopped to help, and he was able to enter the vehicle through the missing rear window. He thought Jane's neck was broken, and carefully reclined her seat to reduce the pressure on her neck. Jane later learned that her friend was imagining the gas leaking out of the damaged car and the car exploding in flames, but Jane was most aware of feeling trapped and wanted to get out of the vehicle. Before the ambulance arrived, a police officer came up to the window and asked for her driver's license and registration. She later learned that the truck driver was cited for improper lane change.

When the ambulance arrived, she was removed from the vehicle and strapped to a gurney. Her friend was transported to the hospital in the same ambulance. The attendant asked Jane why she was shaking, saying "Are you cold?" At the hospital, the friends were separated, and Jane's clothes were cut from her body. She was poked and prodded, and a catheter inserted. She felt like an object rather than a human being, as attendants ignored her during these procedures and spoke over her about what they would order for lunch.

Jane was left in a room alone while she was waiting to be taken for x-rays. At this point, she felt overwhelmed and panicky, and felt her thoughts "catching up." She was worried about her friend, and thought she had heard someone saying her friend's heartbeat was irregular. She eventually got the attention of a nurse and asked the nurse to stay with her while she waited. After x-rays determined her neck was not broken, she was given a cervical brace and paper scrubs to replace her clothes. She and her friend met with a hospital liaison who attempted to provide assistance. Recall they now had no clothes, all their belongings including wallets, and so on, were in the crashed vehicle or strewn about the crash site, and they did not know anyone locally. Jane felt she could not think straight to figure out what to do. The nurse who attended her friend was kind enough to allow both women to stay in her home for a few days, giving them time to retrieve their belongings and contact support. Jane was petrified riding in the nurse's car.

Seeing the crashed vehicle was not nearly as disturbing as seeing the site of the accident, where Jane found her warped and smashed sunglasses. Jane did not want to be alone, and was comfortable only around her friend because they had shared this experience. Particularly since the hospital personnel appeared so detached and insensitive, it was difficult for Jane to believe anyone could understand how she was feeling. Following the trauma, she found that previously routine activities became frightening and overwhelming. She was extremely sensitive to crowds, sounds, lights in such places as grocery stores. She wanted to be in a quiet, controlled environment. She had several nightmares shortly after the accident: in one she was sledding on a course that became more and more complicated and she was going faster and faster, knowing she was about to crash, feeling powerless, hopeless, and terrified. In the other, she was being hung (executed) and awoke, terrified, at the instant her neck was about to snap.

Jane became extremely distressed and hypervigilant in cars as a passenger, feeling as though she had to be watching for other drivers to make a mistake or unsafe maneuver. She did not drive a car herself for more than eight months—at which time she borrowed a car and drove at no more than 25 mph around residential areas for 10 minutes. She drove rarely after that, and avoided interstate highways or any roads where traffic was fast. She became extremely defensive in a car, and on one occasion two years after the accident, when she attempted driving with a friend in the car, her heart rate increased, she became short of breath, was sweating with clenched muscles, and became so dizzy she thought she would pass out and had to pull over.

Jane was unable to afford intensive treatment, and had never heard that PTSD occurred outside of combat situations. She did not feel that anyone could understand what she was experiencing, and did not want to burden others with her concerns. Her friend's visa expired two months after the accident, and Jane found herself isolating from others and becoming more and more reclusive. She did have one session of Eye Movement Desensitization and Reprocessing (EMDR), with no noticeable benefit. She saw a psychologist for two sessions, who provided a workbook on anxiety, and suggested gradual exposure to driving, which Jane did on her own, beginning with very *low speed driving in residential areas, then progressing to busier streets with traffic, and eventually to multi-lane thoroughfares with increasing speed, which was extremely difficult for her.*

Jane also developed intense social anxiety following the accident, which became extreme when she enrolled in school and needed to speak in class. She would have intense physiological reactivity in social situations, feeling as though she would either throw up or pass out. These symptoms led her to consult a neurologist, who prescribed a selective serotonin reuptake inhibitor (SSRI) to manage those symptoms. About seven years post-accident, Jane got a job that required the use of an interstate highway to commute, and she did manage to do so with minimal symptoms. She now sees herself as a very cautious driver and passenger, who would prefer not to drive on high-speed interstate highways but does so when necessary. The social anxiety that seemed to be precipitated by the trauma has diminished.

Reflecting on her experience, Jane felt that she was re-victimized by her callous treatment in the ambulance and at the hospital. The attendant did not appear to recognize that Jane's shaking was symptomatic of shock, and the hospital personnel did not make any effort to reassure or comfort her. Being left alone while waiting for x-rays was psychologically harmful, and also led her to believe that if professionals did not understand how difficult and disturbing this experience was, friends and others surely would be unable to do so. This belief led to the increased social withdrawal. Jane's only source of comfort was her friend, who could say, "Yes, I feel that way too," and help to dispel the sense of going crazy.

Jane felt that some awareness that PTSD was not confined to combat or rape victims only might have encouraged her to feel less alone and perhaps to seek help sooner. The lack of awareness that trauma of all types can result in PTSD made the effects of the event seem bizarre and incomprehensible, whereas, in fact, many who are in traffic accidents experience symptoms of PTSD.

Definitions and Description of the Problem

The first *Diagnostic and Statistical Manual of Mental Disorders* (DSM) to include PTSD defined *trauma* as events "outside the range of human experience" (DSM-III, p. 236). However, the frequency with which trauma occurs belied that definition, and now trauma is defined as "an extreme stressor that involves direct personal experience of an event that involves actual or threatened death or serious injury, or other threat to one's physical integrity" (DSM-IV-TR, p. 463) or witnessing such an event or learning of such an event happening to someone close. Examples of traumatic events are military combat, being assaulted, being kidnapped, a terrorist attack, natural or man-made disasters, serious vehicle accidents, sudden death of a loved one, and learning of a life-threatening illness. Traumatic events overwhelm our adaptive abilities (Herman, 1997) and result in "intense fear, helplessness, loss of control, and threat of annihilation" (Herman, p. 33). Human-caused disasters occur as a result of human error or negligence (dam failures, Chernobyl, etc.), or as a result of deliberate intent to harm (such as September 11, 2001). Mass violence (such as the Oklahoma City bombing) has a greater impact on survivor mental health than other types of disasters (Norris, 2002).

Although this definition above is the "official" one, Carlson (1997) suggests it is not exactly precise or complete. She describes three characteristics of an event that make it a traumatic one; the event must be extremely negative, sudden, and lack controllability.

These characteristics would exist in any event that would be classified as traumatic by the DSM-IV definition, but would include events that might not meet the standard of that definition.

Terr (1991) proposed a distinction between Type I and Type II trauma that is still used by many experts. *Type I trauma* is a single, sudden, unexpected event that results in shock (e.g., an auto accident, witnessing a murder), whereas *Type II trauma* is a series of repeated or long-standing ordeals (living in a war zone, being chronically abused). The type of trauma influences the impact of the event. In addition, the way any individual responds to a trauma is affected by biological factors, developmental level, the severity of the traumatic event, the social context, and other life events.

A technical term that is often used in discussions of reactions to trauma is *dissociation*. Dissociation is a mental process that involves a lack of connection in parts of a person's thoughts, feelings, and memory. For example, daydreaming, being absorbed in a book, and "highway hypnosis" involve a lack of conscious awareness of one's surroundings that most of us have experienced. In a traumatic experience, some people dissociate, or disconnect their physical from their mental experience, so that they avoid the intense psychological pain. The person disconnects the sensory input from emotion or consciousness and memory.

Post-traumatic stress disorder (PTSD) is a mental disorder with a specific set of symptoms in three categories or clusters: re-experiencing the event, avoidance and numbing, and increased arousal. Acute Stress disorder (ASD) is similar to PTSD but is of shorter duration, with an emphasis on dissociative symptoms. This diagnosis appeared for the first time in DSM-IV; prior to that edition, the acute reactions seen in the first month following trauma were not seen as a disorder, and there are some experts (Litz et al., 2002) who do not agree that this addition was helpful. They particularly disagree with the emphasis on dissociative symptoms. Disorders of Extreme Stress, Not Otherwise Specified (DES-NOS) is a proposed diagnosis that was studied for the DSM-IV, and which some experts believe is needed to more completely explain the experience of those who are subject to chronic interpersonal trauma. Figure 7.1 summarizes the symptoms for PTSD and ASD.

Because disasters are traumatic, a definition is appropriate here. A *disaster* is a "sudden event that has the potential to terrify, horrify, or engender substantial losses for many people simultaneously" (Norris, 2002, p. 1). *Natural disasters* are those caused by weather or geophysical events, and have more severe consequences in developing countries where housing and warning systems may be inadequate and few resources for recovery are available. The extent of loss by people experiencing disasters is predictive of psychological distress, and it is clear that losses will always be greater in undeveloped countries and in the poverty-stricken areas in developed countries.

Being a victim of deliberate violence can occur in many ways, and it is beyond the scope of this chapter to discuss the many violent events that can traumatize individuals. Chronic childhood abuse of any kind, particularly sexual abuse, can result in post-traumatic stress symptoms. One type of violence that is not discussed elsewhere in this book, and which may lead to post-traumatic stress symptoms, is *intimate partner violence*. I use this term because *domestic violence* connotes a family context, while "intimate partner" is a broader term. I will discuss this particular kind of violence and its relationship

FIGURE 7.1   **Diagnostic Criteria for Trauma-Related Disorders from DSM-IV-TR.**

Post-traumatic Stress Disorder[1]

A. The person has been exposed to a traumatic event in which BOTH (1) and (2) were present:

1. the person experienced, witnessed, or was confronted with an event that involved actual or threatened death or serious injury or threat to physical integrity of self or others

2. the response involved fear, helplessness, or horror. In children, this may be expressed as disorganized or agitated behavior

B. The event is persistently re-experienced in at least one of these ways:

1. recurrent and intrusive distressing recollections (images, thoughts, perceptions) of the event. In children, this may be repetitive play about the event

2. recurrent nightmares. In children, frightening dreams may lack content

3. acting or feeling as if the event were re-occurring

4. intensive distress at exposure to reminders of the event

5. physiological reactions at exposure to reminders of the event.

C. Persistent avoidance of trauma-related stimuli and numbing of general responsiveness shown by at least three of the following:

1. efforts to avoid thoughts, feelings, or conversations about the trauma

2. efforts to avoid activities, places, and people associated with trauma

3. inability to remember an important aspect of the trauma

4. diminished interest or participation in important activities

5. feeling of detachment or estrangement from others

6. restricted range of emotions

7. sense of a foreshortened future.

D. Persistent symptoms of heightened arousal as indicated by two or more of the following:

1. difficulty falling or staying asleep

2. irritability or outburst of anger

3. difficulty concentrating

4. hypervigilance

5. exaggerated startle response

E. Symptoms have persisted for at least one month.

F. The disturbance causes stress or impairment in social, occupational, or other areas of functioning.

Acute Stress Disorder[2]

A. Same as PTSD

B. During or after the event, three of the following symptoms were present:

1. sense or numbing, detachment, or absence of emotional response

2. reduction in awareness of surrounding (being in a daze)

3. derealization (things do not seem real)

4. depersonalization (feeling as though watching instead of participating)

C. Event is persistently re-experienced as in B for PTSD

D. Avoidance as in C for PTSD

E. Heightened anxiety or heightened arousal as in D for PTSD

F. Same as F for PTSD

G. Duration is a least two days and no more than four weeks

H. The effects are not due to substance use or other disorder

5. dissociative amnesia (cannot recall important aspect of event).

[1]*DSM-IV-TR* (2000), pp. 467–468

[2]*DSM-IV-TR* (2000), pp. 471–472

to trauma in this chapter. This type of violence is unfortunately common enough that most counselors will be providing services to victims at some point in their career.

It is also important to understand the trauma experienced by military personnel in combat situations. The Iraq war (and the ongoing struggle in Afghanistan) is the longest war involving American troops since Vietnam. This war has impacted many soldiers and their families, and so a discussion of this type of trauma will also be included.

It is possible that two people may have the same traumatic experience (they are in the same building during a tornado, for example) and have very different reactions. Factors that influence the way a person is affected by a trauma include previous trauma history, age, sex, sociocultural background, biological influences, individual perceptions of the danger, and social support after the event.

Prevalence

When I think of September 11, 2001, I realize that just about every American experienced a trauma on that day. In fact, as the televisions replayed the attacks over and over again, the images of the day were imprinted on our collective memory. Certainly in the first hours after the first plane hit the first tower, our national adaptive functioning was overwhelmed. We saw experienced newscasters become inarticulate, cities become paralyzed, and a populace fearful of additional previously unimaginable acts. We need to remember that in America, many of our residents and citizens come from parts of the world where such collective trauma has been ongoing for generations, and finding safety on our shores does not obliterate the psychological damage done by years of chronic exposure to trauma and violence in their homelands.

While an exact prevalence rate of trauma cannot be noted, Flannery (1999) estimated that more than half of the population of the United States will experience a traumatic event in their lifetimes, and one quarter of those will experience multiple traumatic events. A higher estimate was cited by Everly (2000), who observed that

90% of Americans will be exposed to a traumatic stressor in their lifetimes. As 25–30% of trauma survivors develop full-blown PTSD at some point, and an unknown number of others will have less severe, but not unimportant, symptoms, helping professionals cannot be uninformed about this issue. The rate of PTSD differs by type of trauma: 5% of persons experiencing the sudden death of a loved one, 13% of rape victims, and 31% of Vietnam combat veterans were diagnosed with PTSD (Carlson, 1997).

Scarpa (2003) provided startling data on the prevalence of community violence (violence in homes, schools, or neighborhoods). For urban youth, 97% had witnessed and 70% had been victims of violence. Similar rates (98% and 65%) were reported by urban adolescents aged 17–19 about their high school years. Most shocking were the rates reported by a "low-risk" sample of rural college students: 96% and 82% reported at least one such experience in their lifetimes, and 90% and 64% reported three or more experiences! A survey of junior high school students (Saltzman, Pynoos, Layne, Steinberg, & Aisenberg, 2003) found that 17% had been hurt badly enough in a violent incident to need medical attention, and 19% required medical attention for injuries sustained in an accident. Twenty-two percent had witnessed someone being badly hurt or killed in a violent incident, 28% had observed someone being shot at with a gun, and 3% had witnessed a murder. Given the increasing multicultural population in schools, it is notable that 4% of the sample said they had lived in a war zone with fighting, injuries, and dead bodies. A useful chart describing possible trauma reactions that might be observed in secondary students (Gurwitch, Silovsky, Shultz, Kees, & Burlingame, 2003) can be found in this source, listed in the references.

It is quite clear that violence is not a rarity in our world or our country. Being a victim of violence or witnessing violence against another is a trauma that counselors are likely to encounter in their clients.

Intimate Partner Violence

Although the vast majority of victims of intimate partner violence are female (Findings, 2000), it is important to note that males are also victimized, if in lesser numbers. Almost all literature about this subject focuses on women, so it is uncertain whether what is observed in women applies to men as well. The National Violence Against Women Survey, conducted in 2000 in the United States found that 22% of women had experienced physical assault by an intimate partner at least once in their lives, and almost 8% reported sexual assault by an intimate partner (Tjaden & Thoenes, 2000).

Symptoms of PTSD are present in 31–84% of women who are victimized by intimate partners (Jones, Hughes, & Unterstaller, 2001). The more severe the violence, and the more serious the injuries sustained, the more intense is the PTSD in the victim (Woods, 2000). Those women who had experienced other traumas (especially childhood sexual abuse) were at increased risk for developing PTSD. Women in shelters for battered women were also at higher risk, perhaps because their situations had reached the extremes of intensity or severity of the abuse. Intensity of exposure in all types of traumas is related to the development of PTSD. Along with PTSD, these women had higher rates of substance abuse and suicide as well as depression and anxiety. Also more likely to experience PTSD were younger, unemployed, low-income women with large numbers of children and little social support. In most cases, the violent event that precipitated a woman's entry at a shelter was not the only violent event she had experienced. Jones and colleagues suggest that the trauma and violence in the intimate relationship exacerbates symptoms from earlier victimization because trauma interferes with developmental processes.

The results of a study conducted with 173 women in Israel have important implications for helping professionals (Sharhabani-Arzy, Amir, Kottler, & Liran, 2003). The participants in the study were divided into three groups: those who had experienced domestic violence and were diagnosed with PTSD, those who had experienced domestic violence but did not have a PTSD diagnosis, and those who had experienced trauma not of an interpersonal nature. More than half the sample (51.6%) met diagnostic criteria for PTSD. In addition to the presence of additional psychiatric symptoms, the group of battered women with PTSD also had higher suicide risk than the group who did not experience interpersonal trauma. Those in the PTSD group also had higher scores on other psychiatric problems as well as suicide risk than the battered women without a PTSD diagnosis. These researchers believe that when violence occurs in an intimate relationship, it is more harmful psychologically than stranger violence or natural disasters because of the damage to basic trust and safety in relationships (see also Woods, 2000). In addition, the authors concluded that PTSD alone was insufficient to describe the impact of domestic violence, and cautioned clinicians to assess for other disorders as well as suicide risk in victims who do meet criteria for PTSD.

Woods (2000) also provides counselors with several insights. This researcher examined three groups of women (53 currently abused, 55 abused more than two years prior to the study, and 52 non-abused women). More of the currently abused group had PTSD than the previously abused group. Other variables such as age, socioeconomic status, race, and ethnicity were not related to PTSD diagnosis. The finding that counselors should attend to is that 44–66% of the previously abused women were found to have PTSD symptoms, even though the average length of time since the end of the abusive relationship was nine years. Counselors should be aware that women with current or past abusive relationships may suffer from PTSD, so routinely screening for a history of intimate partner abuse is important.

A group that may be overlooked in intimate partner violence is the elderly. One survey found that 4–6% of Americans over 50 were in a physically abusive relationship (France, 2006). Cultural values widely held in that age group (one marries for life, for better or worse) keep many of these victims from seeking help. Another growing concern is that of "late onset domestic violence," which refers to abuse that appears in a relationship that long had been peaceful. The violence may erupt when one partner retires, becomes disabled, loses sexual functioning, or has health problems. Additionally, changes in the brain that result from strokes, chronic alcoholism, or Alzheimer's can cause aggressive behavior in previously placid individuals. Finally, there are some cases where the violence has been a feature of the relationship for decades, but the victim never sought help. In the later stages of life, the victim may simply continue to endure what has become ordinary. Victims in this age group are less likely to seek out mental health resources, but physicians should be alert to the possibility that intimate partner violence exists in this group and victims can be helped with effective counseling. Counselors might want to educate physicians in their areas about the need to screen this population and refer for counseling services when appropriate.

It is impossible to discuss this topic without mentioning Lenore Walker's (1979, 1984) work. This psychologist proposed a specific battered women's syndrome, based on her own research. The original volume was published just before the diagnosis of PTSD was added to the DSM-III. Although she has made a significant contribution to understanding this population, the syndrome has never reached the status of a diagnosis, is not in the DSM-IV-TR, and is not always accepted in courts of law. As a result, I recommend that counselors determine whether the client qualifies for a diagnosis of PTSD and also consider other disorders (such as depression) when appropriate.

Trauma in Military Personnel

Since 2000, the Department of Veterans Affairs has seen an increase in the number of cases for disability compensation due to PTSD, with the greatest increase coming since the start of the Iraq war (St. George, 2006). Several researchers believe that the coverage of the Iraq war in the media has triggered symptoms in Vietnam veterans, with one study finding flashback experiences in 57% of a small sample, with 46% experiencing disrupted sleep. Surviving veterans of earlier wars also may have undiagnosed PTSD. One study of 357 former prisoners of war from World War II and the Korean War found rates of PTSD ranging from 26% to 33% depending on the measure used (Engdahl & Eberly, 1994). Many in their sample had enough symptoms to qualify for a PTSD diagnosis but did not find the symptoms distressing. The researchers theorized that those veterans had somehow adjusted to the symptoms. They also reported that many in their sample were relieved to know that their symptoms were not uncommon.

In wars prior to Vietnam, it was widely recognized that some soldiers experienced "shell shock" or "battle fatigue," which in some cases persisted for years after the war and interfered with their functioning. Because the diagnosis of PTSD did not exist until 1980, no figures are available regarding rates of disorders. The current war in Iraq has several characteristics that are different from pre-Vietnam wars: the enemy is not in an identifiable uniform, combat takes place in urban environments where soldiers must avoid harming civilians at the same time as they are confronting enemy attack, and there is no safe place.

Because of developments in protective gear and more skilled acute medical care, more soldiers are surviving their injuries, but are being wounded at a rate of about nine times that of soldiers killed. Some statistics collected in 2003 highlight the degree of trauma experiences: 94% of soldiers have been shot at, 86% knew someone who was killed or seriously injured, 68% have seen dead or seriously injured American soldiers, and 51% found or handled human remains (Hoge, Castro, Messer, McGurk, Cotting, & Koffman, 2004). In addition, 77% shot directly at the enemy, 48% knew they had killed at least one enemy, and 28% knew they had killed a non-combatant.

Soldiers must be hypervigilant, and must make quick judgments about whether apparent civilians are actually combatants. One study found that 62% of soldiers said that they had been in situations where they were threatened but unable to respond aggressively due to concerns about collateral damage. Litz (n.d.) proposes that the ever-stressful environment results in excessive and chronic presence of stress hormones in the system. An additional stressor may be the awareness of the unpopularity of the war with the public. Although, unlike Vietnam, there seems to be support for military personnel at the same time that there is criticism of the war itself, soldiers must be aware that many think their struggles are in vain.

Within the war zone, the military does provide some treatment for "combat stress reactions." The goal is to return the soldier to duty as soon as possible, and the model used is called PIE (proximity, immediacy, and expectations), which means treatment is provided as close to the combat zone as possible, as soon as possible after an incident, with the expectation of recovery and return to duty. However, there is no research that has evaluated this approach, and there is evidence that this does not reduce the occurrence of PTSD (National Center for Post-Traumatic Stress Disorder, n.d.).

Because the current military is an all-volunteer force, many personnel anticipate making a career in the service. This increases the concerns of servicepersons that seeking counseling will result in a stigma that could negatively impact their careers. Hoge et al. (2004) found that only 40% of Iraq and Afghanistan veterans who said they had a mental health problem were interested in getting counseling, and only 26% had done so. Because counseling within the military system is difficult to receive without it being known to superiors, some of these veterans may eventually seek counseling in nonmilitary settings. For those who do not receive counseling services, symptoms may cause problems in relationships and families once they return to non-combat stations, and counselors may be treating partners or children of these servicepersons if not the soldiers themselves.

Developmental Influences

Trauma affects people differently depending on a number of factors, one of which is the developmental stage of the victim. There is evidence that the younger the child when the trauma occurs (if everything else is equal), the more severe the impact will be. Between the ages of 2 and 7, the child's developmental tasks include developing self-control and a sense of self. As a result, this may be a particularly sensitive period for consequences of trauma. In this section, I will discuss how the experience of trauma interacts with development.

Pynoos (1993) developed a typology of the kinds of traumatic events experienced by children. The four categories are: small- and large-scale natural and technological disasters (tornados, hurricanes, nuclear reactor accident), accidents (transportation, injuries from burns, accidental shooting), intra- and extra-familial violence (kidnapping and hostage, community violence, terrorism, torture, concentration camps, witnessing interpersonal violence, and sexual and physical abuse), and life-threatening illnesses and medical procedures.

Infants and Young Children

A relatively specialized line of research has attempted to explain how trauma experiences affect very young children. One estimate of the number of U.S. children who experience trauma in any one year is 4 million (Perry, Pollard, Blakley, Baker, & Vigilante, 1996). The age group with the highest rates of life-threatening trauma is the birth to three-year-old group (Scheeringa, 2004). Trauma in childhood increases the risk of developing a range of psychiatric problems later in life, so it is essential to understand that young children are indeed affected even though they may be unable to express their reactions in words, and do not display fear until about nine months of age (Scheeringa, 2004). There are some who believe that because young children with immature thinking may not understand the extent of the danger, they are not as upset by traumatic experiences as are older children. Others find evidence that despite the absence of verbal or narrative memories in children who are traumatized before the age of 2½ or 3 (when verbal memories can be formed and accessed), there are nonverbal memories that impact future adjustment and behavior (Yule, 2001).

Infants and toddlers do not have the cognitive skills to make an independent appraisal of threat; they observe attachment figures in circumstances where there is some uncertainty about safety. They will respond initially by searching for protective figures. They will exhibit "alarm reactions" (crying, reaching) to gain the attention of parents. Pre-school children who do not find the expected protection often react with "intense fear, rage, or shame and exaggerated motor behavior or extreme passivity" (Pynoos, 1993, p. 211). In some situations, when the pre-school child perceives the danger, the child may use "dissociative" responses to protect him or herself from the overwhelming anxiety. That is, because the child cannot physically escape the traumatic event, he or she may escape mentally, using dissociation (Carlson, 1997).

The most harmful aspect of trauma to infants is the effect on the developing brain. Perry and his colleagues (1996) provide a description of how trauma affects this development. The human brain is an enormously complicated organ containing billions of neurons that are organized into systems that control different functions to ensure survival. Different areas of the brain control thinking, motor activity, and emotional response. One important property of neurons is that they change in response to various signals. This is, in a very simplified version, how learning and memory take place. The kind of information that is stored depends on the type, intensity, and frequency with which the same pattern of neurons is stimulated. More frequent and intense activity makes a stronger impact, and then this pattern filters new activity in the brain. One thing that occurs is that when a particular pattern of neuronal activity is repeated, *sensitization* occurs. That means that the pattern will now be activated by less intense stimulation. This explains how children who are traumatized (repeatedly or very intensely) will exhibit what seem to be exaggerated responses to minor stressors.

Neuron: Specialized cells in the nervous system (brain and spinal cord and nerves) that conduct impulses that allow the brain and body to communicate.

Another important feature of brain development is that it develops in a predictable sequence from the most primitive functions (e.g., breathing) to the most complex (planning, making decisions). There are critical periods for the development of the brain during which the different systems are most sensitive to input from the environment. If disruption (trauma) occurs when more basic systems are developing, those systems will be less able to contribute to the development of the more complex systems. Perry et al. (1996) summarized the importance of these events as follows:

EXPERIENCE CAN CHANGE THE MATURE BRAIN—BUT EXPERIENCE DURING CRITICAL PERIODS OF EARLY CHILDHOOD ORGANIZES

> BRAIN *SYSTEMS*! [Caps in the original, italics added] Trauma during infancy and childhood, then, has the potential effect of influencing the permanent organization—and all future functional capabilities—of the child. (p. 291)

When an infant or child perceives a threat, the brain has instinctive ways to respond. We often hear of the "fight or flight" response that increases heart rate and respiration, and so on when a threat is perceived. But fighting or fleeing would not be in the best survival interest of an infant or small child, who could neither attack the source of the threat, nor escape. The more useful (from a survival perspective) response is to "freeze and surrender." If this response in the brain is activated often, sensitivity will develop, and various neuronal changes will occur. These changes are responsible for observed cognitive, behavioral, and socioemotional effects in traumatized children.

Although infants and toddlers are unable to verbalize their experiences, traumatized children at this age may be more irritable, cry more than usual, and want to be held a great deal. Pre-school children may display fearfulness and insecurity, and may regress behaviorally (return to thumb-sucking, bed-wetting, disrupted sleep, separation anxiety). They are very sensitive to their parents' reactions, and will exhibit more anxiety if the parents are anxious. It is common for children at this age to recreate the trauma in their play, and to do so repeatedly. This is their way of attempting to gain mastery of the situation. Because cause-and-effect thinking has not yet developed, young children may believe their misbehavior caused the trauma.

By age five, the volume of the brain is nearly complete, so interventions prior to that age are critical. Studies have found smaller brains in children with PTSD, and the smallest brains were associated with the earliest experiences of trauma (Cohen, Perel, DeBellis, Friedman, & Putnam, 2002).

Children

A review of 177 research articles on responses to disasters from 1981 to 2000 revealed that school-aged children had the highest rates of severe impairments following disasters (Norris, Byrne, Diaz, & Kaniasty, 2001). For example, a study of children who had been in traffic accidents found trauma-related symptoms at two weeks, with 14% of children still suffering from PTSD three to four months later, and 17% exhibiting traffic-related fears (DiGallo, Barton, & Parry-Jones, 1997). Because this population is at such high risk for serious outcomes, and is often undiagnosed (Stallard, Velleman, & Baldwin, 1999), it is essential to examine the dynamics of trauma in children.

During the traumatic event, children also automatically use the "fight or flight" response or the "freeze and surrender" response discussed above. When in either of those states, brain functioning decreases in two essential areas of the brain: Broca's area (speech) and Wernicke's area (language comprehension) (Baggerly, 2005). As a result, children may have difficulty finding words to describe their traumatic experiences, but may instead have encoded a very clear visual image. Some children may focus their attention on a seemingly small image (e.g., an item of clothing), which becomes a disturbing mental picture that can elicit fear responses. They may also have difficulty with the time sequence when trying to recall the event, and some children will develop a belief in "omens" in an attempt to avoid future trauma (Anonymous,

2002). This means that they believe there were warning signs they just did not notice, but if they are vigilant, they will notice such signs before another trauma can occur. Terr (1981) found this belief to be quite common among the children involved in the Chowchilla school-bus kidnapping incident.

Like younger children, anxiety is often experienced by school-aged children who experience a trauma. They may worry about a re-occurrence of the trauma, and exhibit physical symptoms (frequent headaches and stomachaches, for example). Their school performance may change, and they may ask many questions about death and dying (Gurwitch, Silovsky, Shultz, Kees, & Burlingame, 2006). They may be preoccupied by the traumatic event, talking about it constantly, infuse their writing, drawing, and play with themes of the event. Some young trauma victims will be extremely sensitive to certain sounds (loud noises, thunder, etc.). While such reactions and behaviors are normal responses to trauma, there are children in whom the intensity or duration of those symptoms signals a serious problem. For example, an injury can be a traumatic event for a child, and rates of PTSD diagnosis among injured children range from 13% to 45% (Winston, Kassam-Adams, Garcia-España, Ittenbach, & Cnaan, 2003).

> **Chowchilla incident:** On July 15, 1976, 26 children aged 5–14 and their school bus driver were kidnapped. They were driven around for 11 hours, and then buried underground in an old moving van for 16 hours until they dug their way out. Three kidnappers, apparently planning to request ransom, were convicted of the crime and sentenced to life in prison.

Because children are dependent on adults, they are very sensitive to trauma reactions in adults (Pine & Cohen, 2002). September 11, 2001 was a trauma that affected the entire country, and children were impacted not only by the event but by the ways in which adults and others responded. Thus, when traumas disrupt the family, children are at higher risk for trauma-related psychopathology. And when trauma is inflicted upon children by adults (as in physical or sexual abuse) the child may feel extremely vulnerable. To reduce their anxiety over being so vulnerable, children may engage in fantasies in which they are the powerful aggressor. Some may act out these fantasies, and others may do so when they are older.

Parental psychopathology was found to be the best predictor of psychological problems in children post-trauma (Norris et al., 2001). In their review of the literature on traumatized children, Pine and Cohen (2002) also discovered that girls tend to exhibit more symptoms of mood and anxiety disorders following the event, whereas boys tend to have more behavioral symptoms. A review of the literature on children who witness violence indicated that traumatic events, including witnessing violence, are three times as likely to lead to PTSD when the child is younger than 11. Additional factors that elevated the possibility of PTSD were the frequency of the violent events and the physical proximity of the child to the incident. Reactions are stronger when the child knows the individuals involved; witnessing violence against one's mother was as traumatic for some children as being the victim of abuse themselves (Augustyn & Groves, 2005).

An interesting study revealed the effects of a traumatic event on child victims as well as children who had indirect exposure to a trauma. Twenty-six children in an elementary school near Paris, France were taken hostage by a mentally unstable person (Vila, Porche, & Mouren-Simeoni, 1999). The incident was resolved in two hours and no one was harmed. Researchers investigated the effects on these children over time, and also on twenty-one children from the same school who were not in that classroom during the hostage situation. The researchers found that 96% of children in the hostage classroom experienced symptoms of acute stress, including seven cases of PTSD and eleven cases of subclinical PTSD diagnosed two months after the incident. In the indirectly exposed group of children (those in the other classroom), two cases of PTSD and six cases of subclinical PTSD were diagnosed after the same period, but symptoms in this group had decreased significantly after seven months. PTSD symptoms in the directly affected children were still present after sixteen months. Those children who were psychologically debriefed after the incident fared somewhat better (in terms of severity) than children who were not debriefed. This study provides evidence that children can be traumatized by events even if they are not present when the event occurs.

Symptoms of PTSD in children who experience a trauma may persist if no intervention occurs. In a study of a school-based intervention, researchers found that almost 6% of children in second through sixth grades had significant trauma symptoms two years after Hurricane Iniki (Chemtob, Nakashima, & Hamada, 2002). After the treatment was delivered, symptoms were significantly diminished, and the improvement was maintained at a one-year follow-up.

A different type of trauma was the explosion of the Challenger space shuttle in 1986, which was watched on live television by millions of American students. The flight was re-broadcast many times, so even those children who did not view it at the time it occurred knew about it. Trauma researchers (Terr, Bloch, Michel, Shi, J. Reinhardt, & Metaye, 1999) selected two communities to study: Concord, New Hampshire, the home of Christa McAuliffe, the teacher on board, and Porterville, CA, as a comparison community. A 45-minute structured interview was conducted with randomly selected third- through tenth-grade students immediately following the incident and again one year later. A small group of the Concord students had been watching the launch from Cape Canaveral. The researchers discovered no differences between this group and the other Concord students, so they were combined for the other analyses. East Coast children had significantly more dreams about the incident and drew significantly more pictures about the event. They re-enacted the event in their play significantly more often than the West Coast group, developed significantly more clinging behaviors, and exhibited significantly more fears of space and planes. Interestingly, combining children from both coasts, younger children (versus adolescents) experienced far more symptoms of trauma-related stress problems. All of the following were significantly greater in the elementary-aged children: drawing pictures on their own, avoiding school drawing or writing about the incident, displaying reduced expectations about their personal future, and all fears with the exception of fear of airplanes. For most subjects, symptoms had diminished over the fourteen-month study period, but for school-aged children, diminished interest in space careers remained steady. This study demonstrated that children with more personal interest in an event had more severe symptoms when they were aware of a traumatic public event.

Forty-six people who left Cambodia at age eight to twelve after having lived there during the Khmer Rouge horrors were studied over time by Sack, Him, and Dickason (1999). They also were able to include in their study six students who left Cambodia before the Khmer Rouge took power for comparative purposes. During the

Pol Pot was the leader of the Cambodian communist party (Khmer Rouge). His regime and his repressive policies led to the death of 3 million Cambodians. He died in 1998 before he could go before an international tribunal for his crimes.

twelve-year study period, 67% of those who had lived under the Pol Pot regime had PTSD at some point, while none of the six who left before he took power had the diagnosis. The researchers observed that of the subjects with a PTSD diagnosis, 82% had memories of a specific traumatic event they experienced, while 86% of those without PTSD had memories of the loss and the disruption in their lives, but not specific traumatic incidents. These researchers also noted that a number of their subjects with PTSD had delayed onset, and caution those who work with children who experience trauma that absence of symptoms at one point does not mean they will not develop later. The encouraging outcome was that despite the high rates of PTSD, most of the subjects were functioning well, having obtained educations and jobs.

Adolescents

Adolescents generally react to trauma as do adults. Common responses include flashbacks, nightmares, emotional numbing, and avoidance of reminders of the trauma, depression, increased substance use or abuse. In addition, adolescents may exhibit an increase in problems with peers and some anti-social acting out. Not unusual are withdrawal and isolation from others, suicidal ideation, poor school attendance and decreased academic performance, sleep disturbances, and physical complaints. Some adolescents experience guilt that they were unable to prevent the trauma, and others create fantasies of revenge toward perceived responsible parties.

Like adults, not all adolescents who experience a traumatic event respond in the same way. Previous exposure to trauma, existing mental health problems, and the absence of family support increase the risk for problematic reactions. Research evidence points to high rates of exposure to violence among many adolescents. A study conducted in the midwest found rates of exposure to be similar to those found in an earlier study in Baltimore (Bain & Brown, 1996). Twelve percent of the sample had witnessed a murder, 25% had witnessed an assault with a weapon, and 28% had witnessed a shooting! There were some significant differences by race and gender: females had witnessed fewer shootings, and blacks had witnessed more murders. Augustyn and Groves (2005) cite several studies that confirm the very startling rates at which young people witness violence. Youngstrom, Weist, and Albus (2003) studied exposure to violence in 320 urban adolescents and reported that 79% had witnessed a violent act and 48% had been the target of a violent act. These researchers cite a previous study in which 43% of urban youth reported witnessing a murder. Helping professionals need to inquire about this in adolescent clients, and seek to understand their reaction to the trauma. Recall that some believe that chronic exposure may desensitize adolescents, while others believe exposure to prior trauma interferes with a person's ability to recover from later trauma. Despite possible desensitization to violence, adolescents may experience anxiety, depression, substance abuse, and suicidal ideation even if they do not meet full criteria for PTSD.

A final comment on the experience of trauma in children and adolescents is based on the theory that trauma shatters one's basic assumptions about the world

(Janoff-Bulman, 1992). This will be discussed in more detail in the section on adults. What is important here is that children and adolescents are still forming these basic assumptions, and the relative flexibility of assumptions is both good news and bad news. For many traumatic events, the reactions of parents and other close adults strongly influence the child's interpretation of what occurred. Even when the event separates the child from parents, as in kidnapping, the response and reassurance provided by parents provides protection from damage. It is precisely because primary caregivers have such an influence on the developing worldview of the child that when the trauma is deliberately inflicted by those individuals (as in sexual abuse by a family member) that the damage is so severe. The child's sense of safety and protection is destroyed, and the sense of self is disturbed. In fact, there is evidence that the origin of many personality disorders, particularly borderline personality, is in this type of trauma and the effects it has on one's understanding of the world and oneself in the world.

Adults

The research suggests that approximately 25% of those who experience a trauma will develop symptoms of PTSD (Pine & Cohen, 2002). Risk factors for developing adverse outcomes following a disaster have been identified, and are listed here (as summarized by Norris et al., 2001, p. 8):

- Being female
- Ages 40 to 60
- Little prior experience or training for coping with such an event
- Being a member of an ethnic minority group
- Low socioeconomic status (SES)
- Having children at home
- For women, having a distressed spouse
- Prior psychiatric history
- Severe exposure to the disaster (e.g., injury, threat of loss of life)
- Living in a highly disrupted or traumatized community
- Loss of resources.

Although these characteristics were identified for victims of disasters (floods, tornados, terrorist attacks, etc.), it is clear that many of these would elevate risk of complications in adults who experience a wide range of traumatic events.

There are several opinions on how previous experience with stress and trauma impacts one's ability to cope with a current trauma. One view is that prior experiences make people more resistant to effects of current trauma; perhaps they have developed coping strategies that can be employed in current situations. On the other hand, it is possible that previous experience may deplete the person's psychological reserves, and make it more difficult for them to cope with a current trauma. In addition, stressful circumstances (poverty, discrimination, family problems) after a trauma are likely to complicate a person's recovery (Carlson, 1997).

Herman (1997) emphasized that the most essential characteristic of a trauma is that it causes both terror and helplessness in the victim. It is because of these elements that our capacities and innate systems of self-defense become overwhelmed and disorganized. She theorizes that the features of one's usual responses to danger, because they are not effective in a traumatic situation, remain activated in an "altered and exaggerated" state (p. 34) long after the trauma itself is over. These effects impact physiological arousal, emotion, cognition, and memory system, and also separate these from one another, so that the victim may experience intense emotion without being able to remember the event, or may describe horrific memories with no emotional reaction.

When the impact of the trauma is such that PTSD develops, the diagnostic requirements reflect these dynamics. The first criterion for a diagnosis is that the individual "experienced, witnessed, or was confronted with" one or more events that involved real or threatened death, injury, or threat to physical integrity of self or others, *and* the individual experienced "intense fear, helplessness, or horror" (Diagnostic and Statistical Manual of Mental Disorders (DSM-IV-TR), 2000, p. 467). The other symptoms are grouped into three main categories: re-experiencing (e.g., intrusive thoughts, dreams, reactivity to cues that remind one of the event), avoidance and numbing (avoiding conversation or activities that are related to the event, having feelings of detachment from others), and increased arousal (exaggerated startle response, sleep problems). The symptoms must persist for at least one month to qualify for a diagnosis. That requirement reinforces that many of these symptoms are exhibited by victims of a trauma immediately following the event, but in most cases, they will subside relatively soon after the event.

Very similar criteria are used to diagnose Acute Stress Disorder, with the restrictions that the symptoms are present for at least two days but persist for no more than four weeks following the event. Some studies show that between 14% and 44% of individuals who experience a trauma will qualify for this diagnosis (DSM-IV-TR, 2000).

Another view of the impact of trauma is proposed by Janoff-Bulman (1992), who focused on the effect of a trauma experience on one's "fundamental assumptions" about the world. These personal theories help us make sense of, and interpret, our experience. Human beings tend to resist changing these basic assumptions, but when a trauma occurs, these assumptions may be shattered, causing a psychological crisis. The fundamental assumptions shared by most humans are these: "the world is benevolent, the world is meaningful, the self is worthy" (p. 6). It is these basic beliefs that a trauma destroys. Janoff-Bulman also proposes that although all trauma survivors feel vulnerable and less safe and secure after the event, trauma that is intentionally caused by others (criminal assaults, interpersonal violence, terrorism, war atrocities, etc.) contradicts the belief that human beings are basically good. In fact, survivors may believe that evil is a potent force, and trust in others is no longer easily bestowed. Although this perspective is not reflected in the diagnostic criteria for PTSD or other trauma-related disorders, it is often seen clinically; trauma survivors often grapple with basic existential questions about the meaning of events and their own lives.

When the symptoms of PTSD subside, the person may not be symptom-free. For example, the intrusion symptoms may diminish, but physical complaints, symptoms of arousal and hypervigilance, and depression may still persist and need attention.

Older Adults

Trauma in older adults is a complicated picture. Effects of trauma may be disguised by co-occurring physical health problems, cognitive changes, current stressful life events, and other mental health concerns. This stage of life is characterized by loss (of home, work, physical skills, loved ones, etc.), which may impact the way trauma is experienced. Age also interacts with the social, economic, cultural, and historic context of different settings (Cook, 2002). Most of what is known about elderly trauma survivors is based on studies of three groups: war veterans, Holocaust survivors, and victims of recent disasters (Averill & Beck, 2000; Cook & O'Donnell, 2005). One of the only nationally representative samples of older adults found that 9–21% (depending on cohort, with the lowest rate in the 85+ cohort) had seen something violent happen to someone or had seen someone get killed, and between 16% and 18% had been in a fire, flood, or other major natural disaster (Krause, Shaw, & Cairney, 2004). The researchers found a relationship between exposure to trauma and physical health in late life, with the effects being greatest when the trauma occurred between ages 18 and 30. Those elderly persons who experienced a trauma at those ages had poorer physical health than their non-traumatized peers.

Cook and O'Donnell (2005) highlight obstacles to accurately assessing the effects of trauma (and possible PTSD symptoms) in older adults: self-disclosure was less acceptable in earlier times, self-reliance was the standard, psychological problems were considered to be evidence of weakness, open discussion and information about trauma and PTSD were not available, and mental health problems are frequently attributed to physical concerns in this life stage. Understanding these challenges will help the counselor to understand what might appear to be resistance in these clients, and to respond with understanding and concern.

There is conflicting evidence about whether earlier exposure to trauma is protective or whether it increases vulnerability to later trauma (Busuttil, 2004). Older persons who experienced a trauma at earlier periods of life may exhibit either the development or re-emergence of a variety of trauma-related symptoms, particularly intrusive memories, avoidance of reminders of the trauma, sleep problems, and acute difficulties coping with current loss (Grossman, Levin, Katzen, & Lechner, 2004). Many of these individuals will have showed only mild symptoms when they were younger, but as age-related cognitive declines appear, PTSD symptoms may be amplified. It has been suggested that the symptoms increase because the capacity to inhibit the intrusive memories has been diminished. Other experts believe that with retirement comes more time to reflect on past experiences, which may precipitate PTSD in later life (Busuttil). Various types of dementia affect the pre-frontal cortex, where the mechanisms for stopping thoughts and responses are located. Short-term memory is often impaired while long-term memories perseverate. Another possible explanation for the increased emergence of PTSD is that whatever coping capacities the individual used earlier are no longer functional, allowing the symptoms to emerge.

An interesting study examined the incidence of PTSD in elderly residents of Lockerbie, Scotland during the air disaster there (Livingston, Livingston, & Fell, 2004). The researchers were able to follow the residents at one through three years after the

Lockerbie disaster: On December 21, 1988, Pan Am Flight 103 from London to New York was blown up in the air, with remnants of the plane landing on the town of Lockerbie, Scotland. Two hundred and ten people died, including eleven residents of Lockerbie. Two Libyan nationals were charged, and one was convicted in 2001.

event. At one year after the event, 84% of the elderly survivors met criteria for a diagnosis of PTSD. Symptoms of PTSD declined over the time period, but almost 16% of the sample still met criteria for PTSD three years after the event. This pattern is similar to that found in younger trauma survivors; while many symptoms remit over time, for some they persist for years. There are likely to be many factors involved in predicting which trauma survivors will have persisting PTSD, but some believe that the intensity of exposure (in this case, loss or injury to close friends and family) and the type of trauma (human-caused) are very influential.

Assessment

Helping professionals will generally not conduct a complete assessment for every possible disorder. Carlson (1997) points out that most intake interviews, and even the standard clinical inventories often used at the initiation of treatment are likely to miss symptoms of trauma. Among other problems is that of impaired memory for traumatic events, which is not an unusual occurrence. In fact, a problem with memory of the traumatic event is a symptom of PTSD. In addition, many symptoms (e.g., sleep disturbances, concentration difficulties) of trauma-related disorders can easily be mistaken for those of other anxiety disorders or depression. It is the entire constellation of symptoms that characterizes PTSD, and unless one specifically includes questions about trauma, the important disorder could be overlooked. It would make sense for counselors to routinely use a screening measure to determine whether trauma is involved in the client's history.

However, a very brief screen for PTSD, designed for use by primary care physicians, can be used to determine whether a more in-depth assessment is needed. The PC-PTSD Screen (Prins et al., 1999) is shown in Figure 7.2.

Effective Assessment Instruments

There are many assessment instruments that helping professionals might use to assist them in determining the impact of trauma. (For a thorough review of instruments, see Carlson [1997] and Strand, Sarmiento, & Pasquale [2005].)

One measure that is widely used in research studies about trauma is the *Impact of Events Scale* (Horowitz, Wilner, & Alvarez, 1979). This brief (15-item) measure asks about the frequency of intrusion and avoidance symptoms of PTSD on a 4-point scale with end points at "not at all" and "often." This scale has excellent reliability and validity and has been used with a variety of cultural groups. It is presented in the article cited and can be reproduced at no cost. In addition to research uses, it has clinical applications, and can be used to assess progress in treatment.

A series of assessments developed by John Briere (1995, 1996, 2005) covers the complete age range. These instruments are similar in format, easy to score and interpret,

FIGURE 7.2   Primary Care (PC) PTSD Screen.

In your life, have you ever had any experience that was so frightening, horrible, or upsetting that *in the past month* you

1. have had nightmares about it or thought about it when you didn't want to? YES   NO

2. tried hard not to think about it or went out of your way to avoid situations that reminded you of it?   YES   NO

3. were constantly on guard, watchful, easily startled?   YES   NO

4. felt numb or detached from others, activities, or your surroundings? YES   NO

The screen should be considered positive if the client provides three "YES" answers. It is advisable for the counselor to clarify responses and determine whether the client has experienced a trauma, and to estimate the extent to which the symptoms are interfering with the client's functioning.

and have good psychometric properties. In addition, they are useful regardless of the type of trauma, so the clinician does not need separate measures for each type. The items go beyond the symptoms of PTSD to include other effects of trauma. Computer scoring programs are available as well.

The *Trauma Symptom Checklist for Young Children* (Briere, 2005) is a new measure for evaluating trauma-related symptoms in children as young as 3 years old. This 90-item assessment is completed by a caregiver, and it includes validity scales to ensure accuracy of reporting. The results can be used to assist in making a diagnosis of PTSD, but also alerts the clinician to other symptoms not included in that diagnosis. Norms are available for age groups 3–4, 5–9, and 10–12.

The *Trauma Symptom Checklist for Children* (Briere, 1996) is a self-report measure for use with children aged 8–16. It has been used with both 7- and 17-year-olds; the author cautions against applying norms to 7-year-olds, but provides adjustments for use with 17-year-olds. There are two versions: the full version contains 54 items and includes items assessing sexual symptoms, and the TSCC-A has 44 items and does not make any reference to sexual issues. The items address cognitive, affective, and behavioral symptoms of trauma, and use a 4-point scale and easy-to-use response sheet. Research and psychometric studies support the reliability and validity of this instrument. Scoring and interpretation are straightforward, and there are separate norms for each gender, and by age group. Validity scales are available to check for invalid profiles. Clinical scales measure anxiety, depression, anger, post-traumatic stress, dissociation, and sexual concerns on the full scale. The sexual concerns scales are not available for the TSCC-A.

The *Trauma Symptom Inventory* (Briere, 1995) is designed for adults, aged 18 and over. There are 100 items, although there is an alternate 86-item version that does not make any references to sexual concerns. The profile has 10 clinical scales: Anxious

Arousal, Dissociation Behavior, Depression, Sexual Concerns, Anger/Irritability, Dysfunctional Sexual Behavior, Intrusive Experiences, Impaired Self-Reference, Defensive Avoidance, and Tension Reduction, which are grouped into three larger categories of Trauma, Self, and Dysphoria. There are also 12 critical items to screen for behaviors that would require immediate attention (suicide, self-mutilation), and three validity scales to help the clinician recognize invalid protocol.

The Trauma Center of Brookline, Massachusetts has a packet of assessment tools available to clinicians. This resource is particularly interested in identifying those persons whose condition is better described by the *Disorders of Extreme Stress Not Otherwise Specified* (DESNOS) diagnosis. Although these assessments are likely to be used by clinicians who will specialize in treating clients with this diagnosis, I think it is helpful to be familiar with these instruments because they contain several unique features. For most of these instruments, psychometric properties have not yet been determined, so their utility is for the clinical information generated. Normative data are not yet available.

The *Traumatic Antecedents Questionnaire* is unique in that respondents indicate the extent of their functioning in ten domains at four different developmental periods. Although the person is responding about their memory of earlier time periods, the information is often overlooked in assessment. Preliminary studies found that trauma reported between birth and six years of age was highly correlated with scores on all domains. They also found that sexual, physical, and emotional abuse was most correlated with symptoms of DESNOS, while other traumas correlated more strongly with PTSD. As the DESNOS construct is the framework for these assessments, that finding is confirmation that there are symptoms outside of the PTSD criteria that are experienced by trauma survivors and are problematic for them.

The *Trauma Center PTSD Symptom Scale* asks respondents about symptoms of PTSD experienced within the past two weeks. The items are tied to the DSM-IV criteria for a diagnosis of PTSD. The scale also inquires about lifetime presence of the symptoms, and the respondent indicates both the frequency and intensity of the symptom. It is suggested that this scale might be administered periodically to track a client's treatment progress.

Specifically focused on the DESNOS construct is the Structured Interview for Disorders of Extreme Stress (SIDES), which is also available in a self-report version to be completed by the client (SIDES-SR). This assessment gathers information on past and present functioning of the features of DESNOS: affect regulation, amnesia and dissociation, somatization, disruptions in self-perception, problems in relationships with others, and disrupted systems of meaning. Presence of symptoms in the last month are rated on a scale from 0 to 3; scores of 2 or above indicate clinical elevations. There are several scoring strategies that can be employed depending on the purpose of the evaluation: diagnostic scoring or symptom severity scoring. This measure is the best researched of the group from the trauma center, and there is adequate evidence of validity. Internal consistency coefficients for several of the scales are a bit low, suggesting some caution in interpretation.

A useful set of measures for those treating child trauma survivors is the Parent-Child Weekly Rating Scale (Peebles & Scheeringa, 1996, shown in Scheeringa, 2004), which asks the adult caregiver to rate the children's and their own PTSD symptoms each week as a way to assess progress.

For those interested in a reliable and valid measure of intimate partner abuse, the *Index of Spouse Abuse* (Hudson & McIntosh, 1981) serves the purpose. Despite the title, the wording of the 30-item scale refers to "partner," so it can be used with unmarried couples and with gay and lesbian clients. There are two separate scales, one for physical abuse and the other for nonphysical abuse, and recommended cut-off scores are provided. This scale has been widely used in both research and clinical settings, and as it is included in the article, there is no cost to the counselor for purchasing or scoring. Out of concern that screening for intimate partner violence is often overlooked, McCloskey and Grigsby (2005) present an extensive interview protocol in their appendices. This procedure would be particularly useful for those counselors doing couples work, and according to the authors, should be done routinely. A survey of physicians found that 79% asked about domestic violence if the patient had evidence of injury, but only 10% routinely screened new patients for this common issue (Samuelson & Campbell, 2005). Psychologists also reported low levels of screening unless the client raised the issue. Reasons given for not screening included perceptions that clients would be unwilling to disclose this information, that the psychologist lacked training, fears that the disclosure would be too overwhelming for the client, and that there is not enough time in the intake process.

Treatment Options and Considerations

As I discuss treatment options, there are several points to keep in mind. First, not everyone who experiences a traumatic event will develop a diagnosable disorder. It is important to screen for symptoms in anyone who has experienced a trauma because many people who could benefit from trauma-related treatment are overlooked when their symptoms do not meet the criteria for a diagnosis. Some clients in the immediate aftermath of a trauma or disaster may need less therapy and more assistance in managing the consequences: locating food, shelter, and medical care, gaining access to a wide range of community services, and assistance managing other stressors. It is also important to keep in mind that efficacy studies of even the most successful treatments (cognitive-behavioral therapy (CBT)) found that 50% of clients qualify for the PTSD diagnosis at termination and follow-up (Monson & Friedman, 2006).

Because treatment strategies vary somewhat with the age of the client, I will describe the options by developmental stage.

Children

Cognitive-Behavioral Therapy.   According to Pine and Cohen (2002) there is strong evidence of the effectiveness of CBT in children exhibiting trauma-related symptoms after sexual abuse and physical abuse, but the rigorous controlled studies have not been conducted with victims of other types of trauma. However, these authors state, ". . . based on the empirical database, few other treatments can be recommended for symptoms that specifically emerge in children and adolescents following trauma." Cohen, Berliner, and Marsh (2000) also recommend CBT for both children and adolescents, and note that evidence for medication is weak. They also recommend the inclusion of parents along with treatment of the child. Parental monitoring of the child's symptoms and managing the child's behavior between sessions are helpful adjuncts to direct work with the child. In some cases, parental distress about the child's trauma must be addressed so the parent can be more responsive to the needs of the child. Involving the non-offending parent when the child is a victim of abuse is imperative.

Yule (2001) also agrees that CBT is the recommended treatment for children, but advises caution in the use of *exposure* with this age group. Others disagree, saying exposure is effective with children but note that therapists are reluctant to use it because of the temporary increase of symptoms and because it involves strong negative affect that may be difficult for the therapist to tolerate (Cohen et al., 2000). Yule also emphasizes the importance of distinguishing between trauma responses and grief responses, as the nature of trauma is such that children may experience loss as a result of the trauma experience, and when that is the case, treatment needs to target both issues. Yule also suggests that when large numbers of children are affected (e.g., in disasters), group treatment might be appropriate. He notes that the purpose of such group interventions is not only to express feelings, but to increase children's sense of mastery and control by teaching new skills. Classroom-based psychoeducational interventions, co-facilitated by helping professionals and teachers, are useful as well. While group treatments may not be effective for all child trauma survivors, they do provide a vehicle for screening for those who may need more intensive individual treatment.

> **Exposure:** In CBT treatment, a technique that uses careful, repeated, detailed imagery of the traumatic event. The purpose is to help the client face the fear and gain control over the event.

Two prominent symptoms in traumatized children are the persisting fear responses and the intrusive memories of the event. Research evidence strongly supports the use of CBT to ameliorate those symptoms. Cognitive processing helps the child to "examine and reframe the 'meaning' of the trauma" (Cohen et al., 2002) while exposure techniques are designed to extinguished the conditioned fear responses.

> **Hyperarousal:** High level of physiological and psychological tension that occurs when the nervous system has been overwhelmed. Includes heightened startle reactions, agitation, etc.

To reduce symptoms of hyperarousal (sleep disturbances, restlessness), relaxation techniques have been used successfully. Those techniques may also have a positive effect on physical symptoms that are reported in many children. Cohen and colleagues (2002) theorize that stress is known to suppress normal immune functions, so relaxation may help children decrease the levels of stress hormones in the system, thereby improving overall physical health.

A very clear outline and example of treatment for a child traumatized by sexual abuse is provided in Deblinger, Thakkar-Kolar, and Ryan (2006), which interested readers may want to examine more closely. I will provide a brief summary here. There are three components to treatment: coping skills training, gradual exposure and cognitive processing, and psychoeducation. In this approach, both child and parent are treated with a combination of separate individual and conjoint sessions. Both parent and child are taught emotional expressiveness skills so that they can communicate effectively about feelings. The cognitive coping skills assist clients in recognizing and disputing unhelpful thoughts about the trauma and replacing them with accurate thinking. Survivors may think "I didn't try hard enough to save her . . ." while a more accurate thought might be "If I had tried harder I might have drowned as well." Relaxation skills are taught and practiced to reduce physical tension and anxiety about the trauma.

The gradual exposure and cognitive processing are the key components of treatment. Proponents believe that children need to learn to deal with trauma-related distress rather than avoid it, which is thought to prolong symptoms. Deblinger and colleagues (2006) provide a useful analogy for describing exposure therapy to a child: getting into a cold swimming pool is difficult at first and eventually feels comfortable. Another useful way to explain exposure to children is to compare the approach to a scary movie watched repeatedly; the first time is super-scary, but after repeated viewings it isn't scary at all. These experts stress gradual exposure: talking about the problem in general terms, perhaps reading an age-appropriate book about the type of trauma, and then perhaps having the child create a book about the trauma, which might include narrative and drawings and poems. Giving children choices (such as drawing or writing, or which part of the incident to start with) provides a measure of control that the child needs. In helping children to process the trauma, role playing in which the child plays a therapist helping a child client with the same experience can be used. The therapist would present statements and concerns the client raised earlier, with the child making positive statements and disputing the illogical thoughts. The final component of this approach is education about the issue. In the case of sexual abuse, the child and parent learn personal safety skills to prevent further abuse.

Most of the research in the literature on the use of *flooding* with children is in the form of case studies, and are few at that. Because the procedure may be unfamiliar and counterintuitive to child clients and parents, Saigh, Yule, and Inamdar (1996) remind counselors of their ethical obligation to provide complete and accurate information to clients about the procedures and respond to any questions they may have. They also point out the importance of voluntary participation by clients. Clients' understanding of the goals of this treatment should be checked by asking them to repeat them verbally. Finally, as PTSD symptoms decrease over time in most cases, therapists should be certain that this type of treatment is necessary—typically for severe symptoms that have persisted over a period of time. Counselors should also check for indicators that this treatment is not appropriate—presence of other psychiatric diagnoses, difficulty with imagery, low levels of re-experiencing symptoms are suggested as reasons not to employ this technique.

Flooding: A technique used in CBT in which the client continues to imagine the feared stimulus until the anxiety is extinguished.

Exposure treatments should be used with children only in the context of a strong therapeutic relationship with the counselor. Support and education should also be incorporated into a comprehensive treatment approach. Young children may not be able to focus on traumatic memories, follow instructions in relaxation, or tolerate long periods of anxiety. Saigh and colleagues (1996) suggest that for young children, a helpful modification is to have the children draw pictures of their experience, and then tell stories about their pictures. Also, some therapists have had success with using trauma-related prompts to assist in generating the imaginal memories. An example is the use by a therapist of tape-recorded sounds of increasingly closer artillery explosions to assist in the exposure treatment of a 12-year-old boy whose home had been destroyed in a military battle.

As this chapter includes discussions of intimate partner violence, it might be helpful to examine one approach to treatment of children who are traumatized by family violence (Kerig, Fedorowicz, Brown, & Warren, 2000). The goal of the treatment is to sever the connection between cues to the trauma and the fear or anxious emotional response. The approach is integrative, but is grounded in CBT principles for treatment of trauma. The approach includes exposure, and the authors are careful to distinguish between therapeutic re-exposure and exposure that is re-traumatizing. For example, children who compulsively reenact the trauma in play do not experience symptom reduction because they do not process the event and the resulting feelings. In fact, re-experiencing the event over and over in play (or thought) without therapeutic support may exacerbate feelings of terror and helplessness and impede resolution. Therapeutic exposure is experienced with a supportive therapist with whom a trusting relationship has been established, and exposure is gradual with the child client having some control over the pace. The exposure is accomplished primarily via talking about the incident in great detail. The empathy and calm acceptance of the story by the therapist helps reduce the fear, and the counselor can utilize the talk to identify thinking errors and misconceptions about the incident to help the child gain a more realistic perspective. These authors believe that while drawing and writing can be helpful, a verbal narrative of the story by the client is necessary to avoid distortion and omissions.

The cognitive element is designed to help children correct misconceptions (such as the violence was their fault, they should have intervened, their mother deserved the beating because dinner was not ready on time) and replacing these with accurate information. Children are also educated about strategies to use in the future, and helped to understand and normalize their own reactions to the violence.

Kerig and colleagues (2000) employ systematic sensitization and flooding with some clients, but they point out that there is research evidence that flooding is effective with children with PTSD when the trauma is a Type I (single event) trauma, there is insufficient evidence that that is the case for Type II trauma, which would include domestic violence. Play therapy may be used, especially with younger children, but the authors emphasize that to avoid re-traumatization, the counselor must be very active in interpretation of the play and make explicit the connection between the play and the trauma. They also recommend focusing attention on the feelings that are displayed via play, and engaging in discussion of those and ways to manage them. Another suggestion is to ask the child to play different roles in the re-enactment (e.g., playing the police officer) to reduce feelings of helplessness. To stimulate play that will access the traumatic memories, the counselor might gather specific toys and figures that relate to the incident. Although these authors recognize the value of family therapy to assist the mother–child relationship, they also recognize that this cannot be effective until the mother has progressed sufficiently in her own therapy.

Medication.   Medications for children are usually a last resort because of concerns that many medications that are successful with adult trauma survivors have not been tested with children. Unwanted side effects are also problematic. However, in some severe cases, medication may be considered. Several selective serotonin reuptake inhibitors (SSRIs, particularly Serzone, Prozac, Zoloft, and Paxil) are used with adults, and have recently been FDA-approved as treatments for PTSD, but they are less often prescribed for children. In fact, although there is insufficient research to warrant use of SSRIs in children with PTSD symptoms, a survey reported by Cohen et al. (2002) found that they are the preferred pharmacological treatments for children.

Adolescents

In general, the treatments described for adults are used with adolescents. Counselors should keep in mind that separation from parents after a trauma can be difficult for teenagers, despite their usual strivings for independence. In addition, teenagers may find it difficult to talk about the trauma with parents or peers. The teen may be aware that parents are also upset about the trauma, and may be concerned about causing them additional discomfort by talking about it. Peers may not know what to say, and so may avoid the topic, which can appear to the trauma survivor as lack of interest. A counselor working with adolescent trauma victims will be sensitive to these dynamics and facilitate dialogue between the traumatized teen and parents (Yule, 2001).

While many trauma victims experience depression after a trauma, this tendency is particularly noteworthy in adolescents. Yule (2001) points out that adolescents should be monitored for suicidal thoughts even years after a disaster. He also finds that while an increase in anxiety is typical immediately following a disaster, panic attacks may begin much later. A final concern is for those adolescents whose trauma involved the death of someone close to them. Again, monitoring the level of depression and offering grief counseling when appropriate are important strategies with adolescents. Grief counseling is often an overlooked component of treatment for trauma. Pine and Cohen (2002) observed that CBT is the most effective trauma treatment for adolescents, and suggest that adolescents can write a book about their traumatic experience to be used in the exposure part of the treatment sessions.

Helping professionals should be particularly alert to symptoms of PTSD in children and adolescents who have been involved in accidents. Sabin, Zatzick, Jurkovitch, and Rivara (2006) found that adolescents who experience an injury frequently have many symptoms of post-traumatic stress, as did 30% of adolescents in their sample. Eleven percent also had depressive symptoms, and almost 17% indicated increased alcohol use to problem levels. Symptoms sometimes overlapped, so a total of 39% of their sample reported some level of psychological distress between four and six months after the injury. Importantly, only 55% of those in distress had seen a physician since discharge from emergency treatment, and those physicians did not detect the psychological distress. For school counselors, 64% knew of the student's injury and 60% had met with the student since the injury although only 10% of the meetings were focused on the injury. Counselors also reported that 27% of students received some form of emotional support at school regarding their injury. Because most children and adolescents are in school, school counselors are in a position to identify emotional problems and to monitor high-risk students so that they can be referred for mental health services when necessary. See the section for school counselors later in this chapter.

Adults

Cognitive-behavioral therapy is widely regarded as the most effective treatment for trauma-related symptoms and PTSD. There are several specific components of CBT that are thought to be particularly important: *exposure* refers to repeatedly experiencing the traumatic event, either in imagination or live (depending on the trauma), until the fear and anxiety are extinguished. In PTSD treatment, the client (or the counselor) recounts the traumatic experience as if it were occurring at the moment while focusing on the most disturbing aspects of the trauma. This is done repeatedly until the fear response no longer occurs. This is called *habituation*. The recounting of the event can be tape-recorded so that the client can listen between sessions to increase exposure. Live exposure does not mean re-experiencing the trauma physically, but means facing reminders of the trauma (such as the site of one's house that was destroyed in a hurricane) frequently. Live exposure is often administered in graded increments, starting with less distressing reminders and working up to the most upsetting ones. The goal—habituation—is the same in imaginal and live exposure.

There are several techniques for using exposure in treatment. *Systematic desensitization* is a process in which the counselor and client construct a hierarchical list of memories or cues to the trauma. Then the counselor relates the memories or cues starting with the least distressing one while the client uses muscle relaxation, which has been taught to the client. The theory is that one cannot be both anxious and relaxed at the same time, so hearing the memory while relaxed prevents anxiety from occurring. After many repetitions, the memory is no longer associated with the anxious feelings—and the counselor then moves on to the next one. Eventually, the client is able to experience the memories and cues without the distressing emotional response.

Flooding and *implosive therapy* are other forms of exposure (Livanou, 2001). In flooding, the client is rapidly (as opposed to gradually) exposed to the trauma memory without allowing avoidance. Initial exposure may continue for as many as 100 minutes. Remember that this occurs in the context of a safe situation with a supportive therapist present. Implosive therapy is flooding with additional features: the scenes to be imagined may be exaggerated or created specifically to generate maximum anxiety in the client, and the scenes may be based on psychoanalytic notions of underlying dynamics. Scenes of hopelessness and loss of control may be incorporated.

Prolonged exposure is widely used in treatment of PTSD, and is one of the CBT approaches (Riggs, Cahill, & Foa, 2006). It typically involves nine to twelve individual 90-minute sessions using four procedures: education about trauma and associated conditions, breathing retraining (learning controlled breathing techniques), *in vivo* (in real life settings) exposure to trauma-related but safe situations, and repeated imaginal exposure to the trauma event. The cognitive processing occurs following each session of imaginal exposure. Homework usually includes *in vivo* exposure assignments and listening to tape recordings of the imaginal exposure exercise from the session. There are sources of explicit session-by-session guidelines for using this approach. Riggs and colleagues stress the importance of providing the client with a rationale for this technique. They also indicate that the counselor must convey confidence in the technique, expertise in using it, and confidence that the client has the ability to successfully complete the treatment.

It is also important, as it is with all approaches, to form a strong alliance with the client and to praise and support their efforts and courage in addressing this disorder.

Cognitive therapy for trauma-related symptoms focuses on emotions other than fear (guilt, sadness) that may follow a traumatic experience, helps clients understand the meaning of the trauma, and helps them examine their basic belief structure so that the traumatic memories do not distort the client's view of self and the world. A 12-session protocol is summarized in Shipherd, Street, and Resnick (2006), who provide the source of the full manual and forms that are used in this approach. Cognitive restructuring is a variation of cognitive therapy that teaches clients how to identify faulty thinking (over-generalizing, catastrophizing, etc.), and then how to challenge and change those faulty notions. Sometimes, exposure may be used to test faulty assumptions (Livanou, 2001).

Some therapists incorporate stress inoculation training in treating trauma victims. This technique teaches clients methods to control anxiety. Techniques include slow deep breathing, progressive muscle relaxation, thought stopping, and guided self-talk. Again, exposure is sometimes incorporated (Livanou, 2001).

Because the treatment is controversial for PTSD, and described in more detail elsewhere in this book, I will not discuss EMDR here other than to point out that it is considered by some to be an effective technique for treatment of trauma in children and adults. The quality of the research on the effectiveness of this approach has been criticized, and readers will need to make their own decisions about it.

Older Adults

Research on effective treatments for elderly trauma victims is sparse, so Busuttil (2004) suggests that treatments found to be effective with adults be used until such research is available. Of concern in treating elderly is the likelihood of other psychiatric disorders being present as well, especially depression. Given that physical complaints are also more likely in this age group, consultation with a physician is essential. Medication is often used with the elderly (anti-depressants, mood stabilizers, etc.) but caution is advised. First, it is important to determine whether the elderly client uses alcohol to avoid complications from interactions of prescribed medication with alcohol. An additional concern is prescribing medications to depressed elderly clients that could be used for suicide.

Another issue with the use of common treatment approaches with elderly trauma cases is whether exposure is beneficial (Cook & O'Donnell, 2005). One concern is that the emotional reaction aroused during exposure (intense fear and anxiety) has physiological effects (such as increased heart rate and respiration) that could have a negative impact on the health of an elderly client. Case studies of the effective use of EMDR with traumatized elderly clients have reported positive outcomes, and some proponents of this approach recommend this for elderly clients as a vehicle for life review.

Life review therapy is a treatment approach designed to assist elderly clients to rework conflict from earlier in their lives to reach understanding and acceptance (Cook & O'Donnell, 2005). Several studies found initial evidence of success using this approach with elderly clients with PTSD. Storytelling as a form of treatment is a variant of the life review therapy with four elements that make this useful for resolving historical material.

Cook and O'Donnell note that progress in treatment is typically slower for elderly victims. Also, due to age-related cognitive declines, educational elements should be repeated, and learning of new skills is enhanced when information is provided in several modalities (spoken, written, using diagrams, etc.). These experts also advise therapist flexibility in terms of logistical matters, which may be more challenging for older adults. Telephone consultations may have to replace in-person sessions when mobility is problematic. For this reason as well as other factors of life in old age, support systems may be lacking for elderly clients, and assistance with utilizing available support is an important element of working with this clientele.

Intimate Partner Violence

Mental health problems common among victims of partner abuse are depression, substance abuse disorders, and anxiety disorders, although PTSD is the most common (Rodgers & Norman, 2004). In many cases, when the PTSD is resolved, symptoms of the other diagnoses are no longer observable or are greatly reduced, leading Golding (1999) to suggest that PTSD is the primary disorder, with other disorders best considered PTSD symptoms instead of separate disorders. Hughes and Jones (2000) point out another reason for focusing on the PTSD diagnosis: it locates the cause as outside the client, thus diminishing the stigma of a disorder that has its origin within the individual. This may alleviate the sense of powerlessness that often is a feature of victims of intimate partner violence.

Despite the high rates of intimate partner violence and the prevalence of trauma-related disorders in this population, this group has been neglected in the research on effective treatment for PTSD. A recently developed treatment approach specifically for this population shows great promise in early research (Kubany et al., 2004; Kubany, Hill, & Owens, 2003). The treatment, Cognitive Therapy for Battered Women (CTT-BW), includes elements designed to address PTSD (psychoeducation about the disorder, stress management and relaxation training, self-monitoring of maladaptive thoughts and speech, and talking about the trauma with exposure exercises as homework.) There are also unique components for the battered woman: recognizing and changing dysfunctional beliefs; decreasing negative self-talk, especially related to guilt and shame; self-advocacy techniques; assertiveness training; managing unwanted contacts from former partners; and skills for recognizing potential batterers to avoid future intimate partner violence. Treatment is provided in twice weekly 1.5 hour sessions, and usually includes 8–11 sessions. The studies of treatment effectiveness excluded women who had not been out of the abusive relationship for at least thirty days, who were abusing substances, and who had psychotic disorders. Results were very promising both in the initial evaluation study (2003) and the subsequent study that improved the research design (2004). Both studies included follow-up studies (at three months in 2003 and three and six months in 2004) that found treatment gains were maintained. The samples included ethnic minority women, and no differences in outcomes were detected between whites and minority women. In the second study, both male and female therapists were used, and again no differences in client outcomes were found. Given the strong research evidence of the effectiveness of CBT on trauma-related disorders, and the encouraging outcomes in this well-designed research, this is an approach worthy of attention. There is a manual and client workbook for this protocol, and I encourage any readers who are interested in working with this clientele to investigate this approach more closely.

Because not all women who seek counseling are ready to leave their partners, counselors also must be familiar with models of treatment that do not require that step. Frazier, Slatt, Kowlowitz, and Glowa (2001) applied the Stages of Change model to working with victims of intimate partner violence, but caution counselors to be aware that the client is not the one with the problem behavior—the partner is at fault for the violence. The Stages of Change model views change as a process rather than an event, and proposes stages through which individuals move as they navigate the change process. Those stages are precontemplation, contemplation, preparation, action, and maintenance. Two questions are used to assess the client's stage of change: Have you thought about making changes in your current situation within the last six months? If the answer is "no," the client's stage is precontemplation. If the response is "yes," the next question is asked: "Have you thought about making any changes within the next 30 days?" If the answer is "no" then the client is in the contemplation stage, and if the answer is "yes" the stage is preparation. Interventions for each stage are described that are most likely to be accepted by the client and eventually lead to the next stage. Interested readers can consult this reference for specific strategies that are recommended. Although there are no research data to support the use of this approach with victims of intimate partner violence, it has been found to be successful with other problems, such as substance use.

One issue that is particularly important in treatment of victims of intimate partner violence is that of *secondary victimization*. In this context, the term refers to injustices experienced after the trauma when the victim seeks help for herself. These victimizations place blame on the victim and may not provide the expected support. Hattendorf and Tollerud (1997) give examples of secondary victimization of victims of intimate partner violence: minimization of the trauma and over-diagnosis of psychopathology in emergency rooms. These authors believe that referral for psychotherapy can be a form of secondary victimization, implying that there is something wrong with the woman rather than with the situation. Additional traumatization can be perpetrated by the legal system, that may not prosecute the batterer, or when the case is prosecuted, lack of convictions and light sentences give the message that the woman's trauma is not that serious. Helping professionals should be sensitive to the broader implications of such experiences and assist clients in developing self-advocacy skills.

When treating clients who are victims of intimate partner abuse, the counselor must be certain to determine the client's level of safety, and to ensure that a client's risk for further harm is reduced. It is also important the counselors working with this clientele have links with agencies and services that may be necessary (for emergency housing, legal assistance, etc.) and assist clients in accessing these services as needed (Samuelson & Campbell, 2005).

The perpetrators of intimate partner violence are often less than eager to seek treatment, but may be mandated to do so once the legal system is involved. The Duluth model is a widely used intervention that confronts the attitudes about control that are believed to drive the violence, and educates men about more effective strategies to deal with their partners (Jackson et al., 2003). This intervention is based on the assumption that the causes for intimate partner violence are social or political rather than biological or psychological (Pugh, 2005). Unfortunately, there is persuasive evidence that the program is ineffective. Some experts believe CBT is more likely to have a positive impact on battering behaviors, but to date no such model has been evaluated.

Issues of Diversity

There is evidence that trauma not only affects individuals differently depending on a number of factors, but that there are differences in reactions by gender and race/ethnicity. Several studies have found that females are at higher risk for trauma-related mental health problems than men (Norris, 2002). In a study of 255 survivors of the bombing of the Murrah Building in Oklahoma City in 1995, women had twice the rate of PTSD than men (North et al., 1999). Bolton, O'Ryan, Udwin, Boyle, and Yule (2000) studied the survivors of the sinking of a tour ship on which 400 adolescents from England were traveling, and were able to follow-up with them at five months after the trauma (Yule et al., 2000) and again between five and eight years after the disaster. The five-month post-trauma study found that females had higher rates of PTSD than did the males. Females also had significantly higher rates of any psychopathology, including anxiety and affective disorders, than did the male survivors in the later study. In their study of the effects of both gender and culture on the psychological effects of a hurricane, Norris and colleagues (2001) found that gender explained about 5% of the variance in PTSD symptoms, while cultural group explained less than 1%. A comprehensive study of mental health effects of the September 11 attacks on residents who lived closest to the World Trade Center found higher rates of PTSD and depression in females (Galea et al., 2002).

One concern about the research that readers should keep in mind is the possibility that observed racial/ethnic differences are due to insensitivity of test instruments to cultural differences. For example, in a study of differences in PTSD symptoms between elderly (over 55) whites and African Americans who had been criminally victimized, no differences were detected on rates of PTSD for those who had experienced a physical trauma, while whites had higher rates of PTSD when the trauma was non-physical (Mainous, Smith, Acierno, & Geesey, 2005). In speculating about their findings, the researchers propose two explanations: (1) lifelong experiences create different cultural coping strategies in the two groups that are manifested in the responses to non-physical trauma, and (2) the assessment tool is less sensitive to the symptoms in African Americans.

In addition, Mexican Americans and other Hispanic groups seem to be adversely affected by trauma more than Anglo-Americans, who are affected more than African Americans (Norris, Perilla, Ibañez, & Murphy, 2001). Several studies have found that minority individuals have more and more severe symptoms of PTSD following a trauma compared to European Americans. Pratt, Brief, and Keane (2006) caution that observed differences may be due to a lack of culturally sensitive assessment instruments. They recommend the Harvard Trauma Questionnaire, which is specifically designed for Indochinese immigrants and is available in several languages.

In their review of the literature on racial differences in combat-related PTSD, Frueh, Brady, and de Arrelano (1998) observed that although different rates of PTSD had been found by race in previous studies, further analyses showed that the differences (showing minority veterans had higher rates of PTSD than whites) may be better explained by the levels of stress experienced or pre-existing conditions. For example, in a study in which black veterans reported more distress than other groups, the data showed that blacks had experienced more combat trauma than other soldiers and also experienced racial problems, an additional stressor. An earlier study of Vietnam veterans (Green, Grace, & Lindy, 1990) also found that blacks experienced more combat, more injuries, and greater exposure to gruesome death than did their white counterparts. In addition, a comparison of blacks and whites revealed that whites achieved higher ranks than blacks, even when pre-service variables such as education, employment, childhood trauma were controlled. The authors interpret this finding to suggest that racial discrimination may have been occurring, adding to the stress of black soldiers.

Norris, Kaniasty, Conrad, Inman, and Murphy (2002) were interested in the cultural differences of age effects on PTSD prevalence after a disaster. They studied survivors of hurricanes in the United States and Mexico and flood survivors in Poland. The found that age effects varied by culture such that among Americans, middle-aged participants were most affected, while among Mexicans, younger people had the highest rates of PTSD and among Polish participants, the oldest participants were the most distressed. The results also found that the severity of the trauma was the most important factor in predicting PTSD. The second most important factor was gender, with women in all three samples having significantly more symptoms than men.

An interesting study of earthquake victims in Columbia, South America, measured psychological problems in adolescents using the Spanish version of the Minnesota Multiphasic Personality Inventory–Adolescent (MMPI-A) (Scott, Knoth, Beltran-Quiones, & Gomez, 2003). The earthquake victims had almost all lost their homes (95%); 17% had a family member killed, and 24% were injured in the disaster. A control group was recruited from a school with similar demographics that was not affected by the earthquake. The MMPI-A was administered eight months after the earthquake. At that time, there was no evidence of psychopathology in the earthquake survivors on any scale. Despite the lack of clinical evaluation, there were significant differences between the victims and the controls: victims had higher scores on depression, psychasthenia (anxiety), and schizophrenia (distorted thinking). Females also had significantly higher scores on depression than males. The authors emphasize their main finding that there was no psychopathology in the sample, and suggest that the fact that this was a Type I disaster (single incident), that the sample did not include any adolescents with previous emotional problems, and that family and community support was extremely high. In addition, disaster relief efforts were large and visible, which may have diminished any hopelessness. One other explanation for the findings is offered: the area of Columbia in which the earthquake occurred has an extremely high rate of violence. The repeated exposure to violence may have desensitized the youth to high levels of stress.

In thinking about the differential effects of disaster on racial groups, I only need to visualize the television images of those devastated by Hurricane Katrina. It is plain that African Americans, the majority of residents in the flooded wards, experienced more severe levels of trauma than other residents. Whether this is an effect of race or poverty, that population received more than its share of trauma. Helping professionals must recognize and be sensitive to these disparities if they are to be helpful.

Persons with disabilities experience a variety of trauma at rates higher than the general population. They are victimized by violence at four to ten times the rate of others (Petersilia, 2001) and are more likely to be victims of crime in general (Charlton, Kliethermes, Tallant, Taverne, & Tishelman, 2004). In addition, natural disasters are particularly hard on persons with disabilities (FEMA, 2006). I will review these two types of trauma and their impact on persons with disabilities in turn.

High rates of abuse and violent victimization are reported in people with disabilities around the world (Petersilia, 2001, 2007). Children with disabilities are physically and sexually abused at rates higher than non-disabled children. As law and policies reduced the number of persons with disabilities who are in institutions, one consequence is that some persons with disabilities are forced by poverty to live in unsafe environments. On the other hand, persons in institutions are also very vulnerable to victimization. Persons with disabilities, who are dependent on others for care, including bathing, dressing, and toileting, are particularly vulnerable to abuse by caregivers (Cronin, 2005; Disabled Women's Network Ontario, n.d.), because resistance can result in the withholding of care. Because of their dependence, many persons with disabilities have been encouraged to be compliant with the wishes of caregivers, which makes them an easier mark for those who seek to take advantage.

Persons with physical disabilities may be unable or less able to defend themselves against violence due to challenges with mobility. Those with cognitive limitations may not have the skills to identify high-risk situations, and may lack the vocabulary to provide an accurate account of the crime. And, persons with intellectual disabilities or communication impairments are often not believed if they do report crimes, and even if perpetrators are convicted, sentences tend to be light (Petersilia, 2007). On those rare occasions when a case involving a person with intellectual disabilities does go to court, the person does not receive any assistance with testimony. The adversarial nature of a trial, combined with the presence of the perpetrator, easily overwhelms a person with intellectual disabilities, and the experience can be traumatic and re-victimizing.

Deaf children appear to have higher rates of physical and sexual abuse than hearing children, perhaps because the perpetrators assume they are unable to report the offenses (Durity et al., 2004). Some believe that the greatest risk for abuse occurs in residential schools, which deaf children often attend. Factors that may increase the vulnerability of these children include the inability to partake of "incidental learning." Hearing children learn from overhearing private conversations of adults or siblings and may pick up information from television that is on in the background. Hearing peers may share information by whispering, and the like. These sources of information, that help prepare children to protect themselves from harm and victimization, are not accessible to deaf children. This general lack of information may impair the child's social development and they may have less understanding of what is appropriate in what situations. Further, particularly deaf children of hearing parents (as 90% of deaf children are) may have restricted communication even with family, which may increase their need for intimacy, however inappropriate. In addition to the increased vulnerability of deaf children to abuse, their ability to report and receive therapy is also limited by the limited availability of certified interpreters who can assist. Assessment of disorders is complicated by the lack of measures designed for this population.

In addition to increased vulnerability, Charlton and colleagues (2004) observe that persons with disabilities typically have fewer protective factors that can buffer them from the effects of trauma. In fact, they have been found to be less resilient than non-disabled persons, and are less likely to have appropriate treatment for trauma, particularly if the disabilities are cognitive or involve barriers to communication.

Not only are children with disabilities more likely to be exposed to trauma and violence, but trauma and violence can actually cause some disabilities (Charlton et al., 2004). Child abuse and neglect in infancy increases the likelihood of developmental delays. The brain can be permanently affected by such abuse as "shaken baby," and even neglect can result in decreased brain size and other damage.

Shaken baby syndrome: Constellation of symptoms of violent shaking of an infant or small child, including severe neurological damage and death.

A vignette from the stories of Hurricane Katrina in New Orleans illustrates the challenges of the disabled during a natural disaster.

> During Hurricane Katrina, Benilda Caixeta, a New Orleans resident with quadriplegia, tried for two days to seek refuge at the Superdome. Despite repeated phone calls to authorities, help never arrived for Caixeta. Days later, she was found dead in her apartment, floating next to her wheelchair. (Tady, 2006)

Following the hurricane, many survivors with disabilities had difficulty obtaining accessible housing. On September 26, 2006, a lawsuit on behalf of survivors with disabilities reached a settlement with FEMA to provide them with wheelchair accessible trailers. A telephone number to handle requests from other evacuees with disabilities was set up as part of the settlement.

Although exact figures are not available, it is likely that persons with disabilities were disproportionately affected by natural disasters. In the 9/11 attacks, there is evidence that some people with disabilities were left behind to perish. No plans were in place for evacuating persons with disabilities, who may require special equipment. In the aftermath, those persons with disabilities who lived in the affected areas could not access medical doctors or obtain medications, meals, or other services, and without communication access (telephone service and internet connections were unavailable) they were unable to communicate their needs (Kendall-Tackett, n.d.).

A 2004 report from California on the emergency response to wildfires found that some persons with disabilities could not see the fires, or hear announcements to evacuate, or access transportation to evacuate. Telephones at evacuation sites were not adapted for use by the deaf, and could not be reached by those in wheelchairs. Evacuation plans typically involve some walking or driving, and seeing and hearing, which people with disabilities are unable to do.

A 2006 study determined that only 20% of emergency managers in thirty cities had guidelines for assisting people with mobility impairments during an emergency, and only 27% of these managers had completed a FEMA training course on the special emergency needs of persons with disabilities. An advisory released on March 23, 2006 to provide information on hurricane preparedness for people with disabilities (FEMA, 2006) recommends that individuals plan ahead by gathering emergency supplies into a ready-to-go kit and having food and water sufficient for seventy-two hours. Although this advice is surely helpful, there is no information about how persons would contact emergency officials if services are interrupted. FEMA recommends persons with disabilities create a network of at least three people who can check on a person in the event of a disaster, ensuring these support persons have all necessary information about operating special equipment, working with service animals, and so on. Persons with disabilities, their caretakers, and family members must plan ahead and have procedures in place for both transportation and shelter in the event of a disaster.

For helping professionals who work with persons with disabilities, it would be worthwhile to inquire about past trauma, given the high incidence in the population. It would also be useful to check that such clients do have an emergency plan in place.

Counselor Issues

Vicarious Traumatization

Working with trauma survivors is hard and emotionally taxing. There is controversy about the existence of an actual disorder that develops in mental health clinicians who work with these clients. *Secondary traumatization, vicarious traumatization,* and *compassion fatigue* are terms used to describe the effects of indirect exposure (exposure via hearing detailed accounts of others' traumatic experiences) on counselors (Zimering, Monroe, & Gulliver, 2003). Symptoms of this disorder are the same as those for PTSD, except that the experience itself is indirect. Whether there is a diagnosable disorder seems to me to be less important than the acknowledged stress and psychological reactions experienced by clinicians, which can be considered an occupational risk (Sabin-Farrell & Turpin, 2003). Although the reactions are usually short-lived, for some clinicians they persist and interfere with their ability to do their work.

Two factors have been investigated as contributors to the constellation of symptoms that is experienced by clinicians who have experienced secondary traumatization: personal trauma history and the percentage of trauma survivors treated by the counselor. Although results of the few research studies are mixed on personal trauma history, there is more consensus that the number or percentage of trauma survivors treated by a counselor is directly related to the symptoms of secondary traumatic stress the counselor experiences (Arvay, 2002).

One study examined factors that affected social workers who treated survivors of the World Trade Center attacks on 9/11, and found higher rates of PTSD symptoms in social workers who treated survivors than in those who did not (Boscarino, Figley, & Adams, 2004). These researchers identified several variables that predicted symptom development: degree of exposure (number of clients treated), personal history of trauma, social support available, and environmental (work setting) factors.

Although there is insufficient research to support any specific prevention strategies, Zimering and colleagues (2003) propose four areas that are important: professional strategies, organizational strategies, personal strategies, and general coping strategies. I believe that the professional strategies are crucial. Even if a counselor specializes in trauma work, some limitation on the number of trauma survivors seen at any given time period is essential. In addition, the availability of supervision to allow for debriefing and processing of emotional reactions is another necessity. Organizational strategies include having release time available and ensuring a safe work environment. Personal and general coping strategies are those any counselor should employ regardless of clientele: recognizing one's limits, engaging in self-care activities, and using a personal support system.

Critical Incident Stress Management

Critical Incident Stress Management (CISM) is a structured procedure used immediately following a traumatic event, with the goal of reducing the development of posttraumatic stress symptoms. It was designed for those who work directly with trauma victims, such as police and other emergency services, Red Cross workers, and other first responders. However, the process has been widely applied with trauma survivors. This type of intervention has become so popular that a foundation was created to train about 40,000 people each year in the model.

Critical Incident Stress Debriefing (CISD) is a crucial component of CISM, and is a group review of the trauma event or disaster occurring within days of the traumatic event. It is sometimes used with individual trauma victims. CISD is a structured technique, taking three to four hours, involving seven phases: introduction, fact phase (participants each describe their experience), thought phase (each participants describe their thoughts during event), feeling phase (participants each ventilate emotions), reaction phase (participants each describe any stress reactions), strategy phase (facilitator normalizes response), and the re-entry phase (facilitator summarizes and provides referrals for further help) (McNally, 2004). This approach has been widely adopted, and several school districts I worked in provided training to counselors and psychologists in this procedure. It is important for helping professionals to know that there is insufficient evidence of effectiveness of this process, and some evidence that it can be harmful (Litz et al., 2002). The CISD component is often delivered to all involved personnel, regardless of whether they have symptoms or are experiencing any problems functioning. Although some people undoubtedly benefit, it is not sufficient to prevent trauma-related disorders in all at-risk individuals. Also, this approach may increase stress in some who attend. Although attendance is supposed to be voluntary, there may be subtle pressure to attend. The intervention is facilitated by a trained mental health clinician and a person in the field (or company) that was affected by the trauma. This may create dual relationships and some participants may be uncomfortable in this context. Although participants may give positive ratings for the experience, the fact that the intervention does not reduce psychological problems, and in fact in some cases seems to increase them, is of greater concern.

CISM is also a structured sequence of interventions. The first is pre-incident education, which can be done with groups of individuals who are likely to encounter trauma in their work (police, firefighters, soldiers). This segment is designed to prepare

BOX 7.1

A Note to School Counselors

Most children and adolescents return to school after experiencing a trauma. Given that most will adjust after a period of time, not all will require intervention. For those who do, school counselors are the best equipped persons in the school to provide services, as they are trained in both education and mental health issues (Wong, 2005). A very well-designed study conducted on Kauai two years after Hurricane Iniki devastated the island demonstrated the efficacy of both screening and intervening with large numbers of children (Chemtob, Nakashima, & Hamada, 2002). The researchers were invited to assist school personnel who observed continuing distress among students two years after the disaster. School counselors coordinated the screening procedure, which involved all 4258 elementary children in grades two through six. The screening instruments were administered by regular classroom teachers, who were provided with a lesson on how to respond to self-report inventories so that students were prepared to respond. During administration, all questions were read aloud by the teachers. The six percent of students with the highest scores (reflecting the most distress), 88% of whom met the criteria for a diagnosis of PTSD, participated in four sessions of either individual or group treatment delivered by three school counselors and one school social worker. A manual was created to ensure that all children received the same treatment. Topics of the sessions were: safety and helplessness, loss, mobilizing competence and issues of anger, and ending and going forward. Play, expressive art, and talking were used in both individual and group formats, except that the play was cooperative in the group format. At the end of the intervention, students who completed the intervention had significantly lower scores on the measures. Those lower scores were maintained at a one-year follow-up. Finally, although the outcomes were the same for individual and group approaches, more students in the group format completed the intervention. This study demonstrates that school counselors can be leaders in designing and implementing effective services following a disaster that affects large numbers of students. The most common scenario is for one or a few students to be affected by a traumatic event. Helen Jackson (2004) at Columbia University has a free online training module for helping students cope with trauma and loss that I highly recommend. I have provided access information in the section on additional resources. In that online module, she recommends cognitive therapy techniques, modified depending on the age and situation of the child. All appropriate techniques are mentioned in the section on that treatment approach earlier in this chapter. Particularly recommended are anxiety management strategies, challenging irrational beliefs, and exposure therapy, and working with parents whenever possible. Jackson suggests that interventions address "traumatic reminders," to reduce the anxiety provoked by such stimuli. Traumatic reminders might be holidays, or anniversaries, or even music that may have been playing when the event happened. In addition, school counselors should identify and assist the child with secondary stressors that have emerged as a result of the trauma. For example, has the child had to move? Has a parent become unemployed? If so, the school counselor can help the child understand and cope with these additional challenges.

Traumatic reminders: Things associated with the traumatic event that can trigger reactions of fear and helplessness.

Jackson urges school counselors to be alert to the possibility of vicarious traumatization, discussed in more detail in relation to helping professionals in general, and to recognize when outside help might be necessary.

On September 22, 2005, Richard Wong, the executive director of the American School Counselor Association, addressed a U.S. Senate hearing on helping children displaced by Katrina.

BOX 7.1   **Continued**

He pointed out that school counselors perform valuable service to disaster and trauma victims by being accessible to all students. He observed that school counselors are trained to detect problems that require more in-depth intervention, and to provide assistance and referrals in those cases. Helping children regain some normalcy is important, and by assisting trauma victims in schools, students are able to resume their educational activities as soon as possible.

---

individuals with knowledge about stress and normal responses. Scene support and staff advisement, the next phase, is provided on site of a disaster or large-scale incident. In this phase, trained CISM facilitators allow workers to express feelings, and the facilitator notes any needs (e.g., rest, water) that are detected. The facilitators communicate with other administrative personnel with recommendations, such as shift length, supply locations, and the like. The demobilization phase can only be implemented in certain limited settings, but allows facilitators to communicate basic information before the group leaves the scene. The CISD component occurs 2–14 days after the traumatic event, and includes the steps described above. Further, post-debriefing includes informal interaction between the workers and facilitators. After the immediate incident, community or large-scale debriefing of individuals who were impacted by the trauma is conducted, and support is provided to families as needed. In some cases, assessment and consultation, along with follow-up and referral can be provided to groups who were involved in the CISM (Anonymous, 2005).

It is difficult to study the effects of CISM because of the variability in implementation and because participants in large-scale traumas (such as September 11) are difficult to locate and assess. However, a considerable body of controlled research has accumulated on CISD, and findings suggest that this procedure is not only unhelpful, but may in fact be harmful. Researchers who used a critical incident debriefing procedure with 106 consecutive accident admissions to a hospital found that, for patients with high initial scores on a measure of initial stress reactions (within twenty-four hours of the accident), those who received the intervention had negative effects (more PTSD symptoms) at four months and at three years post-accident than controls who did not receive the intervention (Mayou, Ehlers, & Hobbs, 2000). A meta-analysis that examined published studies on the procedure concluded, "Despite the intuitive appeal of the technique, our results show that CISD has no efficacy in reducing symptoms of post-traumatic stress disorder and other trauma-related symptoms, and in fact suggest that it has a detrimental effect" (van Emmerik, Kamphuis, Hulsbosch, & Emmelkamp, 2002, p. 769). McNally reached a similar conclusion: "Despite repeated attempts to document that psychological debriefing can prevent posttraumatic psychopathology, there is no convincing evidence that it does so. Even if the procedure is not harmful, its continued implementation may delay development of truly effective crisis interventions, while wasting time, money and resources on a method that is, at best, inert" (McNally, 2004, paragraph 12).

I believe the evidence is strong enough that CISD should not be used with individuals. The evidence for group interventions is less clear, but I think it is prudent to utilize the procedure only with voluntary participation. If working with an intact group, such as emergency workers, there may be some benefit in the form of group cohesion, but that is speculative at this point.

Ethical Concerns

Given what is known about CISD, including its popularity and its neutral or negative impact, counselors in schools and agencies may be in a position of being asked to attend trainings or use this approach. I believe that an ethical counselor would inform supervisors or administrators of what is known about the approach, and suggest alternative strategies be explored. Further, the ethical counselor should decline to provide CISD to an individual.

If a counselor works with clients who have experienced trauma in the form of domestic violence, there are two concerns. First, these clients have had their trust and safety deliberately violated, and they are likely to be reluctant to establish trust with anyone else, including the counselor. The counselor needs to be very careful not to misinterpret this reluctance as resistance, and to address the safety issue in sensitive and careful ways and make establishing trust a primary treatment goal.

Because working with trauma victims is so difficult, and the danger of secondary victimization exists, there are two extremes of counselor reactions to this work to which the counselor must be acutely alert. Sometimes counselors over-identify with the victim (Dutton, 1992). This response can lead to problematic emotional responses on the part of the counselor. For example, the counselor may become visibly distressed, causing the client to feel the need to comfort the counselor or be more restrained in sharing information to avoid upsetting the counselor. If the counselor were to express extreme anger at the perpetrator, the client may find herself defending him. The other extreme that sometimes occurs in the counselors who work with these clients is to become emotionally distanced and detached to protect themselves. This stance communicates to the clients that their issues are not that important, and that the violence that the clients experienced is not understood by the counselor. Being alert to these possible responses to working with this clientele will help the counselors avoid unethical behaviors.

It is also essential that counselors focus on the needs of the client. Several authors cited in this chapter express concern that counselors may avoid using exposure treatments because they are unable to cope with the client's negative emotional response. It is unethical to select a treatment approach that is less effective for a client because the counselor has personal difficulty tolerating strong emotions. In such cases, the counselor should not treat trauma cases, and when presented with a client for whom trauma is a central issue, the counselor should make a careful and considered referral to a specialist.

As with many other issues in this book, the counselor's personal history and its effect on the ability to provide ethical services need to be addressed. Secondary traumatization might be more readily experienced by a counselor with a history of trauma and violence, and listening to clients' reports of trauma may be experienced by the counselor as re-victimization. The counselor must be sure that his or her own issues have been resolved before consenting to work with trauma survivors. Both supervision and personal therapy are strategies for ensuring that the personal and professional concerns are separated.

Again the reader must consider the ethical issue is the "boundaries of competence" ethical standard. Counseling trauma victims requires considerable specialized expertise and supervised practice, and counselors interested in this work must get both training and supervised experience in the techniques.

Summary

- Trauma and violence are experienced by most people in the course of their lives. Most people experience acute distress but recover within six months. Some will develop PTSD, and some of those will continue to have the disorder ten years later.

- Disasters, one type of trauma, can be natural or human-caused. Human-caused disasters seem to cause more psychological harm due to the violation of basic assumptions about the world, others, and self.

- Two types of trauma have been identified: Type I traumas are single-incident events (hurricane, criminal assault); Type II traumas are chronic and repeated (as in ongoing sexual abuse or living in the midst of war).

- Many variables influence an individual's response: the severity of the trauma, prior traumatic experiences, mental health prior to the incident, gender, developmental level, and available support systems.

- PTSD is often found in combat veterans and victims of intimate partner violence. These populations have unique issues that should be addressed in treatment.

- A variety of assessment tools are available to screen or diagnose PTSD. The generalist counselor will want to screen all new clients to identify any trauma history.

- The strongest evidence for effective treatment of PTSD and trauma-related symptoms is for CBT Approaches. The use of EMDR is controversial; studies have used weak methodology to measure effectiveness.

- Most CBT approaches incorporate exposure and cognitive restructuring in the treatment protocol. Exposure (systematic desensitization, flooding, and implosion therapy) is designed to disconnect trauma reminders from the distressing emotional response using habituation and extinction. The cognitive elements address faulty thinking about the trauma (e.g., I could have prevented it).

- Females of all cultures are more likely to have problematic or enduring distress following a trauma than males. Some research suggests that minorities experience greater degrees of trauma-related problems than whites, but differences may be due to culturally insensitive instrumentation to measure reactions, or to differential treatment following a disaster.

- Persons with disabilities are at elevated risk for many kinds of trauma, and may have fewer resources to cope with trauma when it occurs.

- Natural disasters impact persons with disabilities disproportionately, as communication impairments and mobility difficulties can interfere with evacuation and sheltering.
- Specialized training is needed to employ trauma-related treatment approaches. Counselors must be alert to their levels of competence, and their own tolerance for horrific content and strong emotions if they are considering specializing in this clientele.

ADDITIONAL RESOURCES

On the Web

- www.trauma-pages.com is a link to David Balwin's Trauma Info pages that contain links to so many other resources there that is truly a one-stop-shopping source.
- http://www.ncptsd.va.gov The National Center for Post-traumatic Stress Disorder in the Department of Veterans Affairs website has material for clinicians and clients and their families. I definitely recommend a visit to the site, which also contains lots of very helpful general material on trauma and PTSD, which is not at all limited to veterans.
- www.istss.org The International Society for Trauma and Stress Studies is useful if you are looking for research or conference information.
- http://www.apa.org/topics/topictrauma.html APA's trauma resource section also posts current information, sometimes in PDF form for downloading. They have current information and reports for psychologists responding to a variety of disasters worldwide.
- http://www.mentalhealth.samhsa.gov/publications/allpubs/SMA-3959/default.asp There is an excellent free resource, *Mental Health Response to Mass Violence and Terrorism: A Training Manual*, available at this site that has many useful assessment tools and ideas for mental health workers. Although designed as a training manual, and certainly valuable for that purpose, it has so many good ideas that readers may want to download it for their own use.
- http://ci.columbia.edu/w0521/index.html For school counselors and others who work with children, I highly recommend the free online course by Helen Jackson. There is no cost, and there are several additional useful modules on loss and grief that are also excellent.
- http://www.ncptsd.va.gov/war/guide/index.html The Veteran's Affairs division has produced the *Iraq War Clinician's Guide* (2nd ed.) that can be ordered or downloaded from this site. For any counselor who will work with military personnel and/or their families, this is an excellent place to start.
- http://www.ncptsd.va.gov/video/index.html has several excellent videos that can be downloaded at no cost. *Hope for Recovery* is a great overview of trauma, and also features some of the experts cited in this chapter. There are programs on medication, assessment, stages of change approach, and general PTSD info. There is an excellent one on *Children on Trauma* (total about 20 minutes). The programs are divided into shorter segments to facilitate downloading.

In Print for Counselors

- *Too Scared to Cry* by Lenore Terr (1992). A classic on trauma.
- *Trauma and Recovery* by Judith Herman (1997) is also widely read and authoritative.
- *Trauma in the Lives of Children* by Kendall Johnson (1998) would be an excellent addition to the library of any counselor who works with children who have been traumatized.
- *Empowering and Healing the Battered Woman* by Mary Ann Dutton (1992) is the most comprehensive and useful book for those who work with female victims of intimate partner violence.
- *Effective Treatments for PTSD* edited by Edna Foa, Terence Keane, and Matthew Friedman (2000) would be a good start for readers who think they might be interested in specializing in treating trauma survivors, and are not sure which approach is best. For each approach, available research is described so that the reader can make informed decisions. Treatments are rated from Level A (best evidence) to effectiveness to level F (recently developed approach with no evidence).
- *Cognitive-Behavioral Therapies for Trauma* edited by Victoria Follete and Joseph Ruzek (2006) has more technical information on using CBT approaches.
- *Post-Traumatic Stress Disorder in Children* by Spencer Eth and Robert Pynoos (1985) is still relevant and provides useful techniques for a variety of types of trauma in children.

In Print for Clients

- *The Post-Traumatic Stress Disorder Sourcebook* by Glenn Schiraldi (2000) is useful for clients, their support system, and the counselor as well. It also helps the client understand different approaches to treatment.
- *I Can't Get Over It: A Handbook for Trauma Survivors* by Aphrodite Matsakis contains four parts: Understanding PTSD, The Healing Process, Specific Traumas (individual chapters on every type of trauma), and Appendices with additional resources.
- *The PTSD Workbook* by Mary Beth Williams and Soili Poijula (2002) is most useful when the client has complex PTSD, as the majority of the book is devoted to topics geared to complex PTSD survivors.

Novels for Counselors and Clients

- *The Kite Runner* by Khaled Husseini (2003) is a favorite of mine. The crucial scene in the book is traumatic for Hassan, but also for Amir. I think reading the book with that in mind would be a worthwhile exercise for those interested in untreated trauma.
- *The Boy Who Loved Anne Frank* by Ellen Feldman (2005) is a moving work of fiction that chronicles the experience of Peter, who was described in Anne Frank's diary. It is an original perspective on a Holocaust survivor, and one I highly recommend.

- *The Return of the Soldier,* is Rebecca West's first novel, published in 1918. She describes the return of a shell-shocked soldier to his elegant English estate. Although we know much more about PTSD now, this short novel gives a glimpse of history that is beautifully written.

Film and Television

- *Jackknife* helps the viewer understand PTSD in Vietnam veterans.
- *The Deer Hunter* is another film about PTSD in veterans of Vietnam.
- *Behind the Lines/Regeneration* provides an example of shell-shock in World War II based on an outstanding novel (part of a trilogy by Pat Barker) about real historical figures.
- *Sophie's Choice* is a classic film about a Holocaust survivor that should not be missed.

EXERCISES

1. Re-read the case study and compare the account with the criteria for a diagnosis of PTSD. Do you think Jane would be diagnosed with this disorder? Defend your position. Based on the available information, what type of treatment would you recommend for her?

2. If you have been persuaded that it is important to inquire about trauma experiences during your initial sessions, how will you do so? If you will use an assessment instrument, which one will you use? If you determine that PTSD is a likely diagnosis, what will be your next step?

3. Assume there has been a shooting (one shooter and one victim, but many witnesses) at a local school. The staff asks for your help, and wants to know how you would approach the situation. What will your strategy be?

4. Assume you are a school counselor whose school includes many military families whose soldiers are deployed in Iraq. What kinds of programming will you devise to educate children and parents about this situation? How would you work with a child whose dad has just returned, and the child reports that the father is "not the way he used to be?"

5. How will you work with the wife of a soldier who has recently returned from Iraq? She reports that her husband is unwilling to come for couples counseling, but she is distressed by his short temper and frequent angry outbursts, none of which he exhibited before his deployment. She also wants to comfort him, but he does not tell her about his experiences, and she sees this as not trusting her.

8

Grief and Bereavement

In the twenty-first century, less than a quarter of Americans die at home; most deaths take place in hospitals or nursing homes. A hundred years ago, death at home was a common event. Bodies were not embalmed, and were viewed at home before burial. Now, funeral preparations take place out of sight of the family, and funerals are typically held away from the home. By the time the body is viewed, it has generally been embalmed and otherwise treated so it appears lifelike (in repose, sleeping), protecting viewers from the reality of death. In the work setting, bereavement leave is often limited to three days, suggesting that is enough time to grieve. These factors all contribute to the difficulty some people experience managing grief.

Grief and loss are about endings. It is appropriate to conclude the book with this chapter, as grief and loss are often associated with the topics covered in previous chapters. Sometimes the loss occurs via death, but one also may grieve lost innocence, lost hopes, lost abilities, lost trust, and so on. Helping professionals must be aware that part of the healing from many of the experiences that bring clients to their offices involves mourning the attendant losses, whether the loss is a person or an ideal.

This topic is different from all of the others covered in this book in that grief is the one experience that counselors are sure to experience personally at some time in their lives. Death and loss are inevitable, painful aspects of the human experience. Because counselors dealing with grieving clients know that this issue is one they have faced or will face personally, self-awareness is particularly important to ensure that it is the client's rather than the counselor's needs that are the focus of counseling. Grieving is not a mental disorder, and individuals who are grieving don't always need counseling. In fact, most people manage this experience without complications and with available support in their environment. However, there are cases when a counselor, grief specialist or not, will encounter a grieving client for whom environmental support is absent or insufficient for their needs. There are also some individuals for whom grief becomes complicated, and these people may seek counseling or be referred for counseling to assist them in returning to an adaptive level of functioning.

Case Study

James was a 21-year-old college senior when his mother committed suicide. She was 50 years old, a professional nurse, in good health. A year or so before her death, her husband of 25 years announced his intention to divorce her. Her husband accepted a new job, and was living in the new city, visiting home on occasion. In addition to James, she had two other sons, one two years older than James, and another who was ten years old at the time of her death.

The summer prior to his junior year, James was working in another state when his father called, asking him to come home because his mother was "not well." When he landed, his mother met him at the airport, and James was confused. Later, James's father told him that she had attempted suicide by taking an overdose of medication, but James had difficulty absorbing that information as she appeared to be fine. He stayed with them for a week, and in an effort to be helpful, arranged for couples' therapy for his parents. He believes they went a few times.

James returned to his summer job, and a month later, his father called to say his mother had "done it again." James left his job and returned home, where he stayed at his mother's hospital bedside for several days. James felt burdened, and then relieved when arrangements were made for her to enter a psychiatric hospital. After a month-long hospital stay, his mother was discharged and arrangements made for her to live with a married sister in another city. James drove his mother to her sister's home, and recalls that on the long trip his mother was obviously sad, and said she wanted to drink. During the drive, James felt trapped and again burdened with responsibility for his mother.

James eventually returned to college and his mother remained with her sister. She found a good job, enrolled her younger son in school, and even received a promotion. James came home for Thanksgiving and Christmas, and his father also visited on those holidays. James had a sense that things were tenuous, but his father was there and he was somewhat reassured. He visited again on his college spring break. At that time, James and his mother discussed plans for James's upcoming graduation in May, and she showed him the dress she had chosen to wear for the occasion. She was concerned about James's plans after graduation, and he told her he was considering either an international position, or teaching in the United States. His mother said that if he decided to teach, he could do so in the city where she was now living, and they could live together. James, ready to begin his independent adult life, said he did not want to do that. James returned to college to complete his senior semester. That conversation haunted him for years after her death; he felt guilty for telling her that he did not want to live with her after graduation, and felt that he had contributed to her decision to end her life.

Shortly after James's visit, James's aunt and uncle wanted to go out of town to visit their own adult children, but were concerned about leaving James's mother alone. She urged them to go, saying her husband would be visiting and they needed the privacy. James's father did indeed visit. Just a few weeks after James's visit with his mother, his father called to say his mother had taken another overdose of medication, and urged James to come home again. One of his college roommates drove James to the hospital, and provided emotional support on the long drive.

James saw his mother in the hospital. His aunt told James that she was not going to make it this time, but he was numb and did not react. James's mother remained in a coma for a week, and then they received the phone call from the hospital telling them of her death. James's father told him that his mother had died of a stroke, and he clung to that explanation, which was easier to accept than suicide. James accompanied his father and uncle to the hospital, returned home, and went to bed, all without crying or really feeling the impact of the loss. The next morning when he awoke, however, he experienced a crushing feeling when he realized she was not there and would never be. The tears and sadness overwhelmed him. When James's father saw him crying, he said "Let me give you this," (a pill, probably Valium) and the tears stopped; they did not return for many years.

James's father eventually gave this account of events: he and James's mother were talking and drinking when his mother announced that she felt tired and cold and wanted to lie down. She went to her upstairs bedroom. When it seemed to his father that she was gone a long time, he went upstairs and found her unconscious and called for an ambulance. When the emergency personnel were taking his mother to the ambulance, they bumped into a grandfather clock, which stopped. After her death, the police came to investigate the death, and the time on the clock turned out to be discrepant with James' father's account of events. The police wondered about foul play and wanted to exhume the body, but James's aunt denied permission to do so. When James learned of the police request about six weeks later, he focused on that situation, believing he would have given permission. He also experienced a shock when he saw the death certificate, with the cause of death given as "suicide." He had chosen to believe his father's explanation of a stroke, and seeing "suicide" on an official document forced him to confront reality. He was embarrassed to tell anyone that his mother died of suicide, and that feeling continued well into adulthood.

James was a co-signatory on a bank account with his mother, so he knew that she had been saving money for the future, and he believed she had goals and was thinking of the future. This added to his confusion about her death.

Many relatives and friends came to the funeral. James viewed his mother's body, but did not touch it. He remained unemotional throughout the funeral and burial rites. He stayed at home for a week after the funeral, and then returned to school and dedicated himself to finishing his courses. He saw a counselor on campus two or three times, and found it helpful to talk to someone about his feelings. He chose not to attend his graduation ceremony.

Another blow came when James's father telephoned him at school two weeks after his mother's death to announce that he had remarried. James was shocked and angry. When he told his concerned roommates what his father had done, one of the roommates reacted, saying how terrible it was for his father to do such a thing. James turned on his roommate, releasing his anger, and the friendship never recovered.

James's emotions focused on his anger at his father's quick remarriage, rather than on his feelings about his mother's death. He thought of his father as selfish and inconsiderate, but did not think much about what his mother's role was in the tragedy. James has kept some reminders of his mother: a vase that she loved, a sweater she knitted for him when he was in junior high school, letters she had written to him, and family pictures.

After graduation, James gladly accepted a position that would take him overseas for four years. He was immersed in learning another language and culture, loved his work, and did it well. During his first year abroad, he had recurrent nightmares about his mother. He came home for a visit after being gone for a year, and had an honest talk with his father, telling him how hard it was to see him remarried and to see his father's new wife using his mother's things. His father listened, and told James to always remember that his mother was a wonderful woman. That comment meant a great deal to James, and the nightmares did not return. When James returned to the United States four years later, he sought psychotherapy to deal with the confusion he felt about his mother's death and his anger toward his father.

James's aunt and uncle were also angry with his father, and James himself eventually withdrew from most of his mother's side of the family. He did not feel welcome in their midst, and he thought he was somehow tainted by his relationship to his father, whom his mother's side of the family, in their grief, hated. It took many years, and several courses of therapy, for him to accept that he was not responsible for his mother's death, and to construct a more balanced and realistic view of both his mother and father.

Definitions and Description of the Problem

Although these are not technical jargon, they nevertheless should be defined clearly. *Grief* refers to the emotional aspect of loss, the painful feelings experienced when a person faces a loss (Dershimer, 1990). Grief is a normal response to loss. Losses other than death can cause the experience of grief, although in this chapter we will focus on the grief experience following death. *Mourning* refers to the actions and behaviors that accompany the feeling of grief in an attempt to adapt to the loss. Mourning is the public expression of grief, and is strongly influenced by cultural and societal rituals and expectations. *Bereavement* is a broader concept, referring to the time period during which the person is in the process of recovering from the death of a significant person in his or her life. *Complicated grief* refers to a condition in which symptoms are more intense and of longer duration than is usual in the culture. This will be discussed in more detail later in the chapter.

Many readers will be familiar with the stages of grief described by Elisabeth Kübler-Ross, whose 1969 book *On Death and Dying* described this theory. Readers should be aware that the stages she described were those experienced by dying patients; these were later applied to grief experienced by survivors after a death. Kübler-Ross' stages were denial, anger, bargaining, depression, and finally acceptance. By now, it is clear that individuals do not progress through such stages in a linear fashion, and that the grief experience is highly individual and difficult to fit into a neat series of stages. In addition, research has not found empirical evidence to support this theory, despite its wide popular acceptance. Nevertheless, her work brought attention to the topic of death and dying, and was the impetus for the development of hospice programs around the country.

Kübler-Ross' stages of grief:

Denial: There is some mistake. I am not dying.

Anger: How can this happen to me?

Bargaining: I promise I will . . . if I get better.

Depression: I don't care anymore.

Acceptance: I am ready now.

Parkes (1998) drew on the attachment work of John Bowlby and proposed phases of the grief experience. Bowlby's attachment theory described the strong emotional bonds between infants and caregivers, which ensures the safety and survival of the infant. These attachments are formed very early and persist over time. Bowlby believed that strong attachments are formed with only a few individuals. Children with a healthy attachment to a parent feel secure enough to explore their environment and move away from the parent, knowing that they may return to the parent for safety when needed. If these attachments are disrupted, the infant tries to regain them by crying and clinging and displays of anger. If those behaviors are not successful in restoring the lost object of attachment, the child experiences despair (Fast, 2003). This is the model for the grief process for all humans. Parkes suggested that individuals first experience numb disbelief, then yearning for the deceased person, disorganization and despair, and finally, reorganization, when a new life without the deceased is structured.

Worden (1991, 2004) conceives of mourning as a set of tasks after a death that need to be accomplished to restore functioning. The four tasks are: accepting the reality of the loss, working through the pain and grief, adjusting to an environment in which the deceased is missing, and emotionally relocating the deceased and moving on with life. Worden's influential work will be the foundation for much of the discussions in the rest of this chapter.

The reader should note that there is some disagreement about these theories of grieving, in which adjustment is measured by how well the individual has broken the bonds with the deceased and returned to normal functioning (see Lindstrøm, 2002; Stroebe, M., Gergen, M. M., Gergen, K. J., & Stroebe, W., 1992). Stroebe and Schut (1999) outline a model that acknowledges the work of Worden (1991) and other theorists (see Figure 8.2). I mention this model here because it adds something to the discussion that appears absent from other approaches. This model postulates a dual process that has *Loss-Oriented* and *Restoration-Oriented* tasks. The loss-oriented tasks are primarily emotional whereas restoration-oriented tasks are more cognitive and behavioral. Both tasks are necessary for the bereaved person to adjust to the changed world that is the result of the death. They include the difficult and essential task of forging a new identity (e.g., wife to widow, child to orphan, partner to single person, etc.) What is new in this model is the idea of *oscillation*, moving back and forth between the two sets of tasks. These authors propose that the oscillation allows the person to take a break from the draining emotional tasks, and that this process helps individuals restore a balance between emotional and cognitive aspects of self. Oscillation is conceived of as necessary for future adjustment, and recognizes that denial is at times purposeful and helpful, as long as it is not extreme or persistent.

> **Oscillation:** Alternating between the loss-oriented emotional tasks and the restoration-oriented cognitive tasks of grieving.

Thus, the helping professional should avoid a rigid idea of what is the "right" way to grieve, and instead appreciate the wide range of ways in which bereavement is experienced. When some form of counseling is indicated, careful listening will alert the compassionate therapist to the individual needs of the client (Stroebe et al., 1992).

What Is Normal Grief?

With wide variability among individuals, there are common elements of a grief response that are often present, which include physical, emotional, cognitive, and behavioral elements. Emotional responses to a death include sadness, although the way this is expressed (e.g., crying) differs markedly from one person to another. Less often recognized, but commonly experienced, is a feeling of anger, which can be anger that there was nothing that could be done, anger at God for allowing this to happen, anger at the deceased for leaving (which is a common reaction in children when an attachment figure leaves them).

While the anger is normal, there is the potential for problems when the anger is misdirected or displaced to someone else, or to oneself. Also normal is the feeling of guilt, which may be realistic but is often irrational. The guilt may focus on what the survivor did or did not do to prevent the death, or how the deceased was treated when alive. This usually dissipates relatively quickly, and if so, does not bode future problems. Many survivors (spouses in particular) may become anxious about how they will survive without the lost person. Existential anxiety about one's own mortality may also be heightened at a time of loss, and is also part of a normal reaction. Loneliness is felt most often when the person was a part of the survivor's day-to-day experience and the

Figure 8.1.   Factors Affecting the Process of Grieving.

Factors Relating to the Relationship between the Deceased and the Survivor

■ *The nature of relationship to the deceased.* The death of a distant relative is different from that of a member of one's immediate family. The losses of different people in one's life are experienced differently because the nature of the relationships differed.

■ *The degree of emotional closeness to the deceased.* The intensity of the attachment is related to the intensity of the grief.

■ *The importance of the deceased to the well-being of the survivor.* If one's self-esteem and security needs were satisfied primarily by the deceased, the loss will be experienced more acutely.

■ *The degree of ambivalence in the relationship.* If there was a high level of ambivalence (love–hate) in the relationship, or a high degree of conflict (particularly unresolved conflict), the grief is usually more difficult.

■ *The way the person died.* Deaths have been categorized as natural, accidental, suicidal, and homicidal (Worden, 1991). The death of a young person may be more difficult than the death of an elderly person who has had a long and full life. Whether the death was expected or unexpected (sudden) affects the bereavement.

Factors Relating to the Survivor

■ *Experience of an earlier loss.* Whether people have experienced the death of someone close before, and how they managed these earlier losses, will affect how they grieve the current death.

■ *Other life changes.* The number of life changes in the year prior to the death also seems to affect mourning, with more changes portending a more difficult grieving process.

■ *Dealing with intense feelings.* How people deal with intense feelings, how they cope with stress, and how they manage anxiety are individual personality factors that will be reflected in the grief and mourning process.

■ *Culture and religion.* For those who have strong affiliations with religious or cultural groups, following the prescribed practices can facilitate a better adjustment to the loss.

■ *The level of social support.* Family and friends can reduce stress by taking on many of the tasks following a death, by providing emotional support and companionship, and by serving as a buffer against environmental pressure.

■ *Level of stress.* If the death comes at a time when there are economic or other stressors already affecting the survivor, it will be more difficult for the person to negotiate the bereavement.

absence is acutely noticed. In some cases, relief is a part of the experience, particularly when the deceased was in pain and suffering prior to the death. Others may feel a sense of liberation, as when the perpetrator of abuse dies.

Physical components of grief often include fatigue, tightness in the chest and throat, feeling short of breath, feeling weak, and lacking energy. In addition to all of these feelings, it is not uncommon for people to report the absence of feeling or numbness. This is similar to the shock experienced when one has a physical injury and pain is not felt. This typically is a short-term initial response to the loss.

Thinking patterns that emerge in bereavement may frighten the bereaved because they are so unlike one's ordinary cognitive style. People may find they initially cannot take in the information about the death, especially an unexpected one. They may convince themselves there is a mistake, for example. This typically is short-lived and is prominent when the news is first received. Confusion and distractibility are also typical of newly bereaved people, and for those who are typically very efficient and organized, the frequent forgetting or confusion may be alarming. It is quite common for survivors to think obsessively about the deceased person, and even to have the sense that the person is nearby. This experience usually diminishes over time. In grieving persons, hallucinations, which are usually considered to be symptoms of serious mental disorders, may occur. These are not problematic unless they persist beyond the first few weeks after the death.

Behaviorally there are also common patterns, which include sleep difficulty, loss of appetite, dreaming of the deceased, and frequent crying. Some people may avoid reminders of the deceased while others may cling to objects that remind them of the deceased.

For an overview of the factors that affect the grieving process, see Figure 8.1.

FIGURE 8.2   A Dual Process Mode of Coping with Bereavement.

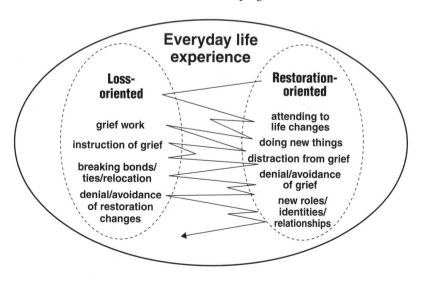

Patterns of Grieving

Martin and Doka (2000) described patterns of grieving, which are influenced by (but not determined by) such factors as gender and culture. The patterns reflect differences in how the grief is experienced internally, how it is expressed, and in the coping strategies preferred. The two primary patterns are intuitive and instrumental. These patterns exist along a continuum, with most people favoring one pattern rather than being exclusively one or the other.

- *Intuitive:* Grievers who are primarily intuitive will feel the loss deeply and intensely, and will experience extremely painful feelings. Their outward expression of grief reflects the intensity of the emotional pain—crying and emotional displays are frequent and open. This type of griever is comforted by sharing their feelings with others. The emotional component of grief is prominent in this pattern, which is often thought of as a female pattern, although many men are intuitive grievers. Intuitive grievers may experience periods of confusion, have difficulty with concentration, and feel disorganized and disoriented at times. They often feel physically exhausted.
- *Instrumental:* Instrumental grievers are less attentive to emotion, and focus on cognition. They try not to become emotional and prefer not to talk about feelings. If any feeling is expressed, it is most likely to be anger. Quiet contemplation is common. Instrumental grievers prefer to direct their energies into problem-solving activities such as planning services and memorials, staying busy, returning to work or school, taking charge of loss-related tasks (working with insurance companies), etc. This pattern is typically thought of as the male approach, although it is seen in both genders. Instrumental grievers also experience periods of confusion and difficulty concentrating.
- *Blended:* This pattern is a combination of the intuitive and instrumental styles, usually with a preference for one style.
- *Dissonant:* The dissonant pattern is one in which the individual's way of coping with grief does not match their internal preferred style. Dissonant grievers suppress emotions, which takes considerable energy. They may be concerned with how others will view their grieving, and strive to demonstrate control and mastery, despite their inner pain. Other dissonant grievers may feel guilty because they do not have the intense emotional reaction they perceive to be "normal." The danger is that this type of dissonant griever will seek unhealthy ways to release emotions—e.g., substance use.

Prevalence

Each year, there are approximately two million deaths in the United States, which means that there are many more than two million Americans grieving in any given year (Harvard Medical School, n.d.). Although grief and loss are universal human experiences, *complicated grief* is estimated to occur in 10–20% of bereaved individuals (Shear, Frank, Houck, & Reynolds, 2005).

Special Cases of Grief

Grief is painful in all cases, but there are some specific types of death that may make bereavement more challenging.

Suicide. Although there are more similarities than differences between survivors of a death by suicide (SOS) and other bereaved individuals, the differences are important and merit attention. Experts differ on whether the differences lead to relatively more cases of complicated grief (Jordan, 2001). Suicide survivors may have some of the same reactions as other mourners, but may experience them more intensely or for longer duration. The differences most often identified are a persistent struggle to make sense of the death, increased levels of guilt and feelings of responsibility for the death, and greater feelings of rejection and abandonment along with anger toward the deceased. In addition, there is a perceived stigma associated with suicide that extends to SOS, so that their social support may be disrupted. Finally, there is an increased risk of suicide among this group of mourners. Van Dongen (1990) noted that there were differences among the SOS according to their perceptions of the risk of suicide. In several of her subjects, the deceased had prior attempts and the survivors were aware of the psychological difficulties. This seemed to lessen the struggle to find meaning in the death.

Some experts note that SOS are more likely to lie about the cause of death in an effort to avoid the negative associations with suicide. In such cases, the family may create a secret that can ultimately be disruptive to family functioning. The case study illustrates many of these common responses to a death by suicide.

The dynamics of grief after a suicide have several clinical implications (Jordan, 2001). One is that group support services are best provided specifically for this group of survivors, who may feel increased isolation in a general bereavement group. Second, because the risk for suicide is greater in this group, this risk should be closely monitored. Third, educational information about suicide and about suicide bereavement should be provided. Next, interventions should target the social network, both from the perspective of teaching skills for dealing with the perceived stigma, and from the position of directly involving the support network in the intervention. Finally, because of the potential for disruption of family processes, intervention should target the entire family system and work toward increasing cohesion.

Worden (2004) advises that helping the survivors test the reality of their guilt may reduce their feelings of responsibility. They may realize they had made more efforts to be helpful than they acknowledged earlier. Survivors may need help avoiding blame as well, as blaming others (particularly other family members) can increase stress on an already burdened family system. Worden also believes it is important to confront the reality of the suicide by avoiding vague or imprecise terms to describe the death. SOS may need assistance in accessing a balanced view of the deceased, rather than a black or white view based solely on this final act. Finally, Worden believes that due to exacerbated feelings of abandonment by the deceased, a mental health professional that has an existing relationship with the survivors should initiate contact and offer support.

Sudden Death. Some experts believe that sudden or unexpected death is, like suicide, more difficult for the survivors than expected deaths. Also similar to suicide is the sense of unbelief and shock that comes with an unanticipated announcement of the death. Guilt also is a common reaction, with thoughts of "If only I had . . ." predominating. For those who may have had angry words with the deceased prior to the death, the unresolved conflict may influence the grieving process and the unfinished business may linger for years. Some may obsess about the wish to have apologized or to put differences aside, for example.

For death by accident or homicide (and to some extent suicide as well) there may be frequent contact with authorities and interactions with the system at a time when the survivors are just learning of the death and attempting to accept the reality of it. For some, the grieving process may be delayed while these matters are the focus. In some cases, the bereavement process will not resolve until there is some resolution to the legal matters (e.g., lawsuit settled, murderer convicted). An additional feeling that is common among survivors of a sudden death is helplessness. Such things are not in anyone's plans, and the sense that there is no order or justice can become overwhelming for mourners. Sometimes these feelings lead to anger and sometimes misdirected blaming of others (e.g., doctors, witnesses).

SIDS and Stillbirth.   There are 5,000 to 6,000 infant deaths each year attributed to Sudden Infant Death Syndrome (SIDS), which is the leading cause of infant mortality in the United States (Paterson, Trachtenberg, Thompson, Belliveau, Beggs, & Darnall, et al., 2006). These deaths occur in apparently healthy babies, and although the deaths are called SIDS, there is no explanation that clearly points to a specific cause of death. Exciting new research by the Paterson group discovered an underlying developmental disorder involving certain brain neurons that puts infants at risk. When this vulnerability is present, infants in the face-down or side-sleeping position appear to lack the protective reflexes for arousal and head turning when they are not getting sufficient air. The authors point to three factors, which, when coupled with this vulnerability, increase risk for SIDS: prone or side sleeping, face-down sleeping, and bed sharing. Mental health professionals who work with new parents might want to be sure they are aware of this new research and take measures to avoid putting their child at risk.

For survivors (parents, siblings, grandparents), the shock of the death is intense and difficult to absorb. In addition, there is often considerable guilt on the part of parents, who believe they could have somehow prevented the death by being more attentive. One client of mine described playing cards with friends in the living room after putting the baby to sleep. When he checked on her later, she was dead. He berated himself for many years, believing he must have waited too long to check on the sleeping baby.

Like other unanticipated deaths, there may be police involvement, questions regarding autopsies, and so on, that elevate feelings of guilt. Parents may have to explain to surviving siblings an event that they themselves do not understand. Different grieving styles in the baby's parents may increase tensions between them at a time when they most need support.

SIDS survivors may benefit from group support with other families who have lost a baby to SIDS. Accurate information should be provided about what is known and not known about SIDS, and an arena to discuss whether or not to have another baby right away can be helpful.

The experience of having a stillbirth is similar in many ways to SIDS death, in that it is often completely unexpected. Parents may feel responsible for the death, and feel confused when there is no medical explanation. Fears about future pregnancies are common, and returning home to a newly equipped nursery without a baby can trigger overwhelming sorrow. If there was ambivalence about the pregnancy, parents may feel they were somehow punished for their feelings, and stress between the couple may increase.

One thing that SIDS deaths and stillbirths share is the absence of a funeral or farewell ritual. Parents may wonder about naming the baby, how to dispose of the body, and how to tell other family members. Many parents choose to spend time with the baby, take photos, and have a service of some kind to acknowledge the death. Support groups may be useful for these mourners, who can talk about their experience with others who understand the impact of such a loss.

An additional complication with a stillbirth is poignantly described by Alison Gardy (2005), who was distressed at the quantity of promotional material for baby products that continued to arrive even after she had notified all possible sources of her information that the baby had died. The onslaught of mail and products was an impediment to this woman's process of grieving, with a great deal of anger directed toward the inconsiderate vendors who continued to send unwanted mail that served only to remind the parents of their loss.

Miscarriage/abortion. Those who experience a miscarriage may not receive the social support that is so critical for good adjustment. It has been my experience that the well-intentioned comments of others often increase the distress of the aggrieved parent. For example, they may be told that the miscarriage is nature's way of taking care of a problem. Many women who miscarry are already worried about their ability to have a healthy baby, and hearing that the baby was likely "damaged" in some way is not a comfort. One young woman I worked with became pregnant with a second child by her abusive husband. When she miscarried, others told her it was a blessing that she would not have any more ties to this man. However, she was excited about the pregnancy, eagerly anticipating the birth, and already imagining how her older child would respond to being the "big brother." The intended reassurance of others was extremely hurtful. An additional challenge with miscarriages is that there is usually no body to see or bury, and no formalized rituals for marking the loss. To the extent that funerals and memorial services assist the survivors in the bereavement process, miscarriage is not accorded those rites. In fact, it is often treated as a medical procedure (e.g., appendicitis) rather than a profound loss. Mental health professionals can be helpful by listening and accepting the loss of the mourner, and sometimes by helping them create a personal memorial or ritual that acknowledges the loss.

Abortion is not always accompanied by grief, but it may occur, and may occur many years later. One client I worked with was a graduate student who had an abortion as a young teenager at her parents' insistence. When she married and began to plan a family with her husband (who knew of the abortion), she was overcome with guilt and feelings of loss. She sought counseling because she became agitated and depressed, and was unable to think about having a child with her husband without becoming overcome with grief. Interestingly, she found a solution to her pain: she volunteered at a neonatal intensive care unit, where she provided contact and holding for very high-risk newborns. She decided that perhaps this work would save infant lives and then she could forgive herself for having the earlier abortion.

If an abortion is chosen as a way to manage an unplanned pregnancy, the woman is often deprived of social support. Although legal, abortion still has a negative stigma in many social contexts, so the woman may not feel able to discuss this with family or friends. Others (parents, partner) may be angry with her for becoming pregnant, so that she receives negative input from others rather than support. One danger in these cases, where guilt may linger, is that the woman will choose to become pregnant again as a way to assuage her guilt. This may not be effective, and may increase her problems. Counselors must understand that despite the reason for the abortion, many women feel a sense of loss and grief, and need a nonjudgmental person to allow them to process their feelings.

AIDS. When Nelson Mandela announced that his son had died of AIDS-related complications, he modeled what many families are unwilling to do, which is to acknowledge the cause of death in AIDS patients. Social stigma and misinformation add to the pain of the loss, often preventing the bereaved from accessing social support networks. In other cases, friends or family may fear that survivors can transmit the virus and avoid contact. Sometimes it is the mourners who fear that the nature of the disease will damage their own ability to receive any social support, and so they withdraw at a time when connections with others are typically helpful. Intimate partners of those who die of AIDS may have the additional burden of fear for their own health status. AIDS victims are often young, so the same feelings about untimely deaths and lost opportunities that arise in other cases of youthful death are added to the equation. Counselors may be able to assist the grieving persons to access safe sources of social support. They may also be able to provide referral information for AIDS-aware support groups and other services. As in the other special cases of grief, the loss of a person with AIDS has more in common with other losses than differences, but attending to those differences can be a valuable service to survivors whose social support may not be available.

Military Deaths. As American troops, including women, are engaged in combat, the need for understanding this type of loss is essential for mental health professionals. There are several unique aspects of the death of a soldier that are important to note (Carroll, 1998). Although the military has well-established procedures and rituals for the death of military personnel, the impact on survivors may not be as well prepared for. First, some family members may be at odds with the notion of a "glorious death," and may feel uncomfortable expressing their anger and frustration. In addition, if the family was living in military housing, they will be forced to relocate after the death, when the supports they have created among friends are most needed. The many changes in lifestyle that are imposed upon military families increase the stress of the death. Carroll is a strong advocate of support groups for military families who have experienced the death of a soldier, as their unique experience can be shared. In fact, she is the founder of Tragedy Assistance Program for Survivors, which has expanded to the use of the Internet to provide support and events for families. See the Resource list below for information about this organization.

Pets.   The last special case to be discussed is the death of a pet. In 1994, a survey found that 53 million households had pets (Sharkin & Knox, 2003). Animals have shorter life spans than humans do, so it is likely that many pet owners will experience the death of at least one pet in their lifetime. There is no doubt that for most pet owners, the attachment to pets is strong and important. Pets provide unconditional love and affection, and give many people a sense of being needed. When a beloved pet dies, people experience many of the same grief reactions as have been described for other losses: sadness, guilt, anger, disruption of daily functioning. However, there are no socially sanctioned rituals for grieving the loss of a pet: no funeral, no bereavement leave from work, few expressions of condolences. People may feel friends and family do not understand the significance of the loss, and that others treat the loss casually, so pet owners may stifle their outward expression of grief. Further, in the case where the pet was euthanized, the pet owner must make a painful decision. Pet owners are often torn between relieving the animal's suffering and the desire to keep the pet with them. These aspects of the death of the pet may make the bereavement difficult.

For people living alone and for children, the loss of a pet can be particularly devastating. The pet may have been the only companion of the person living alone, so the void experienced after the death can be especially large. This is especially likely in the elderly, who may already feel isolated and lonely. The loss of a pet has been found to trigger feelings of grief over previous losses in some individuals, so the feelings experienced may be magnified. For children, the loss of a pet is often the first experience with death. Children often have close bonds with their pets and it is not unusual to hear a child describe a pet as his or her "best friend." Children grieve according to their developmental stages, as described later in this chapter. It should be noted that children's tolerance for strong affect is not as high as that of adults, so they may alternate between periods of sadness and return to usual functioning. Depending on the age, the child may wish to be involved in decisions about the disposal or burial of the remains, and parents will need to decide whether this is appropriate in any given case.

Parents may need assistance in how to help a child with grief when a pet dies. Parents need to know that such euphemisms as "putting to sleep" can be frightening for the child, who might then fear that he or she will die when asleep. Parents can encourage the child to talk about their pet, make a memorial, or whatever seems to acknowledge the importance of the pet in the child's life. Therapists who work with children might want to communicate in their offices their own interest in pets, with posters or photos of animals, and thoughtful questions about pets and their importance in initial interviews with children.

Developmental Aspects

The experience of grief not only varies among individuals, but there are developmental influences as well. People at different times in the life span have different levels of understanding of death, different prior experiences with death and loss, and different needs in the bereavement process.

Children

Children's understanding of death is related to their cognitive and emotional development. Despite their lack of accurate understanding, children may nevertheless have their own ideas about death that need to be taken into account when responding to the death of a loved one in the child's world.

Infants do not have any conception of death, but they do form attachments to the primary caregiver (usually the mother) and will react to the absence of that person. Separation anxiety is common among children in the latter part of the first year of life, and those responses are typical of what these children will exhibit when the loss is of the caregiver: they may cry more than usual, show changes in sleeping and eating habits, and be less active and somewhat withdrawn from contact. Infants are sensitive to changes in others, and will often respond to changes in routines with distress and irritability. As infants approach the end of the first year, their emotional repertoires expand, and they also begin to develop language and symbolic thinking. Like younger infants, they will notice the emotional reactions of others, and be sensitive to changes in their routines. The loss of the primary caregiver will usually result in sadness and distress in the baby.

Toddlers and children up to age five, with their emerging language, are quite literal. They may confuse death and sleep and often believe death is temporary. A client recently told me how he explained carefully to his four-year-old son that great-grandma (who was an important figure in the life of the family) had died and gone to heaven. The child listened very carefully, and then asked how she got to heaven because he wanted to be sure that she knew the way back so she could come to his birthday party. This is a typical response of children at this age. Children who are exposed to television, where death is often temporary (the actor or character appears later in another episode, movie, etc.) may be quite certain of the temporary status of death. In some cases, children of this age who learn that the deceased is buried may become quite distressed and concerned that the deceased will be unable to breathe or eat, and so on. In addition, children of this age may believe their thoughts are powerful enough to cause the death. If they were angry with the deceased, they may believe they caused the death and grief they see in others. Regression to early behaviors (problems with bowel or bladder control, thumb-sucking, etc.) is not unusual in this age group.

Children at this age are very literal in their understanding of language. Adults may say things like "It is hard to lose a parent," while a child may think that means if he or she looks hard enough he can find the "lost" parent. Young children are likely to ask many difficult questions, and answering them carefully and directly will help them adjust.

Children aged six to nine have developed cognitively so that they generally understand that death is permanent. They may be curious about the mechanical aspects of death (what happens to the body) and may think of the deceased as having another form (an angel or a ghost). Because children now understand that death is permanent, they may worry about dying themselves, and may become anxious that others close to them will die. One client, whose primary caretaker (a grandparent) died suddenly and accidentally when the child was three years old developed what appeared to be an extreme case of school phobia years later. She believed that if she stayed at home she could be sure no one else in the family would die. Children of this age may not have the verbal skills to express their feelings of grief, and may act out or become clingy with survivors. Their themes in play may reveal their concerns following a death.

Children aged ten through twelve generally have an accurate cognitive appreciation of death. In this period, they may want more information about rituals observed by families, and may be most concerned with how this death will affect their own lives. Their emotional, physical, cognitive, and behavioral manifestations of grief are more adult-like, but they may be particularly concerned about being different from other children and how their friends will react to the loss. I worked with a ten-year-old child who was convinced that the reason she did not have friends at school was that she was the only one without a mother. Her mother had died several years earlier. Her strong belief about the reason for her rejection prevented her from focusing on her deficient social skills.

Despite their cognitive advances, pre-teens may experience excessive guilt about past misbehaviors toward the deceased, and may still express themselves more behaviorally than verbally. They may be especially sensitive to grieving parents and resist burdening them with their own concerns. Some children, particularly if the deceased is a parent, may feel they must assume the role of the person who died (e.g., become the "man of the house") which can feel overwhelming and arouse resentment.

Adolescents

Although adolescents have the cognitive skills to understand death, their emotional development is not yet adult-like, and grief may be especially disturbing, given their propensity to feel invulnerable. They are also engaged in developing an identity, so depending on the relationship to the deceased (e.g., a parent) they will be concerned with how the death will influence their own lives. Emotional displays can be flamboyant at this stage and withdrawal from social interaction is not unusual for some teens.

Adults

In adulthood, death is understood to be an unavoidable experience, and while the loss of elderly relatives causes grief and sadness, it is usually accepted as part of life. For adults, the difficult losses are those that are unexpected (accidents, murder, suicide) or off-time (death of a young person). For those in middle adulthood, awareness of one's own mortality may increase, and it is not unusual to hear that people check the obituaries of strangers to see how old they are at death. In adulthood, many will have to confront the death of parents, and even among secure adults, the change in status ("Now I am an orphan") can be unsettling.

The Elderly

Among the elderly, bereavement is more frequent than at other life stages. According to Rosenzweig, Prigerson, Miller, and Reynolds (1997), half of all women and 10% of men over age 65 have been widowed at least once. That figure increases to 81% of women and 41% of men over age 85. Many of these elders have also lost friends and various family members. Although not unanticipated, the loss of a spouse at this age can be extremely disorganizing. Consider the loss of a partner of many decades, with whom one carried out daily activities as a unit. Doing those same activities alone can be overwhelming for the elderly person. In marriages of such long duration, it is not unusual for partners to assume certain roles (financial manager, home manager, correspondent, etc.) and when the spouse is gone, the remaining partner may not know how to function solo. If the couple socialized as a unit, the survivor may feel unwelcome among the familiar social group, and may even fear that children or old friends will also abandon them. If the death necessitates relocation of the surviving spouse, this means the loss of familiar surrounding and personal objects, which may further add to the emotional distress. Unfortunately, some elderly persons attempt to cope with the painful feelings by increasing their use of alcohol, sedatives, or tobacco, and thoughts of suicide may emerge. There is also an increased risk for death in the surviving spouse, which peaks from 7 to 12 months following the loss.

Elderly individuals with various forms of dementia may need special assistance when experiencing a loss. One of the troubling features of individuals with dementia is that the memory problems result in their forgetting the death. This means that they experience the shock of learning about the death repeatedly; family members may find this quite disturbing. Those in the advanced stages of the disorder may not understand death at all. To assist these individuals, Lewis and Trzinski (2006) applied two techniques that are reported by staff in nursing homes to be beneficial. The first is a spaced retrieval (SR) learning strategy to help the person with dementia remember that their loved one has died. The second technique is a form of play therapy, "Group Buddies," (puppets or stuffed animals) who attend group treatment sessions with the patient. The group buddy's job is to attend all group sessions, watch, and learn in the group. Staff members reported that in addition to being useful within group sessions, patients were observed using their buddies as confidantes, supports, and comfort objects. Mental health professionals in a consulting role might consider suggesting these techniques, although there is no research evidence yet to support their effectiveness.

Dementia: A mental disorder characterized by loss of intellectual abilities (thinking, reasoning, memory) of sufficient degree to interfere with daily functioning.

Assessment

How does the clinician determine whether the client's grief is within the normal range, or whether it qualifies as complicated grief that may require treatment? There are several conditions that can be used to identify those at risk for complicated grief, and the counselor would be wise to pay attention to these. As social support is so important to the bereaved person, those clients who either have no social support or perceive a high level of non-support from their relationships are more likely to have complicated grieving. If the death occurs under traumatic circumstances, there is a greater risk for difficulties with the grieving process. Finally, if the client is already in crisis at the time of the death, their coping resources may be depleted to the extent that they are unable to cope with the loss.

There are several clues that the grieving process has developed into complicated grief. Complicated grief is likely when the grief is prolonged. Although experts vary in their opinion of what constitutes "prolonged" grief, periods of from one to four years are mentioned in the literature. Complicated grief may reveal itself as behavioral symptoms or somatic complaints, often noticed when the bereaved person visits a physician frequently for vague complaints for which no medical explanation can be found. These symptoms sometimes persist for one to three years (Rosenzweig et al., 1997). When the grieving appears to be excessive or exaggerated beyond what is usual, as noted in the severity and frequency of symptoms and the disruption of life tasks, complicated grief should be considered.

Shear and her colleagues (2005) observed that complicated grief is different from depression and in fact is similar in many respects to post-traumatic stress disorder. Complicated grief causes significant impairment in functioning and is related to negative physical health. One of the characteristics of complicated grief is that it does not respond to standard treatment approaches for depression. Assessment of complicated grief is facilitated by the use of the Inventory of Complicated Grief (Prigerson et al., 1995), which is a 19-item scale in which clients rate how often they have experienced the symptoms described in the statements. A score equal to or above 25 indicates complicated grief. Shear et al. believe this should be administered no earlier than six months following the death.

Treatment Options

The first question to consider is whether and for whom treatment for uncomplicated grief should be provided. Worden (2004) believes bereavement counseling should be offered to anyone who has experienced a loss, particularly if the deceased is a parent or child. Certainly, individuals who seek counseling at such a time should receive services.

Researchers have investigated the effectiveness of treatment for grief. Many of the studies did not meet criteria for rigorous experimental design, but Neimeyer (2000) found twenty-three studies that met his criteria, which were published between 1975 and 1998. The mean number of sessions in the treatments examined was seven, and treatment was initiated from six months to several years after the loss. This study revealed that for people experiencing normal grief, counseling did not show any positive effect, whereas those experiencing traumatic (complicated) grief did show positive effects. In addition, in one of two persons with normal grief, counseling had a negative effect, while this was true for only 17% of the mourners with traumatic grief. Neimeyer concluded that counseling for normal bereavement is "difficult to justify," while for "protracted, traumatic, or complicated grief reactions" (p. 546) such services are appropriate.

When assistance is sought for a normal grief reaction, it is frequently the case that either the individual does not have sufficient social support or he or she believes that it would be unfair to burden others (particularly those who are also mourning) with their own pain. What does a grieving client need? Worden (2004) recommends a number of tasks with which the mourner may need help. The first task is to help them talk about the loss. I have noticed that some clients need to tell the story more than once—many times in fact—as though they want to be sure it actually occurred. They may believe that others in their life get tired of hearing them recount the story over and over, whereas the therapist can allow the necessary repetition. Allowing the mourner to express feelings is also helpful. The mourner may feel that others close to the deceased will not understand their anger, for example, but are relieved to unburden themselves to a nonjudgmental and compassionate professional. When guilt is expressed, the clinician may help the client to determine whether the guilt is really justified. Sometimes, grief reactions include unrealistic guilt (e.g., "If I were there I could have prevented the accident," etc.) and the counselor can help the client test the accuracy of such beliefs. If the grief is not unrealistic (e.g., "I chose not to go to the hospital although I knew he was dying,") the client can sometimes be helped by verbalizing what might have been said to the deceased if they had the opportunity.

Some persons need help figuring out how to manage tasks that the deceased handled before. For example, if the deceased took care of financial matters, the survivor may need a referral to money management resources. Deciding what changes will be necessary and which can wait is a task that a counselor can support. Worden (2004) and others typically advise the mourner not to make major decisions (relocating, for example) until a year or so after the loss, but circumstances do not always allow the mourner that opportunity. Ensuring that the bereaved person has sufficient unbiased guidance (e.g., an attorney) in any necessary decisions is a role the counselor can fill.

In other cases, the survivor may have spent years caring for a chronically ill family member. For those caregivers, the loss they experience involves not only the loss of a beloved person, but also the loss of a major role in their lives. Filling that time and energy can be challenging and frightening for one whose life has been consumed by caring for another. The clinician can recognize that the mourner may feel adrift and may need assistance re-shaping his or her identity when their major life role is concluded.

Finally, Worden believes that the mourner needs to struggle to find a "place" for the deceased so that he or she can move forward. He notes that some people feel that forming new relationships will dishonor the deceased, whereas others feel that no one can replace the person they lost. Even returning to normal routines such as work or school may be difficult if the person makes the deceased the sole focus of their energy. Counselors can help clients sort out these common feelings, and also help them anticipate and prepare for times that are often difficult (anniversaries of the death, holidays, and other special occasions). In addition, the counselor may reassure clients that their experience is normal for those grieving a loss, as it is not unusual for mourners to feel as though they are going crazy. They also need to hear that they will improve, and that support is available as needed.

Therapy for complicated grief is more specialized. Shear and colleagues (2005) note that treating bereavement-related depression has not had significant benefits for complicated grief. These researchers studied the effectiveness of an integrated interpersonal therapy (IPT) and cognitive-behavioral therapy (CBT) approach to complicated grief. The treatment was administered in sixteen sessions held over 16–20 weeks.

The study was carefully controlled and involved 102 bereaved individuals who were randomized to this treatment approach or IPT alone. Fifty-one percent of the treatment group was improved at the end of treatment compared to 28% of the control (IPT) group. Improvement was also more rapid for the specialized approach.

In another randomized controlled study, the effectiveness of an interpretive group therapy was compared with that of supportive group therapy. Interpretive group therapy had a goal of increasing the mourners' understanding of conflicts and trauma that interfered with the grieving process, whereas the supportive group therapy worked to improve the members' adjustment to their new life situations. Improvement was greater for the group receiving interpretive therapy (Ogrodniczuk et al., 2003).

Many communities have self-help groups to assist with bereavement issues. Counselors may choose to lead such groups and/or refer clients to those groups for additional support. Keep in mind, however, that while such programs are often recommended, there is little research evaluating their effectiveness. Schut, Stroebe, Van den Bout, and Terheggen (2001) reviewed the existing literature, and concluded that despite the widespread use of grief counseling, the results have been "disappointing, sometimes even negative" (p. 705). In examining the studies closely, these researchers observed that while primary prevention counseling is beneficial for children, it is not helpful for other age groups. Secondary prevention was somewhat helpful, but the effects were quite temporary. For tertiary prevention (complicated grief) the outcomes were more positive. It is important to note that the participants in these studies were recruited to participate in research, and Schut and colleagues believe that this effected the outcome. They recommend that organizations or counselors not contact the bereaved to offer counseling immediately after the loss. Interventions that were administered after time had passed had better outcomes, so it may be the case that counseling is helpful for complicated grief that does not resolve on its own, but not so helpful in the early stages of normal grief.

Levels of Prevention

Primary prevention: Activities to prevent a problem before it occurs. Death education, and interventions targeted at all who experience a death would be primary prevention.

Secondary prevention: Activities for those at-risk for developing a problem. Counseling for those whose loss is known to be difficult (e.g., survivors of suicide or unexpected death).

Tertiary prevention: Activities designed to reduce the harmful consequences of a problem. Treating complicated bereavement is tertiary prevention.

Mental health professionals should keep this in mind, and avoid routinely advising people who have experienced the death of a loved one to seek counseling.

These results suggest that those providing treatment for complicated grief should have specific training in delivering specialized treatment designed for this group of bereaved individuals, whereas counselors with knowledge of the grieving process who are interested in working with normal grief and loss might be able to provide this service with minimal additional training. Workshops and professional training on grief and loss are often available, and clinicians who expect to do this work would benefit from attending such professional development programs. In many areas, hospice programs offer training to community members, and these tend to be extremely useful for professionals when they are available. Hospice organizations also may have support groups available for the bereaved, including some for specific types of loss (e.g., suicide), and these can be helpful adjuncts to individual therapy. Mental health professionals would be wise to have information about these resources so that they can make accurate referrals.

Issues of Diversity

Funeral practices and mourning rituals vary by culture and religious perspective, but it is important to note that there is more variation within groups than between groups. This means the treatment provider must be careful not to make any assumptions about the client's needs solely based on ethnic or cultural group membership. However, it can be very helpful to have some basic knowledge of various practices to fine-tune one's listening and understanding.

Japanese Americans

There are many different cultural groups among Asian Americans, and discussing each is beyond the scope of this book. However, an example may illuminate some of the ways in which practices might differ from those more commonly seen in European American traditions. Among Japanese Americans, the dead, or ancestors, remain an important part of the lives of survivors (Klass & Goss, 1998). Rituals are practiced for the first forty-nine days following a death to install the deceased and the survivors in their new status. The final memorial service does not occur until the 33rd or 50th anniversary after the death. Between the death and the final memorial service, the spirit of the dead person is purified and elevated until it becomes one of the general ancestral spirits.

The first forty-nine days involve many observances: a service the night of the death, a service during cremation (the method of disposition of the body), and continual services. The rituals are intended to tell the person that he or she is dead and to go away now. A formalized expression said to the survivor at the funeral is, "Now you are experiencing how the end of life is." Cremation occurs within one or two days of the death. Within the first week, the family members gather, the bones are presented on a tray, and two people will pick up the bones using chopsticks and put them in a pot which is then placed in the family tomb. All deceased family members' bones are in the same pot, so the ritual symbolizes the deceased person's joining the family's ancestors.

There are beliefs among the Japanese that newly dead spirits can cause harm to the living if the proper rituals are not observed. Thus, some people will perform rituals for those deceased who have no one to care for them. The Japanese mourner will often experience regret for unmet obligations toward the deceased. It is common for the forty-nine days to include a resolution of "unfinished business," often in the form of a dream that the deceased has forgiven the survivor for any slight. When the survivor is able to relinquish any ambivalent feelings about the dead, the spirit is free to go on with the purification process.

Traditional Japanese households will have an altar containing memorial tablets for the dead ancestors, who still have a presence in the family. The altar also contains "transitional objects" that evoke the dead person, as well as offerings of flowers or foods that were preferred by the deceased. The altar is visited by survivors and is a link to the deceased. There is also a summer festival, in which the dead return for three days to visit the living. Thus, the dead maintain an important role in the family, and the survivors receive continuing support from the community.

Chinese Americans

Chinese American practices stress the importance of performing burial rites appropriately (Klass & Goss, 1998). Funerals for males and heads of households are more elaborate than are those for females. In America, funerals are held in funeral homes, but in China, they would be held in a Buddhist temple or family home.

Friends of the family will come to the home of the deceased as soon as they learn of the death. A family member describes the person's death while mourners listen and dry their eyes. Mourners will take candy that is provided, which they are to eat (and discard the wrapper) before they reach their own homes. The purpose of the candy is to deflect bad luck that might come to those who were near a death. On the day of the funeral, a can of burning paper "spirit money" is placed at the home's entrance, and children will jump over the can as they enter the home.

Among most Chinese Americans, white is the color of grief. If the deceased had a long life, bright colors may be worn in celebration of the deceased's longevity. At the funeral, symbolic items are burned to promote the welfare of the deceased's soul. Women will cry loudly but men remain silent. For up to sixty days following the funeral, women do not wash their hair and men do not shave. Following the funeral, a procession to the gravesite ensues, which begins with loud noises including firecrackers to scare off harmful ghosts. Family members will throw a handful of dirt into the grave, and a procession away from the gravesite symbolizes the return to life of the mourners. A banquet follows the funerals, with the size of the feast commensurate with the degree of success of the deceased.

Post-funeral rituals begin three days later, with survivors leaving food and burning paper money at the grave. There are ceremonies on the 21st, 35th, and 49th day after the death. The family continues to make offerings of food or drink at the gravesite or the household altar on the first and fifteenth days of each Chinese month. Like the Japanese practices, the altar provides a role for the deceased in the life of the family.

Muslim Americans

For Muslims, the purpose of this life is to prepare for the next, and this belief is taught to children from an early age (Raad, 1998). Despite the strong belief that there is a better life to follow, survivors still grieve the death of loved ones. Traditional Muslim practice would have someone reading the Koran over the dying person (who would be facing Mecca), and at the moment of death the eyes are closed and the jaw bound shut. The washing of the body is an important ritual, and may be done by a professional washer or by family members. All items used in the washing must be brand new, and the water used must be disposed of in accordance with prescribed ritual. The body is wrapped in a shroud. The communal mourning period lasts three days, and modern practice advises mourners not to hurt themselves physically, although in some places self-harm still occurs among mourning women. During the period of forty days following the death, most female mourners wear black and cover their heads, although Indian Muslim women wear white.

Jewish Americans

Traditional Jewish rituals around death include burial as soon after death as possible (Grollman, 1998). Embalming, public viewing, and "cosmetization" of the body is against Jewish law, as mourners are urged to remember the dead as they were when alive. Autopsies are also prohibited, so in the case of a death by homicide where the law may require an autopsy, there may be considerable additional distress for the family. The deceased may be buried in regular clothes, but is often buried in a shroud. Male attendees at a funeral generally wear a skullcap (yarmulke) at the funeral as a sign of respect. Flowers are not generally used in modern Jewish funerals (their ancient purpose was to disguise the smell of the decaying body) but a contribution to a charity in the name of the deceased is appreciated. Cremation is not customary, although some modern Jews will choose this method of disposition of the body. In that case, the funeral is still held with the body present and cremation takes place afterwards.

The casket is to be made completely of wood, to hasten the natural process of returning to dust. Family members traditionally would tear their clothing to demonstrate their suffering, but many now cut and wear a black ribbon instead. This is usually worn for from seven to thirty days following the funeral.

The period of mourning immediately after the funeral lasts for seven days and is known as *shiva*. Family members remain home and do not pursue ordinary activities. They will light a shiva candle upon returning from the cemetery, which burns for the seven days. Some Jews cover mirrors during this period to discourage mourners from thinking of themselves rather than the deceased. Friends and family members visit and offer condolences during this period, with the first meal of bread (the staff of life) and hard-boiled eggs (the cycle of life and death). During shiva, the bereaved recite a prayer called the *Kaddish*.

Following this seven-day period, mourners gradually assume their normal activities, but observe a bereavement period of thirty days. When the deceased is a parent, the bereavement period lasts for a full year. On the anniversary of the death, the Kaddish is recited in the synagogue and a candle is lit. The ritual that symbolizes the end of the mourning period is the unveiling of the tombstone or memorial plaque, and is usually held at the end of the first year.

African Americans

Barrett (1998) pointed out that the practices of black Americans will vary according to the religious and cultural affiliation, but suggested that there are some generalizations that apply fairly widely. He also advised that this group often experiences untimely deaths (those of younger individuals) due to poor access to health care. In general, blacks share an acceptance that death is a part of life, and show great reverence toward both the process and the deceased. Funerals are considered to be very important rituals, and attending a funeral is considered a social obligation of members of the community. The dead are typically buried rather than cremated, and ancestors are considered to be present in the spirit world. Honoring the dead is important, and can be demonstrated by naming a newborn after someone who has died, passing babies over the casket, and pouring libations on the ground.

Libation: A liquid used in a religious ritual.

Friends and families will gather at the home of the deceased immediately upon learning of the death to provide support to survivors. It is customary to give food, money, or resources to survivors, but personal attendance at the time of loss is highly valued.

Mexican Americans

Most Mexican Americans observe Catholic traditions of death and mourning. One author (Moore, 1976) described Mexican American funerals as "more emotional" and with more participatory variations of the standard Catholic traditions. She observed that the immediate family of the deceased is visible in the service, usually at the front of the congregation. Children were more likely to be present than in other cultures. Among Mexican Americans, there may be a *velorio*, which is a watch over the body before burial. The rosary is generally said in Spanish the day before the funeral. Some Hispanic groups say the rosary for nine nights after the death, and some families say it every month for a year and on the anniversary of the death thereafter. After the rosary, there is viewing of the body, with touching and kissing not uncommon. Friends and extended family may move to the family's home at that time to provide support. The funeral is a traditional Catholic mass, with pallbearers chosen to be representative of important ties to the community. Following the funeral, there is often a meal or *comida* where mourners will gather and express condolences to the family. In many cases, money to help defray funeral costs is given to the family. In the post-burial period, the family will typically offer special prayers and visit the grave regularly for several months. The family will return to usual activities but limit social activities.

In many communities with large Mexican American populations, the Day of the Dead (*Dia de los Muertos*) is an annual celebration of the lives of the deceased held on November 1 and 2. The deceased's favorite meal may be brought to the gravesite, where family members gather to pray and sing and tend the gravesite. It is a festive occasion that may include confections in the shape of skulls or skeletons, and *pan de muerto* (bread of the dead). Altars are created to commemorate the lives of the deceased, with special mementoes on display in order to attract the deceased to participate in the festivities. Families will socialize with other families with nearby gravesites (Salvador, 2003).

Native Americans

There are hundreds of different tribal groups among the Native American population in the United States and differences in grief and mourning practices vary among tribes. Generalizations are hard to make, but several concepts are relevant. The focus on harmony with the natural world is widespread, and many tribes believe the deceased rejoins the natural world. Traditional spiritual leaders may lead ceremonies for the dead, but some communities observe Christian practices instead of, or in addition to, traditional rituals. Preservation of the body is not central, so embalming is not often practiced. In some tribes, gifts and particular objects are buried with the body to accompany the spirit to the next world. Many Native Americans want to be buried in traditional homelands (Spungen & Piccicuto, 2002).

The Navajo are one of the larger tribes in the United States. Among Navajos, the body of the dead is never touched—this is a very strong cultural taboo. In fact, the word *death* should not be uttered. Navajos believe that when a person is born, the Holy People give it breath or wind. When a person dies, the evil part of the person stays with the body and becomes a *ch'iindi*, or an evil spirit. Only infants or elderly who have lived a long life do not produce ch'iindi. The most dangerous of the *ch'iindi* is the Skinwalker, who is greatly feared. Contact with a *ch'iindi* is the cause of "ghost sickness" that can be cured only by a long and expensive ceremony called the Enemy Way. When a person dies in a *hogan*, the hogan is destroyed. In fact, some families will take the dying relative to a hospital to avoid losing their home (Alvord & Van Pelt, 1999). Consequently, hospitals are seen as places to be avoided. Before mortuaries were readily available, Navajos would ask non-Navajos to bury their dead.

The part of a person's spirit that is good may take a four-day journey to the afterworld (*ciditah*) guided by deceased relatives and friends. The afterworld is an underworld that is very much like the earth and in which the spirits continue with the same activities they were involved in on earth.

It is essential that mental health professionals communicate and demonstrate respect for the varying cultural and religious practices, and acknowledge the importance of these rituals in the lives of many mourners. Encouraging and supporting clients in participating in these practices is ethical and appropriate.

Persons with Disabilities

There are several forms of disabilities that need special attention when a death occurs. People with intellectual disabilities are reported to frequently experience unusual grief reactions, which are then ignored or unrecognized as grief by family and professional caregivers (Clements, Focht-New, & Faulkner, 2004; Dowling, Hubert, White, & Hollins, 2006; Hollins, 1995). Often, well-intentioned adults and family members believe they need to protect the person with disabilities from the loss, so they withhold information or exclude the person from mourning rituals. Because many individuals with cognitive challenges have limited verbal skills, they may be unable to describe their experiences or needs. Caregivers may erroneously assume that the person with intellectual disabilities is incapable of understanding the concept of death, a belief that justifies withholding information. This protective behavior deprives the individual of experiences that increase awareness about death and grief. Lavin (1998) stresses what must be understood by mental health professionals working with persons with learning or intellectual disabilities:

By definition, they have impairments; this does not mean they are without any cognitive ability. They can reason, comprehend, and remember, although they may do so in unique ways. Helping individuals with developmental disabilities cope with loss requires that intervention and support be based on their cognitive strengths. (p. 171)

Particularly when the individual has lived a sheltered existence, the death of a parent or caregiver can be very frightening. The person is likely to have crucial questions about how this death will affect their life, and the lack of involvement of the person in decisions affecting them is commonplace, however hurtful. Lavin (1998) offers some practical suggestions that can assist persons with cognitive disabilities in dealing with the death of a significant person. These tips are useful for caregivers, and mental health professionals can either assist caregivers with these tasks or provide information to facilitate their support of the person with disabilities.

- Use concrete examples to explain the essential concepts about death: irreversibility, universality, and cessation of functioning. The death of a plant or pet can be an opportunity to explain this. Movies and books can be used to create a structured program of death education.
- Prepare the person to attend the funeral or other mourning rituals. Advance discussion may not be sufficient; arranging a private visit with a sensitive person from a funeral home can demystify the event and give the person first-hand experience prior to the funeral event.
- Attend carefully to the terms used to describe the death. Euphemisms may be confusing and can create misunderstanding.
- Many individuals with intellectual impairments think egocentrically, and may believe they caused the death. Be certain to dispel this notion, explaining the cause of death in simple and direct terms.
- Locate a support network. If the parent has died and the person must relocate, this may be challenging, but advance arrangements can ease the process.
- If the person has a religious affiliation, encourage contact with clergy.
- Normalize grief reactions. If the individual has no prior experience with death and grieving, they may not realize that their strong feelings and distress are experienced by everyone who experiences the death of someone they cared about.

A team of researchers (Dowling et al., 2006) tested two interventions for bereaved adults with intellectual disabilities. Although their study was carefully designed, the intervention that involved both family members and care staff at day treatment centers was only actually implemented fully with one individual. The researchers learned that this format was likely too demanding of time from non-clinical persons. The positive findings for the intervention using bereavement counselors, who took a two-day training on working with individuals with intellectual disabilities, are very encouraging. The individual sessions were provided at the location chosen by the client (usually home or treatment center) for fifteen weekly sessions of approximately one hour duration. Counselors used a variety of strategies to communicate with the clients, including drawing, using books and pictures, and making memorial items. The researchers found significant gains in those who received the individual counseling intervention, whereas the others who had originally given consent to participate but did not receive any services either made no gains or actually deteriorated. Both outcome measures assessed changes in behavior, and were completed by family members or caregivers at treatment centers. This seems to be a very promising intervention, and demonstrates that individuals with such disabilities do in fact have grief responses to a death that need attention.

Deaf persons may also have unique difficulties when a death occurs, although the difficulty is more likely to be caused by their treatment by the hearing population than by the deaf themselves (Zieziula, 1998). Although the emotional impact of a death is similar in deaf and hearing people, it is more difficult for the deaf person to communicate his or her experience to others, especially if most other mourners are not deaf. The difficulty communicating with the hearing population extends to getting accurate information. For the deaf person who loses a deaf spouse, the loss can be particularly devastating, as the spouse may have been a "cultural and communication partner" (p. 191). Zieziula notes that most deaf persons have partners or spouses who are also deaf, but may have hearing children. The grief process involves coming to terms with the loss and continuing one's life, changed as it will necessarily be. For a deaf person whose childhood is likely to have involved considerable dependence on others, the death of a partner may cause those dependency issues to resurface.

Counselor Issues

Working with bereaved clients inevitably brings up one's own losses, feelings and fears about death, and heightens our awareness of our mortality. It is essential that counselors clarify their own beliefs and address their own fears prior to engaging with clients. Dershimer's (1990) *Personal Grieving Style Inventory* is a very useful vehicle for exploring thoughts and experiences about grief and loss. It is recommended that this inventory be completed individually, but shared and processed with others. Often training workshops and professional development programs will invite participants to engage in this type of self-exploration, and doing so will raise the counselor's awareness of the kinds of situations and individuals that may present personal challenges for the client. Because the nonjudgmental aspect of grief counseling is so critical, counselors need to pay close attention to their own reactions, and be willing to refer those clients with whom they cannot provide that supportive stance.

Bill Moyer's PBS series *On Death and Dying* is a moving account of the death and grief experience. I show this to my students, who consistently say it is difficult to watch but absolutely necessary. This series can be a stimulus for further discussion with peers about how each counselor copes with loss and responds to grief in others.

Counselors who work with bereaved clients, as a specialty or occasionally, need to be prepared and tolerant of high levels of emotionality. It is important that clients have a safe place to express their feelings, which may be of high intensity.

BOX **8 . 1**

A Note to School Counselors

School counselors have a number of important roles related to death and grief in schools. One of those roles is delivering guidance curriculum. Although some degree of death education would be helpful, some schools will not allow the topic to be presented (Samide & Stockton, 2002). For those school counselors interested in using literature to teach about death, Wilson (1984) includes a list of classic books that would be very useful in today's classrooms. Several Internet sources of children's book titles will be provided in the Resources section later in this chapter. When there has been a death that affects children in school, visiting classes and providing age-appropriate lessons on death can be helpful to students and a relief to teachers who might be uncomfortable doing such lessons themselves.

There are several situations in which the counselor is likely to have a major responsibility: the death of a student or staff member, and the death of a child's parent or sibling. The death of a student can be quite challenging to manage. In a school in which one of my students was interning, a third-grade student died of leukemia only weeks after diagnosis. Several of the children in the class were fearful that they would catch the disease and die as well. Most children were sad, and were shocked to know that someone their age could die. The school counselor was able to visit the child's class and provide information in a sensitive and age-appropriate manner, and to allow for children to express their feelings and ask questions. Some children received additional individual counseling as needed. Another situation occurred at the high school where I worked as a school counselor. A teacher died in a car accident on a weekend. I received the information prior to school convening on Monday morning, and met with teachers first. As this teacher had been at the school for many years, colleagues were deeply saddened, and did not feel able to help students. I delivered the information to students in classroom groups. Students varied in their responses to the news, with those who felt closest to the teacher experiencing the more intense emotional reactions. In addition, several students who had acted out in class recently felt extremely guilty about their behavior and the loss of an opportunity to apologize. Another phenomenon that is quite common is that even those students who did not know the deceased are affected by the memory of losses of their own, and may need support revisiting those events and understanding that such delayed reactions are normal.

Swihart, Silliman, and McNeil (1992) described their experience in a small school when a popular 16-year-old died of leukemia. They point out that although high school students have the cognitive skills to understand death, few had had any direct experience with death, and had also not previously discussed the topic with adults who could provide information. These school counselors found themselves intervening with individuals, providing small groups, and serving the entire system as it coped with this loss. They surveyed the student body eighteen months after the death and gathered data about the students' recalled initial experience and their ongoing responses. They learned that teachers were unable to provide meaningful assistance to students because they were struggling with their own grief. They also discovered that many students believed they needed more opportunity to talk about the death, whereas many others wanted school to proceed as usual and not dwell on the death. These opposite opinions are understandable, given what we know about patterns of grief responses.

Approximately 5% of children will experience the death of a parent before they graduate from high school (When a parent dies, n.d.). In some cases, school counselors are involved when an individual

(continued)

BOX 8.1 **Continued**

student is first notified about a death; the school counselor is the best prepared person on the school staff to be present, and some experts recommend that this task be officially assigned to the school counselor to ensure sensitive and appropriate treatment of the child (Servaty-Seib, Peterson, & Spang, 2003). If the school counselor is present when a student learns of a parental death (from a surviving parent, a relative, a clergyperson), the counselor can assist by giving the child choices about who they want to be notified of the death and what information they wish to be given. They also should be allowed to decide who and how to get their belongings, and the like, and be invited to return to talk with the school counselor as needed.

Usually, the school will receive notification of a death from the family, and the school counselor is likely to be the primary liaison between the family and school. It is not unusual for family members to be consumed with their own grief to the extent that the child's needs go unrecognized. The school counselor can be available to listen to the child and to normalize the grief process. The school counselor also should be an advocate for the student, arranging for appropriate accommodations following the death: allowing time to see the counselor, excusing absences related to the death, making academic allowances for the expected reduced academic performance after the death, and so on (Costa & Holliday, 1994; Samide & Stockton, 2002; Servaty-Seib et al., 2003).

Gray (1988) interviewed fifty students who had experienced the death of a parent while in secondary school. Students had mixed reactions regarding how helpful the surviving parent had been, with equal numbers finding them to be very helpful and not at all helpful. Gray suggests that the school counselor could be helpful in those cases where the relationship is strained by the loss. For most teens, the most helpful person had been a friend or peers in a support group. Many reported that other friends and acquaintances seemed to pull away, which made them feel isolated. Those students who participated in a school support group were much more likely to say that peers understood them better than those who did not participate in a group. One of the disturbing findings from these interviews was that 42% of students said teachers were not helpful. Students appreciated expressions of condolences from teachers when they were given privately, and were appreciative of those who adjusted academic expectations during the bereavement period. Several students reported having been told by teachers to "buckle down and focus on their schoolwork" (p. 188) which was quite unhelpful. School counselors need to educate teachers about the grief process, and provide suggestions for how they might respond to students who have experienced the death of a loved one. Students in support groups found the school counselor to be more helpful than those not in groups, suggesting that the planned, regular contact that occurs with a group was an effective way for students to access their counselors.

Another difficult loss for students is that of a sibling. Balk (1983) observed that much of the literature on grief focuses on the death of a spouse or parent with far less available on this other difficult loss. To understand the impact of the death of a sibling, Balk interviewed thirty-three teenagers who had that experience and discovered that for many of them, the emotional responses continued as long as two years or more after the death. Schoolwork and school motivation deteriorated, a least temporarily, for most of his participants. Like Gray's (1988) participants, students in this study found that peers were most helpful, but some peers withdrew, often as a result of their own discomfort and uncertainty about how to respond. Balk suggests that one role school counselors might take is to meet with friends of the bereaved student to give them suggestions about how they might interact with their bereaved classmate. One comment was made by several participants that would be useful for classmates to know: students emphatically resented being told "I know how you feel," by anyone other than someone else who had lost a sibling. Thus, Balk found that helping the grieving student re-establish social support and helping other students learn how to respond to a peer at a time of grief would be a very useful contribution by the school counselor.

It is clear that some students benefit from bereavement groups in the school setting. The groups in Gray's (1988) study were for those who had lost a parent. Participants believed that those who had lost a loved one who was not a parent would be welcome, but 90% opposed including students who lost a parent through divorce. Samide and Stockton (2002) provide an outline for offering school bereavement groups. They recommend the group be at least eight weeks in duration, and that screening interviews include both students and their parents if possible. These experts recommend that students not participate in school counseling groups for two to four months after the death. Students who have experienced a death, especially younger children, cannot tolerate lengthy sessions with intense affect, so it is important to plan the group so that there are a variety of activities to relieve the intensity. These authors provide an outline of activities for an eight-session group that is flexible and can be adapted to different levels. Gary also offers helpful guidelines for conducting bereavement groups in the schools.

Ethical Concerns

When working with clients experiencing grief, counselors must be sure to adhere to all ethical guidelines of their profession, including boundaries of competence. If counselors find that grief counseling becomes a focus of the work, it is important that they obtain current information by attending professional training and reading the professional literature.

Counselors must be aware of cultural differences, and observe ethical codes for working with multicultural clients. It may be appropriate to attend the funeral or pay a condolence call if a client experiences the death of a loved one. If a counselor is uncertain about the propriety of such a gesture, consultation with a colleague, preferably of the client's cultural background, is strongly recommended.

Perhaps the most important ethical concern regarding grief is the necessity of self-awareness. As grief is a universal experience, counselors must ensure (via consultation and supervision) that they are able to separate their own needs from those of clients. It is strongly recommended that counselors engage in some type of personal growth experience related to grief prior to working with any client. Most professional conferences have sessions on this topic, and there are numerous professional training opportunities specifically focused on grief. There are several online courses on grief that the interested counselor may take if no other training is available.

Summary

- Normal grief involves physical, emotional, cognitive, behavioral, and spiritual components. Most people do not need professional services to deal with grief, but in some cases lack of environmental support will bring mourners to counseling.
- Although the stage theory of Kübler-Ross is best known, it does not accurately describe the individual variations of the grief and mourning experience.

- Worden proposes a task model, suggesting that individuals need to accomplish four tasks to move forward. Those tasks are: accepting the reality of the loss, working through the pain and grief, adjusting to an environment in which the deceased is missing, and emotionally relocating the deceased and moving on with life.
- In addition to normal grief, some individuals experience complicated grief, with longer duration and additional symptoms. There are specialized assessment tools to help the counselor distinguish between normal and complicated grief. These individuals are more likely to receive professional help and require a different approach to treatment.
- The experience of grief changes over the life span as cognitive and emotional development affects people's understanding of death and their ability to recognize and express feelings associated with the loss. Different strategies are indicated for individuals at different developmental levels. The elderly are at risk for complicated grief, and professionals who work with this population should be alert to difficulties and losses.
- Some special cases of grief may require more understanding. Survivors of death by suicide, families of babies who die of SIDS, those who experience miscarriages and abortions, survivors of AIDS deaths and military deaths are among those special cases. In addition, sudden death presents particular challenges, and survivors may need more support and information to manage the grieving process. The death of a pet is sometimes discounted and trivialized, but can be a very painful loss to pet owners. The loss of a pet may be a child's first experience with death and grief.
- Sensitivity to the cultural influences in grieving is important, so that the helping professional does not offend when he or she intends to be helpful. Because cultural practices vary so widely (and because individuals within a culture vary in how closely they follow those practices), the professional would do well to respectfully inquire about relevant practices and beliefs.
- Persons with disabilities may have unique needs when they experience a death, and counselors can help ensure that those needs are met.
- Counselors must be self-aware, so that their own grief issues do not interfere with those of clients. Counselors must be aware of ethical issues in dealing with any client, and with grief counseling, sensitivity to issues of diversity is particularly critical.

ADDITIONAL RESOURCES

On the Web

- http://www.adec.org/ is the site for the Association for Death Education and Counseling. It has training modules available from the organization by well-known experts as well as publications and other resources.
- http://www.centerforloss.com/pg/default.asp is the site of Dr. Alan Wolfelt, who directs the Center for Loss and Life Transition. I have attended his workshops and found them to be very beneficial.

- http://www.mountida.edu/sp.cfm?pageid=307 The National Center for Death Education offers online and residential training.
- http://www.taps.org/or http://www.military.com/benefits/survivor-benefits/tragedy-assistance-program-for-survivors are links to Tragedy Assistance Program for Survivors (TAPS). This is an organization a clinician will want to recommend to families who have experienced the death of someone in the military.
- http://www.nlm.nih.gov/medlineplus/suddeninfantdeathsyndrome.html is an excellent site on SIDS that includes information and links to other sites that have the most current research.
- http://www.sids.org/ is another good website with factual information about SIDS.
- http://www3.baylor.edu/~Charles_Kemp/terminal_illness/childrens_books.htm and http://www.santaclaracountylib.org/kids/lists/death_dying_grieving.html have good lists of children's books on death and dying, coded for age level.
- http://childrensbooks.about.com/od/themesubjectbooksby/tp/petdeath.htm has a list of useful books for the death of a pet.
- http://www.compassionatefriends.org/ For parents and siblings of a deceased child, Compassionate Friends is a wonderful resource. The website of the national organization has much helpful information, and can assist in locating local chapters.
- http://www.dougy.org/ The Dougy Center is dedicated to helping grieving children and teens, and has useful links for kids, teens, and adults. There is information about their programs for training professionals interested in providing services for grieving children and adolescents.
- http://www.helpguide.org/mental/grief_loss.htm is a well-designed website with good information for clients about grief, as is
- http://www.nci.nih.gov/cancertopics/pdq/supportivecare/bereavement/patient/allpages
- http://www.tlcinstitute.org/PTRCchilddevgrief.html is a good site for parents who need information about developmental aspects of grief.

In Print for Counselors

- *On Death and Dying* by Elisabeth Kübler-Ross (1969) is the best-known book on death and grieving and despite the criticism of the book from more modern experts, it is definitely an important one for a counselor to have read.
- *Grief Counseling and Grief Therapy: A Handbook for the Mental Health Practitioner* by J. William Worden (1991) is a classic reference in this field. It is also highly readable and offers specific suggestions for counseling.
- *A Grief Observed* by C. S. Lewis (1989) is the famous author's personal account of his grief upon the death of his wife and is a window into the intimate experience of one man. The film *Shadowlands* is based on this story.
- *The Loss that is Forever: The Lifelong Impact of the Early Death of a Mother or Father* by Maxine Harris (1996) will be helpful for those counselors who may work with children who have lost a parent, and may be appropriate for some adult clients for whom this loss continues to be an issue.
- *Children and Grief: When a Parent Dies* by J. William Worden (2001) is another important and useful reference for working with children.

In Print for Clients

- *Living When a Loved One Has Died* (1995), *Straight Talk about Death for Teenagers : How to Cope with Losing Someone You Love* (1993), *What Helped Me When My Loved One Died* (1982), *Living With Loss, Healing With Hope* (2001), and for children, *A Child's Book About Death* (2001) are all by Earl Grollman, who is a master of speaking to those who are grieving. I often recommend these books to clients who have experienced the death of someone important in their lives. Readers might want to explore the long list of books he has written on this subject.
- *The Fall of Freddie the Leaf: A Story of Life for All Ages* by Leo Buscaglia (2002) is a classic book for children about death that can help prepare them for a loss. This story is also available in Spanish.
- *Talking with Children about Loss* by Maria Trozzi (1999) is an excellent book for parents, but counselors who work with grieving children will find it helpful as well.

Film and Television

- *On Our Own Terms*, A PBS series about death and dying which is available via http://www.pbs.org/wnet/onourownterms/about/index.html Ideally, this series would be the focus of a study group where one could discuss and process the videos. There is a discussion guide available to assist in that process. A follow-up series, *With Eyes Open*, includes an episode that focuses on grief and loss. Information on this series can be found at http://www.pbs.org/witheyesopen/about_the_series.html
- *In America* (2002), is great film about the impact of the death of a child on the parents and surviving children.
- *The Sweet Hereafter* (1997) examines the impact of a sudden tragic loss of many children on the survivors in a small town.
- *Moonlight Mile* (2002) is a good film that focuses on the impact of the death of a woman on her boyfriend and her parents.
- *Corina, Corina* (1994) is about the impact of the death of a wife and mother on the survivors, and the positive effects of the nanny hired by the father on both the grieving father and the daughter.

EXERCISES

1. Apply the concepts in this chapter to the case study at the beginning of the chapter. List the aspects of the situation that contributed to the complications. In what ways did James's experience illustrate Worden's tasks of grief? Imagine you were the counselor James met with right after his mother's death. What are some strategies or interventions you might have used to assist him? What books might you have recommended he read?

2. Watch any of the films mentioned above, and discuss your own responses. What does the film teach you about grief? How would you have worked with the protagonist if you were the protagonist's counselor?

3. Complete individually, and then discuss in a group the Personal Grieving Style Inventory in Appendix A of Dershimer's book.

4. Assume you are a school counselor. One of the teachers in your school was killed in an automobile accident over the weekend. You will be going into her class on Monday morning to work with the students. Plan how you will tell them of the loss, how you will answer their predictable questions, what other services you might offer. Do this exercise as if you were an elementary counselor, middle school counselor, and a high school counselor.

5. Assume you are a counselor in an agency, and one of your adult clients experiences the death of a parent while in treatment with you. How and when will you determine whether the client is experiencing normal grief or complicated grief? What would be some indicators that a complicated grief is likely?

REFERENCES

Chapter 1: Sexual Abuse

Alessi, H. D., & Ballard, M. B. (2001). Memory development in children: Implications for children as witnesses in situations of possible abuse. *Journal of Counseling & Development, 79*, 398–403.

Allison, D. (1992). *Bastard out of Carolina*. NewYork: Dutton.

Alpert, J. L., & Paulson, A. (1990). Graduate-level education and training in child sexual abuse. *Professional Psychology: Research & Practice, 21*, 366–371.

Anonymous. (2004). I'm glad I spoke up. In *Living a lie: Teens write about surviving sexual abuse*. NY: Youth Communication, Inc.

Bass, E., & Davis, L. (1994). *The courage to heal: A guide for women survivors of child sexual abuse* (3rd ed.). NY: HarperCollins.

Blume, E. S. (1989). *Secret survivors: Uncovering incest and its aftereffects in women*. NY: Ballantine Books.

Botash, A. (2006, April 6). Pediatrics, child sexual abuse. Retrieved December 16, 2006, from http://www.emedicine.com/emerg/topic369.htm

Briere, J. (1989). *Therapy for adults molested as children: Beyond survival*. NY: Springer.

Chao, P. (1997). *Monkey king*. NY: HarperCollins.

Classen, C. (1995). Introduction. In C. Classen (Ed.), *Treating women molested as children* (pp. xiii–xxxii). San Francisco: Jossey-Bass.

Cohen, J. D., Mannarino, A. P., Berliner, L., & Deblinger, E. (2000). Trauma-focused cognitive behavioral therapy for children and adolescents: An empirical update. *Journal of Interpersonal Violence, 15*, 1202–1223.

Courtois, C. A. (1995). Assessment and diagnosis. In C. Classen (Ed.), *Treating women molested as children* (pp. 1–34). San Francisco: Jossey-Bass.

Davis, L. A. (n.d.). *People with mental retardation & sexual abuse*. Retrieved December 13, 2006, from http://disability-abuse.com/cando/documents/ABUSEQ&A.rtf

Deblinger, E., & Heflin, A. H. (1996). *Treating sexually abused children and their non-offending parents: A cognitive behavioral approach*. Thousand Oaks, CA: Sage.

Elliott, K., & Urquiza, A. (2006). Ethnicity, culture, and child maltreatment. *Journal of Social Issues, 62*, 787–809.

Engel, B. (1990). *Right to innocence: Healing the trauma of childhood sexual abuse*. Carslbad, CA: Gurze Books.

Feiring, C., Taska, L., & Lewis, M. (1999). Age and gender differences in children's and adolescents' adaptation to sexual abuse. *Child Abuse & Neglect, 23*, 115–128.

Finkelhor, D. (1994). Current information on the scope and nature of child sexual abuse. *Sexual Abuse of Children, 4*, 31–53.

Finkelhor, D. (1995). The victimization of children: A developmental perspective. *American Journal of Orthopsychiatry, 65*, 177–193.

Friedrich, W. N. (1995). *Psychotherapy with sexually abused boys: An integrated approach*. Thousand Oaks, CA: Sage.

Friedrich, W. N. (1997). *Child sexual behavior inventory: Professional manual*. Lutz, FL: Psychological Assessment Resources.

Gibb, C. (1999). *Mouthing the words*. NY: Carroll & Graf.

Gil, E. (1988). *Outgrowing the pain: A book for and about adults abused as children.* NY: Dell.

Gleaves, D. H., Smith, S. M., Butler, L. D., & Spiegel, D. (2004). False and recovered memories in the laboratory and clinic: A review of experimental and clinical evidence. *Clinical Psychology: Science and Practice, 11,* 3–28.

Harvey, M. R., & Harney, P. A. (1995). Individual psychotherapy. In C. Classen (Ed.), *Treating women molested as children* (pp. 63–93). San Francisco: Jossey-Bass.

Hillman, R. J., Tomlinson, D., McMillan, A., French, P. D., & Harris, J. R. (1990). Sexual assault of men: A series. *Genitourin Medicine, 66,* 247–250.

Holmes, G., & Offen, L. (1996). Clinicians' hypotheses regarding clients' problems: Are they less likely to hypothesize sexual abuse in male compared to female clients? *Child Abuse & Neglect, 20,* 493–501.

Huston, A. (Director). (1996). *Bastard out of Carolina* [Motion picture]. United States: BMG.

Isely, P. J., Busse, W., & Isely, P. (1998). Sexual assault of males in late adolescence: A hidden phenomenon. *Professional School Counseling, 2,* 153–161.

Jessie. (1991). *Please tell: A child's story about sexual abuse.* Center City, MN: Hazelden.

Kennel, R. G., & Agresti, A. A. (1995). Effects of gender and age on psychologists' reporting of childhood sexual abuse. *Professional Psychology: Research & Practice, 26,* 612–615.

Kitzrow, M. A. (2002). Survey of CACREP-accredited programs: Training counselors to provide treatment for sexual abuse. *Counselor Education and Supervision, 42,* 107–118.

Krahe, B. (2000). Childhood sexual abuse and revictimization in adolescence and adulthood. *Journal of Personal and Interpersonal Loss, 5,* 149–166.

Lab, D. D., Fiegenbaum, J. D., & De Silva, P. (2000). Mental health professionals' attitudes and practices toward male childhood sexual abuse. *Child Abuse & Neglect, 24,* 391–409.

Leventhal, J. M. (2001). A decline in substantiated cases of sexual abuse in the United States: Good news or false hope? *Child Abuse and Neglect, 25,* 1137–1138.

Lew, M. (1988). *Victims no longer: Men recovering from incest and other sexual child abuse.* NY: Harper & Row.

Lisak, D. (1994). The psychological impact of sexual abuse: Content analysis of interviews with male survivors. *Journal of Traumatic Stress, 7,* 525–548.

Little, L., & Hamby, S. L. (1996). Impact of a clinician's sexual abuse history, gender, and theoretical orientation on treatment issues related to childhood sexual abuse. *Professional Psychology: Research & Practice, 27,* 617–625.

Loftus, E. F. (1993). The reality of repressed memories. *American Psychologist, 48,* 518–537.

Lovett, J. (1999). *Small wonders: Healing childhood trauma with EMDR.* NY: The Free Press.

Manders, J. (2001). *The sexual abuse of children with disabilities.* Retrieved December 16, 2006, from http://childabuse.georgiacenter.uga.edu/both/manders

Morgan, T., & Cummings, A. L. (1999). Change experienced during group therapy by female survivors of childhood sexual abuse. *Journal of Consulting and Clinical Psychology, 67,* 28–36.

Naitove, C. E. (1982). Arts therapy with sexually abused children. In S. M. Sgroi (Ed.), *Handbook of clinical intervention in child sexual abuse.* New York: The Free Press.

Navalta, C. P., Polcari, A., Webster, D. M., Boghossian, A., & Teicher, M. H. (2006). Effects of childhood sexual abuse on neuropsychological and cognitive function in college women. *Journal of Neuropsychiatry and Clinical Neuroscience, 18,* 45–53.

Neimark, J. (2004, August). Are recovered memories real? *Discover,* 73–77.

Nelson, E. C., Heath, A. D., Lynskey, M. T., Bucholz, K. K., Madden, P. A., Statham, D. J., & Martin, N. G. (2006). Childhood sexual abuse and risk for licit and illicit drug-related outcomes: A twin study. *Psychological Medicine, 36,* 1473–1483.

Parnell, L. (1999). *EMDR in the treatment of adults abused as children.* NY: W. W. Norton.

Porter, R. L., Wagner, W. G., Johnson, J. T., & Cox, L. M. (1996). Sexually abused girls' verbalizations in counseling: an application of the client behavior system. *Journal of Counseling Psychology, 43,* 383–388.

ProtectMeFirst.com (n.d.). *Sexual assault of young children as reported to law enforcement: Victim, incident, and offender characteristics.* Retrieved from http://protectmefirst.com/crimestatistics. htm

Rubin, D. C. (1996). *Remembering our past: Studies in autobiographical memory.* Cambridge, UK: Cambridge University Press.

Saunders, B. E., Berliner, L., & Hanson, R. F. (Eds.). (2003). *Child physical and sexual abuse: Guidelines for treatment (Final Report: January 15, 2003).* Charleston, SC: National Crime Victims Research and Treatment Center.

Sgroi, S. (1989). Stages of recovery of adult survivors of childhood sexual abuse. In S. M. Sgroi (Ed.), *Vulnerable populations* (Vol. 2, pp. 111–130). New York: Lexington.

Smith, J. (2002). *Evaluation, diagnosis, and outcomes of child sexual abuse.* Retrieved December 16, 2006, from http://www.childadvocate.net/child_sexual_abuse.htm

Snyder, H. N. (2000). *Sexual assault of young children as reported to law enforcement: Victim, incident, and offender characteristics.* Washington, DC: U.S. Department of Justice Bureau of Justice Statistics.

Sonkin, D. J. (1998). *Wounded boys heroic men. A man's guide to recovering from child abuse.* Cincinnati, OH: Adams Media.

Sullivan, P. M., & Knutson, J. F. (2000). Maltreatment and disabilities: A population-based epidemiological study. *Child Abuse & Neglect, 24,* 1257–1273.

Tyler, K. A., Hoyt, D. R., Whitbeck, L. B., & Cauce, A. M. (2001). The impact of childhood sexual abuse on later sexual victimization among runaway youth. *Journal of Research on Adolescence, 11,* 151–177.

U.S. Department of Health and Human Services, Administration of Children, Youth and Families. (2003). *Child Maltreatment 2001.* Washington, DC: U.S. Government Printing Office.

Williams, L. M. (1994). Recall of childhood trauma: A prospective study of women's memories of child sexual abuse. *Journal of Consulting and Clinical Psychology, 62,* 1167–1176.

Wyre, D. (Producer and Director). (2001). *Ultimate betrayal* [Motion picture]. United States: Hearst Entertainment.

Chapter 2: Self-Mutilation

Acker, D. W., Burck, H. D., & Annis, L. V. (1995). The failure to construct an MMPI-2-based self-mutilative behavior scale. *International Journal of Offender Therapy and Comparative Criminology, 39(4),* 341–351.

Adler, P. A., & Adler, P. (2005). Self-injurers as loners: The social organization of solitary deviance. *Deviant Behavior, 26,* 345–378.

Alderman, T. (1997). *The scarred soul: Understanding and ending self-inflicted violence.* Oakland, CA: New Harbinger.

Allen, C. (1995). Helping with deliberate self-harm: Some practical guidelines. *Journal of Mental Health, 4,* 243–251.

American Psychiatric Association. (2000). *Diagnostic and statistical manual of mental disorders* (4th ed., Text Revision) Washington, DC: Author.

Boyce, P., Oakley-Browne, M. A., & Hatcher, S. (2001). The problem of deliberate self-harm. *Current Opinions in Psychiatry, 14,* 107–111.

Briere, J., & Gil, E. (1998). Self-mutilation in clinical and general population samples: Prevalence, correlates, and functions. *American Journal of Orthopsychiatry, 68(4),* 609–620.

Carr, P. (2004). Living on a razor's edge. In *My secret addiction: Teens write about cutting.* NY: Youth Communication, Inc.

Connors, R. E. (2000). *Self-injury: Psychotherapy with people who engage in self-inflicted violence.* Northvale, NJ: Aronson.

Conterio, K., & Lader, W. (1998). *Bodily harm.* NY: Hyperion.

Cowmeadow, P. (1994). Deliberate self-harm and cognitive analytic therapy. *International Journal of Short-Term Psychotherapy, 9,* 135–150.

Erikson, E. (1950). *Childhood and society*. NY: W. W. Norton.

Evans, K., Tyrer, P., Catalan, J., Schmidt, U., Davison, K., Dent, J., Tata, P., Thornton, S., Barber, J., & Thompson, S. (1999). *Psychological Medicine, 29*, 19–25.

Favazza, A. R. (1996). *Bodies under siege: Self-mutilation and body modification in culture and psychiatry* (2nd ed.). Baltimore, MD: Johns Hopkins University Press.

Froeschle, J., & Moyer, M. (2004). Just cut it out: Legal and ethical challenges in counseling students who self-mutilate. *Professional School Counseling, 7*, 131–135.

Gonzalez, C. (2004). My secret addiction. In *My secret addiction: Teens write about cutting*. NY: Youth Communication, Inc.

Haines, J., & Williams, C. L. (1997). Coping and problem solving of self-mutilators. *Journal of Clinical Psychology, 53(2)*, 177–186.

Hawton, K., Arensman, E., Townsend, E., Bremner, S., Feldman, E., Goldney, R., Gunnell, D., Hazell, P., van Heeringen, K., House, A., Owens, D., Sakinofsky, I., & Traskman-Bendz, L. (1998). Deliberate self-harm: systematic review of efficacy of psychosocial and pharmacological treatments in preventing repetition. *British Medical Journal, 17*, 441–447.

Kress, V. E. W. (2003). Self-injurious behaviors: Assessment and diagnosis. *Journal of Counseling & Development, 81*, 490–496.

Kress, V. E. W., Drouhard, N., & Costin, A. (2006). Students who self-injure: School counselor ethical and legal considerations. *Professional School Counseling, 10*, 203–209.

Lamb, W. (1998). *I know this much is true*. NY: Regan Books.

Levenkron, S. (1998). *Cutting: Understanding and overcoming self-mutilation*. NY: Guilford.

Lieberman, R., & Poland, S. (2006). Self-mutilation. In G. G. Bear & K. M. Minke (Eds.), *Children's needs III: Development, prevention, and intervention* (pp. 965–976). Washington, DC: National Association of School Psychologists.

Linehan, M. M. (1993). *Skills training manual for treating borderline personality disorder*. NY: Guilford.

Martin, P., & Guth, C. (2005). Unusual devastating self-injurious behavior in a patient with a severe learning disability: Treatment with citalopram. *Psychiatric Bulletin, 29*, 108–110.

McCormick, P. (2000). *Cut*. NY: Scholastic Inc.

Mesirow, T. R. (1999). Self-mutilation: Analysis of a psychiatric forensic population. *Dissertation Abstracts International: Section B, 60*, 2354.

Miller, D. (1996). Challenging self-harm through transformation of the trauma story. *Sexual Addiction and Compulsivity, 3(3)*, 213–227.

Morrison, J. (1995). *DSM-IV made easy: The clinician's guide to diagnosis*. New York: Guilford.

Oliver, C., Moss, J., Petty, J., Sloneem, J., Aaron, K., & Hall, S. (2003). *A guide for parents and carers: Self-injurious behaviour in Cornelia de Lange syndrome*. Birmingham, UK: Community Fund. Available online at http://www.cdlsworld.org/books/behaviour/index.php

Rockland, L. H. (1987). Psychodynamically Oriented Supportive Therapy—Treatment of borderline patients who self-mutilate. *Journal of Personality Disorders, 1(4)*, 350–353.

Ross, S., & Heath, N. (2002). A study of the frequency of self-mutilation in a community sample of adolescents. *Journal of Youth and Adolescence, 31(1)*, 67–77.

Sapphire. (1996). *Push*. NY: Alfred A. Knopf.

Sheard, T., Evans, J., Cash, D., Hicks, J., King, A., Morgan, N., Nereli, B., Porter, I., Rees, H., Sandford, J., Slinn, R., Sunder, K., & Ryle, A. (2000). A CAT-derived one to three session intervention for repeated deliberate self-harm: A description of the model and initial experience of trainee psychiatrists in using it. *British Journal of Medical Psychology, 73*, 179–196.

Solomon, Y., & Farrand, J. (1996). "Why don't you do it properly?" Young women who self-injure. *Journal of Adolescence, 19*, 111–119.

Strong, M. (1998). *A bright red scream*. NY: Penguin Books.

Suyemoto, K. K., & Kountz, X. (2000). Self-mutilation. *The Prevention Researcher, 7(4)*, 1–4.

Tyrer, P., Jones, V., Thompson, S., Catalan, J., Schmidt, U., Davidson, K., Knapp M., & Ukoumunne, O. (2003). Service variation in baseline variables and prediction of risk in a randomized controlled trial of psychological treatment in repeated suicide: The Popmact study. *International Journal of Social Psychiatry, 49*, 58–69.

Vesper, J. H. (1996). Ethical and legal considerations with self-mutilating and lethal clients. *American Journal of Forensic Psychology, 14(4)*, 25–38.

Walsh, B., & Rosen, P. M. (1988). *Self-mutilation: Theory, research, and treatment*. NY: Guilford.

Welsh, P. (2004, June 28). Students' scars point to emotional pain. *USA Today*. Retrieved December 23, 2006, from http://usatoday.com/

Wenz, F. V. (1977). Ecological variation in self-injury behavior. *Suicide & Life-Threatening Behavior, 7*, 92–99.

Whitlock, J., Eckenrode, J., & Silverman, D. (2006). Self-injurious behaviors in a college population. *Pediatrics, 117*, 1939–1948.

Whitlock, J. L., Powers, J. L., & Eckenrode, J. (2006). The virtual cutting edge: The Internet an adolescent self-injury. *Developmental Psychology, 42*, 407–417.

Whotton, E. (2002). What to do when an adolescent self-harms. *Emergency Nurse, 10(5)*, 12–17.

Yip, K. (2006). A strengths perspective in working with an adolescent with self-cutting behaviors. *Child and Adolescent Social Work Journal, 23*, 134–146.

Zila, L. M., & Kiselica, M. S. (2001). Understanding and counseling self-mutilation in female adolescents and young adults. *Journal of Counseling and Development, 79*, 46–52.

Chapter 3: Eating Disorders

Abou-Saleh, M. T., Younis, Y., & Karim, L. (1998). Anorexia nervosa in an Arab culture. *International Journal of Eating Disorders, 23*, 207–212.

Agras, W. S. (1993). Short-term psychological treatments for binge eating. In C. G. Fairburn & G. T. Wilson, (Eds.), *Binge eating: Nature, assessment, and treatment* (pp. 270–286). NY: Guilford.

American Psychiatric Association. (2000). *Practice guideline for the treatment of patients with eating disorders* (2nd ed.). Washington, DC: Author.

Anorexia Nervosa and Related Eating Disorders, Inc. *Statistics: How many people have eating disorders?* Retrieved June 18, 2003, from http://www.anred.com/stats.html

Arriaza, C. A., & Mann, T. (2001). Ethnic differences in eating disorder symptoms: The confounding role of body mass index. *Journal of American College Health, 49*, 309–315.

Associated Press. (2003, June 30). Eating disorders threaten Hispanic women. *Las Cruces Sun News*, p. 1.

Attia, E. (2003). Serotonin in anorexia nervosa: A new study supports a familiar hypothesis. *International Journal of Eating Disorders, 33*, 268–270.

Bardick, A., Bernes, K., McCulloch, A., Witko, K., Spriddle, J., & Roest, A. (2004). Eating disorder intervention, prevention, and treatment: Recommendations for school counselors. *Professional School Counseling, 8*, 168–174.

Becker, A. E. (1995). *Body, self, and society: A view from Fiji*. Philadelphia: University of Pennsylvania Press.

Bloomgarden, A. (2000). Therapist's self-disclosure and genuine caring: Where do they belong in the therapeutic relationship? *Eating Disorders: The Journal of Treatment and Prevention, 8*, 347–352.

Braun, D. L., Sunday, S. R., Huang, A., & Halmi, K. (1999). More males seek treatment for eating disorders. *International Journal of Eating Disorders, 25*, 415–424.

Brownell, K. D. (1991). Dieting and the search for the perfect body: Physiology and culture collide. *Behavior Therapy, 22*, 1–12.

Brownell, K. D., & Foreyt, J. P. (1986). *Handbook of eating disorders: Physiology, psychology, and treatment of obesity, anorexia, and bulimia*. New York: Basic Books.

Bulik, C. M., Sullivan, P. F., & Kendler, K. S. (2003). Genetic and environmental contributions to obesity and binge eating. *International Journal of Eating Disorders*, 293–298.

Bulik, C. M., Tozzi, F., Anderson, C., Mazzeo, S. E., Aggen, S., & Sullivan, P. (2003). The relation between eating disorders and components of perfectionism. *American Journal of Psychiatry, 160,* 366–368.

Cachelin, F. M., Striegel-Moore, R., & Paget, W. B. (1997). Comparison of women with various levels of dietary restraint on body image, personality, and family involvement. *Eating Disorders, 5,* 205–215.

Cardoso, P. (Director). (2002). *Real women have curves* [Motion picture]. United States: HBO Independent Productions.

Case, P., & Golding, J. (Co-Producers). (2003). *Perfect illusions: Eating disorders and the family.* United States: PBS.

Claude-Pierre, P. (1997). *The secret language of eating disorders: The revolutionary new approach to understanding and curing anorexia and bulimia.* NY: Random House.

Cooper, P. J. (1993). *Bulimia nervosa and binge-eating: A guide to recovery.* NY: New York University Press.

Costin, C. (1999). *The eating disorder sourcebook* (2nd ed.). Los Angeles, CA: Lowell House.

Crago, M., & Shisslak, C. M. (1996). Eating disturbances among American minority groups: A review. *International Journal of Eating Disorders, 19,* 239–248.

Croll, J., Neumark-Sztainer, D, Story, M., & Ireland, M. (2002). Prevalence and risk and protective factors related to disordered eating behaviors among adolescents: Relationship to gender and ethnicity. *Journal of Adolescent Health, 31,* 166–175.

Crowther, J. H., & Sherwood, N. E. (1997). Assessment. In D. M. Garner & P. E. Garfinkel (Eds.), *Handbook of treatment for eating disorders* (2nd ed., pp. 34–49). New York: Guilford.

Dare, C., & Eisler, I. (1997). Family therapy for anorexia nervosa. In D. M. Garner & P. E. Garfinkel (Eds.), *Handbook of treatment for eating disorders* (2nd ed., pp. 307–326). New York: Guilford.

Eating disorders emerge as problem among American males. (2001, August 16). *The Boston Globe.* Retrieved June 12, 2003, from http://www.intelihealth.com/IH/ihtPrint/EMIHC000/333/342/311308.html

Emerson, E. (2003). Prevalence of psychiatric disorders in children and adolescents with and without intellectual disability. *Journal of Intellectual Disability Research, 47,* 51–58.

Fairburn, C. (1995). *Overcoming binge eating.* NY: Guilford.

Fairburn, C. G. (1997). Interpersonal therapy for bulimia nervosa. In D. M. Garner & P. E. Garfinkel (Eds.), *Handbook of treatment for eating disorders* (2nd ed., pp. 278–294). New York: Guilford.

Fairburn, C. G., & Wilson, G. T. (Eds.). (1993). *Binge eating: Nature, assessment, and treatment.* NY: Guilford.

Farrell, E. (2000). *Lost for words: The psychoanalysis of anorexia and bulimia.* London: Process Press.

Garfinkel, P. E., & Walsh, B. T. (1997). Drug therapies. In D. M. Garner & P. E. Garfinkel (Eds.), *Handbook of treatment for eating disorders* (2nd ed., pp. 372–382). New York: Guilford.

Garner, D. M. (1997). Psychoeducational principles in treatment. In D. M. Garner & P. E. Garfinkel (Eds.), *Handbook of treatment for eating disorders* (2nd ed., pp. 145–177). New York: Guilford.

Garner, D. M., & Garfinkel, P. E. (Eds.). (1997). *Handbook of treatment for eating disorders.* NY: Guilford.

Garner, D. M., & Needleman, L. D. (1997). Sequencing and integration of treatments. In D. M. Garner & P. E. Garfinkel (Eds.), *Handbook of treatment for eating disorders* (2nd ed., pp. 50–63). New York: Guilford.

Garner, D. M., Vitousek, K. M., & Pike, K. M. (1997). Cognitive-behavioral therapy for anorexia nervosa. In D. M. Garner & P. E. Garfinkel (Eds.), *Handbook of treatment for eating disorders* (2nd ed., pp. 94–143). New York: Guilford.

Gottlieb, L. (2001). *Stick figure: A diary of my former self.* NY: Simon & Schuster.

Gowen, L. K., Hayward, C., Killen, J. D., Robinson, N., & Taylor, C. B. (1999). Acculturation and eating disorder symptoms in adolescent girls. *Journal of Research on Adolescence, 9*, 67–83.

Gravestock, S. (2000). Eating disorders in adults with intellectual disability. *Journal of Intellectual Disability Research, 44*, 625–637.

Gravestock, S. (2003). Diagnosis and classification of eating disorders in adults with intellectual disability: The 'Diagnostic Criteria for Psychiatric Disorders for Use with Adults with Learning Disabilities/Mental Retardation (DC-LD)' approach. *Journal of Intellectual Disability Research, 47*, 72–83.

Haas, H. L., & Clopton, J. R. (2003). Comparing clinical and research treatments for eating disorders. *International Journal of Eating Disorders, 33*, 412–420.

Hautzig, D. (1999). *Second star to the right*. NY: Puffin.

Hanauer, C. (1996). *My sister's bones*. NY: Delacorte Press.

Hornbacher, M. (1998). *Wasted*. NY: Harper

Hutchinson, M. G. (1985). *Transforming body image: Learning to love the body you have*. Freedom, CA: The Crossing Press.

Iyer, D. S., & Haslam, N. (2003). Body image and eating disturbance among South Asian-American women: The role of racial teasing. *International Journal of Eating Disorders, 34*, 142–147.

Jackson, T. D., Grilo, C. M., & Masheb, R. M. (2002). Teasing history and eating disorder features: An age- and body mass index-matched comparison of bulimia nervosa and binge-eating disorder. *Comprehensive Psychiatry, 23*, 108–113.

Jantz, G. L. (1995). *Hope, help, & healing for eating disorders: A new approach to treating anorexia, bulimia, and overeating*. Wheaton, IL: Harold Shaw.

Klump, K. L., McGue, M., & Iacono, W. G. (2003). Differential heritability of eating attitudes and behaviors in prepubertal versus pubertal twins. *International Journal of Eating Disorders, 33*, 287–292.

Krentz, A., & Arthur, N. (2001). Counseling culturally diverse students with eating disorders. *Journal of College Student Psychotherapy, 15(4)*, 7–21.

Levenkron, S. (1989). *The best little girl in the world*. NY: Warner.

Littleton, H. L., & Ollendick, T. (2003). Negative body image and disordered eating behavior in children and adolescents: What places youth at risk and how can these problems be prevented? *Clinical Child and Family Psychology Review, 6*, 51–66.

Lock, J., & Le Grange, D. (2005). *Helping your teenager beat an eating disorder*. NY: Guilford.

Manley, R. S., Smye, V., Srikameswaran, S. (2001). Addressing complex ethical issues in the treatment of children and adolescents with eating disorders: Application of a framework for ethical decision-making. *European Eating Disorders Review, 9(3)*, 144–166.

Marcus, M. D. (1997). Adapting treatment for patients with binge-eating disorder. In D. M. Garner & P. E. Garfinkel (Eds.), *Handbook of treatment for eating disorders* (2nd ed., pp. 484–493). New York: Guilford.

McFarland, B. (1995). *Brief therapy and eating disorders: A practical guide to solution-focused work with clients*. San Francisco, CA: Jossey-Bass.

Michel, D. M., & Willard, S. G. (2003). *When dieting becomes dangerous: A guide to understanding and treating anorexia and bulimia*. New Haven, CT: Yale University Press.

Mitchell, J. E., Pomeroy, C., & Adson, D. E. (1997). Managing medical complications. In D. M. Garner & P. E. Garfinkel (Eds.), *Handbook of treatment for eating disorders* (2nd ed., pp. 383–393). New York: Guilford.

Mulholland, A. M., & Mintz, L. B. (2001). Prevalence of eating disorders among African American women. *Journal of Counseling Psychology, 48*, 111–116.

National Association of Anorexia Nervosa and Associated Disorders. *Eating disorder statistics*. Retrieved June 18, 2003, from http://www.eatingdisorderinfo.org/eating_disorders_statistics. html

Norton, K. I., Olds, T. S., Olive, S., & Dank, S. (1996). Ken and Barbie at life size. *Sex Roles, 34*, 287–294.

Omizo, S., & Omizo, M. (1992). Eating disorders: The school counselor's role. *School Counselor, 39,* 217–224.

Owens, L. K., Hughes, T. L., & Owens-Nicholson, D. (2003). The effects of sexual orientation on body image and attitudes about eating and weight. *Journal of Lesbian Studies, 7,* 15–33.

Petty, L. C., Rosen, E. F., & Michaels, S. (2000). Nineteen eating disorder scales: Comparison by focus, ease, response format, and readability. *Eating Disorders, 8,* 311–329.

Piran, N. (2001). Prevention of eating disorders—A dilemma. *National Institute of Nutrition.* Retrieved June 12, 2003, from http://www.nin.ca/public_html/Publications/Rapport/ rapp1_93.html

Polivy, J., & Federoff, I. (1997). Group psychotherapy. In D. M. Garner & P. E. Garfinkel (Eds.), *Handbook of treatment for eating disorders* (2nd ed.) (pp. 462–475). New York: Guilford.

Rintala, M., & Mustajoki, P. (1992). Could mannequins menstruate? *British Medical Journal, 305,* 1575–1576.

Sacker, I. M., & Zimmer, M. A. (1987). *Dying to be thin: Understanding and defeating anorexia and bulimia.* NY: Warner.

Schlozman, S. S. (2002). The shrink in the classroom: Feast or famine? *Educational Leadership, 59,* 86–87.

Shapiro, S., Newcomb, M., & Loeb, T. B. (1997). Fear of fat, disregulated-restrained eating, and body-esteem: Prevalence and gender differences among eight to ten-year-old children. *Journal of Clinical Child Psychology, 26,* 358–365.

Shisslak, C. M., Crago, M., Olmstead, M., & Mays, M. A. (2002, April 29). A longitudinal analysis of patterns of disordered eating among adolescent girls from three ethnic groups. Paper presented at the International Conference on Eating Disorders, Boston, MA.

Smolak, L., & Striegel-Moore, R. (1996). The implications of developmental research for eating disorders. In L. Smolak, M. P. Levine, & R. Striegel-Moore (Eds.), *The developmental psychopathology of eating disorders: Implications for research, prevention, and treatment* (pp. 183–203). Mahwah, NJ: Erlbaum.

Steeves, S. (2000, October 19). Childhood teasing may lead to eating disorders. *WebMD Medical News Archive.* Retrieved June 12, 2003, from http://my.webmd.com/content/article/28/ 1727_62408

Stock, S. L., Goldberg, E., Corbett, S., & Katzman, D. K. (2002). Substance abuse in female adolescents with eating disorders. *Journal of Adolescent Health, 31,* 176–182.

Striegel-Moore, R. H., Garvin, V., Dohm, F. & Rosenheck, R. A. (1999). Psychiatric comorbidity of eating disorders in men: A national study of hospitalized veterans. *International Journal of Eating Disorders, 24,* 405–414.

Treasure, J. (1997). *Anorexia Nervosa: A survival guide for families, friends, and sufferers.* Philadelphia, PA: Taylor & Francis.

Tyrka, A. R., Waldron, I., Graber, J. A., Brooks-Gunn, J. (2002). Prospective predictors of the onset of anorexic and bulimic syndromes. *International Journal of Eating Disorders, 32,* 282–290.

van der Wege, A. J., & Vandereycken, W. (1995). The last word: Eating disorders and 'blindness' in clinicians. *Eating Disorders, 3,* 187–191.

Watson, T. L., Bowers, W. A., & Anderson, A. E. (2000). Involuntary treatment of eating disorders. *American Journal of Psychiatry, 157,* 1806–1810.

Wilson, G. T., Fairburn, C. G., & Agras, S. (1997). Cognitive-behavioral therapy for bulimia nervosa. In D. M. Garner & P. E. Garfinkel (Eds.), *Handbook of treatment for eating disorders* (2nd ed., pp. 67–93). NY: Guilford.

Wonderlich, S. A., Crosby, R. D., Mitchell, J. E., Roberts, J. A., Haseltine, B., DeMuth, G. R., & Thompson, K. M. (2000). Relationship of childhood sexual abuse and eating disturbances in children. *Journal of the American Academy of Child & Adolescent Psychiatry, 39,* 1277–1283.

Yager, A., & O'Dea, J. (2005). The role of teachers and other educators in the prevention of eating disorders and child obesity: What are the issues? *Eating Disorders, 13,* 261–278.

Zerbe, K. J. (1993). *The body betrayed: A deeper understanding of women, eating disorders, and treatment.* Carlsbad, CA: Gürze Books.

Chapter 4: Sexual Minorities

American Academy of Pediatrics. (1993). Homosexuality and adolescence. *Pediatrics, 92*, 631–634.

American Counseling Association. (2005). *ACA Code of Ethics*. Alexandria, VA: Author.

Anderson, J. D. (1994). School climate for gay and lesbian students and staff members. *Phi Delta Kappan, 76*, 151–154.

APA Online. (2005). *Just the facts about sexual orientation and youth: A primer for principals, educators, and school personnel*. Retrieved November 27, 2005, from http://www.apa.org/pi/lgbc/publications/ justthefacts.html

Appleby, Y. (1994). Out in the margins. *Disability & Society, 9*, 19–32.

Baker, J. M. (2002). *How homophobia hurts children: Nurturing diversity at home, at school, and in the community*. NY: Harrington Park Press.

Bauman, S. & Sachs-Kapp, P. (1998). A school takes a stand: Promotion of sexual orientation workshops by counselors. *Professional School Counseling, 1*, 42–45.

Bell, A. P., & Weinberg, M. S. (1978). *Homosexualities: A study of diversity among men and women*. NY: Simon and Schuster.

Besner, H. F., & Spungin, C. I. (1995). *Gay and lesbian students: Understanding their needs*. Washington, DC: Taylor & Francis.

Boden, R. (1992). Psychotherapy with disabled lesbians. In S. H. Dworkin & F. J. Gutiérrez (Eds.), *Counseling gay men and lesbians: Journey to the end of the rainbow* (pp. 157–187). Alexandria, VA: American Association for Counseling and Development.

Bontempo, D. E., & D'Augelli, A. R. (2002). Effects of at-school victimization and sexual orientation on lesbian, gay, or bisexual youths' health risk behavior. *Journal of Adolescent Health, 30*, 364–374.

Bozett, F. W. (1989). *Homosexuality and the family*. NY: Harrington Park Press.

Cass, V. C. (1979). Homosexual identity formation: A theoretical model. *Journal of Homosexuality, 4*, 219–235.

Chan, C. S. (1995). Issues of sexual identity in an ethnic minority: The case of Chinese American lesbians, gay men, and bisexual people. In A. R. D'Augelli & C. J. Patterson (Eds.), *Lesbian, gay, and bisexual identities over the lifespan* (pp. 87–101). NY: Oxford University Press.

Charles, C. (2003). *The Sharon Kowalski case: Lesbian and gay rights on trial*. Lawrence: University Press of Kansas.

Cochran, S. D. (2001). Emerging issues in research on lesbians' and gay men's mental health: Does sexual orientation really matter? *American Psychologist, 56*, 932–947.

Cochran, S. D., Sullivan, J. G., & Mays, V. M. (2003). Prevalence of mental disorders, psychological distress, and mental health services use among lesbian, gay, and bisexual adults in the United States. *Journal of Consulting and Clinical Psychology, 71*, 53–61.

Coleman, E. (1982). Developmental stages of the coming out process. *Journal of Homosexuality, 8*, 31–43.

Corliss, H. S., Cochran, S. D., & Mays, V. M. (2002). Reports of parental maltreatment during childhood in a United States population-based survey of homosexual, bisexual, and heterosexual adults. *Child Abuse and Neglect, 26*, 1165–1178.

Demme, J. (Director). (1993). *Philadelphia* [Motion picture]. United States: Tristar.

Dingfelder, S. F. (2005, December). The kids are all right. *APA Monitor, 36(11)*, 66.

Division 44/Committee on Lesbian, Gay, and Bisexual Concerns Joint Task Force (2000). *American Psychologist, 55*, 1440–1451.

Dworkin, S. H. (1997). Female, lesbian, and Jewish: Complex and invisible. In B. Greene (Ed.), *Ethnic and cultural diversity among lesbians and gay men* (pp. 63–87). Thousand Oaks, CA: Sage.

Dworkin, S. H., & Gutiérrez, F. J. (1992). *Counseling gay men & lesbians: Journey to the end of the rainbow*. Alexandria, VA: American Counseling Association.

Fontaine, J. H. (1998). Evidencing a need: School counselors' experiences with gay and lesbian students. *Professional School Counseling, 1*, 8–14.

Friend, R. (1991). Older lesbian and gay people: A theory of successful aging. *Journal of Homosexuality*, *20*, 99–118.

Garnets, L. (2002). Sexual orientations in perspective. *Cultural Diversity and Ethnic Minority Psychology*, *8*, 115–129.

Gay Lesbian and Straight Education Network. (2002). *Report of the NEA task force on sexual orientation*. NY: Author.

Greene, B. (1997). Ethnic minority lesbians and gay men: Mental health and treatment issues. In B. Greene (Ed.), *Ethnic and cultural diversity among lesbians and gay men* (pp. 216–239). Thousand Oaks, CA: Sage.

Guter, B., & Killacky, J. R. (2004). *Queer crips: Disabled gay men and their stories*. NY: Harrington Park Press.

Gutiérrez, F. J. (1992). Eros, the aging years: Counseling older gay men. In S. H. Dworkin & F. J. Gutiérrez (Eds.), *Counseling gay men and lesbians: Journey to the end of the rainbow* (pp. 49–60). Alexandria, VA: American Association for Counseling and Development.

Harris, M. B. (1997). *School experiences of gay and lesbian youth: The invisible minority*. NY: Harrington Park Press.

Hays, M. (2001, August 2). Visibly queer. *Montreal Mirror*. Retrieved January 1, 2006, from http://www.montrealmirror.com/ARCHIVES/2001/080201/cover.html

Herr, K. (1997). Learning lessons from school: Homophobia, heterosexism, and the construction of failure. In M. B. Harris (Ed.), *School experiences of gay and lesbian youth: The invisible minority*. NY: Harrington Park Press.

Hetrick, E., & Martin, A. (1987). Developmental issues and their resolution for gay and lesbian adolescents. *Journal of Homosexuality*, *14*, 25–42.

Huegel, K. (2003). *GLBTQ*:The survival guide for queer & questioning teens*. Minneapolis, MN: Free Spirit Publishing.

Human Rights Watch. (2001). *Hatred in the hallways: Violence and discrimination against lesbian, gay, bisexual, and transgender students in U.S. schools*. NY: Author.

Hunt, B., Matthews, C., Milsom, A., & Lammel, J. A. (2006). Lesbians with physical disabilities: A qualitative study of their experiences with counseling. *Journal of Counseling & Development*, *84*, 163–173.

Hunter, J. (1990). Violence against lesbian and gay male youths. *Journal of Interpersonal Violence*, *5*, 295–300.

Jacobs, S., Thomas, W., & Lang, S. (1997). *Introduction*. In S. Jacobs, W. Thomas, & S. Lang (Eds.), *Two-spirit people* (pp. 1–18). Urbana: University of Illinois Press.

Kaufman, M. (Director). (2002). *Laramie project*. [Motion picture]. United States: HBO.

Kimmel, D. C., & Sang, B. E. (1995). Lesbians and gay men in midlife. In A. R. D'Augelli, & C. J. Patterson (Eds.), *Lesbians, gays, and bisexual identities over the lifespan* (pp. 190–214). NY: Oxford University Press.

Kinsey, A. C., Pomeroy, W. B., & Martin, C. E. (1948). *Sexual behavior in the human male*. Philadelphia, PA: W. B. Saunders.

Kinsey, A. C., Pomeroy, W. B., Martin, C. E., & Gebhard, P. K. (1953). *Sexual behavior in the human female*. Philadelphia, PA: W. B. Saunders.

Lasala, M. (2000). Lesbians, gay men, and their parents: Family therapy for the coming-out crisis. *Family Process*, *39*, 67–81.

Lawson, W. (2005). *Sex, sexuality and the autistim spectrum*. London: Jessica Kingsley.

Lee, A. (Director). (2005). *Brokeback mountain*. [Motion picture]. United States: Focus Features.

Marans, S. R., & Cohen, D. J. (1991). Child psychoanalytic theories of development. In M. Lewis (Ed.), *Child and adolescent psychiatry: A comprehensive textbook* (pp. 129–144). Baltimore, MD: Williams & Wilkins.

Marsiglio, W. (1993). Attitudes towards homosexual activity and gays as friends: A national survey of heterosexual 15- to 19-year-old males. *Journal of Sex Research*, *30*, 12–17.

Martin, A. (1998). Clinical issues in psychotherapy with lesbian-, gay-, and bisexual-parented families. In C. J. Patterson & A. R. D'Augelli (Eds.), *Lesbian, gay, and bisexual identities in families* (pp. 270–291). NY: Oxford University Press.

Monette, P. (1992). *Becoming a man: Half a life story*. San Francisco: HarperCollins.

Monier, S. S. & Lewis, A. C. (2000). School counselors and sexual minority students. *Q: The Online Journal, 1(1)*, 1–16.

Morales, E. S. (1992). Counseling Latino gays and Latina lesbians. In S. H. Dworkin & F. J. Gutiérrez (Eds.), *Counseling gay men and lesbians: Journey to the end of the rainbow* (pp. 125–140). Alexandria, VA: American Association for Counseling and Development.

Morrison, L. L., & L'Heureux, J. (2001). Suicide and gay/lesbian/bisexual youth: Implications for clinicians. *Journal of Adolescence, 24*, 39–49.

Morrow, D. (1993). Social work with gay and lesbian adolescents. *Social Work, 38*, 655–660.

Muller, L. E. & Hartman, J. (1998). Group counseling for sexual minority youth. *Professional School Counseling, 1*, 38–41.

O'Conor, A. (1994). Who gets called queer in school? Lesbian, gay and bisexual teenagers, homophobia and high school. *The High School Journal, 77*, 7–12.

Orenstein, A. (2001). Substance use among gay and lesbian adolescents. *Journal of Homosexuality, 41(2)*, 1–15.

O'Toole, C. J., & Brigante, J. L. (1992). Lesbians with disabilities. *Sexuality and Disability, 10*, 163–172.

Pennington, D. A. (2002, September). Walking in the fine line. *Counseling Today, 45(3)*, 10–11.

Peplau, L. A., Cochran, S. D., & Mays, V. M. (1997). A national survey of the intimate relationships of African American lesbians and gay men. In B. Greene (Ed.), *Ethnic and cultural diversity among lesbians and gay men* (pp. 11–38). Thousand Oaks, CA: Sage

Peterson, J., & Bedogne, M. (2002). *A face in the crowd: Expressions of gay life in America*. Los Angeles: Prospect Publishing.

Pierce, K. (Director). (1999). *Boys don't cry*. [Motion picture]. United States: Fox Searchlight.

Pilkington, N. W., & D'Augelli, A. R. (1995). Victimization of lesbian, gay, and bisexual youth in community settings. *Journal of Community Psychology, 23*, 33–55.

Price, J. H. & Telljohann, S. K. (1991). School counselors' perceptions of adolescent homosexuals. *Journal of School Health, 61*, 433–438.

Reid, J. (1973). *The best little boy in the world*. NY: Ballantine.

Reynolds, A. L., & Koski, M. J. (1994). Lesbian, gay, and bisexual teens and the school counselor: Building alliances. *The High School Journal, 77*, 88–94.

Rostosky, S. S., & Riggle, E. D. B. (2002). "Out" at Work: The relation of actor and partner workplace policy and internalized homophobia to disclosure status. *Journal of Counseling Psychology, 49*, 411–419.

Russell, S. T., & Truong, N. L. (2001). Adolescent sexual orientation, race and ethnicity, and school environments: A national study of sexual minority youth of color. In K. Kumashiro (Ed.), *Troubling intersections of race and sexuality: Queer students of color and anti-oppressive education*. Lanham, UK: Rowman & Littlefield.

Ryan, C., & Futterman, D. (2001). Social and developmental challenges for lesbian, gay, and bisexual youth. *SIECUS Report, 29(4)*, 5–18.

Sadowski, M. (September/October 2001). Sexual minority students benefit from school-based support—where it exists. *Harvard Education Letter Research Online*. Retrieved October 20, 2002, from http://www.edletter.org/past/issues/2001-so/sexualminority.shtml

Sang, B. E. (1992). Counseling and psychotherapy with midlife and older lesbians. In S. H. Dworkin & F. J. Gutiérrez (Eds.), *Counseling gay men and lesbians: Journey to the end of the rainbow* (pp. 35–48). Alexandria, VA: American Association for Counseling and Development.

Savin-Williams, R. C. (1998). *". . . and then I became gay: Young men's stories*. NY: Routledge.

Sears, J. T. (1992). Educators, homosexuality, and homosexual students: Are personal feelings related to professional beliefs? In K. M. Harbeck, (Ed.), *Coming Out of the Classroom Closet: Gay and Lesbian Students, Teachers, and Curricula* (pp. 29–70). NY: Haworth Press.

Shakespeare, T. (1999). Coming out and coming home. *Journal of Gay, Lesbian, and Bisexual Identity, 4*, 39–51.

Shidlo, A., & Schroeder, M. (2002). Changing sexual orientation: A consumer's report. *Professional Psychology, Research, and Practice, 33*, 249–259.

Siecus (April/May, 2001). Fact sheet: Lesbian, Gay, Bisexual, and transgendered youth issues. *Siecus Report Supplement, 29*, 1–5.

Swartz, D. B. (1993). A comparative study of sex knowledge among hearing and deaf college freshmen. *Sexuality and Disability, 11*, 129–147.

Tafoya, T. (1997). Native gay and lesbian issues: The two-spirited. In B. Greene (Ed.), *Ethnic and cultural diversity among lesbians and gay men* (pp. 1–9). Thousand Oaks, CA: Sage.

Tessina, T. (1989). *Gay relationships*. NY: Putnam.

Tharinger, D., & Wells, G. (2000). An attachment perspective on the developmental challenges of gay and lesbian adolescents: The need for continuity of caregiving from family and schools. *The School Psychology Review, 29*, 158–172.

Thompson, K. & Andrzejewski, J. (1989). *Why can't Sharon Kowalski come home?* San Francisco: Aunt Lute Books.

Thompson, S. A., Bryson, M., & De Castell, S. (2001). Prospects for identity formation for gay, lesbian, and bisexual persons with developmental disabilities. *International Journal of Disability, Development, and Education, 48*, 53–65.

Tobias, A. (1998). *The best little boy in the world grows up*. NY: Random House.

Troiden, R. R. (1989). The formation of homosexual identities. *Journal of Homosexuality, 17*, 43–73.

Tucker, D. (Director). (2005). *Transamerica*. [Motion picture]. United States: IFC Films.

Wainright, J. L., Russell, S. T., & Patterson, C. J. (2004). Psychosocial adjustment, school outcomes, and romantic relationship of adolescents with same-sex parents. *Child Development, 75*, 1886–1898.

Wildman, S. (2000, October). Coming out early. *The Advocate*. Retrieved November 10, 2002, from http://www.advocate.com/html/stories/822/822_comingoutearly.asp

Wolf, T. (1992). Bisexuality: A counseling perspective. In S. H. Dworkin & F. J. Gutiérrez (Eds.), *Counseling gay men and lesbians: Journey to the end of the rainbow* (pp. 175–187). Alexandria, VA: American Association for Counseling and Development.

Chapter 5: Substance Abuse

Alcoholics Anonymous. (2002). *Alcoholics-Anonymous—Big book* (4th ed.). NY: Alcoholics Anonymous World Services.

Anthony, J. C., & Chen, C. Y. (2004). Epidemiology of drug dependence. In M. Galanter & H. D. Kleber, (Eds.), *Textbook of substance abuse treatment* (pp. 55–72). Washington, DC: American Psychiatric Publishing.

Associated Press. (2006, December 22). Study: Teens turning to legal medicines, including cough syrup to get their highs. *The Las Cruces Sun News*, p. 8A.

Athealth, Inc. (2001). Adolescent substance abuse: An interview with Howard A. Liddle, EdD. Retrieved October 15, 2005, from http://www.athealth.com/Practitioner/particles/interview_howardliddle.html.

Babor, T. F., de la Fuente, J. R., Saunders, J., & Grant, M. (1992). *AUDIT: The Alcohol Use Disorders Identification Test. Guidelines for use in primary health care*. Geneva: World Health Organization.

Bartsch, A. J., Homola, G., Biller, A., Smith, S. M., Weijers, H., Wiesbeck, G. A., Jenkinson, M., DeStefano, N., Solymosi, L., & Bendszus, M. (2007). Manifestations of early brain recovery associated with abstinence from alcoholism. *Brain, 130*, 36–47.

Beauvais, F., Oetting, E. R., Wolf, W., & Edwards, R. W. (1989). American Indian youth and drugs, 1976–87: A continuing problem. *American Journal of Public Health, 79*, 634–638.

Bell, T. (1990). *Preventing adolescent relapse: A guide for parents, teachers, and counselors.* Independence, MO: Herald/House Independence Press.

Benshoff, J. J., Harrawood, L. K., & Koch, D. S. (2003). Substance abuse and the elderly: Unique issues and concerns. *Journal of Rehabilitation, 69*, 43–48.

Berg, I. K., & Miller, S. D. (1992). *Working with the problem drinker.* NY: W. W. Norton.

Black, C. (1981). *It will never happen to me.* NY: Ballantine.

Bombardier, C. H., Blake, K. D., Ehde, D. M., Gibbons, L. Ed. Moore, D., & Kraft, G. H. (2004). Alcohol and drug abuse among persons with multiple sclerosis. *Multiple Sclerosis, 10*, 35–40.

Boyle, D. (Director). (1996). *Trainspotting* [Motion picture]. Ireland: Polygram.

Brady, K. T., & Malcolm, R. J. (2004). *Substance use disorders and co-occurring axis I psychiatric disorders.* In M. Galanter & H. D. Kleber, (Eds.), *Textbook of substance abuse treatment* (pp. 529–538). Washington, DC: American Psychiatric Publishing.

Brannigan, R., Schackman, B. R., Falco, M., & Millman, R. B. (2004). The quality of highly regarded adolescent substance abuse treatment programs: Results of an in-depth national survey. *Archives of Pediatrics and Adolescent Medicine, 158*, 904–909.

Burke, P. J., DaSilva, J. D., Vaughn, B. L., & Knight, J. R. (2005). Training high school counselors on the use of motivational interviewing to screen for substance abuse. *Substance Abuse, 26(3/4)*, 31–34.

Butler, K. (2006, July 4). The grim neurology of teenage drinking. *The New York Times.* Retrieved July 4, 2006, from www.nytimes.com/2006/07/04/health/04.teen.html

Campbell, C. I., & Alexander, J. A. (2002). Culturally competent treatment practices and ancillary service use in outpatient substance abuse treatment. *Journal of Substance Abuse Treatment, 22*, 109–119.

Caron, G. G. (Director). (1988). *Clean and sober* [Motion picture]. United States: Warner Bros.

Center for Treatment Research on Adolescent Drug Abuse. (2002). *Multidimensional Family Therapy (MDFT) for adolescent substance abuse.* University of Miami School of Medicine. Retrieved October 30, 2005, from http://www.osophs.dhhs.giv/ophs/BestPractice/ mdft_miami.html

Cloninger, C. R. (2004). Genetics of substance abuse. In M. Galanter & H. D. Kleber, (Eds.), *Textbook of substance abuse treatment* (pp. 73–80). Washington, DC: American Psychiatric Publishing.

Coll, K. (1995). Legal challenges in secondary prevention programming for students with substance abuse problems. *School Counselor, 43*, 35–41.

Conger, R. D. (1997). The social context of substance abuse: A developmental perspective. In E. B. Robertson, Z. Sloboda, G. M. Boyd, L. Beatty, & N. J. Kozel (Eds.), *Rural substance abuse: State of knowledge and issues* (Research Monograph No. 168, NIH Publication No. 97-4177, pp. 6–36). Washington, DC: National Institute on Drug Abuse.

Daisy, F., Thomas, L. R., & Worley, C. (1998). Alcohol use and harm reduction within the Native community. In G. A. Marlatt (Ed.), *Harm reduction: Pragmatic strategies for managing high-risk behaviors* (pp. 327–350). NY: Guilford.

De La Rosa, M. R., Holleran, L. K., Rugh, D., & MacMaster, S. A. (2005). Substance abuse among U.S. Latinos: A review of the literature. *Journal of Social Work Practice in the Addictions, 5*, 1–20.

DeBellis, M. D., Clark, D. B., Beers, S. R., Soloff, P. H., Boring, A. M., Hall, J., Kersh, A., & Keshavan, M. S. (2000). Hippocampal volume in adolescent-onset alcohol use disorders. *American Journal of Psychiatry, 157*, 737–744.

Denning, P., Little, J., & Glickman, A. (2004). *Over the influence: The harm reduction guide for managing drugs and alcohol.* NY: Guilford.

DeWitt, D. J., Adlaf, E. M., Offord, D. R., & Ogborne, A. C. (2000). Age at first alcohol use: A risk factor for the development of alcohol disorders. *American Journal of Psychiatry, 157*, 745–750.

Dimeff, L. A., Baer, J. S., Kivlahan, D. R., & Marlatt, G. A. (1999). *Brief alcohol screening and intervention for college students (BASICS): A harm reduction approach*. NY: Guilford.

Dishion, T. J., McCord, J., & Poulin, F. (1999). When interventions harm: Peer groups and problem behavior. *American Psychologist, 54*, 755–764.

Drug and Alcohol Services Information System. (2005, June 10). *Substance abuse treatment admissionsa-mong Asians and Pacific Islanders: 2002*. Retrieved March 16, 2007, from http://www.oas.samhsa.gov/2k5/AsianTX/AsianTX.htm

Edwards, B. (Director). (1962). *Days of wine and roses* [Motion picture]. United States: Warner Bros.

Edlerly Alcohol and Substance Abuse. (2005). Retrieved March 17, 2007, from http://www.oasas.state.ny.us/AdMed/pubs/FYIInDepth-Elderly,cfm

Ellis, A. (1992). *When AA doesn't work for you: Rational steps to quitting alcohol*. Ft. Lee, NJ: Barricade Books.

Ewing, J. A. (1984). Detecting alcoholism: The CAGE questionnaire. *JAMA, 25*, 1905–1907.

Figgis, M. (Director). (1995). *Leaving Las Vegas* [Motion picture]. United States: United Artists.

Fletcher, A. M. (2001). *Sober for good: New solutions for drinking problems—Advice from those who have succeeded*. NY: Houghton Mifflin.

Foster, S. E., Vaughan, R. D., Foster, W. H., & Califano, J. A. (2003). Alcohol consumption and expenditures for underage drinking and adult excessive drinking. *JAMA, 289*, 989–995.

Franklin, J., & Markarian, M. (2005). Substance abuse in minority populations. In R. J. Francis, S. I. Miller, & A. H. Mack (Eds.), *Clinical textbook of addictive disorders* (3rd ed., pp. 312–339). NY: Guilford.

Friel, J., & Friel, L. (1988). *Adult children: The secrets of dysfunctional families*. Deerfield Beach, FL: Health Communications.

Galanter, M., & Kleber, H. D. (2004). Preface. In M. Galanter & H. D. Kleber, (Eds.), *Textbook of substance abuse treatment* (pp. xvii–xviii). Washington, DC: American Psychiatric Publishing.

Gerard, S. (2005). Prevention and treatment of substance abuse in Native American communities. Presentation at the Phoenix IHS Area Health Summit, Arizona Department of Health Services, June 16, 2005.

Gerler, E. R., Jr., (1991). *The changing world of the elementary school counselor*. Ann Arbor, MI: ERIC Clearinghouse on Counseling and Personnel Services. (ERIC Document Reproduction Service No. ED328824)

Gerstein, D. R. (2004). Outcome research: Drug abuse. In M. Galanter & H. D. Kleber, (Eds.), *Textbook of substance abuse treatment* (pp. 137–147). Washington, DC: American Psychiatric Publishing.

Gfroerer, J. C. (2004, September 16). Substance use among older adults: Current prevalence and future expectations. Presentation at the conference, *Drug abuse in the 21st century: What problems lie ahead for the baby boomers*. Bethesda, Md.

Gfroerer, J. C., Penne, M. A., Pemberton, M. R., & Folsom, R. E., Jr. (2002). The aging baby boom cohort and future prevalence of substance abuse. In S. P. Korper, & C. L. Council, (Eds.), *Substance use by older adults: Estimates of future impact on the treatment system* (chapter 5). Rockville, MD: Department of Health and Human Services, Substance Abuse and Mental Health Services Administration, Office of Applied Studies. Available online at http://www.oas.samhsa.gov/aging/cov.htm

Greene, R. W., Biederman, J., Faraone, S. V., Wilens, T. E., Mick, E., & Blier, H. K. (1999). Further validation of social impairment as a predictor for substance use disorders: Findings from a sample of siblings of boys with and without ADHD. *Journal of Clinical Child Psychology, 28*, 349–354.

Guthmann, D., & Blozis, S. A. (2001). Unique issues faced by deaf individuals entering substance abuse treatment and following discharge. *American Annals of the Deaf, 146*, 294–304.

Hanson, G. R., & Li, T. K. (2003). Public health implications of excessive alcohol consumption. *JAMA, 289*, 1031–1032.

Harm reduction defined (n.d.). Retrieved June 28, 2006, from http://www.ukhra.org/ harm_reduction_definition.html

Health Problems in Hispanic American/Latina women: Alcoholism and illicit drug use. (n.d.). Retrieved October 29, 2005, from http://www.4women.gov/minority/hadrugs.cfm

Higgins, S. T., & Heil, S. H. (2004). Principles of learning in the study and treatment of substance abuse. In M. Galanter & H. D. Kleber (Eds.), *Textbook of substance abuse treatment* (pp. 81–88). Washington, DC: American Psychiatric Publishing.

Hommer, D. W., Momenon, R., Kaiser, B., & Rawlings, R. R. (2001). Evidence for a gender-related effect of alcoholism on brain volumes. *American Journal of Psychiatry, 158,* 198–204.

Jacobson, J. L., & Jacobson, S. W. (2003). *Effects of prenatal alcohol exposure on child development.* Retrieved March 17, 2007, from http://pubs.niaaa.nih.gov/publications/arh26-4/282-286.htm

Kaminer, Y., & Tarter, R. E. (2004). Adolescent substance abuse. In M. Galanter & H. D. Kleber (Eds.), *Textbook of substance abuse treatment* (pp. 505–518). Washington, DC: American Psychiatric Publishing.

Kandel, D. (Ed.). (2002). *Stages and pathways of drug involvement: Examining the gateway hypothesis.* Cambridge, UK: Cambridge University Press.

Kasl, C. S. (1992). *Many roads, one journey.* NY: Harper Paperbacks.

King, J. C. (1997). Substance abuse in pregnancy: A bigger problem than you think. *Postgraduate Medicine Online, 102(3).* Retrieved December 5, 2006, from http://www.postgradmed.com/ issues/1997/09_97/king.htm

Knight, J. R. (1997). Adolescent substance use: Screening, assessment, and intervention. *Contemporary Pediatrics, 14(4),* 45–72.

Knight, J. R., Sherritt, L., Shrier, L. A., Harris, S. K., & Chang, G. (2002). Validity of the CRAFFT substance abuse screening test among adolescent clinic patients. *Archives of Pediatric & Adolescent Medicine, 156,* 607–614.

Knight, J. R., Wechsler, H., Kuo, M, Seibring, M, Weitzman, E. R., & Schuckit, M. A. (2002). Alcohol abuse and dependence among U.S. college students. *Journal of Studies on Alcohol, 63,* 263–270.

Koch, D. S., Nelipovich, M., & Sneed, A. (2002). Alcohol and other drug abuse as coexisting disabilities: Considerations for counselors serving individuals who are blind or visually impaired. *RE:view, 33,* 151–159.

Lê, C., Ingvarson, E. P., & Page, R. C. (1995). Alcoholics Anonymous and the counseling profession: Philosophies in conflict. *Journal of Counseling & Development, 73,* 603–609.

Li, L., & Moore, D. (2001). Disability and illicit drug use: An application of labeling theory. *Deviant Behavior: An Interdisciplinary Journal, 22,* 1–21.

Liddle, H. A. (2002). *Multidimensional Family Therapy for Adolescent Cannabis Users, Cannabis Youth Treatment Series, Volume 5.* DHHS Pub. No. 02-3660. Rockville, MD: Center for Substance Abuse Treatment, Substance Abuse and Mental Health Services Administration.

Loue, S. (2003). *Diversity issues in substance abuse treatment and research.* NY: Kluwer.

Mandoki, L. (Director). (1994). *When a man loves a woman* [Motion picture]. United States: Buena Vista Productions.

Mann, D. (Director). (1955). *I'll cry tomorrow* [Motion picture]. United States: MGM.

Mann, K., Ackermann, K., Croissant, B., Mundle, G., Nakovics, H., & Diehl, A. (2005). Neuroimaging of gender differences in alcohol dependence: Are women more vulnerable? *Alcoholism: Clinical and Experimental Research, 29,* 896–901.

Marlatt, G. A. (2000). Harm reduction: Basic principles and strategies. *The Prevention Researcher, 7(2),* 1–4.

Marlatt, G. A., & Gordon, J. R. (Eds.). (1985). *Relapse prevention: Maintenance strategies in addictive behavior change.* NY: Guilford.

Mason, G. F. (2007). Get sober; stay sober. *Brain, 130,* 8–9.

Maude-Griffin, P. M., Hohenstein, J. M., Humnfleet, G. L., Reilly, P. M., Tusel, D. J., & Hall, S. M. (1998). Superior efficacy of cognitive-behavioral therapy for urban crack cocaine abusers: Main and matching effects. *Journal of Consulting and Clinical Psychology, 66,* 832–837.

McLaughlin, T., & Vacha, E. (1993). Substance abuse prevention in the schools: Roles for the school counselor. *Elementary School Guidance & Counseling, 28,* 124–132.

McLellan, A. T., Kushner, H., Metzger, D., Peters, F., Smith, I., Grissom, G., Pettinati, H., & Argeriou, M. (1992). The fifth edition of the Addiction Severity Index. *Journal of Substance Abuse Treatment, 9,* 199–213.

McLellan, A. T., Luborsky, L., O'Brien, C. P., & Woody, G. E. (1980). An improved diagnostic instrument for substance abuse patients: The Addiction Severity Index. *Journal of Nervous and Mental Disorders, 168,* 26–33.

Miller, G. A. (1999). *The Substance Abuse Subtle Screening Inventory (SASSI): Manual, Second Edition.* Springfield, IN: The SASSI Institute.

Miller, S. D., & Berg, I. K. (1995). *The miracle method: A radically new approach to problem drinking.* NY: W. W. Norton.

Miller, W. R., & Muñoz, R. E. (2005). *Controlling your drinking: Tools to make moderation work for you.* NY: Guilford.

Miller, W. R., & Rollnick, S. (1991). *Motivational Interviewing: Preparing people to change addictive behavior.* NY: Guilford.

Miller, W. R., & Tonigan, J. S. (1996). Assessing drinkers' motivation for change: The stages of change readiness and treatment eagerness scale (SOCRATES). *Psychology of Addictive Behaviors, 10,* 81–89.

Miller, W. R., Wilbourne, P. L., & Hettema, J. E. (2003). What works? A summary of alcohol treatment outcome research. In R. K. Hester & W. R. Miller (Eds.), *Handbook of alcoholism treatment approaches: Effective alternatives* (3rd ed.) (pp. 13–63). Boston, MA: Allyn & Bacon.

National Institute of Drug Abuse. (1999). *Principles of drug addiction treatment: A research based guide.* [NIH Publication No. 99-4180]. Washington, DC: Author.

National Institute of Drug Abuse. (2005). *Inhalant abuse.* Washington, DC: Author.

Nelson, N. T., & Wechsler, H. (2003). School spirits: Alcohol and collegiate sports fans. *Addictive Behaviors, 28(1),* 1–11.

Obert, J. L., McCann, M. J., Marinelli-Casey, P., Weiner, A., Minsky, S., Brethen, P., & Rawson, R. (2000). The Matrix Model of outpatient stimulant abuse treatment: History and description. *Journal of Psychoactive Drugs, 32,* 157–164.

Ogilvie, H. (2001). *Alternatives to abstinence.* NY: Hatherleigh Press.

Onen, S. H., Onen, F., Mangeon, J., Abidi, H., Courpron, P., & Schmidt, J. (2005). Alcohol abuse and dependence in elderly emergency department patients. *Archives of Gerontology & Geriatrics, 41,* 191–200.

Pita, D. D. (1994). *Addictions counseling.* NY: Crossroad.

Poulin, F., Dishion, T. J., & Burraston, B. (2001). 3-year iatrogenic effects associated with aggregating high-risk adolescents in cognitive-behavioral prevention interventions. *Applied Developmental Science, 5,* 214–224.

Preminger, O. (Director). (1955). *The man with a golden arm* [Motion picture]. United States: United Artists.

Prochaska, J., & DiClemente, C. (198). Stages and processes of self-change of smoking: Toward an integrative model of change. *Journal of Consulting and Clinical Psychology, 51,* 390–395

Prochaska, J., Norcross, J., & DiClemente, C. (1995). *Changing for good.* NY: Collins.

Rendon, M. E. (1992). Deaf culture and alcohol and substance abuse. *Journal of Substance Abuse Treatment, 9,* 103–110.

Riley, D. & O'Hare, P. (2000). Harm reduction: Policy and practice. *The Prevention Researcher, 7(2):* 4–8.

Schulenberg, J., Maggs, J. L., Steinman, K. J., & Zucker, R. A. (2001). Development matters: Taking the long view on substance abuse etiology and intervention during adolescence. In P. M. Monti, S. M. Colby, & T. A. O'Leary (Eds.), *Adolescents, alcohol, and substance abuse* (pp. 19–57). NY: Guilford.

Selzer, M. I. (1971). The Michigan alcohol screening test: The quest for a new diagnostic instrument. *American Journal of Psychiatry, 127,* 1653–1658.

Spear, L. P. (2000). The adolescent brain and age-related behavioral manifestations. *Neuroscience & Biobehavioral Reviews, 24*, 417–463.

Spear, L. (2002). The adolescent brain and the college drinker: Biological basis of propensity to use and misuse alcohol. *Journal of Studies on Alcohol, Supplement 14*, 71–81.

Substance Abuse and Mental Health Services Administration. (1998). *TIP 29: Substance use disorder treatment for people with physical and cognitive disabilities* (DHHS Publication No. (SMA) 98-3249). Rockville, MD: Public Health Service.

Tarter, R. E. (1990). Evaluation and treatment of adolescent substance abuse: A decision tree method. *American Journal of Drug and Alcohol Abuse, 16*, 1–46.

Tarter, R. E. (2002). Etiology of adolescent substance abuse: A developmental perspective. *The American Journal on Addictions, 11*, 171–191.

Trimpey, J. (1995). *The small book* (rev. ed.). NY: Dell.

Trimpey, J. (1996). *Rational recovery: The new cure for substance addiction.* NY: Pocket.

United States Department of Health and Human Services, National Institutes of Health. (2003). *Drug use among racial/ethnic minorities.* (Revised). [NIH Publication No. 03-3888. Rockville, MD: Author.

Virginia Department of Mental Health, Mental Retardation and Substance Abuse. (2003). *Reviews to use: Current literature reviews for the substance abuse professional.* Retrieved November 28, 2005, from http://www.dmhmrsas.virginia.gov/documents/OSAS-RETreatmentAfricanAmericans.doc

Volkow, N. D. (2006). Steroid abuse is a high-risk route to the finish line. *NIDA Notes, 21(1)*, 2.

Wallace, J. M., Bachman, J. G., O'Malley, P. M., Schulenberg, J. E., Cooper, S. M., & Johnston, L. D. (2003). Gender and ethnic differences in smoking, drinking, and illicit drug use among American 8th, 10th, and 12th grade students, 1976–2000. *Addiction, 98*, 225–234.

Walton, M. A., Blow, F. C., & Booth, B. M. (2001). Diversity in relapse prevention needs: Gender and rage comparisons among substance abuse treatment patients. *American Journal of Drug and Alcohol Abuse, 27*, 225–240.

Watkins, K. E., Ellickson, P. L., Vaiana, M. E., & Hiromoto, S. (2006). An update on adolescent drug use: What school counselors need to know. *Professional School Counseling, 10*, 131–138.

Wegscheider-Cruse, S. (1989). *Another chance: Hope and health for the alcoholic family.* Palo Alto, CA: Science and Behavior Books.

Westermeyer J., Yargic I., & Thuras P. (2004). Michigan Assessment-Screening Test for Alcohol and Drugs (MAST/AD): Evaluation in a clinical sample. *American Journal on Addictions, 13*, 151–162.

Whelan, G. (2003). A much neglected risk factor in elderly mental disorders. *Current Opinions in Psychiatry, 16*, 609–614.

Whitehouse, A., Sherman, R., & Kozlowski, K. (1991). The needs of deaf substance abusers in Illinois. *American Journal of Drug and Alcohol Abuse, 17*, 103–114.

Whitten, L. (2006). Low-cost incentives improve outcomes in stimulant abuse treatment. *NIDA Notes, 21(1)*, 1, 6–7.

Why elementary counselors. (n.d.) Retrieved January 4, 2007, from http://www.school-counselor.org/content.asp?contentid=230

Widlitz, M., & Marin, D. B. (2002). Substance abuse in older adults: An overview. *Geriatrics, 57*, 29–34.

Wilder, B. (Director). (1945). *The lost weekend* [Motion picture]. United States: Paramount.

Wills, T. A., McNamara, G., Vaccaro, D., & Hirky, A. E. (1997). Escalated substance use: A longitudinal grouping analysis from early to middle adolescence. In G. A. Marlatt & G. R. VandenBos (Eds.), *Addictive behaviors: Readings on etiology, prevention, and treatment.* Washington, DC: American Psychological Association.

Woods, I. P. (1998). Bringing harm reduction to the Black community: There's a fire in my house and you're telling me to rearrange the furniture? In G. A. Marlatt (Ed.), *Harm reduction: Pragmatic strategies for managing high-risk behavior* (pp. 301–326). NY: Guilford.

Zickler, P. (2006). Buprenorphine plus behavioral therapy is effective for adolescents with opioid addiction. *NIDA Notes, 21(1)*, 7–8.

Chapter 6: Suicide

American Association of Suicidology. (n.d.). Some facts about suicide in the U.S.A. Retrieved September 2, 2004, from http://www.suicidology.org/displaycommon.cfm?an=1&sub-articlenbr=44

Bauman, S. (in press). Suicide prevention, intervention, and postvention. In H. L. K. Coleman & C. J. Yeh (Eds.), *Handbook of school counseling*. Mahwah, NJ: Lawrence Erlbaum Associates, Inc.

Blumenthal, S. J., & Kupfer, D. J. (Eds.). (1990). *Suicide over the life cycle: Risk factors, assessment, and treatment of suicidal patients*. Washington, DC: American Psychiatric Press.

Bogue, N. (Producer). (1996). *Choice of a lifetime: Returning from the brink of suicide* [Motion picture]. Canada: Fanlight Productions.

Canino, G., & Roberts, R. E. (2001). Suicidal behavior among Latin youth. *Suicide and Life-Threatening Behavior, 31*, 122–131.

Capuzzi, D. (1994). *Suicide prevention in the schools: Guidelines for middle and high school settings*. Alexandria, VA: American Counseling Association.

Capuzzi, D. (Ed.). (2004). *Suicide across the life span: Implications for counselors* (pp. 95–138). Alexandria, VA: American Counseling Association.

Charlifue, S. W., & Gerhart, K. A. (1991). Behavioral and demographic predictors of suicide after traumatic spinal cord injury. *Archives of Physical and Medical Rehabilitation, 72*, 488–492.

Chung, R. C-Y. (2002). Combatting racism: Speaking up and speaking out. In J. Kottler (Ed.), *Finding your way as a counselor* (2nd ed., pp. 105–108). Alexandria, VA: American Counseling Association.

Conwell, Y. (1997). Management of suicidal behaviors in the elderly. *Psychiatric Clinics of North America, 20*, 667–683.

Curry, J. (2001). Specific psychotherapies for childhood and adolescent depression. *Biological Psychiatry, 49*, 1091–1100.

Davis, D. K. (Producer). (1999). *Remembering Tom* [Motion picture]. Canada: Fanlight Productions.

Davis, T. (2004). Counseling suicidal children. In D. Capuzzi (Ed.), *Suicide across the life span: Implications for counselors* (pp. 211–234). Alexandria, VA: American Counseling Association.

DeLeo, D., Hickey, P. A., Meneghel, G., & Cantor, M. B. (1999). Blindness, fear of sight loss, and suicide. *Psychosomatics, 40*, 339–344.

Dubicka, C., & Goodyer, I. (2005). Should we prescribe antidepressants to children? *Psychiatric Bulletin, 29*, 164–167.

Ellen, E. F. (2002, August). Identifying and treating suicidal college students. *Psychiatric Times, 19(8)*. Available at http://www.psychiatrictimes.com

Ellen, E. F. (2002, October). Suicide prevention on campus. *Psychiatric Times, 19(10)*. Available at http://www.psychiatrictimes.com

Emslie, G. J., & Mayes, T. L. (2001). Mood disorders in children and adolescents: Psychopharmacological treatment. *Biological Psychiatry, 49*, 1082–1090.

Feinstein, A. (2002). An examination of suicidal intent in patients with multiple sclerosis. *Neurology, 59*, 674–678.

Foster, C. A., & McAdams III, C. R. (1999). The impact of client suicide in counseling training: Implications for counseling education and supervision. *Counselor Education & Supervision, 39*, 22–34.

Garlow, S. J., Purcelle, D., & Heninger, M. (2005). Ethnic differences in patterns of suicide across the life cycle. *American Journal of Psychiatry, 162*, 319–323.

Gary, F. A., Baker, M., & Grandbois, D. M. (2005). Perspectives on suicide prevention among American Indian and Alaska native children and adolescents: A call for help. *Online Journal of Issues in Nursing, 10*, 6.

Giles, C. (1997). *Structured Clinical Interview for Suicide Risk (SCISR)* (unpublished scale).

Gliatto, M. F., & Rai, A. K. (1999). Evaluation and treatment of patients with suicidal ideation. *American Family Physician*, March 15.

Goldman, S., & Beardslee, W. R. (1999). Suicide in children and adolescents. In D. G. Jacobs (Ed.), *The Harvard Medical School guide to suicide assessment and intervention* (pp. 417–442). San Francisco: Jossey-Bass.

Goldston, D. B. (2003). *Measuring suicidal behavior and risk in children and adolescents.* Washington, DC: American Psychological Association.

Haley, M. (2004). Risk and protective factors. In D. Capuzzi (Ed.), *Suicide across the life span: Implications for counselors* (pp. 95–138). Alexandria, VA: American Counseling Association.

Hanna, F. J., & Green, A. G. (2004). Hope and suicide: Establishing the will to live. In D. Capuzzi, (Ed.), *Suicide across the life span* (pp. 63–92). Alexandria, VA: American Counseling Association.

Hartkopp, A., Brønnum-Hansen, H., Seidenschnur, A., & Biering-Sørensen, F. (1998). Suicide in spinal cord injured population: In relation to functional status. *Archives of Physical and Medical Rehabilitation, 79,* 1356–1361.

Harrington, R., Whittaker, J., & Shoebridge, P. (1998). Psychological treatment of depression in children and adolescents: A review of treatment research. *British Journal of Psychiatry, 173,* 291–298.

Henderson, D. (2006, September 20). Half of deaf people have felt suicidal, survey finds. *The Herald.* Retrieved January 4, 2007, from http://www.theherald.co.uk/news/70364-print.shtml

Hollon, S. D., Thase, M. E., & Markowtiz, J. C. (2002). Treatment and prevention of depression. *Psychological Science in the Public Interest, 3,* 39–71.

Hurlbut, S. C., & Sher, K. J. (1992). Assessing alcohol problems in college students. *College Health, 41,* 49–58.

Jacobs, D. G. (Ed.). (1999). *The Harvard Medical School guide to suicide assessment and intervention.* San Francisco: Jossey-Bass.

Joe, S., Baser, R. E., Breeden, G., Neighbors, H. W., & Jackson, J. S. (2006). Prevalence and risk factors for lifetime suicide attempts among blacks in the United States. *JAMA, 296,* 2112–2123.

Juhnke, G. A. (1994). Sad Persons scale review. *Measurement & Evaluation in Counseling & Development, 27,* 325–328.

Juhnke, G. A. (1996). The Adapted-Sad Persons: A suicide assessment scale designed for use with children. *Elementary School Guidance & Counseling, 30,* 252–259.

Kaldenberg, J. (2005). Vision-related issues facing baby boomers and the elderly population. Presentation at the White House Conference on Aging Solutions, December 2005. Retrieved January 6, 2007, from http://www.whcoa.gov

Kalichman, S. C., Heckman, T., Kochman, A., Sikkema, K., & Bergholte, J. (2000). Depression and thoughts of suicide among middle-aged and older persons living with HIV-AIDS. *Psychiatric Services, 51,* 903–907.

Kaplan, H. I., Sadock, B. J., & Grebb, J. A. (1994). *Synopsis of psychiatry: Behavioral sciences: Clinical psychiatry* (7th ed.). Baltimore, MD: Williams & Wilkins.

Kessler, R. C., Borges, G., & Walters, E. E. (1999). Prevalence of and risk factors for lifetime suicide attempts in the national comorbidity survey. *Archives of General Psychiatry, 56,* 617–626.

Kirk, W. G. (1993). *Adolescent suicide: A school-based approach to assessment and intervention.* Champaign, IL: Research Press.

León-Carrión, J., Sedio-Arias, M. L., Cabezas, F. M., Roldan, J. M. D., Domínguez-Morales, R., Barroso y Martín, J. M., & Sanchez, M. A. M. (2001). Neurobehavioral and cognitive profile of traumatic brain injury patients at risk for depression and suicide. *Brain Injury, 15,* 175–181.

Mann, J. J. (2002). A current perspective of suicide and attempted suicide. *Annual of Internal Medicine, 136,* 302–311.

March, J., Silva, S., Petrycki, S., Curry, J., Wells, K., & Fairbank, J., et al. (2004). Fluoxetine, cognitive-behavioral therapy, and their combination for adolescents with depression. *JAMA, 292,* 807–820.

Matthews, S., & Paxton, R. (2001). *Suicide risk: A guide for primary care and mental health staff.* Northumberland, UK: Newcastle, North Tyneside and Northumberland Mental Health NHS Trust.

Moscicki, E. K. (1997). Identification of suicide risk factors using epidemiologic studies. *Psychiatric Clinics of North America, 20,* 499–517.

Motto, J. A. (1999). Critical points in the assessment and management of suicide risk. In D. G. Jacobs (Ed.), *The Harvard Medical School guide to suicide assessment and intervention* (pp. 224–238). San Francisco: Jossey-Bass.

Mufson, L., Weissman, M. M., Donna Moreau, D., & Garfinkel, R. (1999). Efficacy of interpersonal psychotherapy for depressed adolescents. *Archives of General Psychiatry, 56,* 573–579.

National Institute of Mental Health. (2003). *In harm's way: Suicide in America.* Bethesda, MD: Author. NIMH Publication No. 03-4594. Available online at http://www.nimh.nih.publicat/harmaway.cfm

National Institute of Mental Health. (2005). *Depression is a serious medical condition . . .* Retrieved March 16, 2007, from http://menanddepression.nimh.nih.gov/clientfiles/menanddep.pdf

Nowack, W. J. (2006, August 29). *Psychiatric disorders associated with epilepsy.* Retrieved January 3, 2007, from http://www.emedicine.com/NEURO/topic604.html

Osgood, N. J., & Thielman, S. (1990). Geriatric suicidal behavior: Assessment and treatment. In S. J. Blumenthal & D. J. Kupfer (Eds.), *Suicide over the life cycle: Risk factors, assessment, and treatment of suicidal patients* (pp. 341–380). Washington, DC: American Psychiatric Press.

Patterson, W. M., Dohn, H. H., Bird, J., & Patterson, G. (1983). Evaluation of suicidal patients: The SAD PERSONS scale. *Psychosomatics, 24,* 343–349.

Poland, S. (1989). *Suicide intervention in the schools.* NY: Guilford.

Potter, L. B., Kresnow, M., Powerrl, K. E., Simon, T. R., Mercy, J. A., Lee, R. K., Frankowski, R. F., Swann, A. C., Bayer, T., & O'Carroll, P. W. (2001). The influence of geographic mobility on nearly lethal suicide attempts. *Suicide and Life Threatening Behavior, 32 (Supplement),* 42–48.

Remley, T. P. (2004). Suicide and the law. In D. Capuzzi (Ed.), *Suicide across the lifespan* (pp. 185–208). Alexandria, VA: American Counseling Association.

Rossello, J., & Bernal, G. (1999). The Efficacy of Cognitive-Behavioral and Interpersonal Treatments for depression in Puerto Rican adolescents. *Journal of Consulting and Clinical Psychology, 67,* 734–745.

Russell, S. T. (2003). Sexual minority youth and suicide risk. *American Behavioral Scientist, 46,* 1241–1257.

Ryan, C., & Futterman, D. (1998). *Lesbian and gay youth: Care and counseling.* NY: Columbia University Press.

Sander, J. W., & Bell, G. S. (2004). Reducing mortality: An important aim of epilepsy management. *Journal of Neurology, Neurosurgery and Psychiatry, 75,* 349–351.

Schonfeld, D. J., Lichtenstein, R., Pruett, M. K., & Speese-Linehan, D. (2002). *How to prepare for and respond to a crisis* (2nd ed.). Alexandria, VA: Association for Supervision and Curriculum Development.

Schwartz, A. J., & Whitaker, L. C. (1990). Suicide among college students: Assessment, treatment, and intervention. In S. J. Blumenthal & D. J. Kupfer (Eds.), *Suicide over the life cycle: Risk factors, assessment, and treatment of suicidal patients* (pp. 303–340). Washington, DC: American Psychiatric Press.

Shea, S. C. (2002). *The practical art of suicide assessment: A guide for mental health professionals and substance abuse counselors.* Hoboken, NJ: John Wiley.

Siehl, P. M. (1990). Suicide postvention: A new disaster plan—what a school should do when faced with a suicide. *School Counselor, 38,* 52–58.

Simon, S. R. S. (2004). Counseling suicidal adults: Rebuilding connections. In D. Capuzzi (Ed.), *Suicide across the life span: Implications for counselors* (pp. 271–304). Alexandria, VA: American Counseling Association.

Simpson, G., & Tate, R. (2005). Clinical features of suicide attempts after traumatic brain injury. *The Journal of Nervous and Mental Diseases, 193,* 680–685.

Spirito, A., Boergers, J., & Donaldson, D. (2000). Adolescent suicide attempters: Post-attempt course and implications for treatment. *Child Psychology and Psychotherapy, 7,* 161–173.

Stefanowski-Harding, S. (1990). Child suicide: A review of the literature and implications for school counselors. *School Counselor, 37,* 328–340.

Stillion, J. M., & McDowell, E. E. (1996). *Suicide across the lifespan: Premature exits* (2nd ed.). Washington, DC: Taylor & Francis.

Thompson, R. A. (1995). Being prepared for suicide or sudden death in schools: Strategies to restore equilibrium. *Journal of Mental Health Counseling, 17,* 264–278.

Waern, M., Rubenowitz, E., Runeson, B., Skoog, I., Wilhelmson, K., & Allebeck, P. (2002). Burden of illness and suicide in elderly people: Case-control study. *British Medical Journal, 324,* 1355–1358.

Webb, L. D., & Metha, A. (1996). Suicide in American Indian youth: The role of the schools in prevention. *Journal of American Indian Education, 36,* 22–32.

Wertheimer, A. (1991). *A special scar: The experiences of people bereaved by suicide.* London: Routledge.

World Health Organization. (2002). *Preventing Suicide: A resource for general physicians.* Geneva: Author.

Chapter 7: Trauma and Violence

American Psychiatric Association. (1980). *Diagnostic and statistical manual of mental disorders* (3rd ed.). Washington, DC: Author.

Anonymous. (2002). *Working with children traumatized by homicide handbook.* Retrieved online June 5, 2006, from http://www.avpphila.org/ovcmanual2002/sec10.crimj.pdf

Anonymous. (2005). Critical Incident Stress Management. Retrieved June 10, 2006, from http://www.psychiatrictimes.com/p040471.html

Arvay, M. J. (2002). Secondary traumatic stress among trauma counsellors: What does the research say? *International Journal for the Advancement of Counselling, 23,* 283–293.

Augustyn, M., & Groves, B. M. (2005). Training clinicians to identify the hidden victims: Children and adolescents who witness violence. *American Journal of Preventive Medicine, 29,* 272–278.

Averill, P. A., & Beck, J. G. (2000). Posttraumatic stress disorder in older adults: A conceptual review. *Journal of Anxiety Disorders, 14,* 133–156.

Baggerly, J. (2005). Systematic trauma interventions for children: A 12-step protocol. In J. Webber, D. D. Bass, & R. Wong (Eds.), *Terrorism, trauma, and tragedies: A counselor's guide to preparing and responding* (2nd ed., pp. 97–102). Alexandria, VA: American Counseling Association.

Bain, J. E., & Brown, R. T. (1996). Adolescents as witnesses to violence. *Journal of Adolescent Health, 19,* 83–85.

Bolton, D., O'Ryan, D., Udwin, O., Boyle, S., & Yule, W. (2000). The long-term psychological effects of a disaster experienced in adolescence: II: General psychopathology. *Journal of Child Psychology and Child Psychiatry, 41,* 513–523.

Boscarino, J. A., Figley, C. R., & Adams, R. E. (2004). Compassion fatigue following the September 11 terrorist attacks: A study of secondary trauma among New York City social workers. *International Journal of Emergency Mental Health, 6(2),* 1–10.

Briere, J. (1995). *Trauma symptom checklist: Professional manual.* Lutz, FL: Psychological Assessment Resources.

Briere, J. (1996). *Trauma symptom checklist for children: Professional manual.* Lutz, FL: Psychological Assessment Resources.

Briere, J. (2005). *Trauma symptom checklist for young children: Professional manual.* Lutz, FL: Psychological Assessment Resources.

Busuttil, W. (2004). Presentations and management of post traumatic stress disorder and the elderly: A need for investigation. *International Journal of Geriatric Psychiatry, 19,* 429–439.

Carlson, E. B. (1997). *Trauma assessments: A clinician's guide.* NY: Guilford.

Charlton, M., Kliethermes, M., Tallant, B., Taverne, A., & Tishelman, A. (2004). *Facts on traumatic stress and children with developmental disabilities.* Louisiana: National Child Traumatic Stress Network.

Chemtob, C. M., Nakashima, J. P., & Hamada, R. S. (2002). Psychosocial intervention for postdisaster trauma symptoms in elementary school children. *Archives of Pediatric and Adolescent Medicine, 156*, 211–216.

Cimino, M. (Director). (1978). *The deer hunter* [Motion picture]. United States: Universal.

Cohen, J. A., Berliner, L., & Marsh, J. S. (2000). Treatment of children and adolescents. In E. B. Foa, T. M. Keane, & M. J. Friedman (Eds.), *Effective treatments for PTSD* (pp. 106–138). NY: Guilford.

Cohen, J. A., Perel, J. M., DeBellis, M. D., Friedman, M. J., & Putnam, F. W. (2002). Treating traumatized children: Clinical implications of the psychobiology of posttraumatic stress disorder. *Trauma, Violence, & Abuse, 32*, 91–108.

Cook, J. M. (2002). Traumatic exposure and PTSD in older adults: Introduction to the special issue. *Journal of Clinical Geropsychology, 8*, 149–152.

Cook, J. M., & O'Donnell, C. (2005). Assessment and psychological treatment of posttraumatic stress disorder in older adults. *Journal of Geriatric Psychiatry and Neurology, 18*, 61–71.

Conroy, P. (1995). *Beach music*. NY: Doubleday.

Cronin, D. L. (2005). Building partnerships for the protection of persons with disabilities. *Critical Response, 2(4)*, 1.

DeBellis, M. D. (1999). Developmental traumatology: Neurobiological development in maltreated children with PTSD. *Psychiatric Times, 169(9)*. Retrieved online June 10, 2006, from http://www.psychiatrictimes.com/p990968.html

Deblinger, E., Thakkar-Kolar, R., & Ryan, E. (2006). Trauma in childhood. In V. M. Follette & J. I. Ruzek (Eds.), *Cognitive behavioral therapies for trauma* (2nd ed.). (pp. 405–432). NY: Guilford.

DiGallo, A., Barton, J., & Parry-Jones, W. L. (1997). Road traffic accidents: Early psychological consequences in children and adolescents. *British Journal of Psychiatry, 170*, 358–362.

Disabled Women's Network Ontario. (n.d.). Family violence against women with disabilities. Retrieved December 28, 2006, from http://dawn.thot.net/violence_wwd.html

Durity, R., Garry, A., Mallah, K., Nicolaisen, J., Oxman, A., Sterritt, M., & Stewart, A. (2004). *Facts on trauma and deaf children*. Louisiana: National Child Traumatic Stress Network.

Dutton, M. A. (1992). *Empowering and healing the battered woman*. NY: Springer.

Engdahl, B E., & Eberly, R. E. (1994, Winter). Assessing PTSD among veterans exposed to war trauma 40–50 years ago. *NCP Clinical Quarterly, 4(1)*, 13–14.

Eth, S., & Pynoos, R. S. (1985). *Post-traumatic stress disorder in children*. Washington, DC: American Psychiatric Press.

Everly, G. S. (2000). Five principles of crisis intervention: Reducing the risk of premature crisis intervention. *International Journal of Emergency Mental Health, 2*, 1–4.

Feldman, E. (2005). *The boy who loved Anne Frank*. NY: W. W. Norton.

FEMA. (2006, March 23). *Hurricane preparedness for people with disabilities*. (Release Number: 1605-199). Retrieved January 3, 2007, from http://www.fema.gov/news/newsrelease.fema?id=24487

Findings from the National Violence Against Women Survey. (2000, July). Retrieved June 15, 2006, from http://infoplease.com/ipa/A0875303.html

Flannery, R. B. (1999). Psychological trauma and posttraumatic stress disorder: A review. *International Journal of Emergency Mental Health, 2*, 135–140.

Foa, E. B., Keane, T. M., & Friedman, M. J. (2000). *Effective treatments for PTSD*. NY: Guilford.

Follette, V. M., & Ruzek, J. I. (2006). *Cognitive-behavioral therapies for trauma* (2nd ed.). NY: Guilford.

France, D. (2006, February). And then he hit me. *AARP Magazine*, 81–85, 112.

Frazier, P. Y., Slatt, L., Kowlowitz, V., & Glowa, P. T. (2001). Using the stages of change model to counsel victims of intimate partner violence. *Patient Education and Counseling, 43*, 211–217.

Frueh, B. C., Brady, K. L., & de Arrelano, M. A. (1998). Racial differences in combat-related PTSD: Empirical findings and conceptual issues. *Clinical Psychology Review, 18*, 287–305.

Galea, S., Ahern, J., Resnick, H., Kilpatrick, D., Bucuvalas, M., Gold, J., & Vlahov, D. (2002). Psychological sequelae of the September 11 terrorist attacks in New York City. *New England Journal of Medicine, 346*, 982–987.

Golding, J. M. (1999). Intimate partner violence as a risk factor for mental health disorders: A meta-analysis. *Journal of Family Violence, 14*, 99–132.

Green, B. L., Grace, M. C., & Lindy, J. D. (1990). Race differences in response to combat stress. *Journal of Traumatic Stress, 3*, 379–393.

Grossman, A. B., Levin, B. E., Katzen, H. L., & Lechner, S. (2004). PTSD symptoms and onset of neurologic disease in elderly trauma survivors. *Journal of Clinical and Experimental Neuropsychology, 26*, 698–705.

Gurwitch, R. H., Silovsky, J. F., Shultz, S., Kees, M., & Burlingame, S. (2003). What to expect after trauma: Possible reactions in middle and high school students. *The Prevention Researcher, 10(2)*, 11.

Gurwitch, R. H., Silovsky, J. F., Shultz, S., Kees, M., & Burlingame, S. (2006). *Reactions and guidelines for children following trauma/disaster*. Washington, DC: American Psychological Association. Retrieved June 5, 2006, from http://www.apa.org/practice/ptguideliens.html

Hattendorf, J., & Tollerud, T. (1997). Domestic violence: Counseling strategies that minimize the impact of secondary victimization. *Perspectives in Psychiatric Care, 33*, 14–24.

Herman, J. (1997). *Trauma and recovery*. NY: Basic Books.

Hoge, C., Castro, C., Messer, S., McGurk, D., Cotting, D., & Koffman, R. (2004). Combat duty in Iraq and Afghanistan: Mental health problems and barriers to care. *New England Journal of Medicine, 351*, 13–22.

Horowitz, M., Wilner, N., & Alvarez, W. (1979). Impact of Events Scale: A measure of subjective stress. *Psychosomatic Medicine, 41*, 209–218.

Hudson, W. W., & McIntosh, S. R. (1981). The assessment of spouse abuse: Two quantifiable dimensions. *Journal of Marriage and Family, 43*, 873–885, 888.

Hughes, M. J., & Jones, L. (2000). *Women, domestic violence, and posttraumatic stress disorder (PTSD)*. Retrieved online June 27, 2006, from http://www.csus.edu/calst/government_affairs/reports/ffp32.pdf

Husseini, K. (2003). *The kite runner*. NY: Riverhead Books.

Jackson, H. (2004). *Helping students cope with trauma and loss*. Online training course available at http://ci.columbia.edu/w0521/index.html

Jackson, S., Feder, L., Forde, D., Davis, R., Maxwell, C., & Taylor, B. (2003). *Batterer intervention programs: Where do we go from here?* National Institute of Justice Special Report, NCJ 195079.

Janoff-Bulman, R. (1992). *Shattered assumptions: Towards a new psychology of trauma*. NY: The Free Press.

Johnson, K. (1998). *Trauma in the lives of children*. Alameda, CA: Hunter House.

Jones, D. (Director). (1989). *Jackknife* [Motion picture]. United States: Kings Road Entertainment.

Jones, L., Hughes, M., & Unterstaller, U. (2001). Post-traumatic stress disorder (PTSD) in victims of domestic violence. *Trauma, Violence, and Abuse, 2*, 99–119.

Kendall-Tackett, K. (n.d.). *The impact of 9/11 on people with disabilities*. Retrieved January 4, 2007, from http://www.apa.org/pi/disability/impactof911.html

Kerig, P. K., Fedorowicz, A. E., Brown, C. A., & Warren, M. (2000). Assessment and intervention for PTSD in children exposed to violence. *Journal of Aggression, Maltreatment & Trauma, 3*, 161–184.

Krause, N., Shaw, B. A., & Cairney, J. (2004). A descriptive epidemiology of lifetime trauma and the physical health status of older adults. *Psychology and Aging, 19*, 637–648.

Kubany, E. S., Hill, E. E., & Owens, J. A. (2003). Cognitive trauma therapy for battered women with PTSD: Preliminary findings. *Journal of Traumatic Stress, 16*, 81–91.

Kubany, E. S., Hill, E. E., Owens, J. A., Iannce-Spencer, C., McCaig, M. A., Tremayne, K. J., & Williams, P. L. (2004). Cognitive trauma therapy for battered women with PTSD (CTT-BW). *Journal of Consulting and Clinical Psychology, 72*, 3–18.

Litz, B. T. (n.d.). *The unique circumstances and mental health impact of the wars in Afghanistan and Iraq*. A National Center for PTSD Fact Sheet. Retrieved June 18, 2006, from http://ncptsd.va.gov/facts/veterans/fs_iraq-Afghanistan_wars.html

Litz, B. T., Gray, M. J., Bryant, R. A., & Adler, A. B. (2002). Early intervention for trauma: Current status and future directions. *Clinical Psychology: Research and Practice, 9*, 112–134.

Livanou, M. (2001). Psychological treatments for post-traumatic stress disorder: An overview. *International Review of Psychiatry, 13,* 181–188.

Livingston, H. M., Livingston, M. G., & Fell, S. (1994). The Lockerbie disaster: A 3-year follow-up of elderly victims. *International Journal of Geriatric Psychiatry, 9,* 989–994.

MacKinnon, G. (Director). (1997) *Behind the lines: Regeneration* [Motion picture]. Canada: Artisan.

Mainous, A. G., III, Smith, D. W., Acierno, R., & Geesey, M. E. (2005). Differences in posttraumatic stress disorder symptoms between elderly non-Hispanic Whites and African Americans. *Journal of the National Medical Association, 97,* 546–549.

Matsakis, A. (1996). *I can't get over it: A handbook for trauma survivors* (2nd ed.). Oakland, CA: New Harbinger.

Mayou, R. A., Ehlers, A., & Hobbs, M. (2000). Psychological debriefing for road accident victims: Three year follow-up of a randomized clinical trial. *British Journal of Psychiatry, 176,* 589–593.

McCloskey, K., & Grigsby, N. (2005). The ubiquitous clinical problem of intimate partner violence: The need for routine assessment. *Professional Psychology: Research and Practice, 36,* 264–275.

McNally, T. J. (2004). Psychological debriefing does not prevent post-traumatic stress disorder. *Psychiatric Times, 21(4).* Retrieved online June 10, 2006, from http://www.psychiatrictimes.com/p040471.html

Monson, C. M., & Friedman, M. J. (2006). Back to the future of understanding trauma: Implications for cognitive-behavioral therapies for trauma. In V. M. Follette & J. I. Ruzek (Eds.), *Cognitive behavioral therapies for trauma* (2nd ed., pp. 1–13). NY: Guilford.

National Center for Post-Traumatic Stress Disorder Fact Sheet. (n.d.). *Treating survivors in the acute aftermath of traumatic events.* Retrieved June 20, 2006, from http:www/ncptsd.va.gov/ facts/disasters/fs_shalev.html

National Center for Post-Traumatic Stress Disorder. (2004). *Iraq War clinician guide* (2nd ed.). Washington, DC: Department of Veterans Affairs.

Norris, F. H. (2002). Psychosocial consequences of disasters. *PTSD Research Quarterly, 13(2),* 1–14.

Norris, F. H., Byrne, C. M., Diaz, E., & Kaniasty, K. (2001). *50,000 disaster victims speak: An empirical review of the empirical literature, 1981–2001.* Washington, DC: Substance Abuse and Mental Health Services Administration. Available online at obssr.od.nih.gov/Activities/911/disaster-impact.pdf

Norris, F. H., Kaniasty, K., Conrad, M. L., Inman, G. L., & Murphy, A. D. (2002). Placing age differences in cultural context: A comparison of the effects of age on PTSD after disasters in the United States, Mexico, and Poland. *Journal of Clinical Geropsychology, 8,* 153–173.

Norris, F. H., Perilla, J. L., Ibañez, G. E., & Murphy, A. D. (2001). Sex differences in symptoms of posttraumatic stress: Does culture play a role? *Journal of Traumatic Stress, 14,* 7–25.

North, C. S., Nixon, S. J., Shariat, S., Mallonee, S., McMillen, J. C., Spitznagel, E. L., & Smith, E. M. (1999). Psychiatric disorders among survivors of the Oklahoma City combing. *JAMA, 282,* 755–762.

Pakula, A. J. (Director). (1982). *Sophie's choice* [Motion picture]. United States: Universal.

Perry, B. D., Pollard, R. A., Blakley, T. L., Baker, W. L., & Vigilante, D. (1996). Childhood, trauma, the neurobiology of adaptation and use-dependent adaptation of the brain: How states become traits. *Infant Mental Health Journal, 16,* 271–291.

Petersilia, J. (2001). Crime victims with developmental disabilities: A review essay. *Criminal Justice and Behavior, 28,* 655–694.

Petersilia, J. (2007). *Invisible victims: Violence against persons with developmental disabilities.* Retrieved January 7, 2007, from http://www.abnet.org/irr/hr/winter00humanrights/petersilia

Pine, D. S., & Cohen, J. A. (2002). Trauma in children and adolescents: Risk and treatment of psychiatric sequelae. *Biological Psychiatry, 51,* 519–531.

Pratt, E. M., Brief, D. J., & Keane, T. M. (2006). Recent advances in psychological assessment of adults with posttraumatic stress disorder. In V. M. Follette & J. I. Ruzek (Eds.), *Cognitive behavioral therapies for trauma* (2nd ed., pp. 34–61). NY: Guilford.

Prins, A., Kimerling, R., Cameron, R., Oumiette, P. C., Shaw, J., Thrailkill, A., Sheikh, J., & Gusman, F. (1999). The Primary Care PTSD Screen (PC-PTSD). Paper presented at the 15th annual meeting of the International Society for Traumatic Stress Studies, Miami, FL.

Pugh, A. (2005, February 17). *Beyond shame and blame: New approach needed for treating domestically violent men: CrossCurrents Winter 2003/04*. Retrieved March 16, 2007, from http://www.camh.net/Publications/Cross_Currents/Winter_2003/beyondshame_crcuwinter2003_04.html

Pynoos, R. S. (1993). Traumatic stress and developmental psychopathology in children and adolescents. In J. M. Oldham, M. B. Riba, & A. Tasman (Eds.), *Review of Psychiatry, 12*, 205–238. Washington DC: American Psychiatric Press.

Riggs, D. S., Cahill, S. P., & Foa, E. B. (2006). Prolonged exposure treatment of posttraumatic stress disorder. In V. M. Follette & J. I. Ruzek (Eds.), *Cognitive behavioral therapies for trauma* (2nd ed.) (pp. 65–95). NY: Guilford.

Rodgers, C. S., & Norman, S. B. (2004). Considering PTSD in the treatment of female victims of intimate partner violence. *Psychiatric Times, 21(4)*. Retrieved online June 25, 2006, from http://psychiatrictimes.com/article/print

Sabin, J. A., Zatzick, D. F., Jurkovitch, G., & Rivara, F. P. (2006). Primary care utilization and detection of emotional distress after adolescent traumatic injury: Identifying an unmet need. *Pediatrics, 117*, 130–138.

Sabin-Farrell, R., & Turpin, G. (2003). Vicarious traumatization: Implications for the mental health of health workers? *Clinical Psychology Review, 23*, 449–480.

Sack, W. H., Him, C., & Dickason, D. (1999). Twelve-year follow-up study of Khmer youths who suffered mass war trauma as children. *Journal of the American Academy of Child and Adolescent Psychiatry, 38*, 1173–1179.

Saigh, P. A., Yule, W., & Inamdar, S. C. (1996). Imaginal flooding of traumatized children and adolescents. *Journal of School Psychology, 34*, 163–183.

Saltzman, W. R., Pynoos, R. S., Layne, C. M., Steinberg, A. M., & Aisenberg, E. (2003). School-based trauma and grief intervention for adolescents. *The Prevention Researcher, 10(2)*, 8–11.

Samuelson, S. L., & Campbell, C. D. (2005). Screening for domestic violence: Recommendations based on a practice survey. *Professional Psychology: Research and Practice, 36*, 276–282.

Saulny, S. (2006, June 21). A legacy of the storm: Depression and suicide. *New York Times*. Retrieved June 21, 2006, from http://www.nytimes.com/2006/06/21/us/21depress.html

Scarpa, A. (2003). Community violence exposure in young adults. *Trauma, Violence, & Abuse, 4*, 210–227.

Scheeringa, M. S. (2004). Posttraumatic stress disorder. In R. DelCarmen-Wiggins (Ed.), *Handbook of infant, toddler, and preschool mental health assessment* (pp. 377–397). Cary, NC: Oxford University Press.

Schiraldi, G. R. (2000). *The post-traumatic stress disorder sourcebook: A guide to healing, recovery, and growth*. NY: McGraw-Hill.

Scott, R. L., Knoth, R. L., Beltran-Quiones, M., & Gomez, N. (2003). Assessment of psychological functioning in adolescent earthquake victims in Columbia using the MMPI-A. *Journal of Traumatic Stress, 16*, 49–57.

Sharhabani-Arzy, R., Amir, M., Kottler, M., & Liran, R. (2003). The toll of domestic violence: PTSD among battered women in an Israeli sample. *Journal of Interpersonal Violence, 18*, 1335–1346.

Shipherd, J. C., Street, A. E., & Resnick, P. A. (2006). Cognitive therapy for post-traumatic stress disorder. In V. M. Follette & J. I. Ruzek (Eds.), *Cognitive behavioral therapies for trauma* (2nd ed., pp. 96–116). NY: Guilford.

Stallard, P., Velleman, R., & Baldwin, S. (1999). Psychological screening of children for post-traumatic stress disorder. *Journal of Child Psychology and Psychiatry, 40*, 1075–1082.

St. George, D. (2006, June 20). Researchers seeing more veterans under stress. *The Washington Post*. Retrieved online June 20, 2006, from http://www.registerguard.com/news/2006/0620

Strand, V. C., Sarmiento, T. L., & Pasquale, L. E. (2005). Assessment and screening tools for trauma in children and adolescents. *Trauma, Violence, and Abuse, 6*, 55–78.

Tjaden, P., & Thoenes, N. (2000). *Extent, nature, and consequences of intimate partner violence: Findings from the National Violence Against Women Survey.* Washington, DC: U.S. Department of Justice, Bureau of Justice Statistics, NCJ 181867.

Tady, M. (2006, August 21). *Disabled people left behind in emergencies.* Retrieved January 8, 2007, from http://www.alternet.org/module/printversion/40443

Terr, L. C. (1991). Childhood traumas: An outline and overview. *American Journal of Psychiatry, 148,* 10–20

Terr, L. (1992). *Too scared to cry: Psychic trauma in childhood.* NY: Basic Books.

Terr, L., Bloch, D. A., Michel, B. A., Shi, H., Reinhardt, J. A., & Metayer, S. (1999). Children's symptoms in the wake of *Challenger:* A field study of distant-traumatic effects and an outline of related conditions. *American Journal of Psychiatry, 156,* 1536–1544.

Terr, L. C. (1981). Psychic trauma in children: Observations following the Chowchilla school-bus kidnapping. *American Journal of Psychiatry, 138,* 14–19.

Tule, W. (2001). Post-traumatic stress disorder in children and adolescents. *International Review of Psychiatry, 13,* 194–200.

U.S. Department of Health and Human Services. (2004). *Mental health response to mass violence and terrorism: A training manual.* DHHS Pub. No. SMA 3959. Rockville, MD: Center for Mental Health Services, Substance Abuse and Mental Health Services Administration, 2004.

van Emmerik, A. A. P., Kamphuis, J. H., Hulsbosch, A. M., & Emmelkamp, P. M. (2002). Single session debriefing after psychological trauma: A meta-analysis. *The Lancet, 360,* 766–771.

Vila, G., Porche, L., & Mouren-Simeoni, M. (1999). An 18-month longitudinal study of posttraumatic disorders in children who were taken hostage in school. *Psychosomatic Medicine, 61,* 746–754.

Walker, L. E. (1979). *The battered woman.* NY: Harper Perrenial.

Walker, L. E. (1984). *The battered woman syndrome.* NY: Springer.

West, R. (1918). *The return of the soldier.* NY: The Century Co.

Williams, M. B., & Poijula, S. (2002). *The PTSD workbook: Simple, effective techniques for overcoming traumatic stress symptoms.* Oakland, CA: New Harbinger.

Winston, F. K., Kassam-Adams, N., Garcia-España, F., Ittenbach, R., & Cnaan, A. (2003). Screening for risk of persistent posttraumatic stress in injured children and their parents. *JAMA, 290,* 643–649.

Wong, R. (2005, September). *Statement of Richard Wong.* Retrieved January 8, 2007, from http:www.schoolcounselor.org/content.asp?contentid=428

Woods, S. (2000). Prevalence and patterns of posttraumatic stress disorder in abused and postabused women. *Issues in Mental Health Nursing, 21,* 309–324.

Youngstrom, E., Weist, M. D., & Albus, K. E. (2003). Exploring violence exposure, stress, protective factors, and behavioral problems among inner-city youth. *American Journal of Community Psychology, 32,* 115–129.

Yule, W. (2001). Post-traumatic stress disorder in children and adolescents. *International Review of Psychiatry, 13,* 194–200.

Yule, W., Bolton, D., Udwin, O., Boyle, S. O'Ryan, D., & Nurrish, J. (2000). The long-term psychological effects of a disaster experienced by adolescents: I: The incidence and course of PTSD. *Journal of Child Psychology and Psychiatry, 41,* 503–511.

Zimering, R., Monroe, J., & Gulliver, S. B. (2003). Secondary traumatization in mental health care providers. *Psychiatric Times, 20(4).* Retrieved August 1, 2006, from http://www.psychiatrictimes.com/showArticle.jhtml?articleID=175802430

Chapter 8: Grief and Bereavement

Alvord, L. A., & Van Pelt, E. C. (1999). *Cutting into sacred territory.* Retrieved July 9, 2005, from http://archive.salon.com/health/books/1999/06/09/cadaver/print.html

Barrett, R. K. (1998). Sociocultural considerations for working with Blacks experiencing loss and grief. In K. J. Doka & J. D. Davidson (Eds.), *Living with grief: Who we are; how we grieve* (pp. 47–56). Washington, DC: Hospice Foundation of America.

Balk, D. (1983). How teenagers cope with sibling death: Some implications for school counselors. *The School Counselor, 31*, 150–158.

Buscaglia, L. (2002) *The fall of Freddie the leaf: 20th anniversary edition*. Thorofare, NJ: Slack.

Carroll, B. (1998). Cultural aspects of peer support: An examination of one program's experience. In K. J. Doka & J. D. Davidson (Eds.), *Living with grief: Who we are, how we grieve* (pp. 207–221). Washington, DC: Hospice Foundation.

Clements, P. T., Focht-New, G., & Faulkner, M. J. (2004). Grief in the shadows: Exploring loss and bereavement in people with developmental disabilities. *Issues in Mental Health Nursing, 25*, 799–808.

Costa, L., & Holliday, D. (1994). Helping children cope with the death of a parent. *Elementary School Guidance & Counseling, 28*, 206–213.

Death of a parent. (n.d.). Retrieved January 3, 2007, from http://coolnurse.com/death.htm

Dershimer, R. A. (1990). *Counseling the bereaved*. NY: Pergamon.

Dowling, S., Hubert, J., White, S., & Hollins, S. (2006). Bereaved adults with intellectual disabilities: A combined randomized controlled trial and qualitative study of two community-based interventions. *Journal of Intellectual Disability Research, 50*, 277–287.

Egoyan, A. (Director). (1997). *The sweet hereafter* [Motion picture]. Canada: New Home Video.

Fast, J. D. (2003). After Columbine: How people mourn sudden death. *Social Work, 48*, 484–491.

Gardy, A. (2005, September 20). Lost baby, and the pain of endless reminders in the mail. *The New York Times*, D5.

Gray, R. E. (1988). The role of school counselors with bereaved teenagers: With and without peer support groups. *School Counselor, 35*, 185–193.

Grollman, E. (1982). *What helped me when my loved one died*. Boston, MA: Beacon Press.

Grollman, E. (1993). *Straight talk about death for teenagers: How to cope with losing someone you love*. Boston, MA: Beacon Press.

Grollman, E. (1995). *Living when a loved one has died*. Boston, MA: Beacon Press.

Grollman, E. (1998). What you always wanted to know about your Jewish clients' perspectives concerning death and dying – but were afraid to ask. In K. J. Doka & J. D. Davidson (Eds.), *Living with grief: Who we are; how we grieve* (pp. 47–56). Washington, DC: Hospice Foundation of America.

Grollman, E. (2001). *A child's book about death*. Centering Corporation.

Grollman, E. (2001). *Living with loss, healing with hope*. Boston, MA: Beacon Press.

Harris, M. (1996). *The loss that is forever: The lifelong impact of the early loss of a mother or father*. NY: Plume.

Hollins, S. (1995). Managing grief better: People with developmental disabilities. *The Habilitative Mental Healthcare Newsletter, 14*. Retrieved December 22, 2006, from http://www.thearc.org/faqs/grief.html

Jordan, J. R. (2001). Is suicide bereavement different? A reassessment of the literature. *Suicide and Life-Threatening Behavior, 31*, 91–101.

Klass, D., & Goss, R. E. (1998). Asian ways of grief. In K. J. Doka & J. D. Davidson (Eds.), *Living with grief: Who we are, how we grieve* (pp. 13–26). Philadelphia, PA: Brunner/Mazel.

Kroen, W. C. (1996). *Helping children cope with the loss of a loved one: A guide for grownups*. Minneapolis, MN: Free Spirit Publishing.

Kübler-Ross, E. (1969). *On death and dying*. NY: Scribner.

Lavin, C. (1998). Helping individuals with developmental disabilities. In K. J. Doka & J. D. Davidson (Eds.), *Living with grief: Who we are, how we grieve* (pp. 161–180). Washington, DC: Hospice Foundation.

Leventry, E. (n.d.). *The revenge of Kübler-Ross*. Retrieved June 28, 2004, from http://www.beliefnet.com/story/151/story_15188.html

Lewis, C. S. (1989). *A grief observed*. San Francisco: Harper.

Lewis, M. M., & Trzinski, A. L. (2006). Counseling older adults with dementia who are dealing with death: Innovative interventions for practitioners. *Death Studies, 30*, 777–787.

Lindstrøm, T. C. (2002). "It ain't necessarily so . . ." Challenging mainstream thinking about bereavement. *Family and Community Health, 25(1)*, 11–21.

Martin, T. L., & Doka, K. J. (2000). *When men don't cry . . . women do: Transcending gender stereotypes of grief*. Philadelphia, PA: Taylor & Francis.

Moore, J. W. (1976). *Mexican Americans*. Upper Saddle River, NJ: Prentice-Hall.

Neimeyer, R. A. (2000). Searching for the meaning of meaning: Grief therapy and the process of reconstruction. *Death Studies, 24*, 541–558.

Nelson, J. (Director). (1994). *Corina, Corina* [Motion picture]. United States: New Line Home Video.

Ogrodniczuk, J. S., Piper, W. E., Joyce, A. S., Weideman, R., McCallum, M., Zaim, H. F., & Rosie, J. S. (2003). Differentiating symptoms of complicated grief and depression among psychiatric outpatients. *Canadian Journal of Psychiatry, 48(2)*, 87–93.

Parkes, C. M. (1998). Bereavement in adult life. *British Medical Journal, 316*, 856–860.

Paterson, D. S., Trachtenberg, F. L., Thompson, E. G., Belliveau, R. A., Beggs, A. H., Darnall, R., et al. (2006). Multiple serotenergic brainstem abnormalities in Sudden Infant Death Syndrome. *JAMA, 296*, 2124–2132.

Prigerson, H. G., Maciejewski, P. K., Reynolds, C. F., III, Bierhals, A. J., Newsom, J. T., Fasiczka, A., Frank, E., Doman, J., & Miller, M. (1995). Inventory of complicated grief: A scale to measure maladaptive symptoms of loss. *Psychiatry Research, 59*, 65–79.

Raad, S. A. (1998). Grief: A Muslim perspective. In K. J. Doka & J. D. Davidson (Eds.), *Living with grief: Who we are; how we grieve* (pp. 47–56). Washington, DC: Hospice Foundation of America.

Rosenzweig, A., Prigerson, H., Miller, M., & Reynolds, C. F., III. (1997). Bereavement and late-life depression: Grief and its complications in the elderly. *Annual Review of Medicine, 48*, 421–428.

Salvador, R. J. (2003). What do Mexicans celebrate on the Day of the Dead? In J. D. Morgan & P. Laungani (Eds.), *Death and bereavement in the Americas* (pp. 75–76). Amityville, NY: Baywood Publishing. Available online at http://www.public.iastate.edu/~rjsalvad/scmfaq/ muertos.html

Samide, L. L., & Stockton, R. (2002). Letting go of grief: Bereavement groups for children in the school setting. *Journal for Specialists in Group Work, 27*, 192–204.

Schut, H., Stroebe, M. S., Van den Bout, J., & Terheggen, M. (2001). The efficacy of bereavement interventions. In M. S. Stroebe, R. O. Hansson, W. Stroebe, & H. Schut (Eds.), *Handbook of bereavement research: Consequences, coping and care* (pp. 705–737). Washington, DC: American Psychological Association.

Servaty-Seib, H. L., Peterson, J., & Spang, D. (2003). Notifying individual students of a death loss: Practical recommendations for schools and school counselors. *Death Studies, 27*, 167–186.

Sharkin, B. S., & Knox, D. (2003). Pet loss: Issues and implications for the psychologist. *Professional Psychology: Research and Practice, 34*, 414–421.

Shear, K., Frank, E., Houck, P. R., & Reynolds, C. F., III. (2005). Treatment of complicated grief: A randomized controlled trial. *JAMA, 293*, 2601–2608.

Sheridan, J. (Director). (2002). *In America* [Motion picture]. United States: Fox Searchlight.

Siberling, B. (Director). (2002). *Moonlight mile* [Motion picture]. United States: Walt Disney.

Spungen, D., & Piccicuto, A. (2002). *Working with children traumatized by homicide: A new paradigm: Participant handbook*. Philadelphia, PA: Anti-Violence Partnership.

Stroebe, M., Gergem, M. M., Gergen, K. J., & Stroebe, W. (1992). Broken hearts or broken bonds: Love and death in historical perspective. *American Psychologist, 47*, 1205–1212.

Stroebe, M., & Schut, H. (1999). The dual process model of coping with bereavement: Rationale and description. *Death Studies, 23*, 197–224.

Swihart, J., Silliman, B., & McNeil, J. (1992). Death of a student: Implications for secondary school counselors. *School Counselor, 40*, 55–60.

Trozzi, M. (1999). *Talking with children about loss*. NY: Perigee Trade.

Van Dongen, C. J. (1990). Agonizing questions: Experiences of survivors of suicide victims. *Nursing Research, 39,* 224–229.

When a parent dies: A guide for patients and their families. (n.d.). Retrieved March 17, 2007, from http://www.hospicenet.org/html/parent.html

Wilson, L. W. (1984). Helping adolescents understand death and dying through literature. *English Journal, 73,* 78–82.

Worden, J. W. (1991). *Grief counseling and grief therapy: A handbook for the mental health practitioner.* NY: Springer

Worden, J. W. (2001). *Children and grief: When a parent dies.* NY: Guilford.

Worden, J. W. (2004). *Grief counseling and grief therapy: A handbook for the mental health practitioner* (3rd ed.). NY: Springer.

Zieziula, F. (1998). The world of the deaf community. In K. J. Doka & J. D. Davidson (Eds.), *Living with grief: Who we are; how we grieve* (pp. 181–198). Washington, DC: Hospice Foundation.

INDEX